D1480415

MONEY, WORK, AND CRIME
Experimental Evidence

MONEY, WORK, AND CRIME
Experimental Evidence

PETER H. ROSSI

Social and Demographic Research Institute
University of Massachusetts
Amherst, Massachusetts

RICHARD A. BERK

Group for Research on Social Policy
Social Process Research Institute and
Department of Sociology
University of California, Santa Barbara
Santa Barbara, California

KENNETH J. LENIHAN

Department of Sociology
John Jay School of Criminal Justice
City University of New York
New York, New York

ACADEMIC PRESS
A Subsidiary of Harcourt Brace Jovanovich, Publishers
New York   London   Toronto   Sydney   San Francisco

ACADEMIC PRESS, INC.
111 Fifth Avenue, New York, New York 10003

United Kingdom Edition published by
ACADEMIC PRESS, INC. (LONDON) LTD.
24/28 Oval Road, London NW1 7DX

Library of Congress Cataloging in Publication Data

Rossi, Peter Henry, Date
    Money, work, and crime.

    (Quantitative studies in social relations series)
    Includes bibliographical references.
    1. Transitional Aid Research Project. 2. Prison
release gratuities––United States. 3. Ex–convicts––
Rehabilitation––United States. I. Berk, Richard A. ,
joint author. II. Lenihan, Kenneth J. , joint author.
III. Title.
HV8887.R67   364.8   80–512
ISBN 0–12–598240–2

To

HOWARD ROSEN

Devoted, Persistent, and Innovative
Civil Servant

Contents

I

THE TRANSITIONAL AID RESEARCH PROJECT EXPERIMENTS: BACKGROUND, DESIGN, AND OUTCOMES

1

An Overview

2

Historical Background of the Transitional Aid Research Project Experiments

3

Design of the Transitional Aid
Research Project Experiments

4

Implementation of Transitional Aid
Research Project Experimental Design

5

TARP Outcomes: Effectiveness Masked by
Unanticipated Side-Effects

II

EX-PRISONERS AND THEIR POSTPRISON EXPERIENCES

6

The World of Ex-Prisoners

7

Participants in the Transitional Aid Research Project

8

Postrelease Social and Psychological Adjustment Patterns
WITH JEFFREY K. LIKER

9

Employment and Earnings

10

Arrests and Arrest Charges

III

MODELING AND ESTIMATING THE EFFECTS OF THE TRANSITIONAL AID RESEARCH PROJECT

11

Model of the Effects of the Transitional Aid Research Project: Theoretical Foundations

12

Estimating Transitional Aid Research Project Models for Texas and Georgia

13

Transitional Aid Research Project Payments, Job Search, and Weekly Wages

IV

CONCLUSIONS

14

The Policy Implications of the Transitional Aid Research Project

V

APPENDICES

A

Data and Instruments 287

B

"Nobody Knows the Troubles I've Seen": Postrelease Burdens on the Families of Transitional Aid Research Project

JEFFREY K. LIKER

C

Women Ex-Offenders in the TARP Experiment

NANCY JURIK

List of Figures

List of Tables

Preface

The Transitional Aid Research Project (TARP) was a large-scale field experiment which attempted to reduce recidivism on the part of ex-felons. Beginning in January 1976, some prisoners released from state institutions in Texas and Georgia were offered financial aid for periods of up to 6 months postrelease. Payments were made in the form of Unemployment Insurance benefits. The ex-prisoners who were eligible for payments were compared with control groups released at the same time from the same institutions. The control groups were not eligible for benefits. Comparisons were made along many lines, including number of arrests for various causes, wages, time unemployed, family status, and living arrangements. All ex-prisoners were followed for one year postrelease.

The assumption that modest levels of financial help would ease the transition from prison life to civilian life was partially supported. Ex-prisoners who received financial aid under TARP had lower rearrest rates than their counterparts who did not receive benefits and worked comparable periods of time. Those receiving financial aid were also able to obtain better-paying jobs than the controls. However, ex-prisoners receiving benefits took longer to find jobs than those who did not receive benefits. Thus, those receiving payments generally worked less during the postrelease year.

This volume reports complete details of the $3.4 million Department of Labor TARP experiment. The reader is referred to Chapter 1 for a description of the project and its findings. We have not supplied a subject index to this volume. Instead, we have included a very detailed table of contents, a list of figures, and a list of tables.

Large-scale field experiments, have been used increasingly in the social sciences over the last two decades to serve the information needs of social policy. Because they combine sample survey techniques, experimental design, and econometric analysis, large-scale field experiments provide better and more trustworthy information than is available through alternative research methods. In the past 20 years, such field experiments have come into use to solve critical issues about whether or not specific proposed social policies are effective in achieving their goals. Their increasing use by policymaking agencies for these purposes, despite their costs, arises out of two developments. First, policymakers are increasingly skeptical about innovations in social policy, an agnosticism born of repeated disappointments with social programs that have not lived up to expectations. Second, the social science research community has learned how to combine effectively the several traditions that contribute to the methodology of field experimentation.

We believe that the TARP experiment makes a strong contribution both to an important policy area, the reduction of crime through reducing recidivism, and to the further development of the field and experiment as a policy research instrument. The reader is, of course, the final judge on both claims.

Acknowledgments

A full accounting of all the persons who played crucial roles in the TARP experiment would lead to a proverbial "cast of thousands." To begin with, there are the more than 2000 persons who agreed to be subjects in the experiment and who repeatedly provided information on what they did the year after being released from the prisons of Georgia and Texas. An additional 2000 never knew they were participants, since we simply kept track of them through their arrest records and Unemployment Insurance earnings files. We hope that all these men and women find that they were benefited by what we have done.

At the other extreme, the TARP experiments owe their existence, in a very direct way, to Howard Rosen, director of research and development in the Department of Labor's Employment and Training Administration. His devotion to a line of research, starting back in the middle 1960s, that sought for ways in which Department of Labor programs could be modified to meet the needs of released prisoners led in a direct line to the TARP experiments. We have experienced his interest in the work of TARP very directly through his constant, good-natured goading and generosity. There can be little doubt that this experiment was carried to a successful completion through his unflagging devotion and support.

Lafayette Grisby of the Employment and Training Administration smoothly provided liaison with the Department of Labor and made our work that much easier to accomplish.

In the states of Georgia and Texas, devoted TARP staffs carried out the administration of the treatments and the collection of data on outcomes. In Texas, Charles L. Smith, Pablo Martinez, and Daniel Harrison headed up a research team under the general leadership of Jack Remeny that supervised the collection and preparation of data and produced a report[1] on the results of the Texas TARP experiment. In Georgia, the team consisted of Jack L.

---

[1] Charles L. Smith, Pablo Martinez, and Daniel Harrison, *An Assessment; The Impact of Providing Financial or Job Placement Assistance to Ex-Prisoners* (Huntsville, Texas: Texas Department of Corrections, 1978).

Stephens, Lois Sanders, and John Doughtie, under George Cox of the Georgia Department of Corrections. Sanders and Stephens were responsible for a report on findings in that state.[2] At the Georgia Department of Labor, Jack Flanigan, Merle Meacham, William McClure, and Eleanor Imlah supervised the data collection.

The analyses of TARP data reported in this volume were carried out at the Social and Demographic Research Institute (SADRI) of the University of Massachusetts at Amherst, and the Group for Research on Social Policy at the University of California at Santa Barbara. At SADRI, Patrick Henry and Jeffrey K. Liker served as research assistants to the senior author. Eleanor Weber-Burdin accomplished sometimes unbelievable feats of virtuosity on our local computer, straightening out errors in a very complicated data set. At Santa Barbara, the second author was helped by Nancy Jurik and Anthony Shih.

The division of labor among the three authors was an extensive one. The senior author supervised the assembly of the data sets and performed the analyses that are contained in Parts I and II. In addition, he has served as the general editor of the volume. The second author performed the analyses described in Part III. The third author constructed the design of the two experiments, served for 3 years as the principal investigator, supervised the fieldwork, constantly visited the two states, provided advice and guidance to the state research staffs, and wrote the basic drafts of Chapters 2 and 3.

At many points, a fairly large number of consultants provided advice to the project staff. In particular, we wish to acknowledge the help provided by Hans Zeisel (University of Chicago), Robert Boruch (Northwestern), Charles Mallar (Mathematica, Inc.), Anne Witte (University of North Carolina), Donald Cressey (University of California, Santa Barbara), Jon Simpson (University of Massachusetts), Harold Watts (Columbia University), James F. Short (Washington State University), Sheldon Olson (University of Texas), and Daniel Glaser (University of Southern California). Hans Zeisel also has provided valuable advice and guidance from time to time during the project, for which we express gratitude. At his request, we note here that in his opinion the approach taken in this manuscript is incorrect and that the conclusions we draw about the results of the TARP experiments are severely flawed by methodological errors. While we cannot agree with Professor Zeisel's opinions, we will note at appropriate points in the text the substance of his disagreements with our approaches.

At SADRI, Jeanne Reinle, Cynthia Coffman, and Laura Martin patiently

---

[2] Jack L. Stephens and Lois W. Sanders, *Transitional Aid for Ex-Offenders: An Experimental Study in Georgia* (Atlanta, Georgia: Georgia Department of Offender Rehabilitation, 1978).

and with good humor typed and retyped the several versions of this manuscript, correcting obvious grammatical errors along the way.

As usual, despite the good advice and excellent help we have enjoyed, we may have gone astray at places in the final product. These errors are our responsibility. We hope that some of the virtues of the volume also can be attributed to us.

I

THE TRANSITIONAL AID RESEARCH PROJECT EXPERIMENTS: BACKGROUND, DESIGN, AND OUTCOMES

1

An Overview

INTRODUCTION

For 6 months starting in January 1976, some of the prisoners released from the state institutions of Georgia and Texas were offered eligibility for unemployment insurance payments for periods of up to 6 months or until they managed to locate employment. These ex-felons were carefully selected as part of an experiment run by the Department of Labor in collaboration with the two states. Other prisoners who were not offered unemployment benefits also participated in the experiment to serve as controls.

The purpose of the experiment was to test a new way of helping persons who had completed their sentences or were released on parole to reintegrate themselves into civilian life. The program was based on the realization that ex-felons were sent out into the world with virtually no reserves of savings or any sort of nest egg that would tide them over until they located work and had earnings on their own. Ex-felons ordinarily got along financially through the generous help of their families and friends who, sharing their own meager resources with the returned prisoners, provided food and shelter.

The ex-prisoners who were offered unemployment insurance benefits were compared with others released around the same time who were not made the same offer. Comparisons included the number of arrests experienced for various causes over the year beyond release as well as amount of unemployment, wages, family status, and living arrangements.

The assumption that the modest levels of financial support ($63 per week in Texas and $70 in Georgia) would ease the transition to civilian life was partially supported by the analysis undertaken on what happened during the year after release from prison. On the positive side, ex-felons receiving benefits experienced fewer arrests on all sorts of charges and managed to get better-paying jobs than their counterparts who worked comparable

3

amounts of time in the postrelease year and were not eligible for unemployment benefits. On the negative side, ex-felons receiving payments took longer than their counterparts to find work and as a consequence worked a shorter portion of the postrelease year.

This volume describes the $3.4-million Department of Labor experiment and presents an analysis of the outcomes in behavior over the postrelease year. In the remainder of this chapter, an overview of the experiment and its outcomes is presented. Part I presents a detailed history of the experiment and the rationale for its design along with a summary of the evidence for the effectiveness of the policy (Chapter 5). Part II provides a detailed account of the participants in the experiments and the events over the postrelease year in their personal lives, employment, and, in some cases, arrest experiences. Part III contains a detailed discussion of the theoretical background of the experiment plus an account of the statistical approaches used to measure the impacts of the payments. Finally, Part IV attempts to draw out the implications of the findings for an effective social policy that would reduce recidivism rates.

THE SOCIAL PROBLEM

In broadest terms, it is the social problem of crime that is the center of concern of this volume. Specifically, however, we will focus on recidivism, the unfortunate tendency of persons convicted of felonies at one point in time to be arrested and convicted again, sometimes to repeat this sequence over and over.

The extent of this problem and its impact on our society are both considerable. The prison population of the United States—including those serving time in both federal and state prisons, but not those serving in county and municipal jails—hovers around 290,000,[1] enough people to fill a modest-sized urban center (in 1970 Rochester, New York, had a population of 296,000). Most prisoners (94%) are men. Now in their middle twenties and serving terms between one and two years, they have usually been in prison before. Most prisoners also have long histories of brushes with the law, starting with arrests as juveniles and often including some time spent in juvenile institutions.

---

[1] As of December 31, 1976, the state prison population was 260,747 and that of federal prisons 30,920: U.S. Department of Justice, Law Enforcement Assistance Administration, *Prisoners in State and Federal Institutions*, National Prisoner Statistics Bulletin (Washington, D.C.: 1979), Table 1.

Three out of five of the felons in state prisons have been convicted of felony charges involving property crimes, the most frequent specific charge being burglary. Another one in five are in prison because of crimes committed against persons, ranging in seriousness from simple assaults to premeditated murder. The remainder have been convicted of a miscellaneous set of charges, among which drug-related offenses are a major subgroup (see Chapter 7).

Property-related offenses are therefore the bulk of the crimes for which persons serve time in prison. Such offenses are even a larger proportion of all crimes recorded, since crimes against persons are much more likely to lead to arrests and convictions. In short, the prison population of the United States is at present largely composed of persons who have been convicted of theft, larceny, fraud, burglary, and similar offenses, all crimes whose common denominator is the fact that it is possible to derive income from the criminal acts involved. Crime may or may not be a way of life for some segment of the United States population of young men, but it most certainly is an alternative occupation from which it is possible to derive a living or at least to obtain some supplementary earnings.

The social costs of crime at this scale are considerable.[2] Besides the losses inflicted on victims and victimized institutions, there is the expense of maintaining police departments, courts, and the staffs of prosecuting attorneys. In addition, there is the cost of maintaining men in prison, which averages $13,500 per prisoner per year in state prisons.

Each year, the state prisons release about 100,000 persons who either have completed their sentences or have been granted parole. Although no one knows for sure how many are ultimately rearrested and returned to prison upon conviction, all estimates of recidivism rates—ranging from 30% to 60%—are unacceptably high from any social-policy viewpoint. Each imprisonment incurs the costs of criminal justice processing and prison maintenance. And each imprisonment represents some larger number of crimes for which no person was apprehended.

While there may be some prisoners who prefer imprisonment to being a free civilian, the overwhelming majority dislike prison intensely, and for very good and obvious reasons. Most leave holding firm resolves not to return. Most probably do not come back. Yet, a significantly large number—at least one in three—do end up back in prison. Those who do return are

---

[2] The annual cost of crimes against persons and property was estimated at close to five billion in the mid 1960s: President's Commission on Law Enforcement and Administration of Justice, *The Challenge of Crime in a Free Society* (Washington, D.C.: U.S. Government Printing Office, 1967).

given longer and longer sentences by the courts and confront parole boards that are less willing to take chances on felons with extensive conviction records. Indeed, recidivism is so prevalent that at any one point in time a large proportion of prisoners are repeaters, many of whom have spent half or more of their adult lives behind bars.

About the only sure knowledge we have of the recidivism problem is that aging and employment are effective antidotes. Older men and ex-felons who find jobs and retain them are less likely to be returned to prison. There is little that any social policy can do about the aging process, but there is much that can be attempted to help ex-felons enter the employed sector of the economy. Indeed, the policy being tested in the study reported here is one of a set of social programs designed to affect the employment chances of ex-felons.

Ex-prisoners might benefit a great deal from steady employment, but they are also not very good employment prospects. To begin with, they all suffer from the stigma of felony convictions, a condition that excludes them from many occupations and lowers their acceptance by employers and co-workers in other jobs. But they also have the disadvantage of coming from groups that have difficulty on labor markets in any event. For example, minority ethnic and racial groups are overrepresented among ex-prisoners. In Georgia about 60% were black, and in Texas 16% were Hispanics with another 48% black. Because ex-felons have spent so much of their adult lives in prison, they have little in the way of job experiences that build up skills and hence reenter the labor market as if they were completely without experience. Finally, average educational attainment levels are low, the typical ex-felon in Georgia and Texas having left school in the ninth grade.

Indeed, the test put to the idea of the Transitional Aid Research Project (TARP) by the ex-felons to which the TARP experiments were directed is a very difficult one. Ex-felons are among the least employable groups in our society.

Given that prison is clearly noxious to almost everyone, and especially noxious to those who have had some direct experiences with prison life, the issue then becomes what causes some ex-felons to engage again in activities that expose them to the risk of additional imprisonment?

The search for answers to that question has produced paradoxical results. On one hand, it has been quite easy to understand why ex-prisoners return. The circumstances facing them as they attempt to fit into civilian life are such that perhaps the question ought to be rephrased to ask why it is that most ex-prisoners do not find their way back into prison. On the other hand, the search for remedies that significantly affect the process has met time and time again with failure.[3] Few programs have been effective in reducing recidivism significantly, consistently, and at reasonable levels of cost.

The TARP experiment described in this volume is one of the more successful attempts both to improve our understanding of the process that leads ex-felons back into prison and to develop a cost-effective program that affects that process in a significant way. TARP is the culmination of more than a decade of effort on the part of the Department of Labor to fulfill the mandate given to it in the Manpower Development and Training Act of 1962 to help ex-prisoners find employment (see Chapter 3).

TARP demonstrated that *the provision of limited amounts of financial aid to released prisoners in the form of minimum unemployment benefit payments for periods of between 3 and 6 months can decrease the arrests experienced by the ex-felons in the year following release by 25% to 50%.*[4] TARP was also able to demonstrate that *the jobs obtained by the ex-felons who received payments paid higher wages and probably had better working conditions.* Apparently, the unemployment benefit payments allowed the ex-prisoners to search more effectively for better employment than could their counterparts who did not receive payments.

The clarity of TARP results was somewhat obscured by the presence of unanticipated and undesirable side effects. Largely because of the regulations governing eligibility for payments from the unemployment insurance system, TARP payments had rather large work-disincentive effects. Essentially, these regulations require that persons be unemployed in order to receive payments (see Chapter 4). Since unemployment raises the probability of recidivism, the positive effects of the TARP payments were offset by the rise in recidivism brought about through increased unemployment. These undesirable side effects can be remedied by appropriate changes in eligibility rules, as we argue in Chapter 14.

The TARP findings are especially trustworthy because of the research design employed. Randomized controlled experiments are the most powerful techniques available for the assessment of the effects of social programs.[5] In addition, TARP was undertaken independently in two

---

[3] Douglas Lipton, Robert Martinson, and Judith Wilks, in *The Effectiveness of Correctional Treatment* (New York: Praeger, 1975), reviewed scores of rehabilitation efforts, finding that no firm evidence for effectiveness exists.

[4] Calculated as the relative decline in the average number of arrests, compared to the numbers of arrests experienced by comparable ex-felons who did not receive payments.

[5] Thomas D. Cook and Donald T. Campbell, *Quasi-Experimentation: Design and Analysis Issues for Field Setting*, (Chicago: Rand McNally, 1979), and Peter H. Rossi, Howard Freeman, and Sonia R. Wright, *Evaluation: A Systematic Approach* (Beverly Hills: Sage Publications, 1979).

states, Georgia and Texas. Similar findings in both instances bolster the trustworthiness of the conclusions drawn. (The design used in the experiments is described in Chapter 3.)

ADJUSTMENT PROBLEMS OF RELEASED PRISONERS

The difficulties faced by released prisoners as they attempt to readjust to civilian life arise partly out of their past histories, which they share with others of the same social origins who have not been convicted of felonies, and partly out of the special circumstances that stem from having been convicted and imprisoned. These conditions are summarized in this section, based on data collected in the TARP experiments. Their significance extends beyond both the period of the study and the geographical limits of Georgia and Texas, however, since their circumstances differ very little from those of convicted felons in any state of the Union. (Chapters 7, 8, 9, and 10 provide greater detail.)

First of all, ex-felons are typically ill-equipped to make much of a go of it outside the prison walls, even if the civil society were to welcome them with open arms. As amply shown in the TARP data presented in Chapter 7, the ex-felons of Georgia and Texas were far below average for their age groups in several characteristics that count on the labor market. Because of their imprisonment histories they have had little opportunity to acquire work experiences, and their sparse work episodes involved employment at the lowest levels of the occupational-skill hierarchy. Their educational attainment averaged ninth grade, but their measured average functional grade equivalent was only sixth grade. Only a minority held valid drivers' licenses, and more than one in four did not know how to operate a motor vehicle.

In addition, a prison record is scarcely an employment recommendation. Some jobs are explicitly barred to ex-felons. Some employers would never hire them for any but the most transient and lowest paying positions. Even when explicit questions about felony convictions are not asked on application forms or at the time of interview, it is often necessary for the released prisoner to account for what he was doing during the period of his imprisonment. Employment about which no questions are asked of applicants consists of jobs that pay so meagerly and have such poor working conditions that employers are willing to take almost anyone who comes in the door.

In short, ex-felons can get into the employed labor force, but the entry points open to them are on the bottom of the pay scale and involve unpleasant working conditions. Indeed, for those who worked during the postrelease year, average weekly wages in Texas were $148 and in Georgia $110 (see Chapter 9). Typical jobs were at the bottom of the skill hierarchy, usually involving unskilled labor in the construction industry. And many were unable (or unwilling) to find any work at all during the entire postrelease year: 11% in Texas and 29% in Georgia.

Legitimate opportunities for earnings therefore compete poorly with illegitimate sources of income. Although we do not know how much can be earned, for example, by being a "full-time" burglar, it is clear that what can be earned by TARP participants from the kinds of jobs typically available to them is the worst competition available on local labor markets.

An additional push toward illegitimate activities arises from the impoverished state in which ex-felons typically leave prison. There are few opportunities for earning money in prison. For example, although at the time TARP began, the Texas prison system required everyone to work at some sort of prison enterprise, no wages were paid. Georgia's prisons had fewer work opportunities, and those who did work were paid less than $.50 per hour. Typically, prisoners got by in prison with the help of friends and relatives who sent small sums that enabled the former to purchase necessities and small luxuries that the prisons did not provide. Very little could have been saved to have on hand when released.

Nor do the prisons provide much to the prisoner on discharge. A discharged prisoner is usually provided with a set of civilian clothes (of indifferent quality), transportation to his home town, and a small amount of *gate money*. Although there are some states that provide as much as $250 upon release, some provide nothing; the average amount is around $50. The Texas prisons were among the more generous, providing $200 in gate money. Georgia was on the low side, with only $25. High or low, the amounts provided were scarcely sufficient to provide for more than a few days of food and lodging. Indeed, the very first problem faced by released prisoners was arranging for the very basic necessities of food and shelter. (Chapter 8 describes these reentry problems as experienced by the exfelons.)

The social insurance systems and the welfare systems ignore or push aside the problem of released prisoners. Unemployment insurance credits that might have accumulated from preprison employment have been wiped out by the ex-felon's stay in prison. Eligibility rules in the public welfare system often specifically exclude young, able-bodied, and unmarried males. Sometimes private charities may assist. Ordinarily, however, the ex-felon is on his own. (Since almost all prisoners are males, we feel justified in using the male personal pronoun throughout this volume.)

The burden of supporting the released prisoner beyond the first few days typically falls on his family. The same relatives who have helped him out in prison provide shelter and food when he is released. Thus, more than two-thirds of the prisoners go back to live with their parents or other close relatives upon release. (The few who are still married upon release generally return to their wives.) Often this means going back into a home where a prisoner's mother is the head of the household.

The ex-felons' families are rarely prosperous. Many are on welfare and trying to get by on less than $100 a week. When breadwinners work, household incomes are less than $150 per week (see Appendix B). An additional mouth to feed and an additional person to house in crowded quarters constitutes a considerable drain on resources that are very meager to begin with. In addition, ex-felons often borrow money or receive small allowances, constituting additional drains on available cash.

The comparatively few who have no relatives or friends to receive them are, of course, even worse off. For these, finding some way to obtain income within a week of leaving prison is an absolute necessity.

For all ex-felons, getting along in the sense of obtaining food and shelter is a problem that looms large within a very short period of time following release from prison. This income bind, mitigated somewhat by the generosity of relatives and friends, constitutes still another pressure in the direction of returning to a life of theft or larceny.

THE TRANSITIONAL AID RESEARCH PROJECT

The Transitional Aid Research Project (TARP) was designed to provide limited financial aid to released prisoners during the critical transition period between prison and full integration into civilian life. It was the culmination of a line of development that started with the Manpower Development and Training Act of 1962, which gave the Department of Labor a mandate to provide programs that would aid released prisoners in obtaining employment. Department of Labor programs initially attempted to provide vocational training within prisons and after release. Evaluations of these attempts to raise the skill levels (and thus enhance employability) of ex-felons indicated that the attempts were hardly successful. Although this general strategy is still being followed by the Department of Labor, with additional projects aimed directly at providing additional training or actual employment opportunities to released prisoners,[6] another strategy, that of providing income support, was also pursued.

---

[6] Notably the Supported Work Experiment, conducted through the joint sponsorship of the Department of Health, Education, and Welfare and the Ford Foundation.

A line of research and development, initiated by Howard Rosen,[7] concentrated on providing some minimum level of income support during the period immediately following release from prison. The aim was to change the balance of incentives in favor of employment and against engaging in property crimes. This was a strategy that recognized severe lack of funds upon reentry as a major source of the postprison adjustment problems of ex-felons and sought a partial solution to this problem by modifying an existing social program, unemployment insurance, through extension of its coverage to newly released prisoners.

The strategy of extending employment insurance coverage had many attractive features. Besides the clear and obvious need for income during the immediate postrelease period, there were also equity reasons for pursuing this strategy. Almost all of the prisoners had lost eligibility or unemployment insurance benefits by virtue of imprisonment.[8] Estimates of the amount of eligibility so forfeited (see Chapter 3) indicated that such amounts were a considerable fraction of the costs of a TARP-like program. In addition, it hardly seemed fair that the burdens of providing for released prisoners largely fell on their impoverished families and that few of the social welfare agencies recognized the income needs of the released prisoners.

In addition, administrative and efficiency considerations made the income strategy attractive. Administratively, the program could be easily delivered by a slight extension of the mandate of an existing set of government agencies—the state employment security agencies, which administered the unemployment insurance benefit system under federal legislation. The state employment security agencies covered every state and had sufficient presence in each state to administer such an extension; a new bureaucracy would not have to be established. The intervention also appeared to be quite inexpensive and showed promise of having very favorable cost-to-benefit ratios even if only moderately successful. The costs of incarceration were so high that even moderate reductions in recidivism could produce savings that could offset the costs of most levels of unemployment insurance payments to ex-prisoners.

The a priori attractiveness of the DOL strategy, however, was not entirely convincing to its originator, Howard Rosen. Appropriately skeptical of interventions, Rosen initiated a set of experiments to test whether extending reasonable amounts of unemployment benefits to ex-felons would in fact make a difference in recidivism. The evaluation strategy was one

---

[7] Director, Research and Development, Employment and Training Administration.

[8] Eligibility rules require that a person be employed in covered employment for two out of the four calendar quarters preceding application. This requirement effectively rendered almost all released prisoners ineligible for benefits since a prisoner was counted as unemployed.

that led to cumulative knowledge through an initial small investment, enlarging the investment of funds and time when the initial returns provided encouraging results.

After a short period of exploratory research, the first experiment in Baltimore was commissioned in 1971. Prisoners released from the Maryland state prisons and returning to Baltimore were randomly allocated to treatments consisting of 13 weeks of payments of $60 per week and/or intensive job counseling and placement services or to a control group that received no payments or counseling. The results of the Baltimore Living Insurance for Ex-Prisoners (LIFE) experiment (described in detail in Chapter 2) were that ex-prisoners receiving payments were less likely to be re-arrested for property-theft-related crimes than those who received only job placement or no services or payments of any kind. This effect led to 8% fewer persons being arrested for such causes, or a relative 25% drop in the proportion arrested for property crimes over a year's period of time.

Although these results were very encouraging, they were also not entirely compelling. First of all, the prisoners used in the LIFE experiment were high-risk subjects, all men whose records indicated that they would very likely end up back in jail. They were not representative of the full range of ex-prisoners. Second, the experiment was administered by a research team whose members were devoted to the intervention and whose skills differed from those of employment security agencies personnel who would administer the program if it were enacted into legislation. Finally, the results were neither very large nor very far from the statistical significance threshold set for the experiment.

Given these doubts, Rosen reasoned that the intervention should receive an additional trial. First of all, the new trial should be administered by the same sorts of state agencies that would be given statutory responsibility if the program were enacted into legislation. Second, coverage should be extended to the full range of prisoners typically incarcerated in state prisons. Finally, the size of the research effort should be enlarged to raise the power of the experiment to distinguish small intervention effects reliably.

The additional trials resulted in two TARP experiments, started in January 1976, in which approximately 4000 ex-felons participated, 2000 each in Texas and Georgia. Released prisoners were randomly allocated to experimental and control groups, as shown in Table 1.1. They were followed for a period of one year beyond release, all through the criminal justice information systems of the states, and a subset, as indicated, were interviewed repeatedly throughout the postrelease year.

Outlines of the experimental design are shown in Table 1.1. There were two levels of treatment, 13 and 26 weeks of eligibility for unemployment

TABLE 1.1
Summary of Benefits Available to TARP Experimental Groups in Georgia and Texas[a]

Experimental groups	State	Maximum weekly payment	Maximum number of weeks	Maximum total allowance	Eligibility period	Forgiveness amount ($)	Tax rate (%)	N
1	Georgia	$70	26	$1820	One year	13.75	100	176
	Texas	$63	26	$1638	One year	8	100	175
2	Georgia	$70	13	$ 910	One year	13.75	100	199
	Texas	$63	13	$ 819	One year	8	100	200
3	Georgia	$70	13	$ 910	One year	—	25	201
	Texas	$63	13	$ 819	One year	—	25	200
4	Georgia	*No Payment Eligibility.* Job placement services available, with up to $100 grants for purchase of tools, special work clothes, etc.						200
	Texas							200
5	Georgia	*Inverviewed Controls.* $15 payment each for prerelease and three follow-up interviews.						200
	Texas							200
6	Georgia	*Noninterviewed Controls.* Postrelease follow-up through arrest records and FICA earnings records.						1031
	Texas							1000

[a] In both states, unemployment payments are conditional on unemployment or on earning less than cut-off thresholds. Eligibility was further conditional on being available for work; that is, not incapacitated by reason of illness, incarceration, or attending school.

insurance benefits; two types of treatments, unemployment insurance and job placement; and two levels of tax rates applied, 100% (in which benefits are reduced dollar for dollar for earnings received) and 25% (in which benefits are reduced $.25 for each dollar of earnings). (Chapter 3 contains additional details about the experimental designs.)

In both states, responsibility for disbursing payments was given to the state employment security agency, while responsibility for data collection in connection with the experiment was given to the Texas Department of Corrections and to the Georgia Employment Security Agency. In both states, the full cooperation of the departments of corrections was given in the assignment of about-to-be-released prisoners to experimental or control treatments and in the collection of data.

In both states, released prisoners falling into one of the payment experimental groups were offered eligibility for payments at the level and for the duration indicated for their groups. A participant received payments by certifying his eligibility with the state employment security agency, indicating that he had been unemployed during the week for which eligibility was claimed and that he was available for employment during that period. These rules of eligibility applied as well to persons ordinarily covered by unemployment insurance benefits in those states. Persons employed partially during a week were eligible for part-payment benefits, with reductions computed according to the tax rates and forgiveness amounts indicated in Table 1.1.

A relatively large amount of data was collected about the participants' experiences throughout the postrelease year. Persons in all experimental groups but one were interviewed before release and three times during the year. All participants were monitored through the computerized arrest records of each state. Earnings subject to Old Age and Survivors Insurance (OASI) taxes were monitored through social security wage records, and those released on parole were followed through the parole department records. (A full accounting of data collection efforts is given in Chapter 3.)

TARP Findings

The guiding idea behind the TARP experiment is the clear understanding that released prisoners are sent back into civilian life without resources that would facilitate their adjustment. The provision of a limited amount of income for a limited period after release is designed to meet that condition and to compensate for it. Beneath this surface, commonsense conception lies a more complicated and theoretically relevant set of ideas. (See Chapter 11 for an extended exposition of the theoretical foundations of the TARP experiments.)

Perhaps most important, TARP is guided by the simple notion that poverty leads to property crime. This hardly startling idea is subscribed to by such diverse scholars as the Marxist sociologist Bonger, writing at the turn of the century, and the neoclassical economist Gary S. Becker, writing more than 60 years later.[9] If one regards participation in property-related crimes as an alternative occupation (or as a supplementary occupation) that carries with it certain risks, then engaging in property-related crimes is bound to be attractive to those whose available legitimate occupations pay poorly, subject one to intermittent unemployment, and involve unpleasant working conditions and activities. Furthermore, if the risks of participation in property crime are low, then property theft may appear to be even more attractive. For released prisoners with urgent needs for income, poor employment possibilities, and high likelihoods of unemployment, property theft may be especially seductive as a source of income. TARP payments were designed to compete with pro-

---

[9] Full references to these and other writers are given in Chapter 11.

perty crimes as a source of income, providing a riskless but modest temporary income.

However, TARP payments not only competed with property crime as a source of income but competed with work in a very direct way. Especially important in heightening the competition between the payments and work were the eligibility rules that made payments contingent on unemployment or partial employment. Payments of $60 or $70 per week with no work may easily have seemed more attractive than before-taxes wages of $100 to $150 per week that included 30 to 40 hours of hard or unpleasant work. Another way of putting this competition is that TARP payments drastically lowered the wage rates (or the value of working) to those who were eligible. Note that work disincentives in the TARP experiment were considerably stronger than in its predecessor LIFE experiment, which had a lower tax rate and a staff that faithfully administered the tax rate and assured that participants were aware of the fact that they were entitled to part payments of benefits if they worked. Indeed, as shown in Chapter 4, we were to discover at the end of the TARP experiments that few participants had adequate knowledge of the TARP rules governing their eligibility for payments.

The work disincentives offered by TARP payments might or might not have had any effect on recidivism, depending on what role unemployment plays in crime. If one envisages the effect of unemployment on crime as working primarily through lack of income, then the work disincentive effects of TARP payments should not have affected recidivism one way or the other since the payments would substitute for earnings and would have had the same effect on recidivism as working.[10] On the other hand, if one envisages crime as at least partially a function of aspects of unemployment apart from earnings, then the work-disincentive effect of TARP payments might have counteracted the property-crime-disincentive effects of the payments. An alternative viewpoint might incorporate both effects: TARP payments might have had a crime-disincentive effect to some degree, but because the payments were so modest, the relative attractiveness of engaging in property crime was not entirely wiped out. In addition, the employment-disincentive effects of TARP payments might have made property crime easier to engage in since there is considerable additional leisure time and thus increased opportunity to engage in that activity.

The increased leisure provided by TARP payments may also have had the effect of inducing those eligible to engage in longer and more thorough

---

[10] Actually, the issues are far more complicated than can be communicated here since the TARP payments are transfers that are not tied to time (as is work) and for that reason have different effects than work. These issues are discussed in greater detail in Chapter 11.

job searches. If this effect did occur, such postponement of work could have been more than compensated for by resultant better jobs with accompanying higher wages and more attractive working conditions.

Two main implications flow from these considerations: First, the TARP experiments were not faithful replications of the earlier Baltimore LIFE experiment, differing sharply in having a strong work disincentive attached to payments. Second, because of the ambiguous role of unemployment in property crime, the outcome of the experiment as far as reduction in property crimes is concerned was problematic.

The overall results of the TARP experiments, as shown in Chapter 5, bore out these expectations. First, there were no significant *overall* differences in either state between experimental and control groups in average numbers of arrests on property-related charges during the postrelease year. Second, there were no *overall* differences in other types of arrests (not related to property). Third, the work-disincentive effects of TARP payments were considerable in both states, with persons in payment groups working considerably fewer weeks over the postrelease year. Finally, there were no very strong differences in the total annual earnings[11] of experimental as compared to control groups, a finding that suggests that the experimental subjects managed to get higher wages when they did work and hence earned about the same amount over the year as the controls even though they worked overall fewer weeks during that period.

These overall findings contain a mixture of good and bad news. On the bad news side, it was clear that the TARP payments, *as administered in Georgia and Texas,* did not fulfill expectations that they would lower recidivism. TARP payments also wielded a strong work-disincentive effect. On the side of good news, it was also clear that TARP payments did not increase recidivism, despite the fact that the payments increased unemployment. *This suggests that the TARP payments did reduce recidivism but that such effects were masked by an increase in unemployment that in turn increased arrests.* (This counterbalancing interpretation of the TARP experiment is described in greater detail in Chapter 5.) The results also suggest that the payments did work to some degree as intended by subsidizing a more effective job search that in turn led to better wages and presumably jobs with better working conditions.

The TARP Counterbalancing Effects Model

The findings suggest that the TARP payments had two effects that opposed each other and balanced each other out. On the one hand, for a given level of employment TARP payments lowered the number of arrests exper-

---

[11] As recorded in employer reports in OASI tax returns.

ienced by persons receiving the payments. On the other hand, because TARP payments increased unemployment, and unemployment increased arrests, the payments produced a side-effect that wiped out the direct arrest-averting effects. The postulated counterbalancing model of TARP effects is shown in Figure 1.1 (and is described in greater detail in both Chapters 5 and 11).

In Figure 1.1, it is important to note that the arrows connecting work and the TARP payments are administratively defined: That is, the rules of eligibility for unemployment insurance benefits in effect make it necessary to be unemployed to obtain payments. The fact that the earlier LIFE experiment did not find a work disincentive in payments indicates that there are some administrative arrangements in which the separation between benefits and work is not so complete. Thus the model shown in Figure 1.1 is consistent with the results of both TARP and the earlier Baltimore LIFE experiment. The model also suggests how an effective program of financial aid to released prisoners might be better designed to enhance the overall recidivism-reduction effects of such help.

The model shown in Figure 1.1 need not remain simply hypothetical. In Chapter 12 we describe an approach that provides estimates of the effects represented by the arrows in that schematic diagram. To do so, it is necessary to write out a set of equations that expresses each of the main variables in Figure 1.1 as a function of the links shown in that table and as a function of additional variables as well. A set of five simultaneous equations were constructed and solved, using three-stage least squares.

The resulting estimates for the full model are entirely too numerous to present here. For present purposes, we have extracted the coefficients of major interest, as shown in Figure 1.2, for each state separately. All the coefficients shown in Figure 1.2 have passed the .05 alpha test, except as indicated.

The pattern and sizes of the coefficients of Figure 1.2 are exactly as the counterbalancing model requires. Furthermore, the results in the two states were very close to each other, adding considerably to our confidence in the

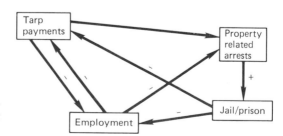

FIGURE 1.1. *Postulated counter-balancing model of TARP payment effects on property-related arrests.*

A. Texas estimates

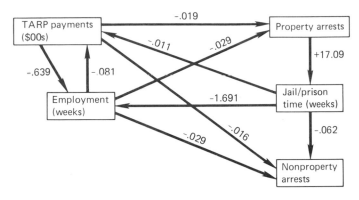

B. Georgia estimates

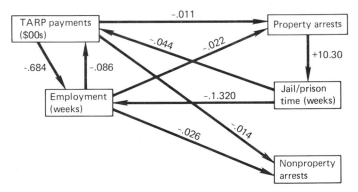

FIGURE 1.2. *Empirical estimates of the counterbalancing TARP effects models for the post-release year. The coefficients for the lines from employment and prison/jail time to TARP payments are averages over the three TARP payment groups. Some of the coefficients that go into these averages are statistically significant at the .05 alpha level, but the overall significances of these averages are difficult to compute in a simultaneous equation framework.*

results. Of special interest are the coefficients for TARP payments: In Texas every $100 of TARP payments lowered the number of property arrests by .019, meaning that for persons who received the maximum total allowance of $910 for 13 weeks, a reduction of .17 arrests on property-related charges was experienced, a hefty 50% proportionate reduction. The corresponding reduction for Georgia TARP members was .09, leading to a sizable 26% fewer arrests proportionately. Also of interest are the sizable coefficients for employment: In Texas each week employed led to .029 fewer property-related arrests; in Georgia, .022 fewer.

Although the counterbalancing model was silent about payment effects on arrests unrelated to property charges, such effects are also shown. They are slightly larger in Texas than in Georgia; there were .016 and .014 fewer arrests in those states, respectively, for each $100 of TARP payments.

If TARP payments had had no counterbalancing effects on employment, the TARP experiment as administered would have had to be declared an unequivocal success. Unfortunately, this was not the case: Every $100 of TARP payments reduced employment by .639 weeks in Texas and .684 weeks in Georgia. Since employment had such strong effects on property arrests, the resulting reduction in employment increased property arrests by amounts that in effect wiped out the arrest-reducing effects of the payments. Because of the effects of other variables affecting both employment and payments, as well as arrests, the actual counterbalancing system is more complicated than we can present here or discuss in any detail. For example, TARP payments set up processes that reverberated widely throughout the system, affecting arrests and employment, which in turn affected returning to prison or jail. And returning to prison affected payment eligibility and employment. Processes of these sorts amplified or dampened the main effects shown here.

Policy Implications

The policy implications of the counterbalancing model are quite clear. First, the payments *are useful* in lowering recidivism. Second, such payments are likely to have attractive benefit-to-cost ratios, being relatively inexpensive and averting costs that are several magnitudes greater. It is cheaper to provide payments between $800 and $1200 to 100 released prisoners than to process about five additional persons through the criminal justice system and provide prison places for them for periods of two and three years, not to mention the costs averted through reduced welfare payments for dependents and other associated costs of imprisonment.

Third, the net effects of employment on rearrest are very strong, as many criminal justice commentators have suggested. The contribution we are able to make through the TARP analysis is to show that the effect of employment holds up strongly net of the many other processes that affect arrests. This finding strongly supports the potential effectiveness of social policies stressing employment for released prisoners. Some sort of supported work strategy, properly administered, apparently has great potential for high payoffs. However, it should be noted that given past failures with work strategies, an effective policy is likely to be relatively expensive.

The policy implications of the TARP experiments lend considerable support to an income-maintenance strategy to reduce arrest recidivism among released prisoners. Specifically, the counterbalancing model suggests that the positive effects of such payments can be fully captured, as in the earlier Baltimore LIFE experiment, if we can strip away the work-disincentive effects that surfaced in the Georgia and Texas TARP experiments. There are a variety of programs that show promise for accomplishing that end. First, it is possible to lower tax rates to provide an incentive for job searches and accepting employment and to insure that participants and administrators are aware of the tax rate. The overall tax rate in LIFE was about 25%, similar to one of the plans in TARP; the crucial difference was that insufficient effort was made in the TARP experiment to make participants aware of the generous tax rate. Whether one could incorporate such a feature into an unemployment insurance system that ordinarily operates with a 100% tax rate may, however, be problematic.

A second possibility is to shift away from the unemployment insurance model to a severance pay model, providing money to prisoners upon release, either as a lump sum, or, perhaps, more sensibly, in the form of installments to be paid out for a limited period of time. For example, each released prisoner could be provided with eligibility for gate money in the amount of $800, $200 of which would be paid upon release and the remainder in 10 weekly installments of $60 each.

A third possibility is to build in positive incentives for working, with bonus payments added on to the severance pay provisions just described that would be paid out on positive demonstration of obtaining employment.

One may add additional wrinkles to such policies, although we suspect that most would mainly be variations on the three themes presented above.

2

Historical Background of the Transitional Aid Research Project Experiments

ORIGINS OF TARP

On January 2, 1976, Edwin L. Dulchin[1] walked into the Texas State Employment Service office in Dallas and was handed a check for $63. Dulchin had just been released from the "Walls"—a state prison in Huntsville, Texas—and was now on his way home, after having served 21 months for a burglary committed in 1973. Dulchin was the first of 4000 released prisoners in Texas and Georgia who would be participating in the Transitional Aid Research Project (TARP), and this was the first of 13 checks he was entitled to receive over the coming year. The purpose of the program was to find out whether providing a limited amount of financial aid to released prisoners would reduce recidivism and help them make the transition from prison life to the world of work.

Although TARP officially began to operate in January 1976, its origins go back at least a decade. The program was the culmination of several years of preliminary research effort and experience. One of the more important beginnings of TARP was the passage of the Manpower Development and Training Act in 1962. Through amendments to the act in subsequent years, vocational training and other services were introduced into the prisons with the hope of increasing employment opportunities after release. Evaluations of these programs, however, did not bear out expectations. No discernible effects of vocational training on subsequent employment or recidivism could be found.[2]

---

[1] A pseudonym.

[2] See, for example, Abt Associates, Inc., *Impact of the Training Program on Trainees. An Evaluation of the Training Provided in Correctional Institutions Under the Manpower Development and Training Act, Section 251*, Vol. III (Cambridge, Mass.: May, 1971); R. Taggart, *The Prison of Unemployment: Manpower Programs for Offenders* (Baltimore: Johns Hopkins University Press, 1972); W. J. Gearhart, H. C. Keith, and G. Clemmons, *An Analysis of the Vocational Training Program in the Washington State Adult Correctional Institu-*

In the early 1960s, the Manpower Administration commissioned George Pownall[3] to study the postrelease work experiences of released federal prisoners. His findings confirmed what many experts had long suspected—it took a long time, measured in weeks or months—for ex-prisoners to find a job. Even after 6 months many prisoners were still unemployed. The study also revealed that prisoners were released with pitifully meager financial resources to tide them over until they found jobs. About half the ex-prisoners in the study had less than $50 when released from prison. Pownall's findings raised the questions of how could they possibly get along until employed, and, was it any wonder that so many ex-prisoners returned to crime and later to prison so soon after release, despite their fresh memories of the harshness of prison life.

The failure of vocational training in prison, high unemployment rates among ex-prisoners, and meager financial resources upon release were all realizations that led Howard Rosen of the Manpower Administration (now the Employment and Training Administration) to consider programs providing limited postrelease financial aid to ex-prisoners in the hope that such aid would ease the transition to employment and successful adjustment to civilian life. To explore this possibility, a pilot study was begun in New York City in 1970 to test the feasibility of conducting a more rigorous experiment at a later time. The aims of the pilot study were to see what administrative difficulties might occur, to develop procedures for random assignment, and to construct screening and interview forms. After a few months of negotiations with New York City Corrections Department officials, access to Rikers Island prisoners was gained. Six men, released during the last week of May 1970, were selected to receive six weekly payments of $60 each. Another 20 men, released at the same time, were selected as controls (no payments), mainly to see if it was possible to interview them during the first week after release and then again 1 month later.

The Rikers Island pilot study was a successful demonstration. Procedures were worked out to recruit subjects, conduct interviews after release, and dispense the weekly checks. At the end of the pilot study a meeting was held between the men who had received payments and several Manpower Administration officials. The six ex-prisoners heartily endorsed the program and said it was badly needed. They also made two recommendations that were heeded in subsequent studies. First, the ex-prisoners recommended that the financial aid should be limited to only 13 weeks rather

---

tions, Research Review No. 23 (Tacoma, Washington: Department of Institutions, State of Washington, 1967).

[3] G. Pownall, "Employment Problems of Released Prisoners," mimeographed (College Park: University of Maryland, 1969). A summary appears in G. Pownall, "Employment Problems of Released Prisoners," *Manpower,* 13, no. 1 (January 1971): 26–31.

than the 26-week period then being considered. They felt that 26 weeks would be too long and that some men would simply "coast along" and not look for jobs. Their second point was that they would much prefer to have jobs than money. Although they appreciated receiving the money when they needed it—gate money at Rikers Island at that time was $.25 and a bologna sandwich—it was a handout. They wanted job-placement services added to the program. These two recommendations—money for only 13 weeks and a job-placement component—were to be incorporated into the following year's more ambitious experiment in Baltimore.

The Rikers Island pilot experience did cause some changes in plans. It had been agreed earlier that heroin users and alcoholics would be excluded from the program out of concern that the media might represent the program as a handout to drug users and one used primarily to support their habits. The program deserved a fair trial without unfavorable publicity. Since prison records indicated that 80% of the persons then being released from Rikers were heroin users or alcoholics (mainly the former), it was necessary to find another site to conduct a more carefully designed test of the program.

Other large cities were approached as potential sites. Several correctional departments, which did not want outsiders looking over their records, withheld cooperation. Other cities had competing programs that might have interfered with the experiment. Finally, the Department of Corrections of Maryland agreed to cooperate. Plans were made to start an experiment in the summer of 1971.

Since financial aid was the essence of the new program being considered, it was necessary to know for planning purposes how much gate money released prisoners received throughout the country. How many correctional departments gave out just bologna sandwiches, or did some vary the menu? More seriously, it was desirable to know the average sum of gate money given on release and how much, if any, savings were typically accrued from working in prison. Glaser *et al.*, in their study of gate money 10 years earlier, had shown that typical amounts were pitifully small (see Table 2.1).[4] It was deemed useful to know whether any states had changed their policies, particularly after the rapid rise in the cost of living during the 1960s. In the spring of 1971 a survey was taken of the correction departments of the 50 states and the District of Columbia (see Table 2.1).[5] Not much had changed in 10 years. The survey found that states typically were

---

[4] D. Glaser, E. Zemans, & C. Dean, *Money Against Crime: A Survey of Economic Assistance to Released Prisoners* (Chicago: John Howard Assoc., 1961).

[5] K. Lenihan, *The Financial Condition of Released Prisoners* (Washington, D.C.: Bureau of Social Science Research, 1974). Also summarized, under the same author and title, in *Crime and Delinquency*, July 1976.

TABLE 2.1
Maximum Legal Cash Gratuities for Prison Releasees ,
United States Jurisdictions: 1961, 1971, 1975

State	1961	1971	1975
Alabama	$2 per yr. served[a]	$2 per yr. served	$2 per yr. served
Alaska	$30	0	0
Arizona	$12.50	$50	$50
Arkansas	0	$10	$25
California	Discharge $40; Parole limit set at official discretion	$68[b]	$200[b]
Colorado	$25	$25	$100
Connecticut	$20	$20[b]	$75[b]
Delaware	0	0	0
District of Columbia	$30	Felons $50; Misdemeanants $10	Felons $50; Misdemeanants $10
Florida	$15	$75	$100
Georgia	0	$25 (Felons only)	Felons $150; Misdemeanants $25
Hawaii	$10	$100	$100
Idaho	$15[b]	$15	$15
Illinois	$50	$50	$100
Indiana	$25	$50	Felons $75; Misdemeanants $30
Iowa	Discharge $25; Parole $5	$100	$100
Kansas	$25	$.05/day earnings saved	$250
Kentucky	$10	$5	$20
Louisiana	Served under 2 yrs., $10; served 2 yrs. or more, $20	Served under 2 yrs., $10; served 2 yrs. or more, $20	Served under 2 yrs., $10; served 2 yrs. or more, $20
Maine	$25	$25	$50
Maryland	$20	$20	$20
Massachusetts	$50	$50	$50
Michigan	$25	$25	$25
Minnesota	$25	$100	$100
Mississippi	Discharge $10; Parole 0	Served 1 yr. or less, $5; 1–10 yrs., $25; 10–20 yrs., $75; over 20 yrs., $100	Served 1 yr. or less, $5; 1–10 yrs., $25; 10–20 yrs., $75; over 20 yrs., $100
Missouri	$25	$25	$100
Montana	$25	$25	$25
Nebraska	$30	$50	$100
Nevada	$25	$50	$50
New Hampshire	$20	$30	$100
New Jersey	$25	$150[b]	$150[b]
New Mexico	$25	$100	$100

TABLE 2.1 (cont.)

State	1961	1971	1975
New York	$20	$40	$40
North Carolina	$25	$25	$25
North Dakota	0	$5	0
Ohio	$25		$50
Oklahoma	$5	$25	$50
Oregon	Discharge $50 Parole $25	$100	$100
Pennsylvania	$10	$10	$10
Rhode Island	$20	$20	$20
South Carolina	0	0	0
South Dakota	$15	$20	$25[b]
Tennessee	$1.50	Discharge $75; Parole $30	Discharge $75; Parole $30
Texas	Discharge $100; Parole $5	$50	$200
Utah	$25	$25	$25
Vermont	$100	$200[b]	$200[b]
Virginia	0	$25	$25
Washington	$40	$40	$40 or $1430[c]
West Virginia	$5	$50	
Wisconsin	$10	$10	$50[b]
Wyoming	Discharge $35; Parole 0	$70	$50
U.S.	$30	$100	$100

Source: American Bar Association, "Back on the Street—From Prison to Poverty," mimeographed (Washington, D.C.: American Bar Association, 1976). This report also surveys financial assistance available under various state and local income-maintenance programs. Note that this table summarizes data from two earlier studies (D. Glaser et al., Money Against Crime, John Howard Assoc., 1961; K. Lenihan, The Financial Condition of Released Prisoners, Bureau of Social Science Research, 1974) as well as data from the ABA 1975 study.

Note: The figures in this table apply to all releasees from state correctional institutions unless otherwise noted.

[a] For all 3 years, Alabama qualifies this gate-money provision with a $10 minimum.

[b] California, Connecticut, Idaho, New Jersey, South Dakota, Vermont, and Wisconsin are jurisdictions in which the limit is not set by statute. In each case the corrections department is delegated authority to determine the ceiling amount. The amount shown for 1975 is the figure in effect on December 31.

[c] $1430 is the maximum that may be given a releasee under a stipend program.

giving between $20 and $30 in gate money. In about half the states, the correction department simply supplemented a man's savings to make a total of $20 or $30; in the other states, a man was given a fixed amount regardless of savings. Not all states were confined to the $20 or $30 bracket; some gave $50 and a very few gave $100 or more. In any case, gate money on hand at release often barely covered a day's expenses and at best merely a few day's. In addition, few prisoners were able to accumulate significant savings in prison, since most prison work paid only $.50 to $1.50 *a day.* Given the cost of shaving equipment, candy bars, cigarettes, and stationary, most prisoners had to supplement their earnings in some fashion (many with gifts from friends and relatives) simply to pay for the few personal articles allowed in prison.

About half the states provided free transportation back to the jurisdiction in which the prisoner had been arrested (or to the state line if the prisoners lived outside the state). The other half did not. Bus fare back home can be expensive, since most state prisons are located in remote rural areas and most prisoners come from urban areas, often several hundred miles away.

In 1975, the American Bar Association conducted another survey of state gate-money practices (see Table 2.1).[6] Although many states had increased the amount of gate money dispensed on release—apparently in response to inflationary trends—the amounts given were still pitifully small. A few states gave nothing. Typical gate money amounts were $50 and $100, with a few generous states giving as much as $250. Thus, as of the time prisoners participating in TARP were released, gate money given to state prisoners was scarcely sufficient to support a single person—much less a person with dependents—for more than a few days beyond release.

In sum, the gate money surveys sustained a *prima facie* case of the need for a program of financial aid; released prisoners were without financial resources, and their first employment after release would take weeks or months to find.

Although there are many benefit programs available to the usual unemployed persons, released felons are typically ineligible. First, their stay in prison has usually resulted in the loss of their eligibility for unemployment benefit payments. Special surveys conducted in both Georgia and Texas at the behest of TARP uncovered the unemployment benefit losses shown in Table 2.2.[7] Among those who had social security numbers, 20% in Georgia and 30% in Texas were eligible for unemployment benefits at

---

[6] Reported in American Bar Association, "Back on the Street—From Prison to Poverty," mimeographed (Washington, D.C.: American Bar Association, 1976). This report also surveys financial assistance available under various state and local income maintenance programs.

[7] Data were collected from newly incarcerated prisoners in reception centers of the Texas and Georgia prison systems by obtaining social security numbers from the prisoners. Since some did not know their numbers or did not have their social security cards or gave invalid social security numbers, data on their eligibility could not be obtained. Eligibility information was obtained by submitting eligibility inquiries in the usual manner through the respective state employment security agencies. See American Bar Association, *Final Report on Activities of the Transitional Aid Research Project* (Washington, D.C.: American Bar Association, 1978), pp. 151–168.

TABLE 2.2
Unemployment Benefit Eligibility of Georgia and Texas State
Prisoners: 1976 Samples of Newly Incarcerated Prisoners

	Texas	Georgia
Number of prisoners sampled	461	4842
Number without known social security accounts	115	1230
Number with valid social security accounts	346	3620
Eligible for benefits	105 (30%)	727 (20%)
Average number of weeks of eligibility	15	13.5
Average maximum eligibility amount	$714	$785

Source: American Bar Association, *Final Report on Activities of the Transitional Aid Research Project* (Washington, D.C.: American Bar Association, 1978), pp. 151-165.

the time of incarceration. Presumably the remainder had not accumulated sufficient covered employment in the relevant eligibility-establishing periods to accrue any amount of eligibility.

Those who were eligible were entitled, on the average, to 13.5 weeks of payments in Georgia and 15 weeks in Texas. The average total amounts for which eligibility was established were $714 in Texas and $785 in Georgia. In short, rather large minorities—from one in five to one in three—lose eligibility by virtue of the period of incarceration, a not inconsiderable loss to the persons involved. It should be noted that if eligibility for earned unemployment benefits were restored to prisoners released, coverage would be almost as much in amount and time for eligible persons as was offered to felons in the TARP program.

Eligibility for help under various income maintenance programs is also usually out of the reach of ex-felons. In many states, Aid to Families with Dependent Children (AFDC) payments are made to families only if there is an absent father. The return of a released prisoner to his family under such circumstances may indeed lead to the loss of payments for his wife and children. Even in states that allow for payments to a family with an unemployed father, the additional payments that accrue to the family unit by reason of his presence usually amount to less than $20 or $30 per week.

Since most released felons are not married at the time of their release, the only programs under which they are eligible for some sort of financial help are those classified as general relief. Payments under such programs are often dependent on proof of some disabling condition and/or a record of local residence. Payment amounts are hardly sufficient for maintenance needs, amounting on the average to less than $100 per month and in some states—for example, Alabama—as little as $37.50 per year.

There are, of course, other sorts of transfer payments that are sometimes available to ex-offenders: food stamps, free medical care, housing subsidies, and the like. Moreover, additional assistance can sometimes be obtained from private agencies. Yet, these hardly put the ex-offender on easy street and are typically difficult to obtain in any case.

In short, prisoners have few resources upon release, and there are few, if any, public programs that can aid them with subsistence until they find employment. Of course, this does not mean that they are completely without aid. For most, it means that their kin and friends are their major sources of financial help. Given the severe poverty backgrounds from which such persons usually come, released prisoners can become an additional burden on households and persons who are already overburdened by problems of their own.

Although the surveys conducted earlier indicated that there was surely a need for some type of support for released prisoners to ease the transition to civilian life, these studies, of course, could not specify what would be an appropriate remedy. There are several directions that responsive policy might have taken. Since gate money was customary, it might have been sensible to urge the states to increase gate money amounts and to adjust such amounts periodically to compensate for inflationary trends. Although such a policy might have made some sense, it certainly would not have been responsive to the congressional mandate that the Department of Labor (DOL) do something related to employment of ex-prisoners.

Another possible policy would have been to modify existing DOL programs to include financial help for released prisoners. In this connection, an extension of unemployment benefits would seem promising. Unemployment benefits are given out to unemployed persons, who have worked more than some minimum period, the rationale being that such payments ease the transition back into the labor force. Such payments to released prisoners would help in two ways: First, they would provide sufficient income to enable the released prisoners to subsist, albeit on a minimal level, and hence lower the pressures to obtain some earnings at any risk. In particular, the temptation to resort to theft crimes would be lessened. Second, the payments would provide the released prisoners with sufficient time to engage in better job searches, making it more possible for them to obtain employment that would take care of their income needs. Both of these effects would lower the attractiveness of property crimes as sources of income and hence lower the probabilities of rearrest on property-related charges. The existing unemployment insurance plans, however, largely ruled out payments to ex-prisoners, since no credits could accumulate while in prison. In addition, some states specifically excluded released prisoners from eligibility until they had accumulated sufficient credits through working after release. Modification of the existing state unemployment insurance programs could have been undertaken through federal legislation that would have set forth general principles and regulations under which the individual states set up their own programs. Aiding ex-prisoners through the unemployment insurance system seemed to Department of Labor officials an appropriate way for that agency to proceed in attempting to discharge the responsibility for the problem given them by the Congress.

In addition, a very good equity argument could be advanced for such an extension of unemployment benefits. As shown earlier in this chapter, persons convicted of felonies typically lost their eligibility for payments as a result of incarceration. Hence, for a fairly large minority of released prisoners, extension of coverage could be regarded as a restoration of rights that were removed under current practices. Such a step could be regarded as part of the general society-wide movement to restore convicted felons to full citizenship rights when released from prison.

Accordingly, a major part of the plan was to test a program that could be administered through state unemployment insurance systems and that would be designed as financial aid to help newly released prisoners through an initial period of unemployment.

Since the Department of Labor also had responsibility for job-placement services through the United States Employment Service, another promising direction would have been to offer some special job-placement services as well as financial aid. Prisoners could be helped to find jobs by placing expert counselors at their disposal. This approach, too, was built into the experiments that were to follow. Like the strategy of providing unemployment benefit coverage, job placement was also an extension of an existing service provided generally throughout the states.

The history of programs designed to lower recidivism was a long series of failures. While the strategy devised by the Department of Labor appeared a priori to be sensible and worth a try, the many other programs that had been tried and failed had also seemed sensible. Under these circumstances, it seemed most prudent to test this new strategy on a relatively small scale. Furthermore, since the program could not be expected to produce extremely large effects on recidivism, given the intractability of this social problem in the past, it seemed best to test it out using methods that would be sensitive to small effects. Hence the decision was made to proceed on a small scale using a controlled experimental design as the testing mode. Although randomized field experiments are difficult to carry out, they have the desirable characteristics of providing definitive estimates of the effectiveness of a program and providing results in which more confidence can be placed than any alternative testing method. Indeed, randomized field experiments are the preferred method for testing programs that are likely to yield results that are difficult to detect because of their size and the possible confounding effects of other events.

THE BALTIMORE LIFE PROJECT

The Baltimore Living Insurance for Ex-prisoners (LIFE) Project started in the summer of 1971. Staff were hired and trained, final arrangements were made with the Maryland Department of Corrections, and in October the program began. It was set up as a true experiment, with random assignment to the various treatment and control groups. In all, there were four groups, three experimental and one control.

GROUP 1: Eligible to receive $60 a week for 13 weeks and offered job-placement services
GROUP 2: Eligible to receive $60 a week for 13 weeks but not offered job-placement services
GROUP 3: Offered job-placement services but no financial aid
GROUP 4: Offered neither financial aid nor job-placement services

This design was set up to test each of the two treatments—financial aid and job placement—separately and jointly. For financial aid, Groups 1 and 2 were the experimental groups, and Groups 3 and 4 were the controls. For the job-placement services, Groups 1 and 3 were the experimental groups, and Groups 2 and 4 were the controls. If there were any interaction effect of financial aid and job placement—that is, something more than the additive effects of each—it would be reflected in the comparison of Group 1 with the sum of Groups 2 and 3.

Administrative responsibility for running the Baltimore LIFE experiment was given to the Bureau of Social Science Research of Washington, D.C., a not-for-profit social-research organization. Direct responsibility for the experiment was in the hands of Kenneth J. Lenihan, who served as principal investigator for the project. Since the main activities and operating offices of the project were located in Baltimore, the LIFE staff operated autonomously throughout the period of the experiment.

Selecting the Study Population

Any prison population contains a wide diversity of people—from those serving a 1-year sentence for shoplifting to those serving 20 years for homicide. Some are first offenders, not likely to get into trouble again, and others are habitual criminals. Since this experiment was to be limited to about 500 subjects, spread across four groups, it was desirable to maximize the chances of detecting any possible effects of each treatment. Thus, the target population was purposely selected to be a high-risk group—ex-prisoners with relatively high probabilities of being rearrested. The logic of excluding low-risk subjects in experiments applies in other fields as well. For example, in testing a drug to prevent cancer, one chooses a population that is highly likely to get cancer; similarly, when testing a new contraceptive, one chooses a highly fertile population. This strategy maximizes the chances that if the experimental treatment is effective, the effects will not pass undetected.[8] If, for example, a population with a rearrest rate of only 10% had been chosen, it would have been difficult to show a statistically significant difference with only 500 cases.

This strategy—using only high-risk subjects—precludes generalizing to other populations, but the chief concern of this program was to test whether payments would work at all. It was not designed to establish national estimates. The essential issue was, "Could financial aid or job placement reduce rearrest rates and increase employment rates?" The LIFE experiment was designed to provide evidence of any support for a positive answer to the question. Generalizing to the total prison population in Maryland or to other states had to await larger field trials.

Selection Criteria

To obtain a high-risk[9] group of subjects, the study population was limited to males under 45 with multiple convictions and at least one arrest on property-related charges. No alcoholics or heroin addicts were included, nor were prisoners on work release for 3 or more months when released. All subjects had less than $400 in savings. For reasons of convenience,

---

[8] Actually, there are two related issues implied in the decision to select high-risk subjects. First, since one cannot reduce the proportion of ex-offenders who are rearrested below zero, there is a floor effect. Thus, one wants to begin with likely proportion well above the floor. In other words, if the initial proportions are near zero, one might be in fact reducing the propensity to commit new crimes, but one's measure would fail to detect it. Second, if one is going to examine the impact of unemployment benefits on rearrests, there must be variance in the outcome measure to explain. Rearrest proportions near zero imply very little variance.

[9] At the completion of the study, rearrest records of low-risk persons who had been excluded from the study were examined. Indeed, they were low-risk candidates: Only 13% of the first offenders were rearrested in the year following on any charge, and only half of these were for robbery, burglary, or larceny. Similarly, persons who had never previously been arrested on a theft charge (typically they had been in prison for murder, assault, or rape) had a rearrest rate of 8% and only 1% for crimes of theft. No one over the age of 45 was rearrested. Among persons who had been on work release, or who had $400 or more in savings, the rearrest rate was 10% and 3% for a theft crime. In contrast, persons who actually became subjects in the study had a rearrest rate of over 50% and 26% for a theft crime. In short, the screening procedures had worked: They yielded a group of ex-prisoners who were highly vulnerable to rearrest.

only persons who were returning to live in the metropolitan area of Baltimore were accepted, since it would have been difficult to conduct interviews, dispense weekly checks, and provide job-placement services throughout Maryland. Also, prisoners who had warrants or detainers were excluded, since they are usually turned over to another jurisdiction on the day of their release. Finally, persons who were released on a court order—as a result of a reduced sentence or a reversal of conviction—were excluded. Such persons are released within 24 hours of the order; in this situation there is not enough time to arrange interviews before release.

Some prisoners excluded themselves by refusing to be interviewed in prison (less than 1%), and others were unavailable for an interview, either being in isolation for violation of a prison rule or working away from prison on a road gang.

Recruiting Subjects

The Correction Department notified the research team a few weeks before each prisoner was to be released, which usually allowed enough time to examine the prison file, determine probable eligibility, and then conduct interviews and determine final eligibility. Research workers identified themselves as working under a federal contract for the Bureau of Social Science Research. Each candidate was asked if he would be willing to participate in a research study for a period of 1 year after release. His participation would require interviews—one while still in prison, and then 12 monthly interviews after release. He would be paid $5 for each interview, plus carfare. Since the payment for the interview prior to release could not be made in prison, he was told he could pick up his payment at an office in Baltimore as soon as he was released.

If he agreed—and almost all candidates did—he was interviewed at that time. The interviews covered such topics as whether he had a job arranged or what kind of job he would be looking for, what his living arrangements would be, and many questions about his past—work experience, education, and family life.

Random Assignment

Eligible candidates were assigned to one of the experimental or control groups by random assignment within one of 16 categories formed by the cross-classification of three characteristics.[10] After a random start, as-

---

[10] The characteristics were (1) work experience (one year or more, versus less than one year); (2) age (20 or less, 21-25, 26-30, 31 or more); and (3) marital status (married versus all other possibilities).

signments were systematic. For example, for persons who had 1 year of work experience, who were between the ages of 21 and 25, and who were not married, the random start was Group 2. Hence the first person falling into that category would receive financial aid but no job-placement service. The next person falling into that category would be assigned to Group 3, receiving job service but no financial aid. The next person would be assigned to Group 4, receiving neither, and, so on.[11]

The interview held in prison verified the subject's work experience, age, and marital status, and hence the group to which he was to be assigned. By checking the sequence of random assignment, the interviewer could determine to which group a subject should be assigned. Persons assigned financial aid were each handed a card with an office address in Baltimore where they could pick up their $5 for the interview just held. Persons assigned to groups with no financial aid were given different cards with another address. The two offices were set up to avoid commingling persons who were receiving financial aid with those who were not.

A few points should be made about these procedures. First, those who refused participation were simply refusing to participate in research—not any particular program—since they were not informed about the various services. Thus refusals do not become a self-selective factor that could interfere with the statistical equivalence among the four groups that randomization produced. Second, assignments could not be affected by the conscious or unconscious preferences of the interviewer since the sequence of assignment was preset. Finally, after the initial interview, the subject was still not informed about what service he would be offered. He was simply asked to report to one of the two offices in Baltimore to pick up his $5 for the prison interview. Information about what services might be available was withheld to preclude discussion of the fiancial-aid program via the prison grapevine.

The Program

The first time a subject reported to one of the two offices he was told about the services, if any, that he was eligible to receive. (If he was in Group 4 and would receive no service, he was asked to report for an interview in 1 month.) If he was assigned to a group receiving financial aid, he was told that he could receive $60 a week for 13 weeks (a total of $780),

---

[11] The purpose of the stratification was to reduce the intergroup variances (treatment groups and control groups) on the stratifying variables, thus increasing the precision of the experiment. Since it appeared a priori that recidivism was related to these variables, assuring that each of the treatment and control groups were identical in these respects reduced the chances that such differences might obscure treatment effects.

assuming he did not find a job during that period. If he did find a job, he was told, his payments would be reduced depending on how much he earned, but eligibility for payments would be extended beyond the 13 weeks until he had exhausted his total amount of $780. For those who found employment, the weekly financial aid was as follows:[12]

Weekly gross earnings	Weekly financial aid
Less than $40	$60
$40–$49	$55
$50–$59	$50
$60–$69	$45
$70–$79	$40
$80–$89	$35
$90–$99	$30
$100–$109	$25
$110–$119	$20
$120–$150	$15
Over $150	0

Each subject was free to spend the money any way he wished, and financial aid was given whether or not he looked for a job. If a person was unavailable for work because he was in school or in other training, or was ill or hospitalized, he still received his full weekly amount. If the person was sent back to jail or prison, his payments were interrupted while he was

[12] This schedule of payments, conditional upon earnings, amounts to rather complicated marginal and gross tax rates. The tax on earnings up to $40 is 0. The tax rate then is sensitive in steps of earnings. As a person enters a step the marginal tax rate is very large (e.g., a person earning $40 loses $5 in payments, that extra dollar earned losing him $5 in payments, equivalent to a marginal tax rate of 500%), but the marginal tax rate declines toward the end of the interval, reaching a low of 10%. Assuming that the midpoint of an interval represents the average tax rate within an interval, the marginal tax rate applying is about 100% for all but the highest intervals, where the tax is somewhat lower. Perhaps a better way of looking at this tax system is by considering the gross tax rate (i.e., dollars of payments lost per income received, in which case the tax rate is seen as a sliding scale ranging from 0% for persons earning less than $40 per week, jumping to 11%, 18%, 23%, 27%, 29%, 32%, 33%, 35%, 33% for subsequent intervals until the last interval, for which it is impossible to calculate the gross tax). In short, although the tax rate for the LIFE experiment has been described elsewhere (K. Lenihan, *Unlocking the Second Gate*, Washington, D.C.: Government Printing Office, 1977) as approximately 25%, in fact the marginal tax rate and the gross rate are quite complicated. Because records concerning payments were not kept, it is not possible to compute the actual marginal or gross tax rates experienced by LIFE participants. If we consider that average weekly wages were somewhere between $100 and $150 per week, then the marginal tax rate faced by LIFE participants was 100%, and the gross tax rate was about 33%.

incarcerated and resumed once he was free. However, each subject was eligible to receive financial aid for only 1 year after entering the study.[13]

On their first visit, subjects receiving financial aid were given their first check and a photo identity check-cashing card. Those who were assigned to receive the job-placement service were told of the assistance available. Two persons from the Maryland State Employment Service were assigned to the LIFE project and were available at the project offices every day. Released prisoners were free to accept or reject the service; no jobs were forced on participants, and they could use the service as often as they wished up to one year after release. About half never used the service; some men had already arranged jobs before release and needed no help. Others simply preferred to look for jobs on their own. But at least half the men who were entitled to the service did talk with the job counselors at some point during the year.

The main source of information about job openings was a "job bank"—a computer-generated list of all job openings, produced daily by the State Employment Service. Job openings listed in the daily newspapers were also used, as well as a list of employers who has indicated willingness to hire ex-prisoners (a list compiled previously by the employment service personnel). This list was augmented by placing ads in business magazines asking for job openings for ex-prisoners. Finally, some job openings came through the Project's own staff (between 15 and 20 jobs) and through some of the subjects who were employed.

It was generally left to the man himself to decide the kind of job he wanted. Men with some previous work experience could usually narrow their interest to two or three acceptable kinds of jobs. Finding suitable work for men who had little or no work experience was more difficult. For those never previously employed it usually took several days of searching discussion and hours of counseling to work out a job plan.

Once an acceptable job opening turned up, every effort was made to help the man get hired. First, the employer was called to get more details about the job and to probe for objections to hiring an ex-prisoner. If bonding was an issue, and the subject would be denied a bond by a private bonding agency, the staff was prepared to get a bond through the state.[14] When a

---

[13] Nine men did not receive the full $780 because they were sent back to prison and remained there beyond the 1-year limit. In addition, two subjects refused to accept any financial aid.

[14] Under a Bonding Program (applicable to all states also financed by grants from the Department of Labor, Employment and Training Division) the Maryland Employment Service could obtain bonds required as a condition for employment if the applicant was denied a bond by a private bonding agency because of his criminal record.

job interview was required, one of the staff usually accompanied the ex-prisoner and spoke to the employer on his behalf.

Sometimes help was given in filling out job application forms—in part because of the limited literacy of some men, but also because their lives had been so disrupted that it was difficult to construct a picture of their past experience. In many instances, a short resumé was prepared that a man could carry with him, containing information likely to be asked for on a job application. Resumés were mailed to potential employers, and training sessions were conducted on how to look for a job and how to handle job interviews.

Some men were helped to get social security cards or drivers' licenses. Physical examinations and special tools were paid for when necessary. Where public transportation was not available, transportation was provided to the job each morning until the person could establish his own way of getting there.

Job placement in the LIFE project was an all-out approach, tailoring efforts to the needs of each man. Some needed very little—given an opening, they could secure a job by themselves. Others were problems; no matter what was done, they were never able to get a job. The job-placement services provided by LIFE were not intended to be reproducible in a large-scale program. The objective was not to test this particular job service (nor how best to secure employment); rather it was to test whether being employed reduced recidivism, no matter how the employment was arranged. The objective was to increase the amount of employment among Groups 1 and 3 to see whether subjects in these groups had lower rates of recidivism than others who did not receive the services.

The recruitment of subjects began in October of 1971 and continued for 21 months, until June 1973, at which time 432 men were in the study (108 in each of the four groups). Beginning in October 1972, as each subject completed his release anniversary, a follow-up was conducted to ascertain new arrests and convictions. Since subjects entered the study over a 21-month period, the follow-up period continued for 21 months, until June 1974.

To obtain arrest and conviction data, the records of the district courts were searched. In Maryland, these records are comprehensive sources since each arrest must be entered in them.[15]

In this experiment an arrest rather than a conviction or a return to

---

[15] We also checked the court records in Washington, D.C. and Wilmington, Delaware, the two largest cities outside Maryland where our subjects were most likely to be arrested. Few arrests outside Baltimore were found. Indeed, one of the surprising findings from the LIFE and the TARP experiments is how unlikely participants were to leave the communities to which they were discharged or to travel long distances.

prison, was chosen as the indicator of failure. This conservative decision counts as failures all possible events that might indicate a return to crime. Many arrests do not result in conviction for technical reasons that have little bearing on what a person's actions may have been. Returns to prison also reflect the fact that persons with previous records are more likely to be returned to prison. There is considerable erosion in numbers from arrests to convictions to prison sentences: Over the postrelease year 53% of the subjects were arrested, 29% were convicted, and 18% were sentenced to prison.

Findings of the LIFE Project Experiment

When follow-ups were completed in the summer of 1974, the main finding was that *financial aid did reduce arrests on charges of theft.* As Table 2.3 shows, an 8% difference between experimentals and controls was found in the number of persons arrested on charges of crimes of theft.[16] However, financial aid had no effect on other kinds of arrests[17]—disorderly conduct, assaults, drug possession charges, driving violations, and a few rape and homicide charges. The Baltimore LIFE experiment appeared to have found a modestly effective treatment. Payments were intended to affect recidivism for economically motivated crimes, and they were shown to have that effect.

The differences between payment groups and their controls are not large, either substantively or statistically. While the difference is statistically significant at the .05 level, assuming a one-tailed test, it is only barely so. In an effort to sharpen the findings,[18] regression analyses were also run in which the dependent variable was whether or not a LIFE participant was arrested on a property-related charge. In addition to whether or not a person was in a payment group, factors that were known from previous studies to affect the probability of rearrest—such as age, parole status, race and so on—were added as independent variables.

Table 2.4 contains the results of the regression analysis. The column headed *b* shows the unstandardized regression coefficients (*b* = coefficients). These coefficients should be interpreted as the increment (or decrement) in the probability of being arrested on property-related charges over

---

[16] Theft arrests included those resulting from any charge in which property was involved, regardless of other charges. Thus armed robbery was classified as a theft arrest even though force or threat of force may have been used.

[17] These are arrests resulting from charges in which *no* property-related charges were involved.

[18] Regression analyses reduce the error sum of squares, thereby increasing statistical power.

TABLE 2.3

Baltimore LIFE Experiment: Arrests during the First Year after
Release in Payment Experimental and Control Groups

Arrest charge	Groups 1 and 2 (received financial aid)	Groups 3 and 4 (did not receive financial aid)	Total	Difference due to financial aid
Theft crimes (robbery, burglary, larceny, etc.)	48 (22.2%)	66 (30.6%)	114 (26.4%)	8.4%
Other serious crimes (murder, rape, assault, etc.)	42 (19.4%)	35 (16.2%)	77 (17.8%)	−3.2%
Minor crimes (disorderly conduct, drinking in public, etc.)	17 (7.9%)	22 (10.2%)	39 (9.0%)	2.3%
Not arrested	109 (50.5%)	93 (43.1%)	200 (46.8%)	7.4%
Total	216 (100%)	216 (100%)	432 (100%)	

TABLE 2.4

Baltimore LIFE Experiment: Regression of Theft Arrest Dummy Variable
on Financial Aid and Other Selected Variables

Independent variables	(Dependent variable = Arrested on property-related charges in post-release year—dummy variable)	
	b	SE
Financial aid (dummy variable for membership in Groups 1 or 2)	−.083*	.041
Baltimore unemployment rate at time of release (3-month average)	.041*	.022
Number of weeks worked in first quarter, full or part-time	−.006	.005
Age at release	−.009*	.004
Age at first arrest	−.010*	.006
Prior theft arrests	.028*	.008
Race (black = 1)	.056	.064
Education (years)	−.025	.022
Had prior work experience of 1 year or more	−.009	.008
Married	−.074	.065
Parole (dummy variable)	−.025	.051
Intercept	.263	.185
R^2	.094*	
N	(432)	

* $p = < .10$

Note that since the experiment was testing directed hypotheses, the .10 level of significance as a two-tailed test is equivalent to the .05 level for directed hypotheses.

the year beyond release that is associated with each unit change in the independent variable involved, net of all other changes contributed by the other independent variables. Thus the b value for financial aid (being in the experimental payment groups) is $-.083$, indicating that being in a payment group lowers the probability of being rearrested on a property-related charge by .083.

Note that the statistical significance of the effect of the experimental treatment is enhanced by holding other factors constant.[19] The effect is almost identical to that shown in Table 2.3, but the standard error is smaller. It should also be noted that all of the independent variables taken together do not explain very much of the variance in rearrest for property-related charges, R^2 for the regression being .094. In short, although the major factors accounting for rearrest are apparently unknown, the payments are known to be effective, although only modestly so.[20]

Whether regarded as a simple outcome, as in Table 2.3, or in regression form as in Table 2.4, the effect of being in an experimental group that received financial aid was statistically significant. In Table 2.4, the probability that the b-coefficient for financial aid was drawn from a population in which financial aid made no difference is .043. Since it was predicted a priori that financial aid would make a difference, it is appropriate to consider a one-tailed test, which lowers the probability to .02. While some might want to have results that were more clearly different from no effect, these were clearly encouraging outcomes for a pilot experiment. Furthermore, the outcomes remained encouraging when examined by alternative outcome measures: Subjects who did not receive financial aid were arrested earlier, were more likely to be convicted, and were more likely to be returned to prison. In addition, a second year follow-up indicated that the rearrest rate differential held over the entire 2-year period: Those in the

---

[19] Because a dichotomous dependent variable necessarily yields heteroskedastic errors under ordinary least squares, the regression coefficients are inefficient, and the standard errors (and thus, t-tests) are biased. Yet, since the distribution on the dependent is not badly skewed, the results are not likely to be misleading. Equally important, Mallar and Thornton (*Journal of Human Resources*, XIII, no. 2 [Spring 1978]:208–236) obtain almost identical results using a probit model that is not subject to the problems associated with the linear probability approach.

[20] Note that one of the major advantages of the randomized experiment is that it is not necessary to know a great deal about the phenomenon that is to be affected by the experimental treatment. Since experimental and control groups are equated through randomization, the same processes and the same mixture of factors can be expected in both groups. Since the groups differ only in the treatment, the effect of the treatment can be estimated net of the combined effects of all other processes. Of course, it is useful to know what are the processes involved, since by specifying such processes, as intended in Table 2.4, the effect can be discerned with greater precision.

payment experimental groups had a property-related rearrest rate of 7.6% less over the 2 years than those who did not receive financial aid. The regression analysis also indicated which other variables in the equation were predictive of these arrests. In particular, the unemployment rate of the city's general population made a difference. (A 3-month average unemployment rate was computed for each man, depending on when he returned to the streets.) If unemployment was high when a man was released, he was more likely to be arrested for theft crime than if unemployment was low. During the course of the study, the 3-month unemployment rates ranged from a low of 3% to a high of 6%. Each percentage point increase in unemployment, on the average, increased the arrest rate of 4%; or, over the full range, unemployment rates made a 12% difference in the rearrest rate for theft. This is a sizable difference, considering only 26.4% of all subjects were arrested for theft during the first year.

It is important to note that this effect of the city's unemployment rate was independent of whether or not the person himself worked (since the number of weeks he worked during the first 13 after release was also included in the equation). Thus, the difference in the arrest rate due to the employment situation should be seen as a contextual effect. Our best interpretation is that the employment situation operates to affect arrest rates through the released prisoners social circle—his family, friends, and relatives—on whom he depends for support after release. If friends and relatives lose their jobs, they can be of little assistance to him. He must survive on his own resources, which are meager. This interpretation, however, must remain speculative since we do not have the data to clinch the argument. But it is clear that some contextual effect was operating since the unemployment rate, independent of whether or not the person worked, affected his chances of being arrested for theft. The regression analysis also suggested that a person's own employment during the first 3 months affected his chances of being arrested for theft during the coming year. (We say "suggested" because the significance level of the coefficient was .178, above the commonly accepted level, and some readers may prefer to ignore it.) The b-coefficient for each week worked during the first 13 was .006; or, each week of work made a difference of .06% in the arrest rate. Since the number of weeks worked ranged from 0 to 13, the difference between those who did not work at all and those who worked all 13 was 7.8%, roughly the same difference that financial aid made. Age also made a difference: Older persons were less likely to be arrested for a theft crime. There was almost a 1% decrease in the arrest rate for each year of age. Similarly, the younger a person was when first arrested, the more likely it was that he would be arrested again. In addition, the greater involvement in crime, as indicated by the number of previous theft arrests, the more likely it was that the person would be rearrested for theft. Several characteristics that are commonly thought to predict rearrest did not appear to have any statistically significant value: race, education, prior work experience, marriage, and parole status (as opposed to being discharged).

A finding that will turn out to be of particular importance in the understanding of later experiments was that those in the payment experiment groups did *not have significantly lower amounts of employment than those in the controls.* Since payments were lowered when a subject in the experimental groups earned money and ceased altogether if he earned more than $150 per week, some degree of work disincentive is offered by the payments. After all, a subject could receive $60 per week for 13 weeks if he did not go to work at all, and such benefits might have turned out to be a temptation. However, there was no statistically significant work-disincentive effect, an outcome that is likely due to the generous tax rates on earnings, whereby almost everyone could receive some payment while working. The released prisoners rarely could earn as much as $150 per week, and hence most persons were eligible for some payments while working. Indeed, except for those who were sent to jail or prison and hence became completely ineligible for payments, all the men in the experimental groups received, by the end of the postrelease year, all of the funds for which they were eligible.

The effects of payment on weeks worked in each of the four quarters of the postrelease year are shown in the regression analyses presented in Table 2.5. In these regressions, the dependent variable is the number of weeks worked in the relevant period. Independent variables used are ones that are likely predictors of postrelease employment, including a mixture of human capital variables such as education and previous work experience as well as status factors affecting employability, such as race and age. Included in each of the regressions is whether or not the participant was in one of the payment groups. The coefficients related to the payment-group membership express the extent to which payment-group members worked more or less than the control-group members—an estimate of the work-disincentive effect of payments.

The coefficients for payment-group membership are negative for the first two quarters and then turn positive for the next two quarters, when the bulk of the payments were disbursed, but the effect is not large enough to be revealed in the LIFE experiment.[21] In short, it appears that no ap-

---

[21] Since one cannot observe negative weeks worked, the dependent variable is truncated at zero. This necessarily leads to biased and inconsistent estimates of the regression coefficients and their standard errors. We will have much to say about such problems in Section III. Suffice it to say here that even with proper adjustments it is very unlikely that work-disincentive effects would surface. The observed effects are simply too small (and of varying sign in any case).

TABLE 2.5

Baltimore LIFE Experiment: Regression of Weeks Worked in Each Quarter and in Total Year of Payment Experimental Groups and Selected Variables

Independent variables	1st Quarter		2nd Quarter		3rd Quarter		4th Quarter		Total post-release year	
	b	SE	b	SE	b	SE	b	SE	b	SE
Payment experimental groups	−.238	.426	−.289	.482	.431	.522	.739	.522	.642	1.543
Age at first arrest	.550*	.061	−.084	.069	−.040	.075	.694*	.080	−.112	.222
Parolee	2.449*	.510	.704	.577	.348	.625	.197	.661	3.698*	1.848
Married	1.356	.674	2.013*	.762	1.622	.825	1.323	.873	6.314*	2.440
Black	−.718	.661	−.224	.748	.290	.810	.631	.857	−.210	2.394
Education	.035	.233	.100	.263	−.036	.285	−.106	.302	−.007	.843
No. of previous theft arrests	−.218*	.086	−.311*	.098	−.276*	.106	−.183	.112	−.988	.313
Age	.060	.040	.112	.045	.683*	.049	.046	.051	.286	.144
Previous work experience	.350*	.087	.482*	.098	.443*	.106	.429*	.113	1.704*	.315
Constant	.803*	.152	1.770	.172		1.186	1.771	.197	6.566	5.490
R^2	.181*		.183*		.122*		.093*		.201*	
N	(432)		(432)		(432) ·		(432)		(432)	

* $p = < .10$

Note that since the experiment is testing directed hypotheses, the .10 level of significance as a two-tailed test is equivalent to the .05 level for directed hypotheses.

preciable work disincentive in the LIFE experiment resulted from being a member of the payment groups.[22]

Despite the considerable efforts of the Baltimore LIFE staff to obtain employment for those in the employment-services experimental groups, job-placement services did not succeed in raising the amounts of employment in those groups.[23] Although these findings do not mean that *any* job-placement service would fail, they do mean that job-placement services are a difficult intervention. Certainly any less intensive set of services would seem as likely to fail at least as much as the very intensive ones offered in Baltimore. Furthermore, since such services are difficult to standardize by their very nature (and hence to reproduce in a large-scale program), job placement did not appear to be a fruitful way to proceed in the development of a program to reduce recidivism.

---

[22] This outcome, which contrasts so strongly with the TARP experiments in Georgia and Texas, is probably due to the fact that eligibility rules were very carefully explained to participants and to the diligence of the LIFE research team who tried to make sure that the Baltimore participants received all of the monies for which they were eligible.

[23] Readers interested in the detailed presentation of these (and other findings) should consult K. Lenihan, *Unlocking the Second Gate*, R & D Monograph 45, U.S. Department of Labor (Washington, D.C.: Government Printing Office, 1977).

Following these findings, a cost–benefit analysis of the Baltimore LIFE experiment was made by Charles Mallar.[24] Any cost–benefit analysis is somewhat inconclusive when many sources of benefits and costs have to be estimated in the absence of relevant empirical data. Hence, Mallar's findings covered a range of cost–benefit ratios varying according to estimates used and perspectives taken. On the most conservative side, Mallar estimated a 4:1 benefit cost ratio, indicating that $4 in savings accrued to society for each dollar expended in LIFE payments. On the most liberal side the computed benefit–cost ratio was 54:1.

FROM THE LIFE PROJECT TO TARP

When the findings of the LIFE experiment were conveyed to Howard Rosen of the Department of Labor in late 1974, and when all concerned were satisfied that the experiment had been conducted properly and that the inferences drawn were appropriate to the findings, the question arose of what policy implications to draw from these findings. Although the findings were encouraging, there were several qualifiers that had to be placed upon them. First, the findings were clearly significant by conventional social-science standards, but certainly not beyond a shadow of a doubt. Second, the findings had been obtained in an experiment administered by an energetic and dedicated research team. A program that was administered by even the best of federal or state agencies could hardly command the same level of effort on the part of program personnel. Third, the subject population in LIFE included only a certain portion of the released prisoner population—all high-risk persons who could best benefit from financial aid. The impact of payments on more representative ex-felons was problematical.

In short, the findings suggested that a policy that would provide some financial aid to ex-felons might be helpful in reducing certain types of recidivism, but the evidence was not strong enough or robust enough to warrant immediate translation into national policy. To obtain advice on what should be the next steps, Howard Rosen sought out two groups of experts.

In January 1975 a meeting was held with members of the National Manpower Policy Task Force. After considering the design, methodology, implementation, and results of the LIFE project, the task force overwhelmingly favored more research. It also urged that new studies be broader in

---

[24] Charles Mallar, *A Comparative Evaluation of the Benefits and Costs from the LIFE Program* (Washington, D.C.: American Bar Association, 1978).

scope, covering the full range of released prisoners, not just high-risk sub-jects. In addition, the new studies were to be conducted in more than one place. Although it would be ideal to have released prisoners from a large number of states, such a research design would be too costly. But at the least, the new studies should cover more than one state.

Most important, the task force recommended that in any new studies, the program administration be carried out by an existing government agency—either an employment service or a correction department; not by a social-research group. Treatment results might be quite different under "normal circumstances" of an existing bureaucracy. Furthermore, a new study should be more oriented to likely policy outcomes. If financial aid was shown to be effective again in a new set of experiments, the new research should test that effectiveness throughout the range of possible practical programs that would be likely to be enacted into policy. The most likely agencies for implementing future programs were seen to be state employment services, which would be given the responsibility by extending unemployment insurance benefits to cover released prisoners. In short, the new research should test what would happen if a financial aid program were carried out by state employment services under the existing rules and regulations of the unemployment insurance programs.

The second meeting was held in February 1975 with an ad hoc group of professionals—economists, criminologists, statisticians, sociologists, government administrators—who had expertise in the areas of crime, employment, or program evaluation.[25] Most participants accepted the find-ings as important and policy relevant. Although some members recom-mended time-series studies as cost effective, there was also general agree-ment that randomized experiments led to more definitive findings, a consideration that offset their greater cost.

Concerning the new research, the ad hoc group made the same recom-mendations as the task force, stressing policy-relevant themes. Some par-ticipants recommended varying the experimental treatment considerably by having several levels of payments (e.g., $60, $80, and $100) and several durations of payment eligibility (e.g., 13, 26, and even 52 weeks). Since it is

---

[25] Attending the meeting were Stuart Adams, Law Enforcement Assistance Administration (LEAA); Peter Barth, University of Connecticut; George Bohlinger, LEAA; Fred Bolton, Department of Labor (DOL); Robert Boruch, Northwestern University; Michael Borus, Michigan State University; John Conrad, Academy for Contemporary Problems; Joseph Epstein, DOL; James Fife, U.S. Parole Board; Lafayette Grisby, DOL; Thomas Joyce, DOL; Kenneth Lenihan and Robert Martinson, City University of New York (CUNY); Sylvia Mc-Collum, U.S. Bureau of Prisons; Howard Rosen, DOL; Leonard Savitz, Temple University; Laura Sharp, Bureau of Social Science Research; Herman Travis, DOL; James Vanecko, Brown University; and Virginia Wright, American Bar Association.

up to each state to set its own payment levels under existing federal unemployment insurance laws, this plan was judged as politically unrealistic, since each state likely would be given the right to set its own payment levels. The group did recommend varying the number of weeks of entitlement—13 and 26 weeks—to see if additional reduction in recidivism could be made by providing aid for the longer period.

One dissenting opinion expressed at this meeting was that no further research be done. The dissentor urged that the Department of Labor, armed with the Baltimore findings, go immediately to Congress to seek legislation for a program of financial aid for all released prisoners. The argument advanced rested not so much on the reductions in recidivism found in Baltimore as on the assertion that the payments were simply a matter of equity. To release prisoners without sufficient resources to survive a period of adjustment was seen as continuing the punishment. In addition, new research might show no recidivism declines. The time to move was now, when both research findings and equity considerations coincided. It was a moral argument. Anyone familiar with the lives of prisoners would find the argument persuasive.

However, the moral argument did not seem politically promising since Congress does not look to the Department of Labor for moral instruction. Singling out released prisoners as deserving of special benefits would require a political constituency to back up the moral claims. But there is no political constituency (to speak of) concerned with released prisoners. It is a transitional status, without an alumni association, and ex-prisoners themselves shed the identity as soon as possible. In any case, arguing for a financial-aid program on the basis of equity did not seem fruitful, and the consensus was that further research, with an eye toward policy decisions, should be undertaken.

With the benefit of hindsight, it appears that the decision of the Department of Labor officials was clearly the right one to take. As we have seen in this chapter, the overall results of applying a version of the LIFE experiment treatment did not result in unequivocal support for the treatment. Rather, as will be shown in later chapters, state employment services did not provide payments to released prisoners in the same way as did the dedicated researchers in the Baltimore LIFE experiment. Furthermore, these differences were critical ones. To have plunged ahead in suggesting policy changes to the Congress would have been to suggest a policy that was at best ineffective and hence inefficient.

It is important to note that the sequence of fact gathering and researches initiated and carried through by the Department of Labor was one that tested a prospective policy on levels that were closer and closer to actual policy as it would most likely be implemented. At any point in the sequence, negative findings would have led to the abandonment of a prospective policy change. Thus, if the initial Rikers Island exploratory phase had indicated that released prisoners were not interested in postrelease financial support, then it would have been highly unlikely that the next step of the Baltimore LIFE experiment would have been undertaken. Rosen and his colleagues would most likely have looked in some other direction for measures that would fulfill the mandate of Congress for the Department of Labor to help integrate released prisoners into the labor force.

The LIFE experiment was designed to be a fine-grained test of the payments leading to easier integration of ex-prisoners into civilian life. It was not a test of the policy as it might actually be implemented but of the policy at its "best," given the population most likely to be affected, administered by a devoted research team that was most likely to implement the policy as completely as possible, and whose beneficiaries would be observed as carefully as possible in the postrelease period. In technical terms, it was research designed to maximize "internal validity."

The successful outcomes of the LIFE experiment meant that it was then known that under some very favorable circumstances payments appeared to be effective in reducing arrests on property-related charges. The next responsible step was to find out whether payments could be integrated into state employment service systems with the same results. In short, the next step was to test the "external validity" of the basic ideas behind the prospective policy.[26] Only if the prospective policy was clearly shown to be effective at this stage and if favorable cost-to-benefit ratios were estimated would the policy be placed before the relevant decision makers.[27]

This strategy clearly recognizes that some policies can be shown to be effective under special circumstances that are difficult to duplicate on a mass scale. It is also a strategy that gives special recognition to the extremely important process of implementation, a usually neglected aspect of the administration of human-services programs.

---

[26] A more complete discussion of the implications of this step-by-step testing of prospective social policies can be found in P. H. Rossi, "Issues in the Evaluation of Human Services Delivery," *Evaluation Quarterly*, 2, no. 4 (November 1978):573–599.

[27] In fact, the outcomes of LIFE were persuasive enough in some quarters that policy changes did result. In particular, legislation was introduced into the California legislature (and passed) extending unemployment benefits to released prisoners in that state with eligibility to be determined by number of days of prison work earned by the released prisoners. The program was started in July 1978. An evaluation of the effectiveness of the program is currently being undertaken by R. A. Berk and his colleagues at the University of California, Santa Barbara.

3

Design of the Transitional Aid
Research Project Experiments

INTRODUCTION

Having decided additional research was needed, the next steps were to design experiments of appropriate power and scope, obtain the cooperation of state agencies, and ensure that the experiments were carried out in ways that were faithful to the design and the central substantive issues of the experiments. At each of these points, decisions made could have conditioned results in critical ways. States could have been chosen that were in some ways quite different from "typical" states, the design could have been insufficiently powerful, the implementation of the design could have led to a deterioration of the power of the treatment, and so on.

The purpose of this chapter is to describe these decisions in considerable detail. Such detail is needed for two reasons: First, it is essential to document how well the experiment was designed and carried out so that anyone may judge whether appropriate procedures were followed. Second, the art of conducting large-scale field experiments is scarcely a well-developed area of social science methodology. It is hoped that the description contained in this chapter contributes to the further development of this art.

EARLY DESIGN CONSIDERATIONS

Without the cooperation of several states, the experiment could not have been carried out at all. Hence, one of the first steps was to ascertain whether there was any interest among any of the states in implementing the experiment. Because the Departments of Labor and Justice were funding the work,[1] the experiment could be carried out at little additional monetary cost to the states. Undoubtedly, however, there would be some nonmone-

---

[1] See Chapter 4 for an accounting of the funds expended.

tary costs to the states, including administrative and managerial disruptions, and it was possible that some of the vulnerabilities of either the state correctional systems or state employment services might be uncovered.

The Department of Labor made inquiries of all but the smallest states (where prison populations were not large enough to provide many releasees over a short period of time). Twenty states replied, expressing at least preliminary interest in running such experiments. With at least curiosity being expressed, the Department of Labor felt it was worthwhile to take the next step of designing experiments to be incorporated into a Request for Proposal (RFP).

Several considerations were incorporated into the design phase. First, the state prison system would have to be large enough to release a sufficient number of prisoners within a relatively short period of time. Since the projected total research time was 2 years (a projection that was quickly abandoned), a sufficient number of prisoners would have to be released over a 6-month period.

Second, following recommendations of the scientific advisory committee, it was decided that the number of weeks of benefits offered should be varied. The LIFE experiment had provided benefits for 13 weeks: The new experiment would provide benefits for two periods: 13 and 26 weeks.

Third, to remain faithful to the idea that the new experiment would offer treatments that would resemble closely what such treatments would be like if enacted into social policy, the benefits would be given out according to the unemployment-benefit rules already established by the state in question. This meant that benefits would be given only to those available to work, excluding students and hospitalized or otherwise incapacitated persons, as well as persons who did not express a willingness to at least consider employment. And it meant that the tax rates applying in the state system would also be used to govern payments to ex-prisoners. Since most states had a 100% tax after a small "forgiveness" threshold, benefits would be reduced dollar for dollar for each dollar earned while working. In addition, payment levels would be set at minimum payments given by the states—$60 to $80 per week. Payments would also be made through the state unemployment-benefit system, meaning that ex-prisoners would come to state employment security offices along with other persons who were receiving benefits. Perhaps the most practical significance of this feature is that the ordinary working hours of the state employment security office —approximately 8:30 AM to 5:00 PM Monday through Friday—would apply.

It should be noted that all these conditions were departures from those followed in the LIFE experiment, which permitted persons unavailable for work to receive payments and which set up separate offices for administering payment, kept project offices open at night and on Saturdays, and applied a graduated tax on earnings that allowed participants to receive some sort of payment until they earned more than $150 per week. To maintain some comparability with the graduated tax provisions of the LIFE experiment, a special experimental group would be added that would experience a 25% tax rate.

Despite the discouraging experience of LIFE with job-placement services, it was also decided to set up an experimental group to which job-placement services would be offered. This decision was made because it was believed that state employment security agencies would be more attracted to participate if job placement, one of their primary missions for the unemployed, was also one of the treatments.

Note that this general outline of the experiment represented some major departures from the LIFE experiment, although it maintained the general thrust of providing financial aid for a limited period of time. The major departures involve more the rules of eligibility and the tax rate than either the amount of payments or the duration of eligibility. In other words, the same treatment, but under different conditions would be administered in the new experiment. The experimental design as described in the RFP that went out to the 20 interested states was as follows:

GROUP 1: To be eligible for financial aid of 26 weeks at minimum payment levels and subject to on-going state unemployment insurance rules, implying work availability and 100% tax.

GROUP 2: To be eligible for financial aid for 13 weeks subject to the same rules as Group 1.

GROUP 3: To receive financial aid for 13 weeks but with a 25% tax on earnings, that is, benefits would be reduced $.25 for each dollar earned.

GROUP 4: To be eligible for intensive job-placement services, including limited money for necessary tools, work clothes, etc.

GROUP 5: No services to be offered—a control group.

Each state was asked to provide 700 released prisoners to be randomly assigned to the five groups—550 to Groups 1 through 4 and 150 to Group 5, the control group.[2] All participants would be interviewed before release from the prison and at the end of the third, sixth, and twelfth months after release. A 1-year follow-up on arrest information would be required.

States would be reimbursed from federal funds for the expenses, salaries, and administrative overhead involved as well as for the payments made. In

---

[2] As the study progressed, these numbers were increased, as indicated in the next chapter.

addition, state agencies were to collect the research data called for and administer the benefit program. A report analyzing the outcome of the experiment would also be prepared by each state and would include copies of the data sets generated. In addition, the states were expected to contribute personnel and other services to the running of the experiment, to the amount of almost one-third of the total cost of the experiment within each state. (See Chapter 4 for a full account of the budgets finally adopted for the states involved.)

Several responses to the RFP were received. An outside panel reviewed all the proposals and recommended awards to the states of Georgia and Texas. The choice was made largely on the basis of an estimate of these states' ability to conduct the experiment and collect the required research data postrelease and on the basis of the suitability of their prison populations. Both states had large prison populations that could easily generate the desired numbers of released prisoners within the time period specified. Both had statewide computerized criminal justice information systems that were regarded as accurate and complete. Other states were passed over because of their size or their unwillingness to accept randomization as the basis for allocating released prisoners to experimental and control groups, or because their criminal-justice systems were reputedly unreliable or not yet on computers.

IMPLEMENTING THE EXPERIMENT

In June 1975, negotiations were started with each of the states to work out the details of responsibilities of the state employment security agencies and the departments of corrections. In Texas the overall responsibility was to be lodged in the Texas Department of Corrections (TDC). The TDC was to be responsible for the selection of subjects, random assignment, interviewing, collecting arrest data, processing all data collected, and preparing a final report. The Texas Employment Security Agency was to be responsible for preparing payments, determining eligibility, and providing job-placement services. Under this arrangement, the Texas Department of Corrections would bear almost all of the research load.

In Georgia, the division of labor was somewhat different. The Georgia Department of Corrections was to select the subjects for the study and carry out random assignment, but the interviews were to be conducted by the Employment Security Agency in the prisons as well as during the first year after release. Data processing was to be carried out by the Department of Corrections, which would also be responsible for a final report. The weekly financial aid and job-placement services were to be dispensed by the Employment Security Agency.

During the negotiations, the design of the research was changed somewhat. The number of persons to be released in each state over a 6-month period was much greater than originally expected. At little additional cost it was possible to add an additional control group (Group 6) of 1000 persons in each state. These additional 1000 persons would not be interviewed. Only data from existing records would be obtained on these persons; that is, information from prison files, a record of earnings subject to unemployment insurance, and arrest information from the statewide computer system.[3] Thus, there would now be two control groups: One group of 200 persons would receive the same number of interviews as those receiving the experimental treatments, and another group of 1000 would be followed up through existing information. All assignments, including those to the new control group, would still be made on a random basis.

Although the administrative responsibilities for the experiment and accompanying data-collection activities were worked out in the final negotiations with each state, a number of details remained to be settled, often while the experiment was under way.

To provide some measure of overall coordination between the two states, the Department of Labor contracted with the American Bar Association (ABA) to oversee the project. The ABA Commission on Correctional Facilities and Services had a staff available which had considerable experience with prison systems and with the issues involved in the experiment. The ABA's commission could also help in providing legal research that would be necessary to prepare new legislation if the findings of the two experiments suggested that new policies should be adopted. Because the ABA staff had little social-research expertise, they had to hire someone to serve as the principal investigator for the two experiments. The principal duties of this person were to oversee and coordinate the activities of the two states. Kenneth Lenihan, who had conducted the Baltimore LIFE experiments, was hired by ABA to perform this role. Lenihan was to spend much of his time over the ensuing 2 years visiting the research staffs in each of the states, coordinating activities and attempting to ensure that the integrity of the experiment was maintained and that research data of high quality were collected by the two states.[4] Finally, a name was provided for the two experiments: Transitional Aid Research Project, or TARP.

---

[3] An additional advantage of this control group was that it could not be affected by interviews and hence could provide an estimate of interviewing effects.

[4] See American Bar Association, *Final Report on Activities of the Transitional Aid Research Project* (Washington, D.C.: American Bar Association, August 1978), for a complete account of ABA activities in connection with TARP.

ESTIMATING THE EFFICIENCY OF
THE TARP EXPERIMENTS

Although the size of the study was set in the first place by the amount of funds available, it would have been futile to carry out the experiments if the sample sizes were not large enough to detect expected effects. Estimates were needed of the expected proportions of persons to be arrested for property and other charges during the first year beyond release from prison. In Texas, a sample of 400 men released from prison during the period of July 1, 1973 to June 30, 1974 were tracked through the state criminal-justice computer for a period of 1 year after release. As shown in Table 3.1, 21.3% were found to have been arrested for a property crime and another 11.2% for other kinds of crime, making a total of 32.5%. In Georgia, using a similar procedure, the results were 24% for property crimes, and 12% for other crimes, making a total of 36% arrested during the first year after release. (These results, incidentally, were lower than the arrest rates actually observed in the 1-year follow-up of TARP participants, as shown in Chapters 5 and 10.)

Following the Baltimore LIFE results, the best expectation was that financial aid would cut property-arrest rates by about one-quarter, or make a difference of roughly 5% between experimental and control groups. If financial aid would cause reduction of this size on Georgia or Texas rates, the planned-for sample sizes would be sufficient to detect such effects and declare them statistically significant. Had the expected rearrest rates been considerably smaller, an increase in the size of the treatment groups would have been called for.

This judgment about the adequacy of group sizes was just an approximation. Since the released prisoners in Texas and Georgia were bound to be different in some ways from the Baltimore participants, the effects of financial aid might be smaller (or larger). In addition, there was no way of knowing whether varying the weeks of eligibility (13 versus 26) and varying the tax on earnings (25% versus 100%) would make any difference in the rearrest rates. The best bet was to use effect estimates based on the Baltimore LIFE experiments since these were the only estimates available.

WORK DISINCENTIVE

Although the evidence from the LIFE experiment was that there was little, if any, work disincentive as a consequence of the payments under the tax system applicable in the Baltimore experiment, there was good reason to believe that the TARP experiments might encounter more work-

TABLE 3.1
Rearrest Rates in Texas and Georgia,
1973–1974 (in percentages)

	Texas	Georgia
Property crimes	21.3	24
Other crimes	11.2	12
Ever arrested	32.5	36

disincentive effects. To begin with, work-disincentive effects were predicted by economic theory. Economists argue that any provision of payments that are conditional upon unemployment lower wage rates and hence the work effort of persons to whom such payments are offered. Thus the offer of $60 per week with a 100% tax on earnings has the presumed effect of making the first $60 earned by a person during a week of eligibility equivalent to working at a wage rate of zero dollars. Persons who earned more than $60 in a week of eligibility had their wage rates lowered accordingly. For example, a person earning $100 per week was in effect working a full week for $40, since without working he would receive $60 in payments.

Payment plans with rigorously enforced 100% tax rates could also be expected to have especially strong work-disincentive effects on ex-prisoners, whose position in the labor market was none too strong and whose job opportunities would largely consist of poorly paid jobs that were unpleasant. As a consequence, ex-felons could be expected to be especially attracted to the choice of leisure (nonworking) as opposed to work.

Of course, these arguments applied as well to the existing unemployment-benefit system as applied to persons who were not ex-felons. Estimating the actual amount of work disincentive, however, is quite another problem. A recent study has shown that persons who were for one reason or another disqualified for benefits upon application had shorter periods of unemployment than those who were eligible, holding a set of relevant worker characteristics constant.[5] But since disqualified workers (persons who quit voluntarily, persons who are fired, etc.) are by that fact different from those let go by their employers on other grounds, the evidence about the work-disincentive effects of unemployment insurance benefits is equivocal.

Thus, although economic theory predicted that TARP payments would have some work-disincentive, the empirical evidence both from the LIFE

[5] Henry E. Felder, *A Statistical Evaluation of the Impact of Disqualification Provisions of State Unemployment Insurance Laws* (Arlington, Va.: SRI International, 1979).

experiment and from analyses of the regular unemployment benefit program showed that economic theory was not at all clear about the size of the
resulting drop in working. The amount of the disincentive effect and its
distribution among subgroups in the ex-prisoner population was problematic. Nor was it possible to get some firm estimates from the analyses of
other types of income-transfer experiments. The New Jersey–Pennsylvania
Income Maintenance Experiment,[6] designed to measure the work disincentive of various income-maintenance plans, found some overall work-
disincentive effect, but the effects were not particularly sensitive to tax
rates and varied somewhat depending on the ethnic background of participants. The income-maintenance experiments had been conducted on quite
different populations (intact poor and near-poor families) with inconclusive
findings; thus, they were little guide to what might be expected from a
released-prisoner population.

The best relevant findings on released prisoners were from the Baltimore
LIFE experiment in which little (if any) disincentive effect had been found
when payments were administered with an approximately 25% tax rate.[7] In
short, previous knowledge and experience did not lead to clear expectations
of whether a work-disincentive effect would appear or how large it might
be. Hence, the TARP design had to be sufficiently powerful to distinguish
between the effects of 26 weeks versus 13 weeks of payments as well as between 100% and 25% tax rates.

At this point, the budget was limited, with only enough money for 150
persons to receive 26 weeks of payments (with 100% tax on earnings) and
250 to receive 13 weeks of payments (half with a 100% tax and half with a
25% tax). If either of these experimental variations had effects, they would
most likely add marginally to the payment effects. Group sizes as then
planned would be too small to detect any but large (and unexpected) effects. To strengthen the design, Howard Rosen of the Department of Labor
sought to obtain more funds in order to increase the sizes of the treatment
groups. But since it would take several months to secure such additional
funds the study began with existing target figures in mind.

GEOGRAPHIC COVERAGE

Both Texas and Georgia are large states. Georgia, with over 50,000
square miles, is the largest state east of the Mississippi; among the 50
states, Texas is second in size only to Alaska. Although released prisoners

---

[6] D. Kershaw and J. Fair, *The New Jersey Income-Maintenance Experiment,* Volume 1
(New York: Academic Press, 1975), and P. H. Rossi and K. Lyall, *Reforming Public Welfare*
(New York: Russell Sage Foundation, 1974).

[7] See Table 2.5 in Chapter 2.

would be returned to all parts of each state, it simply was not practical to provide financial aid and job-placement services in every county in each state. Although it could not be known in advance to which places the TARP participants would be returning, it was possible to use the experiences of previously released prisoners to generate reasonable estimates upon which to base an efficient strategy for providing payments and services to TARP participants.

Georgia has 159 counties and Texas has 254 counties. In many counties, only one or two released prisoners would be expected to return to live. The solution was to extend coverage of the program mainly to places within easy reach of existing employment security offices and to places to which significant numbers of prisoners would be returning.

In Texas, 17 counties were serviced directly by employment security offices located within the county borders. These same counties received about 75% of the released prisoners. The other 237 counties received 20% of the released population (the remaining 5% went outside the state). It was decided that all prisoners returning to the largest 17 counties would be covered. In other counties, only a sample would be eligible. These other counties were formed into clusters of contiguous counties averaging an expected 50 prisoners in each, ending making a total of 15 county clusters. Two of these county clusters were drawn randomly. All prisoners returning to a county in these two clusters were eligible for the study, adding 14 counties to the 17 that were serviced by an employment security office. Thus, coverage was 100% of the 75% of the released prisoners returning to counties served by employment security offices and 13% of the 20% of released prisoners who were returning to other counties. Those going outside the state upon release were excluded from the study.

In Georgia the coverage of employment security offices was more extensive than in Texas. Of the 159 counties in Georgia, 121 were being serviced by an agency office (or one of its satellite offices). These 121 counties accounted for 91% of the released prisoners. Prisoners returning to any of these 121 counties were all declared eligible. Contiguous county clusters were formed of the remaining 38 counties in such a way that each cluster contained an expected 12 released prisoners. In all, there were 12 clusters, and two were randomly chosen. To sum up, 100% of the counties receiving 91% of the released population and a 19% sample of counties that would receive 9% of the population were chosen.

It should be noted that the resulting underrepresentation of prisoners returning to rural counties does not affect the interpretation of experimental results, since residence was not involved in assignment to either experimental or control groups. The resulting underrepresentation does affect estimates of any state parameters that are related to urban or rural residence. Thus, for example, if rural prisoners are more or less likely to return to prison, any estimate of the proportion of prisoners returning to incarceration computed from TARP data will be either an underestimate or an overestimate. As will be shown in later chapters, most of the differences between rural and urban residents among TARP members are either negligible or insignificant.

It bears emphasis that no discretion was allowed to the departments of correction in either state concerning including or excluding any prisoner released during this period who was eligible to be in the experiment under the rules discussed above. *All released prisoners who were returning to the counties specified and for whom there did not exist any detainers or warrants were included in the experiment until the target numbers were achieved.* An occasional prisoner released under court order unexpectedly managed to elude the procedures set up in each state, but the exceptions did not amount to more than a very small number in each state. In short, everyone was included who was eligible until a sufficient number was assigned to one of the six groups.

ASSIGNMENT TO EXPERIMENTAL AND CONTROL GROUPS

Ordinarily, the department of corrections in each of the states knows for some weeks in advance when a prisoner is due to be released.[8] Thus lists of such prisoners could be drawn up in advance, and the necessary processing could be started. These lists were made available to the TARP research teams, who screened them first to identify persons who would be eligible for participation in TARP. All releasees were eligible for inclusion in the study except those who (*a*) were returning to live in an unsampled rural county, (*b*) were returning to live outside the state, or (*c*) had existing warrants or detainers against them.

Eligible persons were then assigned to one or another of the six groups according to a set of procedures that assured both that there was no systematic bias in allocation to any of the groups and that the groups were comparable in certain important respects. This systematic assignment procedure amounted to a stratified randomization of eligible released prisoners. There are several desirable features of the procedures employed. First, the procedure was unbiased: Any released prisoner had the same chance of being assigned to any of the six groups as any other eligible releasee. Second, the stratification procedures assured that the groups

---

[8] Exceptions are prisoners released under court orders who have to be discharged within 24 hours. Such persons were excluded from the TARP experiments.

would be very nearly identical in certain important compositional characteristics. Each would have the same proportions of males and females, parolees and discharged prisoners, and so on. The main advantage of stratification is to increase the precision of the experiment, making it possible to estimate the effects of the treatments with a smaller band of error.[9]

Since the stratified, systematic, randomized assignment procedure differed slightly in the two states, each state procedure will be described separately. In effect, the procedure employed was first to classify each releasee into one of a number of categories formed out of the combination of sex, age group, parole or discharge, and urban or rural residence. Within each of the classes so formed, prisoners were systematically distributed into one or another of the six TARP groups.

In Texas, the first division was made according to whether the person was returning to a county that was serviced by an employment security office; thus persons were either *urban* (serviced) or *rural* (not serviced) residents. Urban eligibles were then further subdivided by sex. Urban males were then classified according to the method of release (parole or discharge), age (22 or less, 23–26, 27–33, 34 or more), and marital status (married versus all others).

Urban women were divided by only one age break (26 or less and 27 or more) and by method of release (parole or discharge). There were too few women in the population to make any further divisions on age or marital status.

Among the relatively small number of persons returning to rural counties (not serviced by an employment security office), only two divisions could be made: age (26 or less and 27 or more) and method of release (parole or discharge).

The stratification scheme in Georgia was slightly more complex. Additional classes could be added because more information about the prisoners was available from prison records. In addition to those distinguished in Texas, an additional, marital-status class was added composed of persons about whom no marital-status information was available. Further, persons in urban counties were subclassified according to whether or not they had been working at the time of the arrest that led to their present sentences.

Prisoners about to be released were systematically assigned to one or another of the six groups in the order in which they appeared on the re-

---

[9] As we noted with reference to the design of the LIFE experiment, the stratification serves to virtually eliminate any correlations between the treatments and stratification variables (since equal proportions of prisoners were allocated) and increases the variance of observed stratification variables. Both enhance statistical power.

TABLE 3.2
Initial Target Allocations among TARP Groups, November 1975

Group	Treatment	Number of prisoners	Proportion of the released population
1	26 weeks' benefits, 100% tax	150	.083
2	13 weeks, 100% tax	125	.069
3	13 weeks, 25% tax	125	.069
4	Job placement	200	.111
5	Interviewed controls	200	.111
6	Noninterview controls	1000	.555

lease lists, using a systematic assignment algorithm.[10] Within each of the classification groups, persons assigned to that classification group were allocated to TARP groups, after a random start, according to the series 1, 6, 2, 6, 3, 6, 4, 6, 5, 6, etc. This allocation procedure was modified slightly by periodically changing assignment rules to produce the proper proportions of intended numbers in each of the TARP groups, as shown in Table 3.2.[11]

As Howard Rosen of DOL was successful in obtaining additional funds for the TARP project on two occasions, the targets for the payment groups were increased twice, necessitating corresponding changes in the allocation algorithm. The final target numbers for the six TARP groups and the actual numbers of persons assigned in each state are shown in Table 3.3. In Texas, the TARP research group managed to obtain the exact numbers desired in each of the TARP groups, whereas in Georgia, because advance information on who was to be released was often late and sometimes incorrect, the target numbers of each of the Georgia TARP groups were off slightly.

Since comparability in data from the two states was highly desirable, much time was spent on getting a standardized instrument to be used in interviewing released prisoners.[12] While the allocation procedures were

---

[10] In both Georgia and Texas the order in which a person appeared on a discharge list was determined by factors (e.g., alphabetic or serial-number orderings) that could not affect allocation to one or the other of the six TARP groups.

[11] Since the intention (in November 1975) was to produce proportions in the TARP groups as shown in Table 3.2, the assignment algorithm was modified every tenth run by adding and deleting assignments as follows: Delete two assignments from Group 1; three assignments each from Groups 2 and 3; add one assignment each to Groups 4 and 5; add five assignments to Group 6. Note that it was the algorithm that was changed before being applied to persons. Once a person was allocated to a TARP group, that assignment was not changed.

[12] Complete standardization was not possible because definitions of conditions varied between the states. For example, Georgia had three release conditions—*discharge, parole,* and *release under supervision.* Texas routinely used the Department of Labor's *Dictionary of Oc-*

TABLE 3.3
Target and Actual Numbers of Persons in TARP Groups
Achieved at End of Recruitment

Group	Treatment	Target number for each state	Georgia actual	Texas actual
1	26 weeks' benefits, 100% tax	175	176	175
2	13 weeks, 100% tax	200	199	200
3	13 weeks, 25% tax	200	199	200
4	Job placement	200	201	200
5	Interviewed controls	200	201	200
6	Noninterview controls	1000	1031	1000
Totals		1975	2007	1975

worked out in detail in each state, work was also proceeding on the pre-release interview schedule. Finally everything was ready. Interviewers were trained. Names of persons to be released in January were transmitted to TARP research staffs in December.

STATE ADMINISTRATIVE ARRANGEMENTS FOR TARP

Although general supervision over the TARP experiments was maintained by the American Bar Association through Kenneth Lenihan, each of the states worked out slightly different arrangements to select participants, to provide payments, and to collect research data. In Texas, the overall direction to the experiment was provided by the research department of the Texas Department of Corrections. A special research staff was hired, and interviewers used for all of the interviews were young, male TDC employees, whose usual assignments were as guards or counselors.

In Georgia, overall direction of the TARP project was assumed by the Georgia Employment Security Agency, which hired the interviewer staffs needed. The Georgia Department of Corrections selected prisoners, made the random assignment of prisoners to groups, and provided a research staff that conducted the data processing and produced a report on the Georgia TARP data.

The collection of research data was carried out in much the same way in the two states. In Texas the TDC interviewers conducted the prison (before release) interviews and made appointments to see each of the prisoners

---

cupational Titles as codes for preprison jobs, whereas Georgia had a special occupational code, presumably custom tailored to the special needs of Georgia.

after their release in the appropriate employment security offices in their home counties. Follow-up interviews were also made by appointment in the security offices. If releasees failed to appear for appointments, the interviewers made efforts to contact them and to arrange for alternate dates.

It should be noted that because the interview sites in Texas were spread widely across the state, the seven fieldworkers had to travel constantly in order to keep their appointments in the several places assigned to them and to track down releasees who were hard to locate.

In Georgia the initial prerelease interviews were conducted by an all-female interviewing team that was hired for that specific purpose. Georgia prisons are not as concentrated geographically as the Texas prisons, and interviewers were hired locally. Another team of 10 persons was recruited from among state employment security personnel to handle the postrelease interviews and the disbursement of payments. In each of the designated agency offices, a single person and an assistant conducted all the interviews of releasees assigned to that office and handled all the contacts with releasees in connection with their payments or job-placement services. Since more than half of the released prisoners in Georgia were assigned to the Atlanta office, the three interviewers and their assistants conducted the bulk of the interviews and contacts in that state.

TARP participants in the two states who were eligible for payments and who wished to receive payments had to report to the designated employment security office and certify that they had not earned more than the threshold amounts and had been available for work during the week for which they wished to claim benefits. At the employment security office they were met by the same person each time (or a designated assistant). In Georgia, the agency employee was the same person who conducted periodic follow-up interviews. In Texas, payments were handled by specially designated and trained employment security clerks.

The descriptions in the preceding paragraphs apply in principle; they outline procedures described in the operations manuals of the TARP programs. One can safely assume that the interviews were conducted as described. At the same time, there must have been some variation from place to place in the way certification and payments were handled. After all, in some Texas offices that handled only one or two TARP participants, the amount of business generated by the participants could only have been a very small fraction of the entire workload of the agency personnel assigned to that function. Under such circumstances, it is easy to imagine that the special rules that applied to TARP participants might not be rigorously and consistently enforced or that other persons might be substituted for the special personnel designated to handle TARP participants on some visits.

RECRUITMENT OF TARP PARTICIPANTS

The interviewing of released prisoners assigned to Groups 1 through 5 began in December 1975. (Group 6 TARP members who were to serve as noninterviewed controls were never approached by TARP staff or interviewers. None of the Group 6 members in either of the states were informed that they were part of any study.) As soon as a person was scheduled for release and the staff assigned that person to one of Groups 1 through 5, interviewers were given the task of recruiting each person to cooperate in the study. Interviewers also conducted prerelease interviews, if prisoners were willing. Once the location of an about-to-be-released prisoner was known, an interviewer was sent out to the prison to conduct a prerelease interview. The state prisons in Georgia are spread throughout the state, whereas in Texas prisons are concentrated around Huntsville; the task of conducting prerelease interviews in Georgia was thus more difficult.

On initial contact with each prisoner, the interviewer asked first whether the prisoner would be willing to participate in a research study for a 1-year period. The prisoner was told that there would be four interviews—one each at the third, sixth, and twelfth months after release as well as one interview while still in prison. If the prisoner agreed, a prerelease interview was conducted on the spot. Prisoners were promised payments ($15 in Georgia, $5 in Texas)[13] for the prison interviews and for each of the three subsequent ones. Payment for the prison interview, however, was to be made only after release. No mention was made at this point about program services that might be offered—either financial aid or job-placement service. In fact, interviewers were not aware of the subject's TARP group assignment, which had already been made by the TARP research staff.

A small number of refusals occurred in each state, less than 1% in Georgia and about 2% in Texas.[14] During the first month of interviewing in Texas, it appeared that Chicanos were refusing to cooperate. The addition of a member of that ethnic group to the interviewing staff soon brought the refusal rate among Chicanos down to about the same level experienced among blacks and whites.

At the close of the interview, the recruited TARP participant was told to report to a specific employment security office at which he could pick up

---

[13] Later raised to $10 for third-month and sixth-month interviews and to $15 for twelfth-month interviews.

[14] The Georgia TARP staff explained that the lower refusal rate in Georgia was because they hired women as interviewers. Prisoners about to be released were anxious to talk to a female. In Texas, under TDC rules, only male interviewers were allowed into prison.

payment for the prerelease interview. The TARP research staff notified the employment security office to prepare appropriate checks for delivery to TARP participants when they appeared at the designated office for their checks. For persons in payment groups (Groups 1, 2, and 3), checks would be the first week's benefits. For the remainder (Groups 4 and 5), the checks would include only interview payments. The employment security office was also notified about the benefits to which a participant was entitled if in an experimental group (Groups 1 through 4) or that he was not to receive any benefits (if in Control Group 5).

On their first visit to the employment security office, participants in the first four TARP groups were told about the benefits for which they were eligible, a summary of which is presented in Table 3.4. Persons in the control group were given their checks containing payment for their prerelease interviews and reminded that they would be contacted for additional interviews at the end of 3, 6, and 12 months.

More than 50 employment security offices were involved in explaining the program to eligible TARP participants. Unfortunately, no systematic effort was made to observe how TARP participants were serviced in these offices. It is therefore impossible at this time to ascertain the care and diligence with which benefits and rules of eligibility were explained to TARP participants. In many of the larger offices, specially designated clerks consistently handled TARP participants, but often in smaller offices any clerk who happened to be available handled the case. In every office, TARP participants were only a very small fraction of the total client load of that office. These characteristics are stressed here because of the contrast presented in the LIFE experiment in which the research staff handled all contacts with participants and such contacts were their only mission.

The benefits to be received as payments varied between the states: The $70-level in Georgia and the $63-level in Texas were set by each state roughly in line with the minimum payments dispensed under that state's unemployment insurance plan. Each state also had a different *forgiveness* amount—$8 in Georgia and $15.75 in Texas—beyond which amount each dollar earned was deducted from the benefit amount. In both states, payments were made conditional on being available for work and on earning less than the cut-off threshold. The availability-for-work provision meant that benefits could not be collected while a person was in school, in the hospital (or otherwise too sick to work), or in jail. In both states, eligibility for benefits was retained for a year beyond the person's release data or until the released prisoner used up the maximum amount of his eligibility, as indicated in Table 3.4.

Persons allocated to Group 4, of course, received no cash benefits but were entitled to special job-placement services. In addition, Group 4

TABLE 3.4
*Summary of Benefits Available to TARP Experimental Groups in
Georgia and Texas*

Experimental groups	State	Maximum weekly payment	Number of weeks at maximum	Total allowance	Eligibility period	Forgiveness amount	Tax rate
1	Georgia	$70	26	$1820	One year	$ 8	100%
	Texas	$63	26	$1638	One year	$15.75	100%
2	Georgia	$70	13	$ 910	One year	$ 8	100%
	Texas	$63	13	$ 819	One year	$15.75	100%
3	Georgia	$70	13	$ 910	One year	$ 8	25%
	Texas	$63	13	$ 819	One year	$15.75	25%
4	No payment eligibility: Job placement services available on request: Some money available for purchase of tools, special work clothes, etc. Four interview payments of $15 each in Georgia and $10 in Texas.						
5	Georgia: Four interview payments of $15 each Texas: Four interview payments of $10 each						

NOTE: In both states payments were conditional on unemployment or on earning less than cut-off thresholds. To receive payments persons had to be available for work, that is, not incapacitated by reason of illness or incarceration or attending school.

members could receive some financial help to purchase work clothes or tools, at the discretion of the job counselor, Unfortunately, no attempt was made to systematically record the kinds of job-placement efforts offered to TARP participants or the kinds of services of this sort actually rendered. We have some information on the grants given for job-related expenses (see Table 4.4 in Chapter 4) but very little else.[15] Hence it is not at all clear what special job-placement services were made available to the Group 4 participants. It is a safe assumption, however, that the placement efforts expended by the local employment security office were several magnitudes less than the efforts expended by Kenneth Lenihan and his research group in the Baltimore LIFE experiment.

Persons in Group 5, the first control group, were simply paid for the prison interview and asked to report again in 3 months for another in-

---

[15] One of the consequences of this information gap is that although we are able to assess the impact of the treatment given to Group 4 and to estimate that impact as essentially nil, it is not possible to judge whether this lack of impact is an effect of a treatment or an effect of the nondelivery of a treatment. See P. H. Rossi, "Some Issues in the Evaluation of Human Services," *Evaluation Quarterly* 3, no. 3 (November 1978), for a general discussion of the importance of measuring the amount of a treatment actually delivered.

terview. Persons in Group 6, the other control group, received no interviews and therefore no payments. They never reported to an employment office. In fact, they were unaware of their participation in the study.

As persons in Groups 1, 2, and 3 reported for their checks in subsequent visits, they were asked a few questions about where they were living. They were also asked whether they had worked during the past week, and if not, whether they were available for work. If a participant reported that he had been working in the past week, then the benefit check to be issued the following week would be reduced according to the formulas shown in Table 3.4.

Interviewing of prisoners who were about to be released continued in both states until July, when the full complement of participants had been recruited in each state. Around April 1, 1976, persons who had been released in January were beng contacted for their first follow-up interview 3 months after release. At the end of June, when the prison interviews were almost completed, 6-month follow-up interviewing began for those who had been first released in January 1976. Twelve-month interviews began in January 1977. At any one time during the year and a half of follow-up, enough interviewing tasks were in the field to keep interviewing staffs quite busy. In the summer of 1977, all interviews were completed. For each person in Groups 1 through 5, four interviews had been completed, starting with the prerelease interview and ending with a 12-month follow-up. Appendix A contains examples of the interview forms used.

In addition, relevant documentary materials were also obtained on all participants, including the uninterviewed Group 6 members. Extracts were made of the prison records of each participant that contained information on previous criminal record, previous employment, and IQ and functional literacy test scores, as well as standard demographic information such as age, sex, race, and place of birth.

Because of the diversity and multiplicity of sources used in the analyses presented in later chapters, it may not always be immediately apparent from which source a particular measure may have been collected. Footnotes to tables are used consistently to indicate the data sources used.

While the follow-up interviewing was proceeding, data on each participant's (including Group 6) wages subject to unemployment insurance coverage were collected through the state employment services. These files contained information by calendar-year quarters on all wages in covered categories of employment. Starting with the calendar quarter in which a person was released, his unemployment insurance wage files were collected for four subsequent quarters.

At the same time, a search began of each state's computerized criminal justice files for each TARP participant's additional criminal records (beyond the time of release) for the entire postrelease year. As the anniversary date of a prisoner's release came up, the criminal justice files were queried about the entries for each participant using the criminal justice serial number that had been established for that person (because of his previous criminal record).

The criminal justice files turned out to have some deficiencies that arose largely out of the fact that local police and court jurisdictions participated in their state systems on a voluntary basis. Since arrests were usually generated locally, the completeness and accuracy of the central state files were dependent, to a great extent, on how faithfully local jurisdictions reported arrests and dispositions to the central state files.

Because of his experience with incomplete records in Maryland, Lenihan instituted a check of completeness in Texas and Georgia. Local records were checked against the machine-readable state file. As in Maryland, the local spot checks indicated that the state files were underinclusive, containing fewer records of arrests than could be discerned in local police departments, sheriffs' offices, and local courts. In addition, it was found that TARP participants in their interviews were reporting some arrests that could not be found on their state records. To make the arrest information as comprehensive as possible, a search of local sources was instituted. The problem was especially severe in Georgia, where the greatest effort was then made to supplement the state files by checking local sources. The cooperation of the police departments in the nine largest Georgia cities was obtained. Each department was sent a list of the approximately 2000 Georgia TARP participants. Police departments were asked to check their arrest records against the list sent and to copy out the arrest record for each person listed. In addition to checking these city police departments, Georgia TARP interviewers were sent out to each of the 119 counties of Georgia to make a comprehensive search of court records and sheriff's office records. Recorded arrests for each of the TARP participants in Georgia were copied when found.

In Texas, where nonreporting was not quite as serious, the search procedure was different. In the major counties—those in which large cities like Houston, Dallas, Fort Worth, and San Antonio are located—there are county computerized files of all arrests. By spot comparisons against local police records the county computer files were found to be essentially complete. These county computer files were then used to supplement information obtained from the state computer file. In the remaining counties— those without computer files—court records were searched and arrest records added to the state central files. In both states, considerable efforts were expended to obtain arrest records as comprehensive and unbiased as possible.

Two additional sets of official records complete the files that were collected on TARP participants. From the agency administering parole in each of the states, information was obtained on terms, conditions, and length of parole given to each paroled TARP participant along with records of parole violations, if any. From the employment security offices, records were obtained on the number, amount, and date of all TARP payments made to eligible members.

The amount of information obtained on each of the TARP participants is considerable. Hence this study is based on a variety of data sources, only some of which come from the released prisoners. First, there are extracts from prison records, provided by the corrections departments, containing much background prerelease information, scores on various tests done in prison, and criminal-record history. Second, for Groups 1 through 5, prison prerelease interviews obtained much additional information about the participants' pasts, especially work experiences, and their future expectations after release: where they were going to live, with whom, job expectations, etc. The 3-month interview covered Group 1 through 5 participants' activities from release date to the time of the interview. The 6-month interview with the same groups covered the period from the time of the 3-month interview until the 6-month interview. Similarly the 12-month interview covered the interval from the 6-month interview to the twelfth. (Copies of representative instruments used are reproduced in Appendix A.)

Third, the wage-file data provide earnings in covered occupations for the quarter in which the person was released and for the four full quarters that followed for all persons in Groups 1 through 6. (Cash, casual labor, civil service jobs, and a few other exempt categories are not reported in these files.) The arrest records of all in Groups 1 through 6 cover one year (365 days) after the release date. They contain information on each recorded charge, the type of charge, dates, dispositions, and whether adjudications took place within the postrelease year. Many adjudications are missing, since the courts had not yet gotten around to hearing the case. Consequently, many sentences are missing. But the arrest record is as complete as humanly possible, and for the purpose of this evaluation it is the main test of the success or failure of the TARP treatments.

The coverage and completion rates for each of these data sources are shown in Table 3.5. For data that come from official records, very high response rates have been obtained. Only in the case of wage-file data for released prisoners for whom no social security identifying numbers existed

TABLE 3.5
Data Files Available and Response Rates for Georgia and Texas TARP
(Entries Are Response Rates)

Group and state	Prison record abstract	Pre-release interview	3-Month interview	6-Month interview	12-Month interview	State arrest file[a]	TARP payment file	Unemployment insurance wage files[b]	Parole record	N
1. Georgia (26 wks.)	100[c]	100[c]	95.4[c]	92.1[c]	89.2[c]	100[c]	100[c]	99.4[c]	100[c]	176
1. Texas (26 wks.)	100	100	99.4	99.4	96.5	100	100	100.0	100	175
2. Georgia (13 wks.)	100	100	93.4	86.9	90.9	100	100	100.0	100	199
2. Texas (13 wks.)	100	100	99.5	99.5	95.5	100	100	98.0	100	200
3. Georgia (13 wks.)	100	100	95.0	88.4	88.4	100	100	98.9	100	199
3. Texas (13 wks.)	100	100	99.5	98.0	94.5	100	100	99.0	100	200
4. Georgia (job placement)	100	100	89.1	83.1	88.6	100	100	99.5	100	201
4. Texas (job placement)	100	100	99.5	100.0	98.5	100	100	96.5	100	200
5. Georgia (control)	100	100	88.6	81.1	88.6	100	100	98.5	100	201
5. Texas (control)	100	100	100.0	98.5	95.0	100	100	91.5	100	200
6. Georgia (control)	100	——————— Not obtained ———————				100	100	92.9	100	1031
6. Texas (control)	100	——————— Not obtained ———————				100	100	91.3	100	1000

NOTE: All figures, except Ns, are given in percentages.

[a] Computerized arrest, adjudication, and commitment statewide files, supplemented in Georgia by record search in local jurisdictions.

[b] Obtained for every TARP participant for whom a social security number was obtainable either in prison records or in subsequent follow-up interviews.

[c] Proportions indicate the percentage of each group (represented in the row in question) for whom data records are available. Included in these percentages are those for whom interviews in a particular period were not necessary (i.e., those dead or in jail/prison the entire period covered by the interview). Also included are cases responding to a mailed questionnaire, including a subset of questions asked in face-to-face interviews (used for TARP participants who moved out of state).

in the files does the response rate fall below 100%.[16] Response rates for
follow-up interviews are extremely high, especially when compared to
response rates for surveys currently conducted on general population
samples. The lowest response rate for any of the waves of interviewing was
81.1% for the Georgia control group at the time of the 6-month follow-
up. All other response rates are over 85%, and most of the response rates
for Texas follow-up interviews are 95% or higher.

It is especially important to note that complete coverage has been obtained for the very crucial data file concerning arrests. Since this file contains data on the critical outcome variable of arrests on property-related
charges, this high level of coverage is particularly important.

ANALYSIS OF TARP DATA FILES

As part of their obligation under their contracts with the Department of
Labor, the two research groups in the states were required to make final
reports concerning the outcome of the TARP experiments in each of the
states. These reports have been completed and submitted to the Department of Labor.[17]

The present analysis in part duplicates the work of the TARP groups in
each of the states, but mainly it goes beyond those reports to accomplish
two additional tasks. First, the report takes into account findings from both
states, pointing out in which respects they were alike and in which respects
different. Second, the state TARP research groups, because of their heavy
operational responsibilities in obtaining these data and processing them,
had little opportunity to look very deeply into the TARP findings. The
present analysis goes considerably beyond the state reports to investigate
more complicated models of the way in which TARP payments functioned.

It should be noted that there are no major contradictions between the
state reports on the TARP experiment and the present volume. Both state
research staffs were kind enough to go over an earlier draft of the volume
to point out differences and, whenever possible, corrections have been
made. Some differences still remain, however, mainly reflecting differences
in the ways in which certain variables were defined operationally.

---

[16] This is mainly because of the absence of social security serial numbers for some of the
ex-prisoners.

[17] Jack L. Stephens and Lois W. Sanders, *Transitional Aid for Ex-Offenders: An Experimental Study in Georgia* (Atlanta, Ga.: Georgia Department of Offender Rehabilitation, 1978);
and Charles L. Smith, Pablo Martinez, and Daniel Harrison, *An Assessment: The Impact of
Providing Financial or Job Placement Assistance to Ex-Prisoners* (Huntsville, Texas: Texas
Department of Corrections, 1978).

OTHER RELATED RESEARCH CONDUCTED UNDER TARP

In addition to the main study of released prisoners described in this chapter, two additional smaller-scale studies were carried out.

The "Significant Woman" Substudy

A small-scale study centered on the reactions of women associated with the released men on their return. The impetus for the study arose out of some suggestions in the Baltimore LIFE study concerning the way in which the payments aided the ex-felons to adjust within the households to which they returned. Although the LIFE study provided relatively good empirical evidence that financial aid reduced arrests on property-related charges, it was not entirely clear how financial aid accomplished this effect. Some hints as to the reasons for the success of financial aid came from some of the responses given by LIFE participants to open-ended questions. In response to such questions about how the payments helped them, participants said that money reduced "pressure at home."

From what could be pieced together, when a man was released and first returned home, he was treated well, much like a returning veteran or graduate from college. There was often a welcoming home party, some gifts of clothing, and a few cash handouts. But this honeymoon period ended soon.

After 2 or 3 weeks he was expected to be out of the house, working and carrying his own weight. It must be remembered that most families to which released prisoners returned were fairly well strapped financially. There was nothing extra in the household, making it difficult to absorb another adult member. A released prisoner needed a bedroom, food, and incidental expense money to get through each day. In Baltimore, released prisoners typically returned to households that were managed by women— mothers, wives, sisters, or other female relatives. These women were the providers within these households. Without jobs or financial aid, the released prisoners became additional dependents. After a few weeks of idleness, the relationship between the ex-prisoners and the women household-heads began to deteriorate. Nagging, antagonisms, complaints, and bitterness ensued. To solve these problems, stemming at least in part from not being able to contribute to household finances, the men turned again to crime, as providing a seemingly easy solution to obtaining some money.

However modest may have been the payments given in the LIFE experiment ($60 per week), they did provide the released prisoners with enough to ease the financial burdens otherwise placed on the household and its meager resources. At the least, the released prisoners did not have to borrow small sums of money in order to have a little spending money, and some may have contributed part of their payment checks to running the households.

There was enough verisimilitude to this explanatory theme running through the comments of LIFE participants that it was thought worthwhile to interview TARP participants' "significant women" to ascertain how payments affected the relationships involved. The study was based on interviews with around 200 women, each designated by a TARP participant as the person with whom he was going to live upon release. The interviews were to take place approximately 3 months after release from prison.

The significant woman study was successful in reaching 198 women. Roughly half of this group were mothers, a quarter were wives, and another quarter were mother surrogates or girlfriends. By design, half the women were connected to men receiving financial aid and half to men not receiving aid. Half were from Houston and half from Atlanta. Findings from the study did not bear out the hunches from the Baltimore study—no differences in the women's attitudes toward men and no differences in reports of TARP participants' behavior could be connected with receiving financial aid. This study was carried out by Russell L. Curtis, Jr. and Sam Shulman at the University of Houston.[18]

A reanalysis of these data was undertaken by Jeffrey K. Liker of the University of Massachusetts research staff. His findings indicate that the payments did help to relieve some of the financial burdens of the significant women and thereby contributed to a greater level of satisfaction among the women with the released prisoners. This effect was especially pronounced among significant women who were mothers (or mother surrogates) of the ex-prisoners.

A summary of Liker's analyses is contained in Appendix B.

Measurement of Public Acceptance of Financial Aid to Released Prisoners

After the TARP contracts were signed, both states formally announced the new projects. When queried by the press, the states provided full descriptions of the studies and their objectives. At no time, however, was there any effort to give these experiments wide attention in the media. It was feared that perhaps some ineligible ex-offenders would get the mistaken idea that they could receive benefits when in fact they could not.

---

[18] This analysis is reported in R. L. Curtis, Jr. and Sam Shulman, *The Impact of Financial Aid on the Home Conditions and Family Relationships of Ex-Offenders*, Center for Human Resources (Houston, Texas: University of Houston, 1978).

Most of all, however, the project staff were reluctant to make the TARP experiment a public issue until much more was known about how it would work. As it happened, however, one of the tabloid national papers ran a story on TARP headlined "Cash for Crooks." It emphasized that murderers and rapists were being given cash handouts by the Department of Labor. This study set off a flurry of inquiries from some congressional offices, but after a full description of the project, as well as its purposes, was made available, congressional concern over the TARP experiment subsided.

Public reaction to this program was nevertheless a matter of considerable interest since public-policy issues would be at stake. The public has shown considerable antipathy toward welfare programs in general, and this program, no matter how it might differ, might seem to be just another extension of the welfare idea.

A public-opinion survey was therefore undertaken to find out what the average person thought about a program of financial aid to released prisoners. Although the general principle of TARP was widely acceptable to criminology and corrections specialists, some thought the idea impractical because it would not be politically acceptable: Certainly, they thought, the public would not approve. Since the TARP experiments were oriented to making policy changes, it was important to find out whether the public supported or resisted the idea. To find out, a few questions were added to a Roper survey of the national population.

In the question sequence used, the general situation that released prisoners face was described. It was stated that prisoners are typically released with $20 to $50 in gate money, an amount which must support them until they find jobs. Each respondent was then asked if he or she would favor or oppose a program that would provide a form of unemployment insurance until the released prisoner found a job. No mention was made of the possibility that such a program might reduce recidivism. Surprisingly, 63% of the respondents said they would favor such a program (see Panel A of Table 3.6). Those who said they were opposed or gave other answers were then asked what their opinion would be if such a program was shown to reduce crime. As shown in Panel B of Table 3.6, 64.1% of those initially negative or undecided said they would favor it. Thus, given the stipulation that unemployment benefits had the effect of reducing recidivism, a total of 78% were found to favor a program that extended such benefits to released prisoners. It looked as if a successful TARP experiment would achieve majority support.

While it may be tempting to read into these results a finding of considerable support for the principles underlying the TARP experiments, some restraint is urged in drawing such implications. The idea of providing financial aid to released prisoners is not one to which the general public has

TABLE 3.6

Public Opinion on Financial Aid to Released Prisoners
in the Form of Unemployment Insurance Benefits

A. *Distribution of Opinions on Initial Question*

"At the present time, most men when released from prison throughout the
country receive between $20 and $50 to start life over. Would you be in
favor of or opposed to providing released prisoners with some form of
financial support, for example, like unemployment insurance, until they
found a job?"

Response	Percentage
Favor	63.0
Opposed	23.5
It depends	
(volunteered)	8.0
Don't know	5.2
No answer	0.3
	100.0 ($N = 2002$)

B. *Distribution of Opinions of Initially Negative or Undecided Persons When*
Possibility of Recidivism Reduction Was Mentioned as Outcome

"If it were shown that such support reduced crime among men coming out
of prison, would you be in favor of it or not?" (Asked only of those who
opposed, did not know, or gave qualified answers to question in panel A.)

Response	Percentage
In Favor	64.1
Not in Favor	22.1
Don't Know	10.3
No Answer	3.5
	100.0 ($N = 741$)

Source: National Sample Survey conducted by Elmo Roper Associates, 1977.

given much thought. Nor was the program implied in the question on the
agendas of public bodies, with the consequence that the moral, political,
and economic issues involved were thoroughly aired. The American public
tends to be generous and openhanded on issues that have not been debated
in public. When issues come up on the agendas of public bodies and when
opponents and proponents have been identified, public opinion may rapidly crystallize into structures that show a great deal less (and perhaps even
more) support for the general principle that motivated the start of the
TARP experiments.

Furthermore, legislation does not exactly follow the majority opinion as
shown in public-opinion polls. Effective opinion may be the articulated

statements of support or opposition on the part of spokespersons for strong segments of the institutional structures of the United States or of regional interests or of whatever interests might somehow become engaged when the issue of financial aid to ex-felons comes before legislative bodies.

The best way to interpret these results is to draw the inference that the general principle of extending unemployment insurance coverage to released prisoners did not meet with initial hostility on the part of the general public. In short, there is no reservoir of existing disapproval that has to be taken into account at the outset.

4

Implementation of Transitional Aid Research Project Experimental Design

INTRODUCTION

It is one thing to design a randomized controlled experiment on paper but quite another to carry out the design faithfully. Indeed, one of the major lessons of the last decade of large-scale field experimentation is that the art of implementation is as demanding in its way as the task of design. Meticulous attention to detail is necessary to insure that random assignments to experimental and control groups are carried out properly. "Random" in this case does not mean "haphazard" but careful and faithful adherence to procedures that avoid any possibility of bias in assignments. Constant attention to the demands of data collection schedules is also necessary to retain as many cases as possible with full information on post-release experiences.

And among the most important implementation issues is ensuring that the "treatment" is delivered appropriately. Fewer than 800 released prisoners in each state were to be offered benefits or job-placement aid by state agencies for which this mission was a small addition to their regular duties. It would be entirely understandable but deplorable if, for one or another reason, TARP participants were lost sight of in a bureaucratic maze and never received some of the payments for which they were eligible.

The purpose of this chapter is to provide some descriptive evidence of the way in which the TARP experiment was carried out. We will first address the issue of randomization, assessing whether there were any biases in the assignment of released prisoners to one or another of the six groups. Next we will take up the issue of payments, considering how well the TARP participants understood the benefit plans for which they were eligible and how much in the way of payment was given out.

RANDOMIZATION SUCCESS

The purpose of the randomizing procedures described in the previous chapter was to ensure the statistical equivalence of the experimental and control groups, a condition in which the six groups would differ from each other only as much as one could expect to occur by chance. That is, in this desired condition, one cannot distinguish between persons in one group and persons in another group through tests of statistical significance. This does not mean that the groups must be identical in all respects but only that they must not vary from each other by more than is to be expected on the basis of chance fluctuation.

A test of whether or not the randomization procedures were successful can be made with a one-way analysis of variance (ANOVA). In brief, if the random-assignment process is properly implemented, the means (or proportions, in the case of dichotomous variables) for a given variable should be nearly the same across all treatment categories. That is, there should be no *systematic* tendency for older ex-offenders, for example, to be found in a particular treatment group; the mean age of ex-offenders in each treatment category should be approximately the same. The means will not be exactly the same because while the *chances* of being assigned to a particular treatment group are identical (within stratification categories), the "luck of the draw" will yield some variation in the means across treatment groups.

Since the means are expected to be the same except for these chance factors, one can test to see if in fact differences in means for different treatment groups can be attributed to chance or whether the randomization has broken down. If the differences in the means are too large to be the likely result of the luck of the draw, one's randomization procedures become suspect. For example, suppose the p-value for the analysis of variance is .50. This implies that if the same group of subjects had been randomly assigned over and over (i.e., if the assignment process were repeated a very large number of times), one would obtain differences between treatment group means as large as those observed 50 times out of 100 (i.e., rather frequently). A p-value of .10 implies that the observed differences between the means would have occurred 10 times out of 100 in numerous reassignments (i.e., rather infrequently). Thus, as the p-value gets smaller, the randomization process is increasingly in doubt. In this instance, we will employ a common social science convention that p-values of less than .05 (5 times out of 100) allow one to reject the null hypothesis that the randomization process was carried out properly.

Tables 4.1 and 4.2 compare the experimental and control groups formed in each of the TARP experiments on a number of measures taken before assignment from the prison records of the participants. None of the

TABLE 4.1

Texas TARP: Experimental and Control Group Differences
at Outset of Experiment Tested by ANOVA

Variable	Group 1	Group 2	Group 3	Group 4	Group 5	Group 6	ANOVA	
							F	p
Age (average)	29.0	29.5	29.6	29.3	29.8	29.7	.208	.96
SD	8.7	9.5	9.8	9.7	9.7	9.8		
Female (percent)	6.9	7.0	7.0	7.0	7.0	6.9	.0017	1.00
White (percent)	37.1	33.0	35.0	36.5	36.0	37.3	.3141	.90
Black (percent)	44.0	53.0	53.0	48.5	46.0	46.8	1.208	.303
Chicano (percent)	18.9	14.0	12.0	15.0	18.0	15.9	.945	.451
Paroled (percent)	52.0	51.5	52.5	53.0	52.0	52.8	.0347	.999
Average PIP rating[a]	116.4	114.3	119.2	119.3	118.0	116.1	1.061	.380
First offenders (percent)	41.3	45.2	55.6	49.8	51.5	47.0	1.962	.082
N	(174)	(199)	(198)	(197)	(198)	(993)		
Average educational achievement score	6.5	6.6	6.7	6.8	6.7	6.8	1.095	.361
N	(172)	(194)	(195)	(195)	(195)	(978)		
Average IQ score	93.6	95.4	93.1	94.1	95.5	95.3	.989	.423
	(159)	(175)	(172)	(171)	(183)	(889)		
Average length of sentence (years)	2.90	2.81	2.66	2.84	2.82	2.75	.203	.961
Number of previous property convictions	1.16	1.08	1.29	1.11	1.02	1.12	1.250	.284
Number of previous personal crime convictions	.14	.13	.13	.16	.11	.12	.391	.855
N	(175)	(200)	(200)	(200)	(200)	(1000)		

NOTE: All information comes from prison records. Ns smaller than total Ns indicate missing values.
[a] PIP rating is a score given to each prisoner based on conduct, work effort, and attitude shown while in prison. Roughly equivalent to a conduct score.

p-values accompanying each of the 25 sets of comparisons is smaller than .08 and most are considerably higher. The overall pattern of findings indicates that within each state the experimental groups and the control groups are statistically equivalent with respect to sex composition, age composition, ethnic mixture, educational attainment, previous criminal record, and IQ scores and as to whether participants were given parole and whether participants were first offenders.

TABLE 4.2
Georgia TARP: Experimental and Control Group Differences
at Outset of Experiment Tested by ANOVA

| | | | | | | | ANOVA | |
Variable	Group 1	Group 2	Group 3	Group 4	Group 5	Group 6	F	p
Black (percent)	53.4	60.3	58.3	58.2	58.7	58.4	.410	.842
Age (average)	27.9	28.8	27.9	28.7	27.8	27.6	.810	.543
Educational attainment (years)	9.4	9.5	9.5	9.2	9.5	9.5	.507	.771
Educational achievement score (years)	5.9	5.7	5.7	5.5	5.8	5.8	.299	.914
N	(117)	(130)	(120)	(140)	(124)	(646)		
Average IQ score	93.6	90.9	91.8	91.4	92.3	94.4	1.59	.161
N	(117)	(130)	(120)	(140)	(124)	(646)		
Average years prior confinement	1.65	1.61	1.93	1.65	.68	1.66	.601	.699
N	(136)	(156)	(151)	(150)	(157)	(804)		
Number of previous property convictions	.86	.70	.65	.68	.61	.64	.713	.614
Number of previous personal crime convictions	.03	.06	.05	.02	.05	.05	.635	.673
Paroled (percent)	37.5	34.1	31.7	32.8	33.3	37.3	.857	.510
Female (percent)	5.7	5.5	7.5	6.5	4.5	5.9	.372	.868
First offender (percent)	72.2	74.9	71.2	72.1	76.6	75.3	.525	.758
Average length of sentence (years)	1.26	1.23	.30	.20	.19	1.13	.956	.444
N	(176)	(199)	(199)	(201)	(201)	(1031)		

NOTE: All information comes from prison records. Ns smaller than total Ns indicate missing values.

The measures shown in Tables 4.1 and 4.2 were selected because previous research has shown each to be related to recidivism and because they were present in the extracts we were furnished from each prison record.[1] Hence if the ANOVA results indicated that experimental and control groups differed on one of these measures, we would be worried that our findings might be reflecting such differences rather than the effects of the payments. Such is not the case.

---

[1] Other measures available in the prison records were not tested since they were not conceivably related to postrelease behavior.

It should be noted that the two states did not yield equivalent groups, reflecting differences between the populations and the criminal justice systems of the two states. Thus, the ethnic compositions of the Texas TARP groups reflect the fact that Texas has a rather large Chicano population. Georgia prisoners are slightly younger, have served shorter sentences, and have had fewer previous convictions than their Texas counterparts.

THE GEORGIA COMMUTATION ORDER

Shortly before the selection of TARP subjects was to begin in Georgia, the governor issued an order that shortened the sentences for certain types of prisoners. The motivation was to speed up the release of prisoners in order to lessen the crowding then existing in the Georgia prison system.

Although the impact of the governor's commutation order on the assignment of prisoners to experimental and control groups was minimal, as the previous section indicated, it did have the effect of producing a different mix of prisoners than would have ordinarily been the case. The governor's order in effect favored quicker releases for persons who were convicted of property offenses. As a consequence, Georgia TARP members are more likely to have been convicted of a property offense, are slightly more likely to be young persons, and more likely to be white and male. Table 4.3 shows the critical characteristics of persons released under the commutation order as compared to those released under ordinary rules governing time of release and parole.

About 44% of Georgia's TARP members were released under the governor's commutation-of-sentence order. The effect of the order was in fact quite favorable for the experiment. Since the run of prisoners participating in the experiment was composed more heavily of those types of ex-offenders who were most likely to "benefit" from the payments, the Georgia TARP experiment's efficiency was thereby increased to some extent.

Since the persons favored by the commutation order were also more likely to have had longer criminal records and slightly longer periods of prison time in previous convictions than the more usual run of Georgia prisoners, the contrasts between Georgia and Texas prisoners are more likely to be stronger than those shown in the previous section of this chapter. Georgia apparently incarcerates persons more frequently for less serious crimes and is less likely to have its prisons filled with old-timers.

While the differences between the two states affect comparisons between the states, within each state the experimental compared with control dif-

TABLE 4.3
Georgia: Characteristics of TARP Member Released
under Commutation Order Compared to Regular Releasees

Characteristics	Released under	
	Regular conditions	Commutation order
Age (average)	29.4	26.0
Female	8.2%	3.1%
Educational attainment	9.5 years	9.5 years
Years of prior incarceration	.12	.37
Total number of arrests	.68	.69
Number of prior property-related convictions	.24	.33
Number of prior personal offense convictions	.05	.04
Total number of prior convictions	.40	.47
Current personal offense conviction	23%	3%
Current property offense conviction	51%	87%
White	37%	48%
Paroled	24%	51%
First offender	76%	72%
N	(878)	(1129)

Source: Prison records.

ferences remain intact. Hence, neither the interstate differences nor the effects of the Georgia governor's commutation order need concern us as we discuss experimental outcomes.

THE EXPERIMENTAL TREATMENTS AND THEIR DELIVERY

The programs offered to released prisoners who were allocated to the first three experimental groups consisted of eligibility for unemployment insurance payments of $70 per week in Georgia and $63 per week in Texas. A fourth experimental group was offered unlimited job-placement help along with grants of up to $100 to offset the expense of acquiring tools and work clothes and to offset other expenses that might be related closely to obtaining employment. To qualify for payments a TARP participant had to report to a local employment security office, certify that he was not employed, and indicate that he was willing and able to accept employment. If he was employed and had earnings above certain amounts during the period for which he was making a claim, his benefits were reduced dollar for dollar if he was in Groups 1 and 2 and $.25 for each dollar earned if he was in Group 3. The several plans are summarized as follows:

State	Group	Maximum payment	Forgiveness[a] amount	Tax[a] (percent)
Texas	1	$63 for 26 weeks	$15.75	100
Georgia	1	$70 for 26 weeks	$8.00	100
Texas	2	$63 for 13 weeks	$15.75	100
Georgia	2	$70 for 13 weeks	$8.00	100
Texas	3	$63 for 13 weeks	—	25
Georgia	3	$70 for 13 weeks	—	25
Texas and Georgia	4	Job placement and grants of up to $100 to cover certain job-related expenses.		

[a] The "forgiveness amount" is the amount of income allowed to a TARP participant to which no tax applies. Thus in Texas, a person was allowed to earn up to $15.75 in any week without any reduction in his benefit. The "tax" rate is the extent to which benefits were reduced if persons had some earnings beyond the forgiveness amount in any week. Thus a 100% tax indicates a dollar-for-dollar reduction and a 25% tax indicates that benefits were reduced $.25 for each dollar earned beyond the forgiveness amount

Note that in order for an eligible participant to receive payments he had to make a positive effort to obtain payments: He had to travel to an employment security office. In addition he had to know enough about the rules of eligibility both to give appropriate answers to office clerks when he arrived and to estimate whether it was worthwhile for him to file for a week's benefits. For example, all participants were eligible if they were available for employment, but that definition excluded attendance at school, time in hospital, time sick, or time in jail or prison. Furthermore, if a participant had earned less than a certain amount in any one week he was still eligible for some sort of partial payment and not an insignificant amount if he were a Group 3 participant.

Group 4 participants were offered job-placement help at the time they received payments for their prerelease interviews and were also told about the grants available for the purchase of tools and for certain other job-related expenses. Although records made available by the state research teams contain data on grants made, there is almost no information on the extent to which members of this group availed themselves of the job-placement services. As shown in the bottom panel of Table 4.4, 5 grants averaging $43 each were made in Georgia and 35 grants averaging $87 each

TABLE 4.4

Payment Eligibility, Actual Numbers of Payments, and Amounts Received
by Period and by Total Year

| | | Payment eligibility | | | Payments received | | | | | | | |
| | | | | | First quarter | | Second quarter | | Last half | | Total year | |
Group	State	Full[a] payment ($)	Number payments	Total amount ($)	Average number	Average amount ($)	Average number	Average amount ($)	Average number	Average amount ($)	Average number	Average amount ($)
1	Texas	63	26	1638	8.6	532	7.2	441	4.4	262	20.4	1236
1	Georgia	70	26	1820	8.3	564	7.4	509	4.5	310	20.2	1384
2	Texas	63	13	819	8.4	517	1.7	97	1.1	67	11.5	682
2	Georgia	70	13	910	7.6	517	2.7	170	1.2	80	11.5	769
3	Texas	63[b]	13	819	9.8	553	2.8	126	1.0	48	13.8	728
3	Georgia	70[b]	13	910	9.3	603	3.7	210	.7	36	13.7	850
4	Texas	Grants up to $100 for tools, work clothes, etc.			5 grants made in postrelease year averaging $43 each							
4	Georgia				35 grants made in postrelease year averaging $87 each							

SOURCE: Payment files from each state.

[a] "Full payment" is the amount paid to persons who earn less than the forgiveness amount in a given week.

[b] Subject to 25% tax. All other groups were subject to 100% tax for earning above forgiveness thresholds.

TABLE 4.5
Knowledge of Payments and Entitlements among
Payment Groups 1, 2, and 3

| | Percentages of persons giving correct answers | | | | | |
| | Georgia | | | Texas | | |
Treatment knowledge item	Group 1	Group 2	Group 3	Group 1	Group 2	Group 3
Amount of weekly payments	93	89	89	84	77	70
Number of weeks' entitlement	45	54	59	33	38	35
Benefit loss if $40 earned	39	46	12	29	30	3
Benefit loss if earned as much as						
benefit ($63 or $70)	53	53	6	48	54	8
Benefit loss if earned $100	61	64	12	72	77	8
Entitlement if sick	7	11	7	13	14	18
Entitlement if in school	12	13	9	12	13	6
Entitlement if arrested	47	41	43	31	40	36
Period of eligibility	63	59	57	68	73	62
Average number of items						
answered correctly	4.2	4.3	3.0	3.3	3.4	1.8
N	(135)	(165)	(161)	(147)	(166)	(156)

SOURCE: 12-month interviews.

were made in Texas. Assuming that each of the grantees involved also used the job-placement services, we have estimated 2.5% and 17.5% minimum usage rates in Georgia and Texas, respectively. Clearly these are lower-bound estimates in each state. Since data on the utilization of job-placement services are so meager, the remainder of this chapter will focus almost exclusively on the three benefit-payment groups.

TARP participants were not very knowledgeable about all the details of the plans they were under, as Table 4.5 indicates. This table shows the proportion of participants in the treatment groups at the time of the 12-month interview who gave correct answers to questions about their benefits. A charitable view was taken of correctness in computing these proportions: That is, if a participant was approximately correct he was marked as correct; an incorrect answer was one that went wide of the mark. It should also be borne in mind that these questions were asked at the end of the postrelease year. Most of the participants had used up their benefits some months earlier, and their recall of the details of the plans they had been under may have suffered as a result of decay over time.

Almost all participants knew the amounts of the maximum weekly payments of $70 and $63 for which they were eligible. About one-half of the Georgia participants knew how many weeks of eligibility they were given, but about one-third of Texas participants got that number correct. One-half to two-thirds knew the correct period of eligibility and about two-thirds of Groups 1 and 2 participants had a more or less correct idea of how much of their benefits would be lost if they earned $100. Perhaps this level of knowledge was enough for most participants to get by in the sense of knowing more or less what they were entitled to, for how long, and some of the conditions of eligibility.

Relatively poor levels of knowledge were shown by Group 3 participants. In particular, they appeared not to be aware of the fact that a rather generous tax rate applied to their benefits and that they could get partial payments if they earned up to $212 per week in Texas and $200 per week in Georgia.

Most participants seemed not to know that they were not eligible for payments while in school or while sick. Most participants were not very knowledgeable about the tax rates involved in their plans, although Groups 1 and 2 had more knowledge than Group 3.

At the bottom of Table 4.5 we have shown the average number of items that participants answered correctly. Participants in Georgia Groups 1 and 2 average about 4 out of 9 items, with Group 3 getting 3 out of 9 correct. Levels of knowledge in Texas were lower than those in Georgia, all groups getting one less item correct than their Georgia counterparts. One may speculate that the higher knowledge of the Georgia participants reflects the fact that the employment service personnel that dealt with that state's participants were specially detailed for that purpose and thus may have provided more informed service. Whether or not such was the case, of course, is impossible to tell at this point.

Although it is difficult to assess whether the levels of knowledge shown in Table 4.5 are high enough for the experiment to work as planned—assuming that detailed knowledge of benefits makes the treatments more effective—it is especially disappointing that Group 3 participants did not sufficiently appreciate the fact that a rather generous tax rate applied to their benefit eligibility. The tax rate in this group was expressly designed to encourage persons to work. It seems unlikely that it could have had such an effect if eligible participants did not know about it and understand how it worked.

Special analyses wre undertaken to determine the extent to which knowledge about the benefit plans was differentially distributed among TARP participants. Findings indicated that better educated, older participants knew slightly more than less educated, younger persons. In addition, holding age and education constant, Texas Chicanos were slightly less knowledgeable than other persons. These tendencies were so slight, however, that few consistently survived statistical significance thresholds when other variables were held constant. (In order not to clutter up the text these findings are not reported here.)

The impact of knowledge about the TARP payment plans on the amounts of money received is shown in Table 4.6, in which correlations of knowledge with the total number of payments and the total amount of cash received are presented. By and large, the correlations are positive but quite modest, indicating that the more the participants knew about TARP payment plans the more payments and the more money they received. The impact of knowledge on payments is especially strong in Group 3, which was under the most complicated of the three plans, indicating that for this group knowledge made more of a difference.

The interpretations in the last few pages are based on the assumption that knowledge affects payments. Since knowledge was measured at the end of the postrelease period, an equally tenable assumption is that the number and amounts of payments affected knowledge: TARP members who had more experience with the steps involved in making claims and collecting checks presumably accumulated more knowledge of how benefits were calculated. At this point we cannot say what may have been the direction of influence between knowledge and payment. We can only say that they are related.

It is possible, however, to assert with considerable confidence that knowledge of TARP payment plans and obtaining the benefits were not very highly related. There were many other events in the lives of TARP members that affected whether or not they received a large amount of cash or a large number of payments. Knowledge of the TARP payment plans may have played a role, but it was certainly not a very large one, as the modest size of the correlation coefficients indicates.

Still another way of looking at how well the experiment worked in the sense of delivering payments to eligible participants is illustrated in Table 4.4. In this table we show for each payment group the average numbers of payments made and the average amounts paid out of benefits. In the last two columns of Table 4.4 we present the numbers of payments and dollar amounts paid out over the entire postrelease year. Note that Group 1 and 2 participants did not receive, on the average, the full number of payments to which they were entitled. Of course, this average covers a great deal of variation—a few participants took no payments and a few took more payments than their entitlement, some apparently being partial payments that extended their eligibility beyond 26 and 13 payments.

But also note that Group 3 members, while showing such a low level of knowledge about their tax rates, apparently took advantage of that provision in sufficient numbers to raise the average number of payments beyond 13 and to obtain more money in total benefits than their counterparts in Group 2. Of course, this finding may only indicate that employment security personnel in Texas and Georgia knew the regulations involved and helpfully provided participants with the benefits they were entitled to.

TABLE 4.6

Correlations of Knowledge about Payments with Number of
Payments Received and Total Amounts of Payments Received

	Georgia	Texas
A. *Group 1 (26 weeks of eligibility)*		
1. Correlation with number of payments	.09	.25
2. Correlation with total amounts received	.12	.26
B. *Group 2 (13 weeks of eligibility)*		
1. Correlation with number of payments	.20	.20
2. Correlation with total amounts received	.21	.18
C. *Group 3 (13 weeks of eligibility*		
and 25% "tax")		
1. Correlation with number of payments	.32	.23
2. Correlation with total amounts received	.21	.33

SOURCE: Payment file and 12-month interviews.

There are virtually no differences between the two states in the numbers of payments given out to each group. The differences in dollar amounts of benefits are also negligible, once the fact that Georgia payments were slightly more generous than Texas is taken into account.

The remaining columns of Table 4.4 show how benefits were given out during various periods over the postrelease year. Group 1 members used up about 60% of their eligibility in the first 6 months and the remainder in the last half of the year. Group 2 members used up the bulk (75%) of their benefits in the first 6 months, only small amounts, on the average, were paid out in the last half of the year.

It is especially interesting to note that the patterning of payments for Group 3, subject to a 25% tax rate, differs from those of Group 2. To some degree, Group 3 members did take advantage of the more generous partial payments that were available to them, as noted above. The tax rate also apparently made it possible for the members of this group to use up their eligibility faster; they received about 90% of their total eligibility within the first 6 months after release. Group 3 members also used up a greater proportion of their total eligibility at the end of the postrelease year than either of the other two groups—about 92% as compared to about 75% for Groups 1 and 2. Indeed, the Group 3 experience is quite similar to the Baltimore LIFE experiment, in which all but a small handful of participants used up all of their eligibility by the end of the postrelease year.

The evidence presented in Table 4.4 is that the state agencies in Texas and Georgia were able to deliver the treatments, especially when the eligibility provisions, as in Group 3, made it possible to make partial payments when participants were working. It should also be noted that since the tax provisions used in Group 3 were different from the ordinary provisions of the unemployment benefit systems of the two states, their demonstrated ability to administer the special provisions is even more impressive.

Did the payments fulfill the needs they were intended to meet? This question, unfortunately, will have to remain unanswered, at least for the time being. The data presented in Table 4.4 are consistent with a variety of interpretations. On one hand, since we know that released prisoners generally have a hard time finding work, the fact that TARP participants used up at least some of their eligibility for benefits must mean that the payments averted some weeks with zero income. On the other hand, perhaps the best result would have been if TARP participants had used up even less of their eligibility because they quickly found jobs to support themselves and their dependents. We can infer that something along these lines occurred from the fact that few of the participants in Groups 1 and 2 received all of the benefits to which they were entitled. Indeed, the central question, to which we will return time and time again throughout the remainder of this report, is what the balance was between the work-disincentive effects of the payments and the income-producing effects of the payments.

TARP COSTS

The total costs of running the TARP experiments, including payments to participants and research costs, amounted to a little more than $3.4 million. Of this amount, approximately $1 million was spent in benefit payments to TARP participants in the treatment groups. Of the remainder, it is difficult to sort out expenditures for administration from expenditures for the collection and analysis of data. Our best guess is that about two-thirds of the $3.4 million (or about $2.28 million) went for research purposes and the remainder to support the administrative costs of running the benefit system in the two states. As detailed a breakdown as possible of the costs of the TARP experiments is given in Table 4.7.

As field experiments go, the TARP experiments were quite inexpensive. For example, the 3-year-long income-maintenance experiment in New Jersey and Pennsylvania cost about $8 million, with about $3 million going to 1300 families as transfer payments.[3] The Experimental Housing Allowance Experiments have cost more than $34 million to date, with

---

[3] P. H. Rossi and K. Lyall, *Reforming Public Welfare: A Critique of the Negative Income Tax Experiment* (New York: Russell Sage Foundation, 1976).

TABLE 4.7
TARP Experiment Expenditures as of July 1979

A. Texas TARP:		
1. Benefit payments to TARP participants	$495,845	
2. Texas Employment Commission administrative expenses	162,717	
3. Texas Department of Corrections expenses (includes payments to TARP participants for interviews)	547,335	
Total Texas TARP expenditures		1,205,897
B. Georgia TARP:		
1. Benefit payments to TARP participants	574,063	
2. Interview payments to TARP participants	35,385	
3. Administrative personnel costs (includes interviewer payments)	738,530	
4. Other Expenditures (supplies, space, computer, etc.)	174,309	
Total Georgia TARP expenditures		1,522,287
C. American Bar Foundation:		
1. Administration and ABA research	183,875	
2. Principal investigator and staff	174,274	
3. Special studies ("significant women" study, cost-benefit analyses, etc.)	101,539	
Total ABA expenditures		459,688
D. University of Massachusetts:		
1. University of Massachusetts personnel	79,306	
2. Subcontract to University of California, Santa Barbara	42,300	
3. Computer and other expenses	91,886	
Total Massachusetts expenditures		213,492
E. Grand Total		$3,401,364

TABLE 4.8
Sources of TARP Funds as Budgeted

	Dollars	Percentage
Contributed by DOL	2,131,379	62
Contributed by LEAA	500,000	15
Contributed by State of Georgia[a]	400,000	12
Contributed by State of Texas[a]	400,000	12
Total	3,431,379	

SOURCE: Budgeted amounts as furnished by Department of Labor.

NOTE: Funds shown in this table are budgeted amounts. Since actual expenditures totaled less than the amounts budgeted, grand totals in this table and in Table 4.7 differ.

[a] Donations primarily in the form of services of personnel allocated to experiment plus facilities and computer services.

several years of expenditures yet to go. Other field experiments may be even more expensive.

Not all of the funds used in the experiment were furnished by the Department of Labor. All sources of funds are shown in Table 4.8, in which the separate contributions of the states and the Law Enforcement Assistance Administration of the Department of Justice are also shown. While the majority of the funds were provided by the Department of Labor, significant contributions were made by the Law Enforcement Assistance Administration and the states of Georgia and Texas.

Of course, the key issue is not so much what was expended but whether the sums involved yielded information that in some sense justified the outlays involved. It will take some years for the final returns on the benefits of the experiment to be fully appreciated; for the present, however, the reader is invited to make his or her own assessment.

SOME CONCLUSIONS CONCERNING IMPLEMENTATION

The purpose of this chapter was to assess the extent to which the TARP experiments were properly implemented. We have presented considerable evidence that at least at the start of the postrelease year, the randomization procedures that were followed resulted in experimental and control groups that were statistically equivalent. And an examination of the payment records revealed that the state agencies were able to deliver the benefits despite the rather hazy notions that the participants retained of the terms of their eligibility.

5

TARP Outcomes: Effectiveness Masked by Unanticipated Side-Effects

INTRODUCTION

The policy-related purpose of the TARP experiments was to test whether the provision of limited amounts of financial support could lower the recidivism rates for property-related offenses committed by released prisoners. The encouraging results of the Baltimore LIFE experiment were to be tested under conditions resembling more closely those that would obtain if the policies involved were to be incorporated into state unemployment insurance schemes.

This chapter examines the postrelease-year arrest records of TARP participants and assesses the extent to which the expectations of lowered recidivism were fulfilled. As we have already noted, the findings indicate that the payments, *as administered*, were *not* successful in lowering arrest rates for persons receiving benefits.

The important message of this chapter is that conditions were not as they appeared on the surface. We will show that the payments actually did lower arrests, but that this effect was counteracted by the fact that payments also indirectly increased arrests by fostering unemployment. The empirical evidence supporting this counterbalancing theory of TARP effects will be presented, along with some of the policy implications of the model.

OVERALL EXPERIMENTAL OUTCOMES

The rationale for the TARP experiment was that the provision of modest amounts of financial aid would help released prisoners to make an acceptable adjustment to civilian life. It was thought that such aid would lower rates of property-related crimes and ease the transition to gainful employment. Ideally, one would want to judge the success of the TARP payments by contrasting the crime-commission rates of those eligible for payments with the control groups who were not given any payments. Of course, since the "true" crime-commission rates are not possible to estimate for any given individual or for identifiable groups, it is necessary to use, as in the Baltimore LIFE experiment, a criterion that, although clearly related to the true crime rate, is at least one step removed. Arrests recorded in the states' criminal justice information systems are the best measure available.

Arrests are made by the police either on the complaint of some witness to a possible criminal act or on the basis of some direct evidence uncovered by the police. As is well known, not all crimes committed are reported to the police or witnessed by them. Furthermore, for those crimes in which there are ordinarily no direct witnesses—for example, in most burglaries—citizen reports do not often lead to arrests of suspected criminals. Hence, arrests are undoubtedly biased downward, representing only some portion of the crimes actually committed.

There also may be some compensating biases related to the fact that TARP members are ex-felons and hence more likely to be arrested by the police as likely suspects. However, these are biases that are not related in any conceivable way to membership in any of the experimental or control groups. Hence, although arrests are not exactly identical with crimes, the differences in rates of arrest among the experimental and control groups are not biased by being confounded with membership in TARP groups.

Tables 5.1 and 5.2 present data on arrests of various sorts experienced by TARP members in the year following release. The top panel (Panel A) of the tables contains the proportions ever arrested and the average number of arrests on property-related charges experienced by TARP participants in each of the six groups. On the average, 24% of the Georgia TARP members and 23% of the Texas members were arrested on property-related charges at least once during the year after release. The percentages within each of the subgroups of the experiment vary somewhat but in no systematic way. Thus, the lowest arrest proportion in Georgia was for Group 5, a control group, but in Texas, the lowest proportion shown was for Group 4. In fact, *in neither state were there systematic differences between experimental and control groups* that passed the statistical significance tests represented by the analyses of variance tests displayed in the last two columns of the tables. The *p*-value for Georgia is .44 and for Texas .63, indicating, respectively, that patterns of differences as large as shown would have arisen by chance 44 and 63 times out of a hundred random samples of the appropriate size from the same population.[1]

---

[1] These results and those in the tables that follow are subject to several important caveats. First, for *descriptive purposes*, the comparisons across treatment and control groups are fully valid and can be taken at face value. However, inferences to the parameters of the underlying

TABLE 5.1

Georgia: Arrests on Various Charges during Postrelease Year
in Experimental and Control Groups

| Variable | Experimental groups | | | | Control groups | | ANOVA | |
	1	2	3	4	5	6	F	p
A. *Property-related arrests*								
Percentage ever arrested	29.0	24.1	27.6	22.4	18.9	23.0	1.50	.19
Average number of arrests	.41	.39	.38	.31	.28	.34	.97	.44
SD	(.77)	(.88)	(.68)	(.68)	(.70)	(.73)		
B. *Offenses against persons*								
Percentage ever arrested	5.1	10.6	10.0	9.0	10.0	8.6	.90	.48
Average number of arrests	.06	.15	.13	.10	.10	.10	1.30	.26
SD	(.31)	(.49)	(.40)	(.33)	(.32)	(.35)		
C. *"Significant" arrests*[a]								
Percentage ever arrested	40.3	37.2	37.2	35.3	32.3	34.7	.69	.63
Average number of arrests	.59	.64	.64	.56	.48	.57	.75	.58
SD	(.88)	(1.2)	(1.1)	(.93)	(.84)	(.98)		
D. *Arrests on all charges*								
Percentage ever arrested	49.9	49.2	49.2	49.1	48.4	48.7	.76	.58
Average number of arrests	.69	.72	.71	.73	.62	.68	.24	.94
SD	(.97)	(1.2)	(1.1)	(1.3)	(1.2)	(1.2)		

SOURCE: Computerized arrest records, corrected by records search.

NOTE: No values are missing. Ns for each group equal the Ns shown in Table 3.4.

[a] Includes crimes against person, property-related crimes, and such serious offenses as the use of weapons and drugs. Primarily excludes drunk and disorderly behavior and traffic-related offenses.

The second row in the first panel of Tables 5.1 and 5.2 contains the average numbers of arrests on property-related charges in Georgia and Texas, respectively. The analysis of variance results indicate that the experimental and control groups did not differ significantly on this measure either. *In short, there were no overall differences in property-related arrests between those who received the experimental treatment and the controls.*

---

causal processes must be handled cautiously. For nominal outcomes (reported as percentages), one necessarily has heteroskedastic residuals and hence, biased standard errors. Therefore, the significance tests (and their p-values) are not precisely correct. However, we spot-checked several of the more important null findings with logit models and conclusions remained virtually the same. For outcomes truncated at zero (e.g., the number of arrests, weeks employed), both the comparisons across treatment and control groups and the standard errors are biased and inconsistent. Again, however, the inferential distortions are apparently not substantial. In Part III we make appropriate adjustments for the effects of truncated dependent variables much like those reported here (in several cases the variables are identical), and the same basic patterns (and lack of patterns) emerge.

TABLE 5.2
Texas: Arrests on Various Charges during Postrelease Year
in Experimental and Control Groups

	Experimental groups				Control groups		ANOVA	
Variable	1	2	3	4	5	6	F	p
A. *Property-related arrests*								
Percentage ever arrested	22.3	23.5	27.5	20.0	22.0	23.2	.70	.63
Average number of arrests	.27	.30	.43	.30	.33	.33	1.15	.33
SD	(.54)	(.60)	(.94)	(.74)	(.74)	(.72)		
B. *Person offenses arrests*								
Percentage ever arrested	5.1	3.0	4.5	3.0	4.5	2.0	1.87	.10
Average number of arrests	.05	.03	.05	.04	.05	.02	1.41	.22
SD	(.22)	(.17)	(.24)	(.26)	(.24)	(.17)		
C. *Total personal and property arrests*								
Percentage ever arrested	44.1	43.4	46.4	41.9	43.7	42.9	.99	.42
Average number of arrests	.32	.33	.48	.34	.38	.36	1.24	.29
SD	(.57)	(.64)	(.96)	(.79)	(.77)	(.75)		
D. *Drinking-related charges*								
Percentage ever arrested	4.0	6.5	5.0	5.0	5.0	5.9	.34	.86
Average number of arrests	.05	.09	.19	.07	.06	.06	1.52	.18
SD	(.23)	(.34)	(1.8)	(.37)	(.25)	(.26)		
E. *Total arrests on all charges*								
Percentage ever arrested	37.7	38.0	42.5	34.0	36.5	35.5	.87	.50
Average number of arrests	.63	.53	.69	.70	.66	.59	.68	.64
SD	(1.01)	(.80)	(1.12)	(1.11)	(1.16)	(1.01)		

SOURCE: Texas computerized arrest files.

NOTE: No values are missing. Ns for each group equal the Ns shown in Table 3.4.

The remaining panels of Tables 5.1 and 5.2 summarize arrests on non-property charges. The expectation was that the payments were to be effective primarily in averting arrests on property-related charges. Frequently, however, the charge entered upon arrest is not the charge made at the time of the incident. Thus, for example, a person may be arrested on a "driving while drunk" charge but later be charged with a burglary when evidence is uncovered of possible participation in a burglary incident. As the evidence from the analyses of variance indicates, however, experimental and control groups cannot be distinguished on a variety of other kinds of arrests. In Georgia, a little less than half of TARP members in each of the groups experienced at least one arrest in the postrelease year. In Texas, a little more than one-third of the participants were arrested at least once. Within each state, it does not appear that members of the groups receiving payment or job placement were significantly different in these respects when compared to the control groups.[2]

Quite a different story emerges when the postrelease employment and earnings of TARP participants are considered, as Tables 5.3 and 5.4 illustrate. *TARP payment eligibility clearly had strong effects on work effort.* Panel A in each of the tables contains the average number of weeks worked by members of each of the five groups. TARP members of Group 1 who were eligible for 26 weeks of benefit payments worked an average of 12.3 weeks in Georgia, as compared with 24.3 weeks for controls; the corresponding figures in Texas were 20.8 and 28.3 weeks. These patterns over the postrelease year amount to a reduction of work effort (compared to controls) of about 51% in Georgia and 27% in Texas. On the average, Groups 2 and 3, who were eligible for 13 weeks of payments, worked more than Group 1 but still less than the controls. Finally, Group 4, eligible for special job-placement efforts, worked slightly more than the controls in Texas but less than their controls in Georgia.

Indicating substantial work-disincentive effects of TARP payment eligibility, these patterns become even more pronounced when separate periods within the postrelease year are examined, as in Panels B through E of Tables 5.3 and 5.4. The differences between groups eligible for payments and control groups were especially striking during the first 14 weeks after release, when all members of those groups retained their eligibility for payments. In later periods, Group 1, given 26 weeks of eligibility for payments, tended to stand out as evidencing less work effort, with the other payment groups becoming closer and closer to the controls.

For some not quite understandable reason, Group 4 in Georgia, eligible for intensive work-placement services, had a consistently lower work effort than the controls throughout the postrelease year. The same group in Texas, however, was indistinguishable from the controls.

Data on weeks worked in the postrelease year came from follow-up interviews with TARP participants who were queried in detail on work during each of the follow-up interviews.[3] For this reason, no information

---

[2] The information available in TARP data sets does not permit an interpretation of the differences in total arrests between the two states. These differences may represent partly the differential efficiencies of the two information systems and partly the greater unemployment rates in Georgia during the period in question. (See Chapter 9 for a description of the state unemployment rates in this period.)

[3] These data were subject to errors of recall. In addition, TARP members in the payment groups may have underreported employment because payments were not supposed to be made to persons who were employed. To test the amount of distortion entered into the reports of weeks worked, we correlated number of weeks worked with employment insurance wage files separately for payment groups and for controls (who presumably had no motive to under-report work effort). The patterns of relationships for the payment groups and the controls

TABLE 5.3
Georgia: Employment and Earnings in Postrelease Year
for Experimental and Control Groups

Variable	Experimental groups				Control groups		ANOVA	
	1	2	3	4	5	6	F	p
A. *Total weeks worked during postrelease year*								
Average weeks worked	12.3	17.4	17.7	19.6	24.3	—	10.71	.0000
SD	14.2	15.7	16.5	16.2	17.3	—		
N	(142)	(155)	(155)	(146)	(154)	—		
B. *Weeks worked first 6 weeks postrelease*								
Average weeks worked	1.0	1.0	1.2	2.1	2.3	—	16.15	.0000
SD	1.9	1.0	1.2	2.1	2.3			
N	(167)	(186)	(188)	(179)	(177)			
C. *Weeks worked 7th to 14th week postrelease*								
Average weeks worked	1.4	1.8	1.9	2.8	3.6	—	16.51	.0000
SD	2.6	2.8	2.9	3.0	3.2			
N	(167)	(186)	(188)	(179)	(177)			
D. *Weeks worked 15th to 25th week postrelease*								
Average weeks worked	2.5	4.0	4.5	5.2	6.5	—	13.47	.0000
SD	4.6	5.0	5.2	5.4	5.5			
N	(157)	(171)	(171)	(164)	(164)			
E. *Weeks worked last 26 weeks postrelease*								
Average weeks worked	6.8	9.5	10.4	8.8	11.1	—	4.23	.0022
SD	9.2	10.4	10.5	10.3	11.2			
N	(152)	(179)	(171)	(174)	(176)			
F. *Earnings and work unemployment insurance wage file data*								
Percentage with some earnings	53.7	60.8	62.4	62.5	65.2	61.2	1.14	.33
Earnings	$1064	$1525	$1433	$1088	$1553	$1531	2.50	.03
SD	2094	2277	2148	1784	2134	2336		
N	(175)	(199)	(197)	(200)	(198)	(958)		

SOURCES: Panel A through E: Weeks worked as reported in postrelease interviews with TARP participants; Panel F: Earnings recorded in unemployment insurance wage files.

on weeks worked was available for Group 6; members of this group, it will be recalled, were not interviewed.

Data on all TARP participants who had valid social security numbers were available on wages earned that were covered by the state unemployment benefit system. These data were available in the form of total covered wages during each of four calendar quarters. Since prisoners were released

---

were essentially alike. In short, it appears that weeks worked, as constructed from recall, is not biased toward underreports in the payment groups out of motivation to receive benefits illegally.

TABLE 5.4

Texas: Employment and Earnings in Postrelease Year
for Experimental and Control Groups

	Experimental groups				Control groups		ANOVA	
Variable	1	2	3	4	5	6	F	p
A. *Total weeks worked during postrelease year*								
Average weeks worked	20.8	27.1	24.6	29.3	28.3	—	6.98	.0000
SD	17.6	16.3	17.8	17.1	18.5			
N	(169)	(191)	(189)	(197)	(189)			
B. *Weeks worked first 6 weeks postrelease*								
Average weeks worked	1.8	1.9	2.0	2.8	2.9	—	11.08	.0000
SD	2.2	2.2	2.2	2.3	2.2			
N	(174)	(199)	(199)	(200)	(199)			
C. *Weeks worked 7th through 14th week postrelease*								
Average weeks worked	2.2	3.0	3.2	4.2	4.2	—	14.36	.0000
SD	3.0	3.0	3.2	2.8	3.0			
N	(174)	(199)	(199)	(200)	(199)			
D. *Weeks worked 15th through 25th week postrelease*								
Average weeks worked	4.5	7.3	6.8	7.4	7.6	—	10.4	.0000
SD	5.3	5.0	5.4	5.4	5.3			
N	(174)	(199)	(196)	(200)	(197)			
E. *Weeks worked last 26 weeks postrelease*								
Average weeks worked	12.4	14.8	12.7	14.9	13.9	—	2.18	.0695
SD	10.6	10.5	10.8	10.5	11.0			
N	(169)	(191)	(189)	(197)	(190)			
F. *Earnings and work unemployment insurance wage file data*								
Percentage with some earnings	67.4	78.6	69.7	73.1	66.1	66.2	2.84	.02
Earnings	$1922	$2215	$2242	$2069	$1960	$2043	.39	.86
SD	2941	2455	2242	2069	2698	3034		
N	(175)	(196)	(198)	(193)	(183)	(913)		

SOURCES: Panels A through E: Weeks worked as reported in postrelease interviews with TARP participants; Panel F: Earnings recorded in unemployment insurance wage files.

continuously throughout the period from January through July 1976, it is not possible to match the unemployment insurance wage files precisely with the postrelease year. Although adjustments were made to obtain better estimates of covered wages earned during the postrelease year, some degree of inaccuracy existed in the files.[4] In addition, certain types of

---

[4] Adjustments consisted of allocating an appropriate proportion of the ending quarter of unemployment insurance wages. Thus a person whose postrelease year ended the second week of May, 1977 was credited with half the wages earned during the second quarter of 1977. This amount added to the wages reported for the first quarter of 1977 and the last three quarters of 1976 was that person's estimated covered wages during the postrelease year.

employment were not covered by the unemployment benefit system, notably state and local government jobs, transient labor paid in cash, and certain types of agricultural employment. It is also possible that some TARP participants had several social security numbers, opened under various aliases, and that others made errors in reporting their social security numbers to the prison records clerks.

The proportion of persons with at least some earnings reported during the postrelease year is shown in the top line of Panel F in Tables 5.3 and 5.4. This proportion represents the percentage who were employed at least once during the postrelease year in a covered employment circumstance. No significant difference appeared in this respect in Georgia, but in Texas it appeared that the control groups (Groups 5 and 6) had slightly lower proportions, indicating that the controls were more likely not to work at all, although the differences were rather slight.

The second row of Panel F in Tables 5.3 and 5.4 contain the average covered earnings recorded for each of the six groups. In Texas, no significant differences in average earnings were revealed. In Georgia, Groups 1 and 4 were sufficiently lower in average covered wages received to produce statistically significant analysis of variance results.[5]

The findings presented in Tables 5.3 and 5.4 suggest that TARP payments had considerable work-disincentive effects, but that this lessened work effort tended to disappear toward the end of the postrelease year, Furthermore, it appears as if the lessened work effort of those in the payment groups did not lead to correspondingly lowered annual earnings, a suggestion that payment-group TARP members found employment that paid somewhat better than did those in the control groups.

As a summary of the gross, overall outcomes of the experiment, the following statements may be made:

- The TARP payments, *as administered*, did not decrease arrests for property-related offenses in either state.
- TARP payments, *as administered*, neither decreased or increased arrests on charges for a variety of other kinds of offenses.
- TARP payment eligibility exerted a clear and strong work-disincentive effect, with participants in the payment groups clearly working fewer weeks in the postrelease year.
- TARP participants in payment groups did not earn consistently less than controls over the postrelease year. No statistically significant dif-

---

[5] Again we see that Group 4, as in the analysis of weeks worked, showed a lower work effort than the controls as well as two of the three payment groups. No explanation for this pattern comes easily to mind.

ferences were found in Texas. In Georgia, Groups 1 and 4 earned less than other groups in the experiment.

In short, the benefits extended under the provisions of the TARP experiment failed to produce their intended effects of lowering arrest rates on property-related charges, and, by extension, of lowering the participation in economically motivated crime that lies behind such arrest rates.

Given the more successful results from the previous Baltimore LIFE experiment, it is also apparent that payments are effective in some contexts, for example, those provided in the LIFE experiment. This consideration leads us to place qualifications on the generality of the TARP findings: Payments *as administered under the TARP plan* are apparently ineffective for the intended purposes of lowering arrests on property-related charges.

It should be noted that the results presented in Tables 5.3 and 5.4 do not provide complete comfort for pessimists. First, although the payments did not reduce property-related arrests, they also did not increase such arrests. A policy that would provide transitional financial aid to released prisoners on equity grounds would certainly be sustained by these findings. In other words, it is not contraindicated to provide money to prisoners to ease the transition to productive civilian life, especially since those burdens fall heavily on the families and spouses of the released prisoners.

Second, we may note that although the number of weeks worked in the postrelease year was decidedly less for TARP payment groups, there was no corresponding consistent drop in earnings over the entire year. This suggests that the payments may have had the effect of allowing persons to obtain better employment, as reflected in the fact that at the end of the year those with payment eligibility earned as much as those in the control groups. TARP payments may have allowed some of the participants the leisure to conduct better job searches, to turn down poor jobs that were available, and in the end to receive higher wage rates than those in the payment groups.

WHY DID TARP APPEAR TO FAIL? AN ARRAY OF POSSIBLE EXPLANATIONS

It must be emphasized at the outset that when we discribe TARP as having failed, we refer specifically to the failure of *payments as administered in the TARP experiments.* In other words, the payments were successful in reducing arrests, but the system of administering payments, including the eligibility rules, used in the two experiments produced unwanted side effects that masked the arrest-reducing effects of the payments.

As administered and implemented in two states, the TARP plan failed to produce the overall desired effects. It is not the first program designed to reduce recidivism that has failed: Indeed, successes are rare among the many that have been tried. It might be easy to dismiss the basic idea that lies behind TARP as simply another notion that has had its day, except for the fact that an earlier version of TARP did show some success. The seeming contradiction between LIFE and TARP encourages some thought about why payments should succeed in the one instance and fail in the other.

There are many reasons why social programs fail.[6] A review of some of these reasons may provide leads to an explanation of failure in this particular case.

To begin with, the TARP experiment may have been a success but through effects that were so feeble they could not be detected statistically. Or the data collected may have had so many measurement defects that the true effects of the treatments were obscured. This set of possible explanations may be quickly dismissed on several grounds. First, there were few signs in the arrest outcomes that the effects were pushing at the threshold of statistical significance. Indeed, there was more evidence (but not statistically significant) that the payments increased arrests for property thefts than the other way around. Second, the fact that results were identical in the two states argues against feeble effects that were too weak to be measured.[7] Third, although there were undoubtedly measurement defects in both TARP experiments, such errors were at a minimum in the analysis of the main effects of the experiment on property-related arrests. We are quite certain that there were no errors in classifying an individual as receiving TARP payment eligibility and that errors in the arrest data were at a minimum.[8] In short we are confident that the experiment as conducted has not falsely rejected as ineffective a truly effective treatment because the research design was not powerful enough to detect that effectiveness.

Turning to another source of failure, a program may fail because it is based on an incorrect understanding of the processes involved in the phenomena in question. In the TARP case, the basic ideas underlying the

---

[6] See Peter H. Rossi, "Some Issues in the Evaluation of Human Services Delivery Programs," *Evaluation Quarterly*, 3, no. 3 (November, 1978).

[7] In addition, we combined the data for both states, effectively doubling the size of the experiment and increasing the power of the statistical test by a factor of 1.4, without essentially changing the results. The combined Georgia and Texas TARP experiments also did not show statistically significant differences among experimental and control groups.

[8] The inclusiveness of the Georgia and Texas criminal justice information systems was tested by checking arrest records at the local jurisdiction level. In Georgia, where we found many errors, we supplemented the criminal justice information arrest files with a hand search through local jurisdiction records. (See Chapter 2 for an account of these measures.)

provision of money during the early parts of the transition to civilian life may be incorrect. TARP assumes that for released felons property crimes are an important source of income, a source that competes quite favorably with legitimate jobs, in the sense of being more available than such jobs and more attractive than many available jobs. Hence, the provision of funds may help released felons to get through a period of postrelease unemployment without resorting to property theft. TARP findings provide little that contradicts this view, since persons in payment groups who received benefits were no more likely to be arrested.

The TARP findings, however, do indicate that it is very easy to compete with the kinds of jobs typically available to released prisoners. The TARP payments were quite modest in size yet were still quite effective in lowering the work effort by magnitudes up to 50%. Jobs typically available to TARP members paid between $100 and $150 per week and were likely to involve unpleasant tasks. Hence, $63 or $70 per week with no work was frequently seen as better than such jobs.

In designing the TARP experiments, apparently little consideration was given to the possibility that payments might have a strong work-disincentive effect. The designers were led to think along these lines because the Baltimore LIFE experiment did not produce a strong or consistent work-disincentive effect. Almost as a cautionary measure, Group 3—which received 13 weeks of payments with a generous 25% tax—was added to provide closer comparability to the LIFE experiment's generous tax rate. In any event, the fact that the TARP designers did not anticipate so great a work-disincentive effect is a clue that the conceptual model underlying TARP may have been at least partially at fault.

Another potential source of trouble in the conceptual model underlying TARP was its failure to specify completely the role of employment in recidivism. TARP looked at employment primarily as a source of income. Men who work do not commit crimes because the main motivation to commit crimes is to obtain financial resources. However, employment competes with crime in other ways as well. For one thing, employment occupies time and thus reduces opportunities to commit crimes. Were the crime-averting effects of employment solely the effect of earnings, then the substitution of payments for earnings (assuming a generous payment level) should bring about the same crime-averting effects produced by employment.

A third source of social-program failure lies in defects of implementation. In this respect, there appears to be an important deficiency in the way in which TARP was administered in both Georgia and Texas. TARP participants were not aware of certain critical aspects of the TARP payments. As shown in Chapter 4, TARP participants only dimly understood the terms under which they were eligible for payments and how payments were reduced if participants had earnings during a given period of eligibility. This deficiency was particularly serious for Group 3 participants, for whom the nominal tax rate of 25% should have provided a clear incentive for working. Indeed, this stands out in stark contrast to the earlier LIFE experiment in which the research team went to great lengths to ensure that participants were aware of their eligibility for partial payments in the event of employment. (For example, each LIFE participant was given a chart that showed clearly how his earnings would affect payment size, and participants were reminded frequently that they did not necessarily lose all their benefits if employed.)

Finally, it is conceivable that overall findings reflect conflicting results among subgroups or conflicting processes that work in opposite directions. There may have been subgroups or participants for whom payments provided sufficient incentive to abstain from property thefts; in other subgroups, the opposite incentives may have obtained. Or, it may be that payments provided contradictory incentives to TARP participants in payment groups.

The main sources of failure in the TARP experiment appear to be in implementation and in the underlying theoretical model. Thus in the next section, we will review the conceptual links between earnings and crime. We will construct a model that will attempt to explain the overall findings of the TARP experiment yet remain consistent with the outcomes of the earlier Baltimore LIFE experiment.

A CONCEPTUAL REINTERPRETATION OF THE TARP EXPERIMENTS

As mentioned earlier, an important assumption underlying the designs of both the LIFE and TARP experiments was that persons commit property thefts largely out of economic need. This is not to deny that other elements may be at work in the case of particular individuals or in the case of particular crimes. It merely asserts that on the average, persons in need are more likely to commit property crimes than persons who are not in need.

Persons newly released from prisons are especially likely to commit property crimes because they are so frequently in financial straits. Ex-offenders have few occupational skills, meager job experience, and the stigma of a criminal record, and they are equipped with very modest levels of gate money and savings upon release. At best they are faced with an indifferent labor market and, in some cases, a hostile one. They have been in close contact with other convicted felons whose experiences with property theft have most likely been shared. They are also returning to an environment that presents many opportunities for property crime. Clearly, newly released prisoners are faced with an array of economic opportunities, legitimate and illegitimate, in which the latter must appear particularly attractive. The balance of economic incentives favors a return to criminal activities. High recidivism rates are the likely outcome, and experience with released prisoners bears that expectation out.

Both the LIFE and the TARP experiments were designed to shift the balance of incentives to favor legitimate as opposed to illegitimate activities. This was to be accomplished by providing income that would lower financial need while released prisoners explored their local labor markets in search of legitimate job opportunities. The major differences between the two experiments lay more in how the financial help was provided and the rules under which eligibility for payment was established. These differences have been discussed in earlier chapters.

It is unlikely that many social scientists would quarrel fundamentally with a working hypothesis that people steal in part from economic necessity. As the Marxist political economist William A. Bonger wrote early in this century,

> If a man has not sufficient food, if he has not (at least in non-tropical countries) clothing to protect him against the cold, if opportunity for rest is lacking, etc., his life is in danger. In our present society there are always a number of persons who are in want of the strict necessities of life, and who are therefore obliged to steal if they do not wish to succumb to poverty. It is evident that the word "poverty" is not to be taken in the most limited sense, so that one who can still buy a morsel of bread, and yet steals, may still be considered a thief from poverty.[9]

Fifty years later, the neoclassical economist Gary S. Becker, working from a very different underlying perspective and with a far less monolithic set of causal factors, reached roughly similar conclusions:

> This approach implies that there is a function relating the number of offenses by any person to his probability of conviction, to his punishment if convicted, and to other variables, such as the income available to him in legal and illegal activities, the frequency of nuisance arrests, and his willingness to commit an illegal act....
>
> For example, a rise in the income available in legal activities or an increase in law-abidingness due, say, to "education" would reduce incentives to enter illegal activities and thus reduce the number of offenses.[10]

---

[9] William A. Bonger, *Criminality and Economic Conditions* (1916; reprinted, New York: Agathon Press, 1967), p. 564.

[10] Gary S. Becker, *An Economic Approach to Human Behavior* (Chicago: University of Chicago Press, 1976), p. 47.

Yet, it is one thing to document support for the general idea that people may steal in response to their economic circumstances and quite another to develop a formal model of the impact of the TARP experiment. To begin, there are a host of problems involving operationalizing of economic need. Should one focus on absolute or relative deprivation, an issue raised by Leon Radzinowicz?[11] Is the relevant causal mechanism unbridled egosim fostered by our economic system, as Bonger suggested, or a mismatch between what society promises and what it delivers, as proposed by Robert K. Merton?[12] In short, it is not clear precisely what problem financial aid is supposed to solve.

Second, if the problem is not well defined, the solution will of necessity be poorly articulated. For example, TARP payments may reduce economic need and consequently reduce the motivation to steal. Hence, fewer property crimes will be committed overall. Alternatively, TARP payments may raise the opportunity costs of apprehension, which means that the impact of TARP payments cannot be understood outside the context of local law-enforcement practices. Since apprehension and conviction means that payment eligibility will be lost, one of the risks taken upon entry into illegitimate activities is that loss of payment eligibility. Hence the provision of TARP payments increases the costs of entering upon illegitimate activity.

Third, the TARP experiment was embedded in a set of complicated relationships that link criminal activities to a number of other factors. In particular, if the TARP payments are viewed in economic terms, the role of employment must also be considered. If income derived from the treatment is supposed to reduce property crime, should not income derived from work have much the same effect? Yet, once the impact of employment is introduced, the ultimate benefit of the TARP treatment become more ambiguous. Economists would predict that the provision of any sort of financial aid would lower labor-force participation. If, as in the case of TARP payments, such financial aid is made contingent on lack of earnings or if such payments are reduced if there are earnings (as in the case of Group 3 participants who were subject to a 25% tax) then the work-disincentive effect of providing financial aid should be very strong. With the cushion of TARP payment eligibility, newly released prisoners would be less inclined to seek work immediately upon release and less likely to take jobs as long as some eligibility for payments remained.

---

[11] Leon Radzinowicz, "Economic Pressures," in L. Radzinowicz and M. Wolfgang, *The Criminal in Society* (New York: Basic Books, 1971).

[12] Robert K. Merton, "Social Structure and Anomie," in R. K. Merton, *Social Theory and Social Structure* (New York: The Free Press, 1957).

The effect of reduced employment on property crime depends on two additional links. First, if the payments are not large enough to compensate completely for the income derivable from property crime, properly corrected for the risks involved, then some incentive for engaging in illegitimate activities would remain. Second, if part of the crime-averting effects of employment operate through nonincome effects of employment—for example, the effects of the time spent working or the effects of differential association with noncriminals—then the provision of income through TARP payments would not completely substitute for employment in the prevention of property crimes. In short, it is possible that the induced unemployment produced by TARP payments could actually increase the number of property crimes committed.

In other words, TARP payments could have had two opposing effects on the number of property crimes committed by those who received payments: *a direct effect reducing property crime by lowering financial need* and *an indirect effect increasing property crime by increasing unemployment.* Were this the case, it would be possible to observe no overall reduction in property crime as a result of the experiment.

The counterbalancing model of the effects of TARP implied above is shown graphically in Figure 5.1. Note that each of the arrows in the diagram postulates an effect. The sign (positive or negative) given to an arrow indicates whether the effect in question raises (+) or lowers (-) the measure at the head of the arrow. Thus the negatively signed arrow connecting "TARP payments" and "property-related arrests" indicates that the payments act to lower arrests on property-related charges. Similarly, the positively signed arrow leading from "property-related arrests" to "jail or prison" represents the quite obvious positive relationship between being arrested and spending time in prison or jail.

The counterbalancing model shown in Panel A of Figure 5.1 postulates that TARP payments will have two effects on property arrests: a direct effect, lowering arrests through the provision of income; and an indirect effect increasing arrests by lowering employment. The model postulates a relationship between employment and property arrests in which increased employment leads to decreased property arrests. The corollary of this is that decreased employment leads to increased arrests.

Some of the arrows in the Panel A diagram derive from the eligibility rules of the TARP experiment. For example, a person is ineligible for TARP payments while he is in jail or prison. The negative arrows connecting "employment" and "TARP payments" are also ones that are imposed by TARP payment eligibility rules, since earnings reduce payments and payments imply unemployment.

The model postulated to account for the LIFE findings is shown in Panel

A. TARP Model—Counterbalancing Effects:

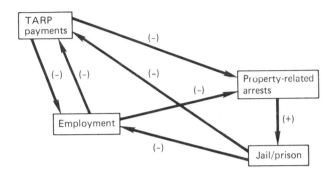

B. LIFE Model:

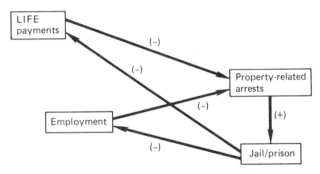

FIGURE 5.1 *Postulated models of TARP and LIFE payment effects on property-related arrests and employment.*

B. Note that the model is identical with that postulated for the TARP experiments except that there are no arrows linking "employment" and "LIFE payments." Since the LIFE experimenters administered that program under quite generous tax rates and made strong efforts to acquaint participants with their rights to partial payments when they were working, the work-disincentive effects of the payments were minimized to the point where they did not appear as statistically significant (as we saw in Chapter 2).

The conceptual scheme constructed as an interpretation of the TARP findings emphasizes criminal activity as an attractive alternative to legitimate employment for the released prisoners who participated in the experiment. It should be emphasized that this model does not pretend to explain crime but only the tendency to engage in criminal activities under certain circumstances. It is especially appropriate as a model for explaining the postrelease behavior of released prisoners faced with the benefits to which they were eligible under the TARP financial aid plan.

Theories that have been constructed to explain criminal behavior in the general population tend to be irrelevant when dealing with a population of ex-offenders. Our subjects were all convicted felons who had served at least a year in prison. For many, this prison term was the latest in a series of brushes with the law, some of which had resulted in previous prison terms. Clearly, these are men (and a few women) who had been in close contact with other convicted criminals in jail and prison. Hence, for example, theories based on differential association can hardly hope to explain postrelease criminal activity, since all subjects had been in close association with other convicted criminals.

Nor can we be helped by other theories of criminal behavior. TARP participants come from much the same backgrounds—from neighborhoods and communities with high crime rates. As we will see in later chapters, they often come from families in which parents and siblings also have criminal records.

TARP participants are also very homogeneous with respect to socioeconomic background. There are few sons and daughters of the middle class among them. The vast majority have had little formal education and have histories of erratic employment in low-status, low-paying jobs. Consequently, if there is something about socioeconomic background and family history that affects the propensity to engage in criminal activities, TARP participants will scarcely manifest such differences since they tend to be homogeneous in those respects.

Nor is this a group for whom deterrence theory can be helpful in understanding criminal activity postrelease. For one thing, these are persons who have not been deterred earlier by the prospect of imprisonment or other punishment. Within each of the states they all face the same criminal justice system with a more or less uniform set of procedures. While there may be some difference from locality to locality within each state (and we will see that there are some differences along these lines in Texas), by and large all face the same prospects of punishment for committing crimes.

Finally, even if early childhood experiences help explain participation in crime, one must keep in mind that we are observing TARP members well after childhood and after at least one demonstrated failure to stay out of serious trouble. If childhood factors make a difference, for this group the differences have already been made. That is, we really have no "successes"; we cannot compare law-abiding citizens with law breakers. We have a sample of adults who have been convicted before and can consider only whether they have additional brushes with the law or change their ways. The relevance of early socialization is therefore at best unclear.

For these reasons, our reinterpretation of TARP findings rests heavily on economic theory. TARP participants are too homogeneous in many relevant respects to consider models that rely on other factors as sources for criminal behavior. But most important of all, the TARP treatment itself is an economic variable. Hence, if it is at all effective it must operate through economic mechanisms.

TESTING THE TARP COUNTERBALANCING MODEL

So far the counterbalancing model shown in Figure 5.1 is a reasonable but not yet demonstrated hypothesis that can seemingly account for both the TARP and LIFE results. However, the model need not remain on the level of an unproven hypothesis since it is possible to use the TARP data to estimate coefficients for each of the links shown in Figure 5.1.

In order to construct such estimates it is necessary to write a set of simultaneous equations that express each of the main variables in terms of each other, as applicable, and in terms of factors not shown in Figure 5.1. These additional elements, derived from our understanding of what affects postrelease behavior, make it possible to estimate coefficients for each of the links shown. The additional factors considered are shown schematically in Figure 5.2. Note that this diagram embodies a considerable amount of information derived from prison records and from other data collected during the follow-up interviews.

The actual solution of the simultaneous equation model implied in Figure 5.2 is presented in greater detail in later chapters. For present purposes it is merely necessary to consider whether the factors incorporated into the model make sense in some a priori way. That is to say that on the basis of what is known about the recidivism of released prisoners, do the arrows as drawn in Figure 5.2 make sense?

The extended model shown in Figure 5.2 can be regarded as composed of three sectors: prerelease exogenous factors, postrelease exogenous factors, and postrelease endogenous factors.

Prerelease exogenous factors, listed in the box on the extreme left of the diagram, consist mainly of ex-prisoner characteristics as determined at the outset of the experiment (and hence exogenous). Such personal characteristics as race, age, sex, previous criminal record, and human capital factors (education, employment experience, acquired job skills, and the like) are all characteristics of the released prisoners that we believe affect both their employment chances and their recidivism. We know from previous research that men are more likely to be recidivists than women, that older

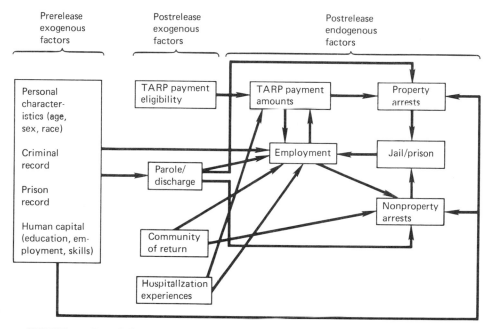

FIGURE 5.2 *Extended model of counterbalancing TARP payment effects.*

ex-offenders are less likely to be returned to prison than younger ones, and so on.

Postrelease exogenous factors are events and conditions that occur after release and that affect employment and arrest but are not themselves affected by employment and arrest experiences. For example, being placed in an experimental group and offered eligibility for benefit payments is clearly an exogenous event determined wholly by the systematic randomization procedures described in Chapter 3. While parole status is determined before release, the experience of parole occurs after release. Similarly, the community to which the ex-prisoner returns is an exogenous situation that might effect both employment opportunities and arrest, depending on the state of local labor markets and the patterns of law enforcement pursued locally. Sickness and hospitalization experiences are also shown here as postrelease exogenous events that affect both employment and TARP payments.

Postrelease endogenous factors are essentially the elements contained in the TARP counterbalancing model. Note that nonproperty arrests are included among these factors. While the economic theory that underlies the TARP model does not make the same predictions about nonproperty arrests as it does about property arrests, it is conceivable that such events may be affected by both employment and TARP payments. For example, the provision of some income support through TARP payments may reduce interpersonal conflict that might arise over finances within the households to which prisoners return. Certainly, by preempting time, employment may reduce nonproperty arrests by lowering the opportunities for getting into trouble. TARP payments certainly raise the opportunity costs of nonproperty crimes.

Coefficients for each of the lines shown in Figure 5.2 have been estimated but are too numerous and complicated to present here (see Chapter 12). Of particular relevance for our purposes in this chapter are those coefficients for the lines connecting postrelease endogenous factors. Figure 5.3 shows these coefficients separately for Texas and Georgia. Note that Figure 5.3 presents only those coefficients that have passed the .05 level of significance threshold, except as indicated.

The pattern and sizes of the coefficients of Figure 5.3 are exactly as the counterbalancing model requires. Furthermore, the results in the two states are very close to each other, adding considerably to our confidence in the results. Of special interest are the coefficients for TARP payments. In Texas every $100 of TARP payments lowered the number of property arrests by .019, meaning that for persons who received the maximum total allowance of $910, there was a reduction of .17 property-related arrests, a hefty 50% proportionate reduction. The corresponding reduction for Georgia TARP members was .011, leading to a sizable 26% proportionate reduction.

Of special interest are the sizable coefficients for employment. In Texas each week employed led to .029 fewer property-related arrests, and in Georgia, .022 fewer. It should be emphasized that this finding concerning the effect of employment on rearrest for both property and nonproperty crimes is quite important. In a way, the TARP studies may be viewed as experimentally inducing unemployment through the work-disincentive effects of payments. Hence the estimated effects of employment on postrelease arrest are better estimates than have been provided in previous research. This finding also has important policy implications, as we will discuss in greater detail later on in this book. An employment strategy that would successfully provide employment for released prisoners is very clearly supported by this finding.

Although the counterbalancing model was ambiguous about payment effects on arrests unrelated to property charges, such effects are also shown, slightly larger in Texas than in Georgia, amounting to .016 and .014 fewer arrests for each $100 of TARP payments.

Were there no counterbalancing effects of TARP payments on employment, the provision of financial aid would have to be declared an une-

A. Texas estimates

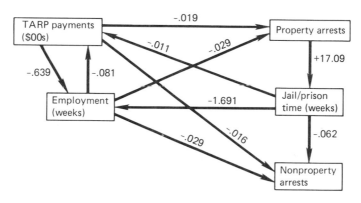

B. Georgia estimates

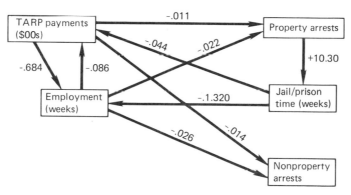

FIGURE 5.3 *Empirical estimates of the counterbalancing TARP effects models for the post-release year. The coefficients for the lines from "employment" and "jail/prison time" to "TARP payments" are averages over the three TARP payment groups. Some coefficients contained in these averages are significant at the .05 level, but it is difficult to compute the overall significance of the averages in a simultaneous equation framework.*

quivocal success. Unfortunately such is not the case: Every $100 of TARP payments reduced employment by .639 weeks in Texas and .684 weeks in Georgia. Since employment has such strong effects on property arrests, the resulting reduction in employment increases property arrests by amounts that in effect wipe out the arrest-reducing effects of the payments. Because of the effects of other variables—which affect both employment and payments, as well as arrests—the actual counterbalancing system is more complicated than we can present here or discuss in any detail. For example,

TARP payments set up processes that reverberated widely throughout the system, affecting arrests and employment, which in turn affected returning to prison or jail, which in turn affected payment eligibility and employment. Processes of these sorts amplify or dampen the main effects shown here.

POLICY IMPLICATIONS OF THE LIFE
AND TARP PROJECTS

The policy implications of the counterbalancing model are quite clear. First, payments did lower recidivism. Second, such payments are likely to have attractive benefit-to-cost ratios, being relatively inexpensive and averting costs that are several magnitudes greater. It is cheaper to provide payments of between $800 and $1200 to 100 released prisoners than to process about five additional persons through the criminal justice system, provide prison places for them for periods of 2 and 3 years, and cover other associated costs of imprisonment as well as welfare payments for dependents.

Third, the net effects of employment on rearrest are very strong, as many criminal justice commentators have suggested. The contribution we are able to make through the TARP analysis is to show that the effect of employment holds up strongly net of the many other processes that affect arrests. This finding strongly supports the potential effectiveness of social policies stressing employment for released prisoners. Some sort of supported work strategy, properly administered, would appear to have great potential for high payoffs. However, it should be noted that given past failures with work strategies, an effective policy is likely to be relatively expensive.

The policy implications of the TARP experiments lend considerable support to an income-maintenance strategy to reduce arrest recidivism among released prisoners. Specifically, the counterbalancing model suggests that the positive effects of such payments can be fully captured, as in the earlier Baltimore LIFE experiment, if it were possible to strip away the work-disincentive effects that surfaced in the Georgia and Texas TARP experiments. There are a variety of potential programs that show promise to accomplish that end. First, it is possible to lower tax rates to provide incentives for job searching and for taking employment when offered. It would also be necessary to insure that participants and administrators are aware of the tax rate. The overall tax rate in LIFE was about 30%, similar to one of the plans in TARP; the crucial difference was that insufficient effort was made in the TARP experiment to make participants aware of the generous tax rate. Whether one could incorporate such a feature into an unemployment insurance system that ordinarily operates with a 100% tax rate, however, may be problematic.

A second possibility is to shift away from the employment insurance model to a severance-pay model, providing money to prisoners upon release, either as a lump sum, or, perhaps more sensibly, in the form of installments to be paid out for a limited period of time. For example, each released prisoner could be provided with eligibility for severance pay in the amount of $800, $200 of which would be paid upon release and the remainder in 10 weekly installments of $60 each.

A third possibility is to build in positive incentives for working, with bonus payments added on to the severance pay provisions just described that would be paid out on positive demonstration of obtaining employment.

There are additional wrinkles one may add to such policies, although we suspect that most would mainly be variations on the three themes laid out above.

Before we plunge into the enactment of any of the programs suggested above, it should be borne in mind that the counterbalancing model was fitted to the TARP data with a considerable amount of custom tailoring and creative stitching (at least so we believe it to be). While we did most of our creative tailoring on the Texas data and then applied the model to Georgia, a procedure which tends to reduce the possibility of Type I and Type II errors, we cannot be thoroughly confident that the model is robust enough to survive yet another replication. In addition, despite the positve precedent of the earlier Baltimore LIFE experiment, we cannot be entirely sure that it is possible to detach work disincentives from payments. Hence, although we run the risk of sounding like yet another set of self-serving researchers, we would strongly urge another round of policy-oriented researches, this time testing a larger family of payment plans, varying more widely the amounts of payments and testing the efficacy of several alternative methods of detaching work disincentives from payments. The end result of such an additional round of research would be to capture fully and more definitively the desirable arrest-averting effects of transitional income-maintenance payments to ex-prisoners.

II

EX-PRISONERS AND THEIR
POSTPRISON EXPERIENCES

6

The World of Ex-Prisoners

In the next four chapters, many readers will inhabit a world that is vastly different from the world of their own experience. Most men (and women) who have served terms in our state prisons are quite unlike the average American citizen in a variety of ways. As a result, their experiences on return to civilian life are not comparable to the experiences, for example, of people who have shifted from one community to another or who have returned to civilian status after military duty.

AN OVERVIEW OF PART II

To begin with, released prisoners differ from other Americans in that they have served at least one term in our state prisons after having been convicted of, usually, a felony. But, perhaps more important, they are not representative of all Americans nor of their own age and sex. To understand what happens to these people when they leave prison, we must understand from what segments of our society they have come and what special acts brought them to prison. Thus Chapter 7 will examine the backgrounds of TARP participants and the crimes of which they were convicted.

The rest of Part II provides an account of how the prisoners fared after release. Chapter 8 looks at the sorts of living arrangements they were attracted to and the persons with whom they shared their lives. Many readers will be surprised to know how far behind their age peers these young men and women were in family formation and independence. Chapter 8 also considers some subjective aspects of adjustment to civilian life in the form of self-ratings of how well the ex-prisoners felt they were getting along socially, emotionally, and economically.

In Chapter 9 we consider the postrelease employment and earnings experiences of TARP members. Again, readers may be surprised to learn that a large number of TARP participants found no employment throughout the year. Moreover, those that did work did so erratically, typically, in low-status and low-paying jobs. On the average, released prisoners' earnings were considerably below the poverty level and thus much below average earnings for persons of their age and marital status. If poverty breeds crime, it is abundantly clear that ex-prisoners occupied fertile territory.

Finally, in Chapter 10 we consider the postrelease experiences of TARP members with the criminal justice systems of their states. Data on arrests experienced, charges brought, and disposition of cases are given. Many TARP participants quickly had contact with the law and were on their way back to prison before the end of the year. The majority, however, managed to stay clear of the police and the courts, at least for the first year.

There are several reasons for spending so much time on the descriptive tasks of Part II. First, the conditions of ex-prisoners set the stage for an understanding of why the TARP payments worked the way they did. After all, $63 and $70 is scarcely enough to get by on. Yet the fact that the payments did make significant differences in their lives indicates the extent to which these lives were impoverished. Second, the data contained in Part II help us to understand how to construct the equations we need to compute the models described in overall terms in Chapter 5. We will draw heavily upon that knowledge in Part III of this volume. Finally, the information is of interest in and of itself. The TARP data files provide more and better information on the postprison experiences of ex-offenders than has been available up to this time.

A TECHNICAL NOTE

A considerable portion of the data presented in Part II is derived from interviews obtained from TARP members before release and at intervals throughout the postrelease year. Although prison records are available on all TARP members, along with unemployment insurance wage files, parole records, and arrest records, only Groups 1 through 5 were interviewed. Hence, in some cases all 4005 TARP participants are represented. Often, however, only Groups 1 through 5, composed of roughly 2000 persons, will be represented. It should be borne in mind, however, that persons in Groups 1 through 5 are not a biased subset of all TARP members.

In addition, the interviewers' success in reaching persons for postrelease interviews varied.[1] Hence, case bases tend to decline as data from interviews conducted later in the postrelease year are considered.

Each of the tables in Part II contains a source note indicating from which data source the information was obtained. The tables also present case bases for all the data, from which an appreciation of missing data may be obtained.

---

[1] Even when a TARP member could not be reached, it was often possible to obtain important status information on that person. Short questionnaires were mailed to persons who left the state. Persons who had returned to prison and who could not be interviewed were considered to have neither employment nor earnings during the period of imprisonment.

7

Participants in the Transitional
Aid Research Project

INTRODUCTION

To persons familiar with the criminal justice literature, the characteristics of prisoners are well known.[1] The TARP participants were not very different from other released prisoners; they came from the same socio-economic and age groups as prisoners in other states. Readers who are familiar with the many existing descriptions of convicted felons may want to skim rapidly through this chapter, noting only the ways in which the TARP participants differed from their counterparts in other states. A more general reader likely will find the descriptive statistical portraits presented in this chapter of considerable interest, constituting an introduction to a world very different from the ordinary citizen's experience.

Throughout Part II, *all readers should bear in mind that TARP participants, like other convicted felons, were overwhelmingly drawn from the bottommost socioeconomic levels. One's knowlege of labor-force behavior, family formation, household composition, occupational performance, and so on—whether it derives from personal experience or from literature that focuses on central tendencies in our society—does not apply, or not without considerable qualification, to TARP participants.*

As a preview of the contents of this chapter, the following outline presents the salient characteristics of TARP participants:

1. Most (94%) were males.
2. Many grew up in broken homes or with foster parents.
3. Less than half were serving time for their first offenses.
4. Most had been arrested several times before the arrest that led to their current imprisonment.

---

[1] See, among others, U.S. Dept. of Justice, *Handbook of Criminal Statistics, 1977* (Washington, D.C.: Government Printing Office, 1977); and Charles Silberman, *Criminal Violence, Criminal Justice* (New York: Random House, 1978).

5. The average TARP participant was in his late twenties and had served much of his time since late adolescence in prison.
6. Few had steady work experience: Almost half were unemployed at the time they were arrested for the crime that sent them to prison.
7. A minority were currently married. Most were still living in their parental homes when arrested.
8. According to Texas and Georgia population characteristics, minority groups were overrepresented among TARP members.
9. Typically, TARP members had not completed high school but had dropped out after completing the ninth grade.
10. TARP members were typically imprisoned after conviction on a property-related charge, of which burglary constituted the most frequent category.
11. About half of the study members had been released on parole and hence would be under parole supervision for at least half of the year following release.
12. TARP participants left prison with little more than the gate money gratuities provided by the state prison systems: $25 and $200 in Georgia and Texas, respectively.

Serving time in a state prison or jail is clearly an experience reserved mainly for young men of low socioeconomic backgrounds and of minority race and ethnicity.

AGE AND SEX

The most salient characteristics of the TARP participants are that they were overwhelmingly young and male, as shown in Tables 7.1 and 7.2. The average age of Georgia participants at time of release was 27.9 and of Texas participants, 29.6. These ages were also skewed toward the lower side: Half the Georgia participants were 24.8 or younger; the corresponding figure for Texas is 26.7. The proportion of males was 94.1% for Georgia and 93.1% for Texas.

The age differences between the two states reflected mainly the effect of the commutations given to certain prisoners by the governor of Georgia just before the experiment began.[2] As a consequence, the Georgia TARP participants contained younger persons who were more likely to have been given short-term sentences.[3]

---

[2] See Chapter 4 for an account of this and other Georgia–Texas differences.
[3] See Table 7.12, which shows that the average term served by Georgia participants was lower than that served by Texas counterparts. It should also be noted that sentences given did not vary as much as did the terms served.

TABLE 7.1

*Sex Composition of TARP Members Compared to State Prison
and State and General United States Populations*

	Percentage of males in	
	Georgia	Texas
TARP members	94.1	93.1
100%	(2007)	(1975)
State prison population (1975)	96.2	96.3
General state population (1970)	48.6	48.9
General United States population (1970)	48.7	

SOURCES: For TARP members: prison records; for state prison population: U.S. Department of Justice, Law Enforcement Assistance Administration, *Sourcebook of Criminal Justice Statistics: 1977* (Washington, D.C.: Government Printing Office), p. 629, Table 6.39; for state and United States populations: U.S. Bureau of the Census, *Census of Population: 1970*, Vol. I, *Characteristics of the Population* (Washington, D.C.: Government Printing Office) Part 12, p. 57, Table 19; Part 45, p. 105, Table 19; and Part 1, p. 265, Table 265.

TABLE 7.2

*Age Composition of TARP Participants Compared to
State and Federal Prison Populations and to
State and United States General Populations*

	Average age		Median age	
	Georgia	Texas	Georgia	Texas
TARP members[a]	27.9	29.6	24.8	26.7
State prison population (1973)	30.5	31.9	24.9	26.1
Federal prison population (1973)	30.9		25.3	
State general population				
Ages 18–74 (1970)	41.3	41.8	36.6	37.5
United States general population				
Ages 18–74 (1970)	42.7		38.9	

SOURCES: For TARP members: prison records; For prison populations: U.S. Department of Justice, Law Enforcement Assistance Administration, *Census of Prisoners in State Correctional Facilities: 1973* (Washington, D.C.: U.S. Government Printing Office, 1977), pp. 12–13; for general population: U.S. Bureau of the Census, *Census of Population: 1970*, Vol. I, *Characteristics of the Population* (Washington, D.C.: Government Printing Office) Part 12, p. 58, Table 20; Part 45, p. 106, Table 52; Part 1, p. 269, Table 52.

[a] Ns are shown in Table 7.1.

Table 7.1 presents a dramatic picture of the great contrast in sex composition between prison populations and the general population. Prisoners were more than nine to one males, while the general population sex ratio for either state or for the country as a whole is less than one to one. The two TARP samples had slightly more females than either their parent prison populations or the general U.S. prisoner population: This slight disparity reflected the fact that women were in prison usually for shorter sentences and hence were likely to be more plentiful in any year's run of releases.[4]

Table 7.2 shows that TARP participants were slightly younger than the prison populations from which they were drawn and younger than state prisoners generally. This difference in age also would be characteristic of released prisoners in any year, since prisoners with shorter sentences would tend to be a larger proportion of any year's releases and also somewhat younger than the larger prison population from which they were drawn. TARP participants, like prisoners in general, were considerably younger than the adult populations of their states and of the United States. Crime (or being convicted of a crime) is clearly a young man's business.

RACE AND ETHNIC COMPOSITIONS

The race and ethnic composition of the TARP groups, shown in Table 7.3, will come as no great surprise to many readers. Compared to the general population of Georgia, prisoners and TARP participants were much more likely to be black. Almost three out of five Georgia TARP participants were black, compared to slightly more than one out of four in the general Georgia population. Proportionately, there were somewhat more whites in the TARP population than in Georgia's state prisons in general, possibly indicating that whites were imprisoned for shorter periods of time.

The ethnic composition of the Texas TARP group reflected the fact that Texas has a large Hispanic component, made up primarily of Chicanos, and one that is concentrated in the western part of the state. Sixteen percent of TARP participants were Hispanics, 48% black, and 36% white, mirroring quite closely the general Texas prison population but strikingly different from the general Texas population.

There may have been many reasons for the overrepresentation of blacks and Hispanics relative to whites in the TARP groups. The main reason, however, as we will show, lay in the socioeconomic position occupied by these groups within their states. As groups, blacks and Hispanics occupied the lowest rungs of the socioeconomic ladders of Texas and Georgia, and their representation in the TARP groups reflected that fact primarily.

---

[4] A special analysis of women in the TARP experiments, undertaken by Nancy Jurik, is summarized in Appendix C.

TABLE 7.3
Race and Ethnic Origins of TARP Participants

	White	Black	Hispanic	Other	N
A. *Georgia*					
TARP participants	42%	58%	—	a	(2,007)
Georgia prison population	39%	61%	—	a	(11,023)
Georgia population (1970)	74%	26%	—	a	
B. *Texas*					
TARP participants	36%	48%	16%	0	(1,975)
Texas prison population (1975)	38%	45%	17%	a	(18,935)
Texas population (1970)	72%	12%	15%	a	
C. *United States*					
Federal prison population (1973)	48%	48%	—	4%	(172,627)

SOURCE: For TARP participants: prison records; for Georgia prison population: Georgia Departments of Corrections and Offender Rehabilitation, *Annual Report: 1975;* for Texas prison population: Texas Department of Correction: *Annual Statistical Report: 1975,* p. 102 and p. 116; for general population: U.S. Bureau of Census, *Census of Population: 1970,* Vol. I, *Characteristics of the Population* (Washington, D.C.: Government Printing Office), Part 12, p. 12, Table 19; Part 45, p. 65, Table 19; and Part 1, p. 262, Table 48; for federal prison population: U.S. Department of Justice, Law Enforcement Assistant Administration, *Census of Prisoners in State Correctional Facilities: 1973* (Washington, D.C.: U S Government Printing Office, 1977), pp. 16 217.

a Less than 1%.

FAMILY BACKGROUNDS OF TARP PARTICIPANTS

Corresponding to their low social origins, TARP participants came disproportionately from families that had experienced some degree of disruption. Table 7.4 shows that many were reared in broken homes. Persons responsible for participants' rearing at the ages of 5 and 15 are shown in Panel A. At the earliest period, two-thirds of Texas members were being brought up in intact households, but by early adolescence (age 15), less than half were living in such arrangements. At the latter age, one out of four was being brought up by his mother alone, 5% were in foster homes or institutions, and 12% were being reared by other relatives. It is striking to note that at that the fairly young age of 15, 5% were already on their own.

Georgia participants, while coming from slightly more stable families than Texas members, also experienced considerable disruption during their childhood. At the earliest period, three-quarters of Georgia members were being reared in intact households; by early adolescence (age 15), this proportion had declined to 59%. At that age, one out of five was living in a

TABLE 7.4
Family Backgrounds of TARP Participants

	At age 5		At age 15	
	Georgia	Texas	Georgia	Texas
A. *Person(s) who reared TARP participants*				
Mother and father (including stepparents)	76%	68%	59%	47%
Mother alone	14%	17%	22%	27%
Father alone	1%	1%	4%	3%
Foster home or institution	1%	1%	2%	5%
Other (e.g., other relatives, nonrelatives)	8%	12%	13%	12%
On one's own	—	—	—	5
100%	(765)	(761)	(800)	(800)

	Georgia	Texas
B. *Welfare status during childhood*		
Ever on welfare	26%	12%
N	(965)	(771)
Average number of months on welfare		
(for those ever on welfare)	12	—
N	(251)	
Proportion on welfare 12 months or more		
(among those ever on welfare)	—	91%
100%		(93)
C. *Family size*		
Average number of siblings	4.6	—
D. *Family members' prison experiences*		
Proportion with some family member		
having prison experience	32%	—
100%	(975)	
Average number of family members		
mentioned	1.19	—
Persons mentioned as having been		
in prison[a]		—
Father	17%	
Mother	1%	
Brother	84%	
Sister	4%	
Wife	1%	
Child	2%	
Other relative in prison	9%	

SOURCE: Texas and Georgia follow-up interviews.

[a] Percentages based on number of mentions. Hence 17% of relatives mentioned as having been in prison by TARP members were members' fathers.

female-headed household, and 17% were living with their fathers or other relatives. It is clear that as in Texas, a large proportion of Georgia participants were living in disrupted families at some time during their childhood.

We know very little more about the families in which participants were reared. Georgia participants grew up in large families—the average number of brothers and sisters was 4.6, indicating that typically the participant grew up in a household of about six to seven people. Of course, this estimate does not take into account other relatives living in the household or the fact that single-parent households were quite common.

The socioeconomic levels of participants' families are only poorly indexed by the proportion who were ever on welfare; 26% in Georgia and 19% in Texas. Of course, it is difficult to judge whether this degree of prevalence is at all unusual for other households with the same characteristics, that is, mother-headed families. (Our impression is that these rates are high, but we may be mistaken.) Those TARP participants' families who were on welfare were supported for relatively long periods: It is estimated that on the average, Georgia participants were on welfare for 12 months; in Texas 91% of participants were on welfare for a year or more.

Panel D of Table 7.4 summarizes Georgia participants' answers to the question of whether any other members of their families had served prison terms. Almost one out of three cited one or more family members who had been in prison (the average number of mentions being 1.19). Among persons mentioned, brothers were cited most frequently (84%) with fathers coming in second (17%). Mothers and sisters were mentioned by 1% and 4%, respectively, and 2% mentioned having children who had served time in prison. Finally, "other relatives" were claimed as sometime prisoners by 9% of the Georgia participants.

These fragmentary data on TARP participants' families of origin clearly indicate deprivation.[5] Many participants were brought up in disrupted households and in large families in which quite frequently other household members had been convicted of criminal offenses. These were also families who garnered some of their support from welfare payments.

---

[5] Further corroboration for this assessment of the low socioeconomic status and poverty of the homes from which TARP participants came can be found in the "Significant Woman" study referred to in Chapter 3 and summarized in Appendix B. For example, the median educational attainment of mothers of the TARP participants is about eighth-grade level, and less than one-third had completed high school. Mothers' earnings, when employed, were typically less than $100 per week. Mothers were often the main support of these households, as indicated by the fact that total household income was less than $150 per week in almost two-thirds of the cases studied.

EDUCATIONAL ATTAINMENT AND IQ

Educational attainment is a critical individual characteristic in our society. First, formal educational attainment above a certain level is often a
qualification for above-the-minimum jobs. All other things being equal,
employers prefer to hire high school graduates for such jobs rather than
those who have dropped out. Second, educational experiences are usually
the means by which one acquires the critical verbal, reading, and
calculating skills necessary to be in touch with the world and to function
within more skilled job contexts. Finally, completing school may often
mean that an individual is able to function within a relatively structured
environment, complete assignments, give concentrated attention to tasks,
and live within certain regulations.

The educational deficiencies of the two TARP groups were quite striking,
as Table 7.5 shows. Georgia TARP members typically had gotten half-way
through the ninth grade, and their Texas counterparts had left school a few
months earlier than that. Even more striking as an evidence of educational
deficiency was the participants' tested grade-level equivalance:[6] Georgia
TARP participants tested as functioning at almost the sixth-grade level.
Texas participants did a bit better, testing at about half-way through sixth
grade. In short, not only did TARP members fail to progress very far
through the educational systems of their states but their tested level of
educational achievement fell considerably below their formal accomplish-
ments.

The low educational attainment of TARP participants does not appear to
have been due to correspondingly low IQs, as the average and median
scores shown in Table 7.5 seem to indicate. Although IQ tests have been
disputed as measures of "pure" intellectual capacity, most critics would
view IQ test performance as a good measure of the ability to absorb the
content of contemporary formal schooling successfully. It is in this connection that the average and median IQ scores of the TARP groups do not appear to have been particularly low; the averages were 93 and 95 in Georgia
and Texas, respectively.[7] The very poor educational levels of the young

[6] Grade-level equivalence was tested by standard educational achievement tests administered in each prison system at the time of admission to prison. Results are shown in terms
of grade levels achieved on the average by persons who have received those scores.

[7] By convention, IQ tests are normed with the mean score set to equal 100 and with standard deviations of 10. Thus, two-thirds of a normal population would achieve scores between
90 and 110. Assuming that the tests used in the Georgia and Texas prison systems are fair
measures for adult populations, the average scores for TARP participants do not differ from
the average for adults by very much.

TABLE 7.5
Educational Attainment and IQ Levels of TARP Participants

	Georgia		Texas	
	Average	Median	Average	Median
Years of formal education	9.5	9.7	9.1	9.2
N		(1725)		(1610)
Tested years of educational equivalency[a]	5.8	5.6	6.7	6.9
N		(1277)		(1929)
Tested IQ scores[a]	93.2	97.0	94.9	97.3
N		(1277)		(1749)

SOURCE: Prison records.

[a] Tested when incarcerated. Short-term prisoners in Georgia are not likely to be tested; thus the N for these measures falls quite short of total TARP participants. It is also possible that some prisoners whose literacy skills were very poor could not be tested.

TARP participants thus appear not to have been due to any marked deficiency in the ability to absorb the contents of educational experiences.

Without additional specific information we can only speculate at this point on why participants' educational attainments fell behind their tested abilities. On the one hand, school involves more than just intellectual tasks. To finish high school one must attend regularly, do assignments, submit to the discipline of the classroom, and so on. On the other hand, schools are not passive institutions; they select, channel, and reject students. Some of the TARP participants may not have been able to submit to the regimen of the school and others may have been forced out by schools that rejected them.

Educational attainment is often regarded, particularly by economists, as a kind of human capital. Investing time and effort to attain a diploma means accumulating skills and aptitudes that are regarded by employers as useful in the occupational world. Hence, someone who has accumulated more human capital through educational attainment can be expected to command better jobs at higher pay rates. The amount of human capital held by TARP participants at the point of release was impressively low. The difficulties of TARP members in the labor market were at least partially attributable to these deficiencies in educational attainment, especially when seen in stark contrast to the average levels of attainment achieved by persons of comparable age in their localities.

PREIMPRISONMENT WORK EXPERIENCES

The low socioeconomic backgrounds of TARP members, along with their poor records of educational attainment, presage a set of correspondingly poor employment records, as the data displayed in Table 7.6 indicate. Prior to imprisonment, participants' employment appears to have been intermittent labor at jobs requiring low levels of skill and paying relatively low wages.

Detailed direct information is not available on the amount of unemployment experienced by TARP members from the time they first entered the labor market. Table 7.6 contains the only direct data available. Almost all members had been employed at one time or another; only 1% had never held any job at all. However, at the time they were arrested for the offenses for which they were imprisoned, almost half (48% and 47% in Georgia and Texas, respectively) were unemployed.[8] Although unemployment rates for young men are known to be high, ranging from 25 to 35% for young black males under 21, these proportions are considerably higher and especially so when we take into account that TARP members were usually older than 21.

For those who were employed, the average skill levels of jobs held were low. Although the information available in the TARP files does not permit very fine occupational distinction, it is quite clear that most TARP members worked at jobs that were either unskilled or required semiskilled qualifications, the proportions being 93% in those categories in Georgia and 77% in Texas.[9]

Average wage levels for those who were employed bear further witness to the relatively poor jobs held by TARP members. Average weekly wages were $136 in Georgia and $148 in Texas. The distributions were weighted to the low side, however, as the median weekly wages of $119 and $125 indicate.[10] The typical annual earnings of TARP members, assuming employment continually over a 52-week period, ranged between $6000 and $8000 (using the lowest median and the highest average shown in Table 7.6).

Typically, TARP members were employed in low-skilled construction jobs. Indeed, the most frequently cited specific job was that of plasterboard installer.

---

[8] Of course, we cannot tell whether these bouts of unemployment were really withdrawals from the labor force or whether they represent an inability to find work.

[9] Occupational title coding in Texas was considerably more precise than in the Georgia TARP data files; hence the Texas proportions are probably more accurate concerning skill levels.

[10] Unfortunately, the interviewing instruments used in both Georgia and Texas did not specify whether wages were to be reported in net terms (after taxes) or gross (before taxes). In any event, since these wages were very much on the low side, taxes and other employer withholdings are likely to be proportionately small.

TABLE 7.6

Preimprisonment Work Experiences of TARP Participants

	Georgia	Texas
A. *Longest period of employment on any preimprisonment job*		
Number of months of job held for longest period of time		
Average	33.4	28.6
Median	24.0	17.6
Proportion who never held any job	1%	1%
N	(971)	(971)
B. *Employment at time of arrest*		
Proportion unemployed at time of arrest	48%	47%
N	(971)	(971)
Type of employment at time of arrest[a]		
Unskilled labor	45%	15%
Semiskilled labor	48%	62%
Skilled labor or skilled white collar	6%	17%
Professional, technical, or managerial	2%	6%
100%	(507)	(520)
Reported wages earned per week on job held at time of arrest[b]		
Average	$136	$148
Median	$119	$125
Reported weeks worked on job held at time of arrest		
Average	$88	$64
Median	$41	$22

Source: Prerelease interviews with Groups 1 through 5.

[a] Employment classification is based on recombinations of codes used by Texas and Georgia TARP staffs and is not comparable, except in a very approximate way, to usual census occupational classifications.

[b] Data obtained in prerelease interviews under conditions that make it impossible to determine whether wages reported were gross (before taxes and other deductions) or net (after taxes and deductions).

Assuming full-time employment over the year, TARP participants appear to have had earnings that were about 15 to 25% lower than average earnings for men in the 25–29 age groups in their respective states.[11] However, there is every indication that the assumption of full-time employment over the year is hardly warranted. Half were unemployed at the time they were arrested, an indicator that levels of unemployment were most

[11] Median annual earnings (1969) for men aged 25 to 29 in Texas and Georgia were, respectively, $6920 and $6639, as reported in the 1970 Census. Corrected for inflationary trends up to 1974, median earnings were $8789 and $8432. (Bureau of the Census, *Census of Population: 1970*, Washington, D.C., GPO, Vol. 1, *Characteristics of the Population*.) Comparisons of this sort are difficult to make because of the considerable mix of ages, length of imprisonment, and so on, within each TARP group.

likely high at any time. In short, while their average wage rates appear to be low, their earnings were most likely even lower because of intermittent employment and corresponding stretches of unemployment throughout the year.

FAMILY ARRANGEMENTS OF TARP PARTICIPANTS AT ARREST AND ON RELEASE

By the time males in the adult population of the United States have reached the ages of typical TARP participants, most have married and set up their own families and households. In 1970, among American males between the ages of 25 and 29, 71% were currently married, another 25% were still single, and another 4% had been divorced, had separated from their wives, or had become widowers. Not so for TARP participants, however. At the time of arrest, only about one in three was married (or living in a common-law arrangement), slightly more than half of the Georgia members were still single (46% in Texas), and the remainder had been married and were currently divorced or separated (see Table 7.7).

TABLE 7.7

Family Status of TARP Participants at Time of Arrest Including Some Comparisons with the General Population

	Georgia	Texas	United States males (Ages 25-29)
A. *Marital status*			
Single (never married)	51%	46%	25%
Married (including common-law relationships)	34%	36%	71%
Formerly married and widowed	15%	19%	4%
100%	(1773)	(1903)	
B. *Number of children*			
Average number of children	1.11	1.18	
N	(976)	(975)	
C. *Living arrangements*			
Mother and father	14%	—	
Mother only	23%	—	
Father only	3%	—	
Other relatives	10%	—	
Wife	23%	—	
Friend(s)	10%	—	
Alone	18%	—	
100%	(962)	—	

SOURCE: Prison records.

Accordingly, a very large proportion were still living in parental house-holds. Forty percent of the Georgia TARP members were living with one or both parents at the time of their arrest; another 10% were living with other relatives. Among the half who had left their families of origin, 23% were living with wives, 10% with friends, and 18% alone. Note that the propor-tion living with wives was only about two-thirds of the proportion who claimed to be married at the time of arrest.

TARP members were decidedly out of step with the typical progression along the average family life cycle. Of course, their imprisonment experi-ences—both the current imprisonment and previous prison sentences—had helped to retard their progression toward the typical marital status of age peers in the general population. After all, if one spends a large proportion of one's adult years in prison, the opportunities for marriage are limited. Also, however, the marriages entered into by TARP members appeared to be fragile and easily broken. The proportion who had separated from or divorced their wives is more than three times that for the general male population.

By the time of their release from prison, as Table 7.8 shows, TARP members had fallen still further behind, as wives and common-law rela-tionships dropped away. The proportion separated or divorced had risen from 15% to 24% in Georgia and from 19% to 29% in Texas. There was also a slight rise in the proportion of TARP participants who claimed to be single, possibly representing common-law relationships that had withered away.

In short, TARP members were typically far behind their age counterparts in life-cycle stage. large proportions were single, many had failed mar-riages, and a plurality were still living with their parental families at the

TABLE 7.8

*Marital Status of TARP Participants at Time of Release
Compared with the General Population*

	Percentage of participants		Percentage of United States males (Ages 25–29)
	Georgia	Texas	
Single, never married	52	50	25
Married (including common-law relationships)	24	21	71
Formerly married and widowed	24	29	4
100%	(976)	(975)	

NOTE: Data were derived from prerelease interviews. Note that the proportion who claimed never to have been married at time of release is slightly larger than those who were classified in that group according to their prison records (see Table 7.7). We suspect that some who had been divorced or whose common-law liaisons had been broken while in prison later classified themselves as single.

time they were arrested. Prison experience, perhaps mainly the sheer amount of time spent in such institutions, was an important factor in their failure to keep pace with their civilian counterparts. There may also have been an element of social ineffectiveness involved: For whatever reasons, the TARP participants appear to have had some difficulty establishing and maintaining steady arrangements with members of the opposite sex.

TARP members' plans at the time of release, as shown in Table 7.9, were to return to arrangements much the same as those they had left. In both states, few were going to set up separate households, either by themselves or with spouses—25% in Texas and 19% in Georgia. The extent to which marital ties had been further weakened by imprisonment can be seen in the contrast between the proportion who claimed to be married at time of release and the proportions who intended to live with their spouses. In Georgia, 24% claimed to be married but only 18% intended to live with their spouses; the corresponding proportions for Texas were 29% and 14%.

The largest group in each state's TARP contingent intended to return to their parental households. In Georgia 54% intended to go back to live with their mothers and/or fathers. In Texas, the proportion was somewhat lower, 41%, perhaps expressing the slightly greater age of Texas TARP participants.

The setback in family life-cycle progression of the young men in the

TABLE 7.9
Planned Living Arrangements at Time of Release

| | Percentage of TARP participants | |
	Georgia	Texas
Parental families		
Mother and father	27	16
Mother alone or father alone	27	35
Total with parental families	54	51
Spouse or common-law wife/husband	18	14
Siblings	7	11
Other relatives	9	[a]
Friends	3	4
Alone	7	5
Miscellaneous	2	16[a]
100%	(974)	(975)

SOURCE: Prerelease interviews of Groups 1 through 5.

[a] Texas prerelease interviews do not permit distinguishing "other relatives" as a separate category and, hence, such living arrangements are included in the category "miscellaneous." Also included in the latter category are intended residence in halfway houses.

TARP experiment apparently continued, at least at the point of return to civilian life. We will see in later chapters that some changes occurred in the first year beyond release.

The postprison living arrangements of the TARP members were the focus of the "Significant Woman" study to which we have referred and which involved interviews with the women in the lives of a small subsample of TARP members. Depending on their postprison living arrangement plans, wives or mothers were interviewed about 3 months after the prisoners' release to obtain data on how TARP members were getting along with the women they going back to. (See also Appendix B.)

PREVIOUS CRIMINAL RECORDS OF TARP PARTICIPANTS

TARP members represented the full range of persons who were released from Georgia and Texas prisons over a 6-month period. For some, this confinement had been their only prison experience. For others, this particular confinement was only the latest in a long series of prison terms. Indeed, one of the Texas TARP members claimed more than 100 previous confinements.

For the typical TARP member, then, the present confinement did not result from a first brush with the law (see Table 7.10). Georgia TARP members claimed an average of about 7 previous arrests, and the corresponding number for Texas participants was considerably higher—15.4 previous arrests. Because these averages were affected strongly by a few participants with very high previous arrest records, the median numbers of arrests, 4.1 and 8.2 for Georgia and Texas, respectively, were perhaps more characteristic of TARP members. Nevertheless these medians indicate that

TABLE 7.10
Previous Criminal Justice Records of TARP Participants

	Georgia		Texas	
	Average	Median	Average	Median
Number of previous arrests[a]	7.4	4.1	15.4	8.2
N	(934)		(975)	
Number of previous convictions[a]	2.9	1.9	6.1	3.0
N	(976)		(975)	

SOURCE: Prison records.

[a] "Previous" means before current arrest or conviction for which participant was serving time at release.

the typical TARP member had been in trouble with the law repeatedly in his adult years.

These brushes with the law had resulted in a number of previous convictions, averaging 6.1 in Texas and 2.9 in Georgia, as shown in Table 7.10. The typical TARP participant has failed to make it outside the prison world on several occasions.

These records suggest that TARP members had long histories of contacts with the criminal justice systems of their states. And, indeed, such was the case, as the data shown in Table 7.11 indicate. Georgia TARP participants experienced their first arrest at the average age of 19 and Texas members at the average age of 16.7. The median ages at first arrest are somewhat lower than these averages, indicating that half the Georgia members had at least one arrest by the time they were halfway through their seventeenth year, whereas Texas members reached that point at age 16.

Typical first convictions followed closely upon first arrests for Georgia members (comparable statistics for Texas TARP members are not available), occurring about 90 days after such arrests. However, since not all convictions resulted in imprisonment, age at first conviction did not represent the start of prison experience for all those who were arrested.

Table 7.11 also contains average ages at which participants' first conviction started and current conviction ended. These are presented here to pro-

TABLE 7.11
Ages of TARP Participants at First Arrest, First Conviction,
and at Start of Current Incarceration

	Georgia		Texas	
	Average	Median	Average	Median
Age at first arrest	19.1	17.5	16.7	16.0
N	(972)[a]		(975)[a]	
Age at first conviction	19.3	17.7	[b]	[b]
N	(969)		—	
Age at beginning of current incarceration	26.3	23.2	26.8	24.0
N	(1930)		(1974)	
Age at release from prison	27.5	24.4	29.6	26.7
N	(1930)		(1974)	

SOURCES: Prison records and prerelease interviews.

[a] Data available only from TARP participants in Groups 1 through 5.

[b] Data not available in Texas prison records or in Texas TARP interviews.

TABLE 7.12
Confinement Records of TARP Participants

	Georgia		Texas	
	Average	Median	Average	Median
Total years of current imprisonment	1.2	.8	2.8	1.9
N		(2007)		(1974)
Total years ever confined	2.8	2.0	5.2	3.5
N		(976)		(975)
Proportion of adult years (17 to current age) spent in confinement	.36	.29	.47	.40
N		(976)		(975)

SOURCES: Prison records and prerelease interviews.

vide an estimate of the number of years over which the typical criminal justice records extended. In Georgia, about 7 years elapsed between the TARP member's first arrest and the beginning of his current imprisonment; the corresponding number for Texas was 10 years.

Given their youthfulness and their early contacts with the police and the courts, it is not at all surprising that a large portion of TARP members' adult years have been spent in confinement. The average time spent in prison during their current confinement was 1.2 years in Georgia and 2.8 years in Texas (see Table 7.12). Since their current confinement was likely to have been the result of only the latest in a series of brushes with the law, the total amount of confinement ever experienced was likely to have been much greater. Indeed, on the average, Georgia members have been in prison 2.8 years and Texas members 5.2 years.

Expressed as a proportion of adult years (age 17 to age at release from current confinement), *Georgia TARP participants had spent more than 1 out of 3 of their adult years in prison, and Texas participants had spent almost 1 out of every 2 years in prison.* Of course, it should be kept in mind that these are *averages;* some prisoners spent larger portions and some prisoners spent smaller portions of their adult years in prison.

The findings in Table 7.12 help to explain some of the earlier descriptions of TARP participants. Having spent so many of their adult years in prison, it is not at all surprising that their progress along the family life cycle was so retarded or that their employment records were so meager. Although TARP members were in their late twenties when released from prison, their "functional age," computed by deducting prison time from their ages at release, was only a little over 24 years.

OFFENSES OF CONVICTION

The charges of which TARP members were convicted and for which they were serving prison time are shown in Tables 7.13 and 7.14. Although most prisoners were convicted of one charge only, there were sufficient convictions on several charges to bring the average number of charges to 1.25 in Texas and 1.39 in Georgia.[12]

The predominant charges involved property crimes. In Texas, 72% of the charges consisted of property crimes, of which 40% were burglaries. Indeed, more than one out of three Texas TARP participants had been convicted of burglary (among other charges), and more than two out of three were convicted of one or another felony involving property. Similar proportions can be computed for Georgia members. One out of three were convicted of burglary, and about two out of three were convicted of all property crimes, burglary included.

Offenses involving drugs comprised the next largest group of crimes of which TARP members were convicted—13% and 12% of the offenses in Texas and Georgia. Offenses against persons, 11% and 9%, and the third largest group.

The seriousness of the felonies of which TARP members have been convicted ranged widely. At one extreme, a small group—about 2% in each state TARP contingent—were convicted of murder or homicide, regarded as the most serious of felonies. At the other extreme were a few persons who were sentenced for possession of marijuana; there is currently little consensus as to whether such possession should be regarded as a criminal offense.[13] Typical offenses lay somewhere between these two extremes and ordinarily involved taking someone's property, usually by burglary.

The preponderance of the charges of which TARP members were convicted involved theft-related crimes—72% in Texas and 60% in Georgia. Given also that these charges are likely to have been only the latest in a series of arrests and convictions that go back to late adolescence, it is likely that many TARP participants have committed theft after theft, some to the

---

[12] The Georgia prisoner contingent contained not only felons but misdemeanants who had been convicted by state courts and given prison sentences. It is difficult to make a clear distinction between felonies and misdemeanors in the Georgia criminal justice system, and we suspect that much of the difference arose out of the plea-bargaining positions of accused offenders.

[13] P. H. Rossi et al., "The Seriousness of Crimes," American Sociological Review, 39 (1974): 224–237.

TABLE 7.13
Texas TARP: Offenses of Current Conviction

	Number of persons convicted	Percentage of total convictions
Homicide and manslaughter	125	
Assault and battery	52	
Sexual assault	55	
Total crimes against persons	232	9
Robbery	354	
Arson	8	
Burglary	706	
Larceny	381	
Vehicle theft	48	
Forgery	147	
Fraudulent activity	107	
Embezzlement	10	
Receiving and possession of stolen property	5	
Damage to property	9	
Total crimes against property	1775	72
Drug offenses	326	13
Sex offenses	25	
Family offenses	3	
Gambling	2	
Commercial sex	1	
Obstructing police or courts	5	
Flight, escape	9	
Bribery	1	
Weapons offenses	56	
Miscellaneous	27	
Total other offenses	129	5
Total convictions	2462	
Average number of charges	1.25	
($N = 1975$)		

SOURCE: Prison records.

point that theft may be their major occupation while out of prison. For many others, income through theft may have supplemented their meager job earnings. In either event, if TARP payments were intended to lower motivation to engage in further property thefts after release, TARP members appeared to be an appropriate test group. If the plan were to work with these released prisoners, many of whom have had long histories of property crimes, the test would be a critical one.

TABLE 7.14
Georgia TARP: Offenses of Current Conviction

A. *Number of charges*

Felonies	Number of convictions	Misdemeanors	Number of convictions
Homicide	18	Assault and battery	74
Manslaughter	69		
Kidnapping and terrorism	12	Theft by taking	107
Assault and battery	154	Robbery and burglary	4
Total crimes against		Fraud and forgery	34
persons	253	Receiving stolen goods	7
		Criminal trespass	28
Robbery	213	Total property crimes	180
Burglary	684		
Theft by taking	219	Sex offenses	5
Forgery and fraud	134	Drug offenses	45
Arson and property damage	33	Motor vehicle driving	
Receiving stolen goods	66	violations	37
Motor vehicle theft	134	Driving under influence	74
Total property crimes	1483	Concealed weapons	64
		Drunkenness	10
Sex offenses	40	Abandonment and non-	
Drug offenses	292	support	44
Escape and aiding escape	72	Escape and aiding escape	20
Criminal attempt and criminal		Miscellaneous misdemeanors	14
conspiracy	60	Total misdemeanors	567
Miscellaneous felonies	26		
Total felonies	2,226		

Total offenses of conviction = 2793
Average number of charges = 1.39
(N = 2007)

B. *Proportions*

Felonies and misdemeanors combined

Against persons	11%
Against property	60%
Drug offenses	12%
Other offenses	17%
Total	100%

SOURCE: Prison records.

CONTINUING TIES: PAROLE AND DISCHARGE

For many former prisoners, release from prison does not mean the immediate end of ties to the criminal justice system. About half of the TARP participants were released on parole (see Table 7.15), a condition that places some restrictions on their freedom[14] and which lasts for varying periods beyond release. Typically, a prisoner released on parole is in that condition for a period that equals that unexpired portion of his sentence. A person on parole resides in a kind of legal limbo: Although outside prison, he may be called back without going through the same processes of arrest and trial that sent him to prison in the first place. If one or more of the numerous parole conditions are violated, and if his parole supervisor believes that the violations are sufficient to indicate that he is in danger of reverting to a criminal career, then he may be returned to prison, presumably to serve out the remainder of his original sentence.

The length of time a released prisoner is placed upon parole status depends partially on how much time remains to his sentence on release from prison and on the parole practices within state parole-granting agencies. As shown in Table 7.15, Georgia TARP participants tended to receive shorter periods of parole time; 46% were given less than 6 months as compared to only 13% for their Texas counterparts. Correspondingly in Texas, three out of five releasees were given more than a year as compared to only 25% for Georgia TARP members.

As will be shown in later chapters, whether or not a TARP member was given parole strongly affected his postrelease behavior. In part, these effects occurred because the prison systems and parole boards selected some prisoners for parole based on whatever the ruling assumptions were concerning which prisoners were more likely to be successful after release. In part, parole status may have affected subsequent behavior because parole conditions acted as a deterrent to improper behavior postrelease.

Granting parole to a prisoner is ordinarily a decision made in an indi-

---

[14] Although parole conditions in the two states varied somewhat, there were many parallels. Violations of parole conditions could lead to parole revocation and return to prison. Parole conditions included the following requirements: consistent and timely reports to parole supervisor; permission from parole supervisor needed for marriage, job, and residence changes; operation or ownership of a motor vehicle; possession and/or use of alcohol (to excess in Georgia) or narcotics; association with persons of "bad character" or "known criminals" forbidden; ownership or possession of weapons forbidden; and so on. It is difficult to imagine that any released prisoner would not violate one or another of the conditions of his parole at some time. Hence, the actual enforcement of parole conditions is at the discretion of the parole supervisors, a situation that some commentators have deplored as inequitable (Rosemary J. Erickson *et al.*, *Paroled But Not Free* [New York: Human Sciences Press, 1973]).

TABLE 7.15
Parole Status of TARP Participants at Time of Release

		Percent of TARP participants	
		Georgia	Texas
A.	*Parole status*		
	Full discharge (no parole)	51	48
	Parole	49	52
	100%	(932)	(969)
B.	*Length of parole given*		
	26 weeks or less (up to 6 months)	46	13
	27–51 weeks (6 months to 1 year)	29	26
	One year or more	25	62
	100%	(486)	(503)

SOURCE: Parole files.

TABLE 7.16
*Regression of Parole on Selected Prerelease
Offender Characteristics: Texas*

Independent variables	b	SE
Male	$-.129^*$	.059
Education	$.021^*$	.007
First offender	$.159^*$	.032
Black	$.067^*$	.031
Job arranged at release	$.269^*$	.031
Age	.001	.002
Intends to live alone postrelease	$-.278^*$	.073
Total PIP score[a]	$.002^*$	.0005
Property offense conviction	.045	.033
Participated in "approved" social organizations in prison[b]	$.143^*$	.032
Intends to live with wife	$-.067$	.047
Intends to live with parents	$.091^*$	.036
Has drivers license	$-.044$	.032
Constant	.020	.131
R^2	$.201^*$	
N	(957)	

SOURCES: Prison records and prerelease interviews.

[a] PIP Score consists of points given to prisoners for good time served, good behavior, performance on prison jobs, etc.

[b] "Approved" social organizations include participation in religious activities, Boy Scouts, and other civic service organizations while in prison.

* $p = < .05.$

142

TABLE 7.17
*Regression of Parole on Selected Prerelease
Offender Characteristics: Georgia*

Independent variables	b	SE
Male	− .018	.071
Black	− .116*	.346
Education	− .025	.007
Maximum security classification[a]	− .400	.257
Age	.002	.002
Job arranged postrelease	.219*	.034
First offender	.181*	.039
Intends to live alone	− .107	.007
Intends to live with wife	− .061	.056
Property offense conviction	.031	.037
Has a driver's license	.045	.034
Intends to live with parents	− .019	.045
Constant	.384*	.142
R^2	.128	
N	(833)	

NOTE: Dependent variable = parole dummy variable: 1 = parole, 0 = not paroled.

[a] Classification of prisoner at time of entry for placement in maximum-security prison.

* $p < .05$.

vidual case and is based upon an assessment of whether or not the parolee has a reasonable prognosis of remaining free and clear of further entanglements with the criminal justice system. Some prisoners are never granted parole, but serve to the limit of their sentences; others become paroled as soon as their minimum sentences are served.

Although a thorough analysis of who received parole is not essential at this point in our discussion, some indications of the parole-granting patterns in the two states are presented in Table 7.16 and 7.17, which contain the results of regression analyses in which the dependent variable was the question of whether or not parole was granted. The analyses vary from state to state because we do not always have parallel information in the two TARP data bases.

The coefficients shown in Tables 7.16 and 7.17 have a direct meaning that is easily apprehended. Each coefficient in the column headed "b" represents the increment (or decrement) in the probability of being given parole that is associated with each of the independent variables. Thus the coefficient for being male in Table 7.16 indicates that males had .127 less (minus sign) of a chance of being granted parole compared to females. The coefficients are net, that is, they measure the effect of the independent variable, holding everything else constant. Thus the chances for males are

.127 less than for females, when we hold being a first offender constant, regardless of length of sentence, and so on through the list of independent variables.

Several findings stand out in Tables 7.16 and 7.17. First, it is possible to predict (retrospectively to which persons parole was given. Given these data, however, such predictions can be undertaken with only modest accuracy, as the R^2 values at the bottom of the two tables indicate.[15] Second, the two prison systems heavily weighted previous criminal behavior: First offenders were favored over repeated offenders. Third, attention was also paid to prison behavior (although our information on this score came mainly from the Texas records, which are more complete on this issue than Georgia records). Prisoners who had good conduct records within the Texas prisons and who participated in "approved" activities were more likely to be granted parole. Fourth, parole authorities were somewhat concerned with intended postrelease behavior: Texas prisoners intending to live alone were less likely to be paroled. Georgia authorities were not sensitive to the issue of living arrangements. Apparently, however, both states favored persons who had jobs arranged prerelease. Finally, there is some evidence that blacks were less likely to be granted paroles in both states, although the tendency to slight members of that group was stronger in Georgia than in Texas.

Note that the generalizations made above concern the net effects of each of the factors discussed; that is, they obtained holding all other things in the equations constant. Thus, a first offender was more likely to be granted parole independent of the length of the original sentence imposed, independent of his prison behavior, and so on.

Of course, we do not know whether parole authorities consciously took these factors into account when they made their decisions. All we can say is that their decisions were made *as if* these factors counted in their decision making concerning prisoners in the two states.

It should also be noted that the comparisons made in Tables 7.15 and 7.16 are between persons who were released on discharge and those who were released on parole. Those who were discharged presumably had been denied parole at a previous point in time and hence had served longer sentences. They are not the persons who were considered for parole at the same time that the parolees in our sample were considered: At the least, they were older. One can make the case that age is the only difference between the two groups, those discharged being identical with prisoners who were considered and rejected for parole at the same time as the parolees in

---

[15] The higher R^2 on a scale from .00 to 1.00, the better the prediction afforded by the set of independent variables included in the analyses.

the two state samples, except for age. In any event, the comparisons made in Tables 7.16 and 7.17 are not the most appropriate ones for the purpose of definitively determining the principles employed by parole boards in making parole decisions.

In later chapters, analyses are presented that document the extent to which the factors that affected obtaining parole also play roles in predicting adjustment to civilian life. For the time being, it is perhaps useful to note that prison behavior played much less of a role in postprison adjustment than in parole decisions.

GATE MONEY AT RELEASE

Upon release, each prisoner is furnished with a set of civilian clothes, (the outfit furnished varies with the seasons and from medium to low quality), typically with a bus or train ticket to a destination within the state, and with a small amount of gate money, a gratuity that is supposed to provide some funds to tide the prisoner over until he finds productive employment. The amount of gate money furnished varies somewhat from state to state. A recent (1975) survey found that the average gate money was $75, with some states providing considerably more and others nothing.[16]

In 1976, Texas and Georgia were among neither the most generous nor the least generous of all states. Georgia was considerably less openhanded, giving each prisoner $25 upon release, in contrast to Texas, where gate money amounted to $200. Of course, there were other funds available to prisoners upon release. Gifts sent by relatives and friends could have been saved. In Georgia, prison work earned wages. In addition there was some trade or enterprise among prisoners that could also have led to accumulated funds. Finally, some prisoners may have had savings that predated imprisonment.

As shown in Table 7.18, most TARP prisoners had only gate money upon leaving prison. In Georgia, three out of four had only $25 upon release.[17] The remaining one in four had managed to save a little more, half accumulating up to $75 in addition to gate money. Texas prisoners were considerably better off on release, but a little more than half exited only with the gate money of $200. Texas prisoners also appear to be more enterprising and

---

[16] Robert Horowitz, *Back on the Street—From Prison to Poverty* (Washington, D.C.: American Bar Association, Commission on Correctional Facilities and Services, 1976). See also Chapter 2 of this book.

[17] A handful claimed that they had not even been considered eligible for the gate money, possibly because their sentences were too short to establish eligibility.

TABLE 7.18
TARP Participants: Money Held at Time of Release

	Georgia	Texas
Amount of money available to prisoner at time of release		
Average	$115.62	$419.64
Median	25.00	200.43

Georgia		Texas	
Amount of money held	Percentage of TARP participants	Amount of money held	Percentage of TARP participants
$25 or less	73	$200 or less	53
$26 to $50	9	201–225	16
$51 to $75	4	226–250	9
$76 to $100	2	251–275	2
$100 and over	12	276 and over	20
100%	(950)	100%	(973)

SOURCE: Prerelease interviews. Amounts consisted typically of "gate money" given to prisoner by the state prison system, plus earnings and other savings accrued while in prison and savings available in outside accounts. Note that many of these figures are very rough estimates.

apparently had accumulated a lot more money than Georgia prisoners. One out of five had at least $75 more than the Texas gate money (or a total of $275). Indeed, a handful claimed that they would have more than $1000 at release. In both states the few who had managed to accumulate some funds while in prison (or preserve savings in outside repositories) drove the average of money at hand up to $115.62 in Georgia and $419.64 in Texas. More typical, however, were the median amounts available to the released prisoners, $25 in Georgia and a few pennies more than $200 in Texas.[18]

The typical amounts of money available to TARP members were far from adequate to support a person through any period of transition. Georgia prisoners, who typically had $25 when they were released, did not have enough funds to support themselves for more than a day or two. Even the considerably better-off Texas releasees at most could have supported themselves at a low level of comfort for perhaps two or three weeks. This

---

[18] Analyses of the distribution of gate money within each of the states shows that some types of prisoners were more likely to accumulate money than others. In particular, the better educated and older prisoners were more likely to have greater sums of money on release. In addition, men had more money than women (possibly representing better employment opportunities) and blacks and Chicanos (in Texas) were not likely to accumulate much in the way of funds.

fact raises the very serious question of how those released prisoners who were not eligible for TARP payments would manage to get along. The answer has been provided in this chapter, for we have seen that a large proportion of the prisoners intended to live with their parents or other relatives when they were released. The burden of the transition to civil life was to be borne by the impoverished families of the released prisoners. Whether they wanted to or not, TARP members were not able to strike out on their own. Their financial resources were too meager to support them. The next chapter will take up the postrelease living arrangements of TARP members in greater detail.

It is to this financial problem of providing for the basic needs of released prisoners that TARP payments were addressed. TARP payment eligibility in Texas provided a sum of $819, which unemployed members in two of the experimental groups could rely upon, and $1638 for those in the treatment group given 26 weeks of eligibility. In Georgia the corresponding payment eligibility amounts were $910 and $1820. In both states, TARP payments were several multiples larger than money on hand at release and were intended to provide funds to aid successful adjustment to civilian life. It should also be noted that TARP payments did not provide for living standards at even the poverty line, for they were doled out as weekly payments of $63 and $70, respectively, in Texas and Georgia. Nevertheless, low as the TARP payments were, they were still generous in comparison to the gate money amounts provided by Texas and Georgia and were several magnitudes larger than savings accumulated by prisoners.

EPILOGUE

The purpose of this chapter has been to present the backgrounds of TARP members and their characteristics at time of release from prison. The image that emerges outlines the typical TARP participant as a young male, with a disadvantaged employment and family background, who has repeatedly been in trouble with the law since adolescence. Likely as not, he was released on parole but was given only enough funds to get by for a few days after leaving prison.

There were more resemblances than differences between the TARP participant groups in Georgia and Texas. Although race and ethnic mixes differed in the two states, this was mainly because the parent-state populations differed in the same ways; in both states TARP participants were drawn from the lowest levels of their local societies. Georgia ex-prisoners reflect the poorer socioeconomic level of that state in lower preconfinement wages, compared to their Texas counterparts. Since wage rates are sensitive to levels of employment, the comparatively greater prosperity and lower unemployment rates in Texas meant that the employment situations faced by the two groups of released prisoners were different. TARP participants in Georgia faced a much harder time finding any employment than their Texas counterparts. Under those circumstances, TARP payments may not have had the same sort of effects in Georgia that they did in Texas.

This chapter has described the men (and the few women) to whom the TARP payments were offered in the hope that this limited amount of financial aid would make a difference. In some ways, the description of typical TARP members is discouraging to those expectations. These were persons who have been in and out of prisons several times and have failed to be "rehabilitated" on several previous tries. The occupational skills they command are meager, and they have had few opportunities to deepen those skills in actual job experiences. They were also free of the steadying influences of family responsibilities. Indeed, at the time of their release, they were destined to become (again) the responsibilities of their families.

In other ways, the description of typical prisoners who had become involved in the TARP experiments leads to optimism. First, there was certainly room for improvement. Second, these are persons typically who had become involved in property-related crimes. There were also many who had not yet fully settled into a lifetime criminal career for whom the financial help of the TARP payments might have made a critical difference. Finally, there was abundantly clear evidence that the released prisoners needed financial help.

8

Postrelease Social and Psychological Adjustment Patterns
WITH JEFFREY K. LIKER

INTRODUCTION

There are many striking contrasts between the prison world the ex-felon leaves behind and the free world he enters upon release. From a highly regimented world of fixed schedules, he enters a life where routines are his to set at his discretion. Prison is a single-sex, narrow-age-band world; civilian life is bisexual and contains children and older persons. No prison provides a life of luxury, but every prison provides at least shelter, clothing, and subsistence. In the free world, it is necessary either to provide for oneself or to find some way of obtaining help from others.

Perhaps even more important are the expectations that are built up in prison about what freedom will mean. There are few, if any, prisoners who reluctantly leave the walls. Almost all look forward to freedom with positive expectations. As described by many commentators, the departing prisoner has most likely thought much about what freedom would bring, what he would do to celebrate his release, what friends and kin he would try to see, what places he would visit, and so on.[1] Those who are fortunate enough to have retained close ties to friends and relatives probably have made some arrangements for a place to stay, at least temporarily (as the living-arrangement plans described in the last chapter indicate). Others have tried with varying degrees of success to arrange for jobs.

Most go forth generally optimistic that they will never return to prison. They will "make it" this time.

But for many the optimism is hardly met by the experience of postrelease

---

[1] See Donald Clemmer, *The Prison Community* (Boston: Christopher Publishing House, 1940); John Irwin, *The Felon* (Englewood Cliffs, N.J.: Prentice-Hall, 1970); Charles Silberman, *Criminal Violence, Criminal Justice* (New York: Random House, 1978); John Irwin and Donald R. Cressey, "Thieves, Convicts and the Inmate Culture," *Social Problems* 10 (Fall, 1962): 142–155; Daniel Glaser *et al., Money against Crime* (Chicago: John Howard, 1961).

life. The arranged job falls through. The room they were planning to stay in is no longer available. Old friends have changed—perhaps married and developed different interests and friendship circles. The wives or lovers they thought were waiting found better things to do. Even their parental families have often changed, living in new places and with new interests, and perhaps having acquired a stepparent to whom the ex-prisoner would be an unwelcome stranger in the house.

The transition to civilian life can be viewed as stressful even when it goes well and according to optimistic expectations. The larger the gap between expectations and experience the higher stress levels often are. Stresses can arise from a variety of circumstances: finding a place to live, getting a job, relations with others, sickness and accidents, and so on through a litany of all the events, good and bad, that happen to someone trying to regain a place within civilian life.

This chapter shows some of the points at which adjustment problems arose for TARP members in the year after release. Living arrangements are discussed first, along with their changes over the year. Marital status and relations with the opposite sex are next discussed. Finally we consider changes in how the ex-prisoners react to the world about them in the form of measures of their perceptions of problems in finding their way economically and their problems in feeling comfortable with themselves. Of course, these do not constitute the only stress points in the prisoner's existence. Chapters 9 and 10, respectively, take up employment and arrest patterns, topics that are so important from the viewpoint of the goals of the TARP experiment that they are given special attention.

POSTRELEASE MARITAL STATUS AND LIVING ARRANGEMENTS

An important part of the process of adjustment to freedom is the establishment of living arrangements and the reestablishment of old ties and bonds to family, spouses, and friends. As indicated in Chapter 7, the majority of TARP members had plans at the time of release to return to their parental households. Even some of those who were then still married did not plan to live with spouses but were going to live with their parents. There are undoubtedly many reasons for this reliance on blood ties, among which not the least is the lack of resources to strike out on one's own. It is a tribute to the strength of kinship ties that so many TARP members intended to return to their parental households. Kinship ties appear to be those that one can count on regardless of what has happened in the past.[2]

One might expect that, once free and given a little time to reorient themselves to civilian life, TARP members would move rapidly to set up their own living arrangements and to bring themselves more into line with the ordinary life-cycle stages of their age peers. However, as shown in Table 8.1, there were apparently fewer dramatic changes in marital status during the year following release from prison than might have been expected. In Georgia 52% were single at time of release and 48% were single at the end of the year following release. In Texas, changes were more dramatic: The proportion of single persons dropped from 50% to 32% from the beginning to the end of the first postrelease year.

In both states most of the changes in marital status involved net shifts from being single to being married. In Georgia the proportion married started out at 22% at time of release and ended up at 29% at the end of the year. In Texas, the net changes were greater, starting with 17% married and ending with 34%. It should be recalled that Texas TARP members had been in prison longer and were two years older on the average than their Georgia counterparts. Hence they were more likely to have gone through a marital disruption while in prison. In addition, because of their greater age, Texas ex-prisoners may have been anxious to catch up with their age peers.

The net changes described so far conceal a great deal of shifting back and forth among marital statuses. Although more of the ex-prisoners were married at the end of the year, many who started off being married separated and were later divorced. Some started up liaisons that were later ended, and so on. Correlations that measure the stability of marital status from one point in time to another are shown in the bottom panel of Table 8.1. These coefficients express the extent to which the marital status of individuals remained unchanged from interview to interview: The higher a coefficient the more stable a marital status is from the earlier to the later interview involved. Thus in Georgia, a person who is single at time of release

---

[2] Donald Cressey, commenting on an earlier version of this manuscript, remarked that if the provision of financial aid helped any of the prisoners to remain out of dependence on their parents, the result would be beneficial both to the parents and to the ex-prisoners. The addition of another adult could not but add to the financial burdens of the poor households involved and, hence, if ex-prisoners could be helped to set up their own households, so much the better for their parents' financial solvency. In addition, the ex-prisoners would be better off as well since if the parental household contributed anything to their criminal behavior, providing them with the means to avoid returning to that environment would aid to their successful adjustment to civilian life.

TABLE 8.1
Marital Status at Selected Points Throughout Study Year

	Georgia				Texas			
	At release	3 mos.	6 mos.	12 mos.	At release	3 mos.	6 mos.	12 mos.
A. *Marital status distributions*								
Single, never married	52%	53%	50%	48%	50%	49%	45%	32%
Married and common-law	22%	23%	27%	29%	17%	20%	25%	34%
Separated, divorced,								
widowed	26%	24%	23%	23%	34%	31%	30%	34%
100%	(976)	(895)	(800)	(776)	(975)	(929)	(92)	(837)
B. *Correlations across periods*[a]								
Single versus all other								
statuses								
At release		.81	.76	.70		.82	.76	.65
3 months			.81	.74			.79	.68
6 months				.77				.67
Married versus all other								
statuses								
At release		.61	.50	.40		.52	.41	.31
3 months			.74	.59			.69	.51
6 months				.69				.57

SOURCE: Follow-up interviews.

[a] Product–moment correlations.

is more likely to be still single 3 months later (.81) than at the end of the year (.70). Being single is apparently a more stable status than being married. All the correlation coefficients for the married status are lower than for the single status. In short, single persons were more likely to remain single throughout the postrelease year, married persons were likely to shift out of the married state, and the nonmarried into that state. Indeed, the lower coefficients for Texans express partially the fact that there was a stronger trend toward being married in that state over the postrelease year.

It should be borne in mind that marital status shifts were measured in the TARP study over relatively short periods of time. It usually takes some time for a person to get married and usually even longer to get divorced. Hence the fact that there was so much change in the marital arrangements of the TARP sample reflects the general instability of their lives, other indicators of which are presented throughout this chapter.

Several attempts were made by the research staff to discern the predictors of changing marital status among TARP participants in the two states. In particular, there was considerable interest in the impact that TARP payment eligibility might have had on either changes in marital status or in enhancing the stability of marriages.[3] These efforts were not rewarded with any significant success. For married ex-prisoners, it appeared that TARP payments or work had no effect on marital stability, neither enhancing stability nor fostering breakups. Nor was it possible to find any other factor relating to the stability of TARP marriages. The main determinant of getting married was age: The younger the TARP participant, the more likely he was to get married if he was released as single or formerly married. Payments had no effect nor did the amount of work effort or any other condition of postrelease life for which indicators were available in the TARP files. In short, it looked as if the processes that led to changes in marital status were independent of employment and TARP payments.

As we discussed in Chapter 7, the majority of TARP members intended to live with their mothers and/or fathers, 54% in Georgia and 51% in Texas (see Table 7.9). Shifts in living arrangements from intentions at time of release through the end of the postrelease year are shown in Table 8.2. The major changes occurring in the postrelease period involved moving from parental households into other living arrangements. In both Texas and Georgia, the main shift was toward setting up a new household through marriage. The proportion living with spouses started at 18% in Georgia and finished at the end of 12 months at 32%. The corresponding figures in Texas were 14% and 32%. The complementary decline in those living with parents was a drop from 54% to 36% in Georgia and from 51% to 29% in Texas. There were also some slight changes in the other categories: The proportions living alone rose from 7% to 9% in Georgia and from 5% to 11% in Texas.

This trend highlights the importance of the part played by parental households in absorbing the costs of the transition to civilian life. TARP members returned to those homes because they had no other place to which they could lay a claim. As the transition was made, more or less successfully, TARP members moved out to set up their own households or to share households with siblings or peers.

The net result of these changes at the end of the year was to divide TARP participants into roughly equal thirds: One in three were still living with their mothers and/or fathers, another third were living with spouses and/or in common-law relationships, and the remaining third were living in some other arrangements.

---

[3] Evidence from the Seattle and Denver Income Maintenance Experiments appears to indicate that the income-maintenance payments enhanced marital instability, especially when the payments were meager. See M. Hannan, N. Tuma, and L. Grueneveld, "Income and Independence Effects on Marital Dissolution," *American Journal of Sociology* 84, no. 3 (November 1978): 611–633.

TABLE 8.2
*Household Living Arrangements at Selected Points
during Year beyond Release*

	Living arrangements (percentage of participants)							
	Alone	With spouse	With one parent	With two parents	With other rels	With siblings	Other	100%
A. *Georgia TARP*								
At Release								
(intention)	7	18	27	27	9	7	5	(974)
At 3 months	7	22	27	21	3	9	12	(895)
At 6 months	8	27	25	18	2	9	11	(800)
At 12 months	9	32	20	16	8	4	7	(774)
B. *Texas TARP*								
At Release								
(intention)	5	14	35	16	[a]	11	16[a]	(975)
At 3 months	8	23	22	20	12	4	10[b]	(970)
At 6 months	11	28	20	17	10	4	10[b]	(966)
At 12 months	11	32	16	13	7	3	10[b]	(936)

SOURCE: Follow-up interviews.

[a] Texas TARP data did not permit separate designation of other relatives as a living arrangement at time of release. The category "Other" includes persons who intended to go to or were residing in halfway houses.
[b] Includes TARP members who were in jail, as coded by Texas TARP research group.

The shifts in living arrangements and marital status described above were usually necessarily accompanied by changes in residence. Hence, we can expect that TARP members were a very mobile group in their first year beyond release. Indeed, such was the case, as Table 8.3 shows. At each follow-up interview, TARP members were asked how many places they had lived in during the period since their last interview. In Georgia, about two-thirds had lived in only one place in each of the periods involved. In Texas, TARP members appeared to have moved about somewhat more, with 60% being stable in the first three months following release and 54% in that condition during the last half of the postrelease year. Note that the ex-prisoners tended to be somewhat more stable during the last half of the postrelease year, averaging 1.53 and 1.8 residences in Georgia and Texas, respectively. Since the 12-month interview covered a 6-month period of time, residential location appears to have been somewhat more stable in that period.

This amount of residential shifting far exceeds the general levels of mobility within the U.S. population. According to the Current Population Survey, about 20% of the U.S. population has shifted residence at least once during the period of a year, with about two-thirds of those shifts in-

TABLE 8.3
*Residential Mobility of TARP Participants at
Various Periods of Postrelease Year*

	Georgia	Texas
A. *Number of places lived during first 3 months*		
One residence	69%	60%
2 residences	16%	22%
3 or more	15%	17%
Average number of residences	1.50	1.60
N	(897)	(952)
B. *Number of places lived during second 3 months*		
One residence	71%	65%
2 residences	16%	24%
3 or more	13%	12%
Average number of residences	1.44	1.53
N	(786)	(857)
C. *Number of places lived during last 6 months*		
One residence	64%	54%
2 residences	24%	31%
3 or more	11%	14%
Average number of residences	1.53	1.80
N	(760)	(824)

volving changes in residence within the same county. With about half of
the ex-prisoners having made at least one residential shift during the year
after release, the mobility rate for the subjects of the TARP study must be
considered far in excess of what can be expected typically.

The findings presented in this section amount to a description of a group
of men and women who are very much in flux as far as their personal lives
and living arrangements are concerned. Of course, many of these changes
were to be expected. Some of the TARP members had been in prison for an
extended time, and it would be too much to expect that they could have
simply moved back with their families or their spouses and renewed old
stable patterns. For one thing, "old patterns" in many cases had been patterns of instability. For another, the released prisoners, as well as their
families, had changed in the interim. Clearly, these two considerations
alone would lead one to expect that places of residence would have been
changed frequently as the TARP members tried out different arrangements
of their personal lives. As we will see in subsequent analyses, these changes
were sensitive to some extent to other events occurring in their lives,
especially employment experiences.[4]

---

[4] See also the "Significant Woman" study reported in Appendix B.

ILLNESS AND HOSPITALIZATION

The marginal lives led by TARP members before imprisonment were sufficiently hazardous that a fairly large proportion were classified by their state's prison system as having a disability sufficiently severe to limit the kinds of work or other duties they would have been assigned in prison. Eleven percent of Georgia TARP and 12% of Texas TARP participants had been so classified while in prison. How large these proportions were can be appreciated by contrast with corresponding proportions in the general population derived from the census: In Georgia in 1970, 1.6% of males between the ages of 25 and 34 suffered disabilities that impeded their working; in Texas the proportion was 1%.[5] Even if we assume that the prisons were overly conservative in declaring a person disabled, the prevalence of disability among TARP members appears to have been considerable.[6]

The hazardous nature of TARP members' lives continued after release. Among Texas TARP members, five died during the postrelease year, and there were nine deaths among Georgia members.[7] When we consider that the general death rate for males of that age range is about 5 per 100,000, these deaths (amounting to a rate of 500 per 100,000) appear to have been excessive. While we did not collect data systematically on the causes of deaths among TARP members, we do know from field reports that most died through violence and some in automobile accidents and from drug overdoses.

The TARP follow-up interviews did not collect data on the specific illnesses and injuries suffered over the year. However, it is likely that such data would further corroborate the generalization that TARP members led lives that were fraught with physical threats from illness and injuries. Information is available, however, on the number of incidents of disabling sickness and hospitalizations and their accompanying durations.[8] Table 8.4 contains the average number of weeks TARP members in each state were sick or in hospital, as well as the proportion of persons that had such episodes in each period.

---

[5] Bureau of the Census, *Census of Population: 1970*, Vol. 1, *Characteristics of the Population* (Washington, D.C.: Government Printing Office), Part 12, pp. 803–804, Table 169; and ibid., Part 45, p. 1537, Table 169.

[6] Of course, differences in the meaning of disability between the prison systems and the census would also affect these comparisons.

[7] These deaths among the interviewed TARP groups—976 in Georgia and 975 in Texas—came to the attention of interviewers or were found in documentary records. Undoubtedly other deaths escaped notice.

[8] Subjects were asked whether they were in hospital or were sufficiently sick at any point to be unable to work.

TABLE 8.4
*Time Spent in Hospital or Too Sick to Work during
Postrelease Year by Periods*

Time period	Georgia			Texas		
	Average weeks	Percentage of persons	N	Average weeks	Percentage of persons	N
First 6 weeks	.017	1	(897)	.064	4	(967)
Next 7 weeks	.038	2	(897)	.175	9	(967)
17–26 weeks	.575	12	(795)	.366	17	(936)
Last 6 months	1.051	13	(770)	.863	23	(886)
Total year	1.740	23	(683)	1.466	38	(883)

SOURCE: Follow-up interviews.

Georgia TARP members spent, on the average, 1.7 weeks (or 12 days) sick or in hospital during the postrelease year, involving 23% of the men and women concerned. The corresponding figures for Texas were 1.5 weeks, or 11 days. Thirty-eight percent of Texas TARP members had a disabling sickness or hospitalization incident, a rate that appears to be somewhat higher than Georgia's.[9] This level of disabling incidents of illness or injury is considerably greater than is ordinarily experienced by males of comparable age groups in the United States.[10] This illness incidence was not simply a continuation of conditions that led some to be classified as disabled while in prison. The sicknesses and hospitalizations appear to have been largely new conditions acquired postrelease, with most of the evidence pointing to a considerable contribution of newly acquired illnesses and injuries.[11]

---

[9] This may reflect differences in the state health-care systems for poor people, with the Texas poor making more use of hospitals for illnesses and injuries while in Georgia outpatient facilities may be utilized more frequently.

[10] Estimates of sickness episodes for a comparable population group within each of the two states are not available in published literature. However, for the United States as a whole, it is estimated that on the average about 5 days are lost per year for reason of sickness or hospitalization for persons in the labor force: (U.S. National Center for Health Statistics, *Vital and Health Statistics*, series 10, no. 100 (1975). Another estimate computed from data presented in J. Hedges, "Absence from Work," *Monthly Labor Review* (October, 1977) provides a projection for the same group of slightly less than 7 days a year lost from work either for illness or for "personal reasons." Either estimate is about half that recorded for TARP members. When we consider that national estimates include persons of a much wider age range, whose average age is in the low 40s, the illness prevalence in the TARP groups seems to have been very high.

[11] The correlation between being classified as disabled and the number of days lost from illness and injury is low enough (around +.2) in each state to indicate that while persons

In sum, the evidence is quite compelling: In their first year after release, TARP members led lives that were fraught with more than ordinary levels of illness and/or injury. A larger number died than ordinarily would have been expected. The typical TARP member spent more than 1 week out of 52 too ill to be available for employment.

SELF-ASSESSMENTS OF ADJUSTMENT

The adjustments that ex-prisoners made to freedom are reflected directly in life events that took place during the postrelease year. Adjustment problems were also mirrored in ex-prisoners' subjective experiences of difficulties in achieving what they wanted to obtain in a variety of life spheres. Adjustment, therefore, has both an objective side, consisting of the flow of life events, and a subjective side, consisting of the assessments of satisfying or problematic outcomes of those experiences. So far this chapter has been concerned primarily with recording the flows of events. In this section we turn to the subjective side of adjustment, consisting of the views expressed by TARP members about the ways in which they were experiencing satisfactions or troubles in the main areas of life.

Self-reports of satisfaction with these areas of life tend to be biased upwards. That is, persons usually report high levels of satisfaction with any particular condition at any one point in time, since persons who had been highly dissatisfied can be expected to move out of those conditions as quickly as possible.[12] Nevertheless, such assessments are useful in making comparisons across time periods and across subgroups.

In each of the follow-up interviews, TARP participants were asked to assess how well they had gotten along in a number of specific areas during the periods immediately preceding the interviews. For example, during the 3-month interviews, each was asked how much of a problem it had been to get a job and how frequently he had felt lonely or angry or depressed. An appreciation of some of the problems experienced by TARP members during the first 3 months after leaving prison can be gleaned from the responses shown in Table 8.5. Although it is difficult to assess how much

---

classified as disabled in prison were more likely to experience more disabling days in the postrelease year, the contribution of this group was not great enough to be the completely determining factor.

[12] Since a person's "satisfaction" with a particular state is constantly being adjusted, either by changing states or changing assessments of that state, it is to be expected that without constraints, persons would tend toward the satisfied assessment of their states. At any point in time, it is to be expected that more satisfaction than dissatisfaction is to be found in any population concerning areas of life over which the individual can exercise some control.

TABLE 8.5

Self-Assessed Adjustment Problems in First Three Months after Release

| | Percentage of participants (100% in parentheses) | |
	Georgia	Texas
A. *Acknowledge "serious problems" in*		
Finding a job	52 (861)	40 (948)
Getting along financially	27 (890)	31 (948)
Having enough clothes	15 (890)	22 (948)
Finding a place to live	13 (885)	18 (947)
Staying out of trouble	6 (888)	7 (947)
Transportation (getting around one's city)	20 (754)	31 (944)
B. *Acknowledge that "very often" or "sometimes" the following conditions occurred:*		
Not getting along with spouse (if married)	36 (241)	33 (213)
Not getting along with girl/boyfriend (if applicable)	23 (471)	24 (498)
Feeling depressed	59 (888)	62 (947)
Feeling lonely	33 (887)	40 (948)
Being treated as an "ex-con"	31 (884)	26 (948)
Feeling strange and awkward	33 (756)	41 (947)
Feeling uncomfortable in stores and restaurants	15 (757)	24 (948)

SOURCE: Three-month follow-up interviews.

more difficult life appeared to TARP members (as, say, compared to others of their age and sex), it is also clear that in some areas of life, TARP members experienced considerably inflated levels of trouble.

Slightly more than half (52%) of Georgia TARP members reported that getting a job had been a serious problem, and two out of five (40%) Texas members expressed the same difficulty. Clearly, getting a job was a problem, much more so than we would expect to find among the general population. Georgia members found the employment problem more serious than those in Texas, a finding that is much in line with the actual experiences with employment in those two states, as shown in Chapters 5 and 9. Georgia's unemployment rate in 1976 was, in some localities, more than twice the rate in Houston, which is the best city in Texas to go to for employment. Georgia TARP members reported working considerably less than their Texas counterparts, a condition that was also reflected in their reporting considerably more difficulty in obtaining employment.

Of course, there is undoubtedly a reciprocal relationship between getting a job and reporting difficulties in finding a job. On one hand, if it is difficult to find a job, then one is less likely to work. On the other hand, the less one works, the more difficult it may seem to find employment. This reciprocity can be discerned in the fact that persons in the TARP payment groups (Groups 1 through 3) reported much more difficulty in finding work than those in the controls, despite the fact that within each state both experimentals and controls (by definition) were facing exactly the same objective employment situation.[13] Analyses not reported in this volume have established the fact that the reciprocity is slightly lopsided; that is, employment experiences affected the assessment that finding a job was a serious problem less than the belief that employment was a serious problem affected the level of work effort.[14]

As shown in Table 8.5, getting along financially was rated a serious problem by about 30% in each of the two states. It is difficult to know whether this level of dissatisfaction was high or low in comparison to what might have been reported by other persons of the same age in the two states. The levels appeared high, especially in relation to other problems listed in Panel A of Table 8.5. It should also be noted that the experimental and control groups did not vary significantly in their ratings of finances as a serious problem. Apparently the payments made little difference in this respect.[15]

In Panel A, the only other area in which significant proportions of TARP members indicated that they faced serious problems concerned transportation. Twenty percent in Georgia and 31% in Texas reported great difficulties in getting around their communities (in a physical sense). It is interesting that the levels of complaints were higher in Texas than in Georgia, possibly reflecting the well-developed public transportation in Atlanta, to which nearly half of the Georgia members returned after release.

In contrast, having enough clothes, finding a place to live, and staying out of trouble appeared to be viewed rarely as serious problems.

Panel B of Table 8.5 shows the proportions of TARP members who experienced at least some difficulties either in relations to significant other persons or within themselves. More than a third of the TARP members who were married quarreled with their spouses. Close to three out of five

---

[13] This difference is seen in an analysis of variance test showing that the differences on this item across experimental and control groups were statistically significant in Georgia at the .0001 level and in Texas at the .0064 level.

[14] See J. K. Liker and Peter H. Rossi, "Reentry Blues: The Complex Role of Legitimate Employment During the Ex-Prisoner's Transition to Civil Life" (Unpublished paper presented at the 1979 Annual Convention of the American Sociological Association, Boston, 1979).

[15] Of course, since persons in the experimental groups worked less and therefore had less earned income in the first quarter, this equality of level of complaint may only mean that the payments compensated for the lowered employment (see Chapter 9).

said that occasionally they felt depressed. A third of the Georgia TARP members and two out of five of the Texas members acknowledged some occasions of feeling "lonely," and about the same proportions also complained of times when they felt "strange and awkward," and so on.

The general portrait that emerged was that of a fairly large minority— somewhere between a third and a half—who experienced some difficulties with loneliness, depression, and "feeling strange." Going along with those subjective states were troubles relating to their spouses and boy/girlfriends, as applicable.

Clearly, the first few months out of prison were not entirely joyful ones. Prisoners may have been glad to be released, but the road ahead was not without its troubles, at least for a fairly large minority of them.

The fact that these questions were repeated largely unchanged in the remaining follow-up interviews facilitates observations on changes in adjustment over the course of the postrelease year. Rather than present the findings question by question, we have formed some of the items shown in Table 8.5 into a pair of indices (presented in Table 8.6). Each index is constructed from the items contained in the two panels of Table 8.5. Those in Panel A of Table 8.5 were formed into a *Practical Adjustment Index*, which measured how well the members indicated they were doing with respect to getting a job, doing well financially, finding a good place to live, and solving their transportation problems.

The questions in Panel B of Table 8.5 were formed into a *Personal Adjustment Index* which assessed the degree to which they did not experience loneliness or depression, feel uncomfortable about being an ex-convict, and so on.[16]

This division of the subjective assessment questions into two domains was justified not solely on a priori reasoning but also because inspection of the correlations among these items indicated that items in each index tended to be consistent with each other. Interitem correlations tended to be relatively high.[17] The items formed two clusters, one composed of the items (or equivalents) in Panel A and the other composed of items in Panel B. Practical problems of getting along in the world seemed to be the common theme in the one, and psychological problems of feeling states appeared to be the common theme in the other cluster. Hence, the two names used for the indices, *Practical Adjustment* and *Personal Adjustment*. These clusters

---

[16] Unfortunately, changes were made from interview to interview in the questions included and sometimes in the form of the question or answer categories allowed.

[17] On the basis of responses in the 3-month interview, we found average interitem correlations for Texas and Georgia respectively were 1) .35 and .34 between items in the economic difficulties cluster; 2) .33 and .31 between items in the feeling-states cluster; and 3) .20 and .19 on the average across the two clusters of items.

were strikingly similar across states and time periods, indicating an inherent stability.[18] For each cluster, an index was constructed out of the simple sum of responses to relevant items. That is, responses to the five questions of each index were added together and then standardized to range from 0 to 100 points.[19] The result was that 100 is the best score and represents the case of a participant reporting no practical or personal difficulties. In contrast, a score of zero indicated the least satisfaction with one's adjustment.

Note that these scales have an arbitrary metric, and hence, particular scores are difficult to interpret. Clearly a score of 100 on either scale means that a person either felt completely adjusted in "practical" terms or felt quite good about himself in "personal" terms. A score of zero, on the other hand, meant a participant felt quite badly about himself or about his ability to get along in practical terms. Scores in between the two extremes, where most of the score values fell, indicate that some difficulties had been experienced—the lower the score, the greater the number of difficulties.

Perhaps the best way to obtain an appreciation of the meanings of these scores is to consider the score averages on the two indexes in Georgia and Texas as computed from the 3-month follow-up interview. (These data are shown in abbreviated form in Table 8.6.) In Georgia the average scores on *Practical Adjustment* and *Personal Adjustment*, respectively, were 62.8 and 68.1. It seems that Georgia TARP members had a higher level of adjustment in their personal sphere than in the practical one. For Texas the corresponding scores were 60.3 and 63.6, indicating the same trend within the state but also a slightly lower level of adjustment in both spheres of life as compared to Georgia. Average scores in the sixties indicate that a sizable minority of participants expressed difficulties in practical and personal adjustment.[20] Differences between the states were significant only for the *Personal Adjustment Index.*

---

[18] Taking responses from the 3-month interview, the corresponding correlations across states computed for pairs of interitem correlation was about .85.

[19] The computational formula used to calculate the adjustment indices was as follows:

$$\text{INDEX} = \frac{\sum_i I_i}{K I_{max}} \times 100$$

where:

INDEX	= Adjustment Index (practical or personal)
I_i	= Response to item i
I_{max}	= Maximum possible value of items
K	= Number of items used in index

[20] The fact that Texas members have lower adjustment scores is also consistent with Table 8.5, in which Georgia members are worse off with respect to employment but better off with respect to every other item.

TABLE 8.6
Trends in Subjective Quality of Life by Age Groups

	Texas			Georgia		
	21 and under	22–29	30 and over	21 and under	22–29	30 and over
A. *Average scores of adjustment indexes*						
Practical Adjustment Index						
3-Month	59.6	57.8	63.5	63.7	61.5	63.8
N	(137)	(454)	(351)	(235)	(385)	(269)
6-Month	68.9	63.8	71.1	63.7	63.4	66.1
N	(131)	(419)	(338)	(211)	(332)	(243)
12-Month[a]	69.5	68.3	75.9	67.0	65.7	69.2
N	(118)	(327)	(306)	(194)	(309)	(224)
Personal Adjustment Index						
3-Month	59.5	62.3	69.1	66.0	67.2	71.2
N	(140)	(454)	(351)	(234)	(385)	(265)
6-Month	66.5	66.8	74.1	74.2	74.8	78.8
N	(131)	(421)	(340)	(214)	(332)	(248)
12-Month[b]	63.9	66.5	72.1	73.6	74.0	78.2
N	(118)	(367)	(306)	(191)	(304)	(308)
B. *Difference in adjustment index means across interviews*						
Practical Adjustment Index						
3–6-Month	+9.3*	+6.0*	+7.6*	0.0	+1.9	+2.3
6–12-Month	+0.6	+4.5*	+4.8	+3.3	+2.3	+3.1
3–12-Month	+9.9	+10.5*	+12.4*	+3.3	+4.2	+5.4*
Personal Adjustment Index						
3–6-Month	+7.0*	+4.5*	+5.0*	+8.2*	+7.6*	+7.6*
6–12-Month	−2.6	−0.3	−2.0	−0.6	−0.8	−0.6
3–12-Month	+4.4*	+4.2*	+3.0	+7.6*	+6.8*	+7.0*

NOTE: Indexes range from 0 to 100, where 100 is the case of a respondent who answers "No problem" or "Never" to all items.

[a] In Georgia items were available in an agree–disagree format only. Since both forms were available in the Texas 12-month interview, we used the percentage difference between these alternative forms to adjust the Georgia 12-month practical index. Adjustments were made separately within each age group.

[b] Since the 12-month personal index was based on items different from those in the only available 3-month personal index, shown above is an adjusted 12-month equal to: 12-month personal (alternative) + (6-month personal [alternative] − 6-month personal). This approximates the metric used in the 3-month personal and the 6-month personal shown above, and therefore comparisons can be made across time.

* $p < .05$.

Trends in the adjustment indexes over the year are shown in Table 8.6.[21] In this table TARP participants were divided into three age groups based on expectations that adjustment levels would be age related. The intervals were chosen to distinguish very young participants—under 21—who would be having considerable difficulties with employment because of their age, from older—over 30—persons, many of whom would ordinarily be leaving behind their criminal careers. The middle group—those between the ages of 22 and 29—were expected to be persons for whom adjustment was most critical and for whom the alternatives between crime and employment would be most evident.

The *Practical Adjustment Index* averages show a pattern of differences in adjustment by age that was curvilinear in form and consistently so across time periods and states. The oldest group scored the highest, possibly because past experience enabled older releasees to cope with the problems of reentry. The youngest group (average age 20) was next, scoring less than the oldest but higher than the middle group (average age 25). Thus the middle group seems to be the hardest hit subjectively by practical difficulties.

The *Personal Adjustment Indexes* shown in the lower part of Panel A in Table 8.6 exhibit a somewhat different pattern across age groups. The oldest group was still ahead of the younger groups across state samples and time periods. However, there was virtually no difference in personal difficulties experienced between the two younger age groups.

Comparing across state samples, notice that all age groups in Georgia started the postrelease year higher in practical adjustment than their counterparts in Texas. These differences are not large enough to be statistically significant.

This ranking of state samples did not hold up over time. Superior labor-market conditions enabled Texas members to progress to a greater extent than Georgia releasees, and by the 6-month interview, those in Texas scored higher in practical adjustment across age groups. The Texas group

---

[21] A problem in looking at trends across time was that items were added and removed across interview schedules. One set of items, identical in form, was common to the 3-month and 6-month schedules but was omitted from the 12-month interview. A somewhat different set that was common to the 6-month and 12-month interviews was not included in the 3-month interview. Fortunately the 6-month interview, which included both sets of items, provided a bridge between the 3-month and 12-month interviews. Indexes from both sets were constructed and intercorrelations across alternative forms were high. To standardize to a common metric, the 12-month indexes were adjusted by the difference between the alternative measures in the 6-month interviews.

gained an additional edge in the second 6 months and was still further ahead in practical adjustment 1 year after release.

These changes over time are summarized in Panel B of Table 8.6 as score differences across time periods in the adjustment indexes. The third row in this panel shows the change between the 3- and 12-month measurements. While the Texas group improved over the year by 10.9 practical-adjustment points on the average across age groups, the equivalent figure for Georgia was only 4.3 points. Indeed, all of the Texas 3-month to 12-month differences and only one of the Georgia differences were statistically significant.

As one might expect, personal adjustment was less sensitive than practical adjustment to market conditions and other state differences. Across age groups and time periods, the Georgia sample had higher average personal-adjustment scores than those released in Texas, a difference that was statistically significant. The smallest difference across states was for the oldest group. For this group the Georgia sample scored 76.1 points on the average across time periods, and the oldest Texas group scored 71.8, a difference of 4.3 points. The largest difference across states was between scores for the youngest age group—those affected most by the commutation order in Georgia. The youngest age group scored 71.3 on the average in Georgia and only 63.3 in Texas, a difference of 8 points. The middle group scored 72 on the average in Georgia and 65.2 in Texas, a difference of 6.8 points.

Summarizing, the oldest age group in both states was clearly best able to adjust subjectively to the problems associated with reentry. The oldest age group scored highest on practical and personal adjustment across time periods, and improved across time to the greatest extent on practical adjustment. The youngest age group had slightly fewer practical difficulties compared to the middle group, which was the worst off of the three. Thus releasees in the 22 to 29 age group, who probably had neither the parental support of the youngest group nor the coping experience of the oldest group, faced the most serious economic difficulties.

Within these average trends, there was considerable variation from individual to individual in subjective assessments of practical and personal problems. To understand some of these differences, regressions were computed using the scores derived from the 12-month interview as dependent variables. The 12-month indexes were used since they represent the end result of the adjustment processes under way during the postrelease year. In other words, these analyses are concerned with what made a difference in making a better adjustment over the entire postrelease year. These analyses may be viewed as indicating some of the factors that led to more or less satisfaction with adjustment as experienced at the end of the post-release year.[22]

Table 8.7 displays the results of regressing the 12-month *Practical Adjustment Index* on a number of individual characteristics.[23] In both Texas and Georgia only modest amounts of variance in the index were accounted for, as the R^2 values of .24 and .27 indicate. The most important correlate of positive scores on practical adjustment was the number of weeks worked during the year. This factor alone accounted for about 40% of the explained variance in each of the states. In Texas, for every week worked, the adjustment index was increased by .71 and in Georgia by .86, net of all the other factors included in the equation. Hence a Texas participant who worked 26 weeks gained 18 score points and, in Georgia, 22 score points, compared to someone who had not worked at all during the postrelease year. Employment experiences led to higher self-assessments of getting along in the practical sphere.

Of the remaining independent variables in the equation of Table 8.7, the only ones that were significant in both states were the fact of being black, a condition that lowered the practical adjustment score by about 5 points in Texas and 6 points in Georgia, and the number of residential moves experienced during the year—the more moves, the lower the score.

In Texas, weeks spent in jail or prison over the year unaccountably raises the positive sense of practical adjustment, whereas going to the big metropolitan centers of Dallas-Fort Worth and Houston, lowers the scores received. In that state both educational attainment and age increased the self-ratings of adjustment. In contrast, Georgia participants were affected by none of these factors, the only significant determinants being the ones mentioned earlier and the money at hand at the time of release.

It is important to note that in neither state did the amount of TARP payments affect the self-ratings of adjustment in the practical sphere. Additional analyses (not presented here) also show that the TARP payments did not affect ratings one way or another at any of the interview periods, including those in which payments were prevalent. Of course, TARP payments were not designed to directly affect the sense of well-being of the recipients, although one might have expected that payments would have affected at least the sense of economic well-being by providing a minimum level of income during the period of eligibility. However, it should be

---

[22] Additional analyses currently underway will examine self-assessments at each of the follow-up interviews as affected by events (e.g., unemployment, arrest, shifts in marital status) occurring in the intervals between interviews.

[23] Characteristics were selected because they were policy relevant (e.g., TARP payments) or theoretically relevant.

TABLE 8.7

Twelve-Month Practical Adjustment Index Regressed on Selected Independent Variables

Independent variables	Texas		Georgia	
	b	SE	b	SE
Total TARP cash received all year ($)	0.002	0.002	0.001	0.002
Weeks worked all year	0.71**	0.09	0.86**	0.09
Total social security wages all year ($)	0.001	0.00	0.00	0.001
Total number of arrests all year	−1.81	1.30	−0.30	1.34
Weeks in jail/prison all year	0.28**	0.11	0.19	0.13
Weeks in hospital all year	−0.10	0.25	0.37	0.20
Money on hand at release ($)	0.001	0.001	0.009*	0.004
Parole[a]	1.55	2.24	3.41	2.54
Married at release[b]	1.72	3.15	3.18	3.27
Single at release[b]	−0.01	2.53	2.95	3.03
Number of times moved all year	−1.05*	0.52	−1.43*	0.68
Went to Dallas/Ft. Worth (Savannah)[c]	−6.47*	2.69	−2.26	5.63
Went to Houston at release (Atlanta)[c]	−6.14*	2.76	0.38	2.51
Male	−3.56	4.23	−0.50	4.93
Black[d]	−5.10*	2.39	−6.41**	2.45
Chicano[d]	−2.90	3.43		
Years of education	1.20*	0.55	1.02	0.55
Physical handicap at release[e]	−1.28	3.42	4.48	3.77
Total months ever incarcerated	−0.02	0.02	−0.06	0.05
Age in years	0.44**	0.15	0.24	0.16
Commuted sentence			3.18	2.39
Constant	36.39**	9.53	26.82**	9.66
R^2	.238**		.266**	
N	(728)		(637)	

[a] Compared to prisoners whose sentences were completed (dischargees).

[b] Compared to prisoners divorced, separated, or widowed at release.

[c] Compared to prisoners who claimed they were returning to any place other than Dallas/Ft. Worth (Savannah) or Houston (Atlanta) in the prerelease interview.

[d] Compared to whites.

[e] Compared to those claiming no physical handicap in the prerelease interview.

* $p \leq .05$, two-tailed test.
** $p \leq .01$, two-tailed test.

borne in mind that the adjustment indexes being analyzed here were taken at the end of the postrelease year, long after most of the eligibility periods had been exhausted. The effects of the payments, if any, are most likely to be found during the first 3 months of the year, when most of the participants assigned to Groups 1 through 3 were eligible for payments.

Table 8.8 presents the results of regressing the personal problems index scores on the same variables. Scores on this index were more poorly ac-

TABLE 8.8

Twelve-Month Personal Adjustment Index Regressed on
Selected Independent Variables

Independent variables	Texas		Georgia	
	b	*SE*	*b*	*SE*
Total TARP cash received all year ($)	−0.002	0.001	0.00	0.002
Weeks worked all year	0.15**	0.05	0.44**	0.09
Total social security wages all year ($)	0.00	0.00	0.00	0.001
Total number of arrests all year	−2.07**	0.74	−3.82**	1.31
Weeks in jail/prison all year	−0.06	0.06	0.05	0.13
Weeks in hospital all year	−0.22	0.15	0.20	0.19
Money on hand at release ($)	−0.001	0.001	0.004	0.004
Parole	0.35	1.28	4.21	2.48
Married at release	0.95	1.80	4.29	3.20
Single at release	0.59	1.44	2.26	3.00
Number of times moved all year	−0.80**	0.30	−1.13	0.66
Went to Dallas–Ft. Worth (Savannah) at release	4.34**	1.54	−12.09*	5.50
Went to Houston (Atlanta) at release	−0.99	1.58	3.61	2.45
Male	2.68	2.41	5.35	4.81
Black	0.73	1.37	−1.58	2.39
Chicano	−1.08	1.96		
Years of education	0.63*	0.31	−0.19	0.54
Physical handicap at release	−3.24	1.95	0.90	3.68
Total months ever incarcerated	−0.017	0.012	−0.001	0.04
Age in years	0.21**	0.08	0.05	0.15
Commuted sentence			1.36	2.34
Constant	46.72**	5.44	57.62**	9.44
R^2	.179**		.141**	
N	(724)		(632)	

* $p \leq .01$, two-tailed test.
** $p \leq .05$, two-tailed test.

counted for by the equation, R^2 values for Texas and Georgia being .18 and .14, respectively.

Several findings contained in this table were worth noting. First, in neither Georgia nor Texas did TARP payments make any difference in personal adjustment. TARP payments neither impeded nor facilitated self-assessments of personal adjustment. Second, employment was the strongest single determinant: the more weeks of employment, the higher the self-assessment of getting along on the personal level. Third, arrests (for whatever cause) lowered the personal problems index in both states. In short, a participant who worked during the postrelease year and who did not become entangled again with the law felt a lot better about himself at the end of the postrelease year.

The remaining determinants of personal adjustment vary in Georgia and Texas. The number of residential moves made lowers personal adjustment in Texas significantly. Being released to the Dallas–Fort Worth area increased personal adjustment as did being older and better educated. In contrast, going to Atlanta lowered personal adjustment among Georgia TARP participants, but nothing else in the equation seemed to make enough difference to cross thresholds of statistical significance.

About the most that can be made of these findings concerning self-assessments in the two states is that employment played a crucial role both in the practical adjustment and personal adjustment processes. The more weeks worked, the more easily solved were the practical problems of everyday life and the better TARP participants felt about themselves. It was also abundantly clear that if the TARP payments helped participants, they did not do so by raising either the participants' self-esteem or their sense of being able to come to grips with the practical problems of their lives.

ADJUSTMENT IN THE POSTRELEASE YEAR

The data presented in this chapter provide a description of how the released prisoners got along in certain areas of their lives and of their own assessments of their progress. There was a steady trend in the postrelease period toward independence from parental households, upon which ex-prisoners depended heavily during the period immediately after release. Ex-prisoners moved around a great deal, and during the last half of the year a third married and were living with their spouses.

The troubles ex-prisoners experienced were partially those involving employment, especially in the earliest period, with some difficulties in self-confidence. Large proportions experienced bouts of depression and feelings of being strange and awkward.

Perhaps the most important finding of this chapter is its additional emphasis on the importance of employment. The more weeks a member worked over the postrelease year, the better adjusted he felt himself to be both in practical and psychological terms. The fact that TARP payments did not have a similar effect indicates that it was probably not the earnings that derived from employment that made the difference; otherwise, payments should make up for some of the unemployment in the earlier periods of the year. Rather it appeared to be some other effects of employment. A person may be more than his work, but working appears to help a person feel better about himself.

9

Employment and Earnings

INTRODUCTION

As the account of the postprison lives of TARP members unfolds, the importance of employment looms ever larger. Especially important were the very positive effects of employment on arrest. The more a TARP member worked, the less likely he was to be arrested, as was shown in Chapter 5. We have also seen that employment made a difference in how the ex-prisoners felt about themselves and their adjustment problems: The more weeks worked, the more positive they felt. Of course, findings giving so much importance to employment are not unique to the TARP study. Almost all the literature on postprison adjustment provides abundant documentation that major obstacles to successful adjustment are the many difficulties ex-prisoners enounter in finding and holding jobs. Failures in the job market lead to recidivism.

The major reasons for such difficulties are obvious. A prison record is hardly an asset on the job market, especially in respect to the better jobs for which employers look more closely at past histories. But there are other problems as well. As Chapter 7 indicates, TARP members were not prime candidates for jobs at even the lowest skill levels, prison records or not. The skills they held were meager, as were their previous employment histories and levels of educational attainment. Perhaps even their marital statuses were handicaps, as employers may believe that married persons are more reliable workers than those who are single or who have experienced marital disruptions.

All these considerations lead one to expect that TARP members would have experienced difficulties connecting well with the labor market. It is understandable that finding jobs and holding them would have been serious problems for the ex-prisoners in the TARP study.

FINDING A JOB

Despite these obstacles, however, jobs for prisoners were not impossible to find. As Table 9.1 shows, 47% of Georgia's TARP members and 40% of Texas TARP members claimed in prerelease interviews to have had jobs arranged before being released from prison. As many criminologists have noted, some of these jobs may have been convenient fictions arranged by prisoners' friends and relatives in órder to meet the requirements of eligibility for parole.[1] Indeed, as Panel B of Table 9.1 shows, persons who were released on parole in each state were much more likely to have claimed an arranged job. Yet some of these jobs must have represented more than either conveniences or the products of wishful thinking.

Indeed, some of the TARP participants met with success almost immediately after release. As Table 9.2 shows, within the first 2 weeks one out of five Georgia members and two out of five Texas members were already on their first jobs. Within the first month and a half (7 weeks), 43% in Georgia and 67% in Texas had started on their first job. By the middle of the year, 62% in Georgia and 85% in Texas had started working at least once.

It was not as easy for all prisoners (or not all prisoners tried equally hard). At the end of the postrelease year, goodly proportions in both states had *never* started on any job: 29% in Georgia and 11% in Texas.

There are several patterns of particular interest in Table 9.2. First, it was clearly easier to get a job in Texas. One of the reasons for this difference was that Georgia TARP members were younger on the average and suffered from some of the unemployment disabilities of young people. But there were also motivational differences as well. Though a great majority of TARP members in both states aspired to obtain some type of job after release, a larger proportion of Georgia releasees either did not intend to look for work or had no particular type of job in mind, 8% in Georgia as compared to 1% in Texas. Finally, a major factor was the difference between the employment situations in Georgia and Texas. Men and women with these very meager employability characteristics were much more likely to be especially affected by the unemployment rate. As marginal workers or workers with marginally desirable characteristics, they were likely to be the last persons hired and the first fired as employers adjusted their work forces to production needs. In a tight labor market, as in Texas,

---

[1] In Texas, close to 60% of the jobs were arranged for by family or friends; in Georgia that proportion was 50%. Although both prison systems maintained some job-placement services, only very small minorities (less than 5%) obtained their postrelease-arranged job through such services. Former employers were also frequently cited as sources for the prearranged jobs, and a small minority also somehow obtained jobs on their own.

TABLE 9.1
Jobs Arranged at Time of Release

| | Percentage of participants | | | |
| | Georgia | | Texas | |
	Parole	Discharge	Parole	Discharge
A. *Job arrangements by type of discharge*				
Job arranged	66	38	53	24
No job arranged	34	66	47	76
100%	(324)	(638)	(509)	(466)
B. *Prearranged jobs*				
Job arranged before release	47		31	
Job tentatively arranged			9	
No job arranged	53		60	
No job arranged but does not intend to work			1	
100%	(963)		(975)	

SOURCE: Prerelease interviews.

TABLE 9.2
Number of Weeks from Release to First Employment

| | Georgia | | Texas | |
	Percentage	Cumulative percent	Percentage	Cumulative percent
Number of weeks to first employment				
Less than 2 weeks	21	21	41	41
2 to 3 weeks	10	31	14	55
4 to 5 weeks	7	38	7	62
6 to 7 weeks	5	43	5	67
8 to 9 weeks	3	46	3	70
10 to 13 weeks	5	51	6	76
14 to 26 weeks	11	62	9	85
27 to 51 weeks	9	71	4	89
Never held a job in frst year after release	29	100	11	100
100%	(976)		(965)	
Average number of weeks to first job (for those who obtained at least one job in first year)	10.0 weeks		6.4 weeks	
Median number of weeks to first job (for those who obtained at least one job in first year)	5.2 weeks		2.7 weeks	

SOURCE: Follow-up interviews.

TARP members fared quite well; in Georgia they did not do nearly as well.

Table 9.3 presents unemployment rates separately for the postrelease destinations planned by 5% or more of TARP members. Overall in this period, Georgia unemployment rates were at least 50% higher than those in Texas. In particular, Atlanta's rates (to which about a third of Georgia TARP members went upon release) were almost twice those of Houston in 1976 and still more than 50% higher in 1977. Indeed, the two most frequent postrelease destinations of Georgia TARP members, Atlanta and Savannah, each had unemployment rates in 1976 and 1977 that were higher than the more common home destinations of Texas TARP members. Only in San Antonio did unemployment rates reach the same magnitude as in Atlanta or Savannah.

There are very good reasons to believe that TARP members' employment would have been quite sensitive to the unemployment rates in the cities to which they were released, and especially sensitive to decreases in such rates when the initial rate was low. TARP members were marginal workers who had poor skills and lacked experience. It is to be expected that their employability would have gone up drastically as the labor market became increasingly tight from the employer viewpoint. After all, when the last man has been hired, it is because the end of the line has been reached. Ex-prisoners tend to be on the tail of the queue.

A second point to note in the findings of Table 9.2 is that many TARP members were able to find jobs within very short periods of time after release. One of five of Georgia's TARP members were employed within 2 weeks and one in three of Texas participants were at work in that period.

TABLE 9.3
Average Unemployment Rates in Texas and Georgia,
1976 and 1977

	1976	1977
Georgia		
Atlanta	8.21	7.09
Savannah	8.4	6.8
Remainder of Georgia	7.94	7.33
Texas		
Houston	4.5	4.5
Dallas–Fort Worth	5.68	4.85
San Antonio	7.5	7.0
Remainder of Texas	5.22	4.92

Source: State Employment Services.

TABLE 9.4
Number of Weeks to First Job, by Experimental Groups

	Georgia			Texas		
Experimental group	Average number of weeks[a]	Percentage who never held job	N	Average number of weeks[a]	Percentage who never held job	N
Group 1: Eligibility for 26 weeks	26.7	35	(157)	16.6	18	(173)
Groups 2 and 3: Eligibility for 13 weeks	21.3	14	(370)	11.7	10	(392)
Groups 4 and 5: No payment eligibility	14.3	17	(367)	8.5	9	(400)

[a] Averaged over all TARP participants in relevant experimental groups, including those who never held job during first year (arbitrarily given 52 weeks as time to first job). These averages are undoubtedly an underestimate of time to first job after release since persons still never employed at the end of the postrelease year have undoubtedly experienced unemployment beyond the end of their first anniversary of release. Differences between experimental and control groups in both states are highly significant statistically. ($p < .0001$).

Subsequent periods did not produce increments that large to the proportion who had started on at least one job.

Finally, we may note the average work experiences for those who did get at least one job. In Georgia the average number of weeks unemployed before working was 10 weeks, with a median number of weeks of 5.2. In Texas, the corresponding numbers were considerably smaller, an average of 6.4 weeks and a median of 2.7 weeks to first jobs.

The work-disincentive effects of the TARP payments apparently acted at least partially by lengthening the periods of unemployment before first jobs, as Table 9.4 indicates. In Georgia, those who were offered 26 weeks of TARP payment eligibility were out of work for an average number of 26.7 weeks before getting their first jobs. In Texas the average number of weeks to first job for the same group was 16.6. Those in the experimental groups who were offered 13 weeks of TARP payment eligibility were unemployed 21.3 and 11.7 weeks before their first jobs in Georgia and Texas, respectively. In contrast, control group TARP members, who were offered no payments, went 14.3 and 8.5 weeks to their first jobs in Georgia and Texas, respectively.[2]

---

[2] These average weeks to first employment are considerably higher in Table 9.4 when compared to Table 9.2. These discrepancies arise because persons who never went to work during the postrelease year were given the arbitrary time to first job of 52 weeks in the computations of Table 9.4. They were omitted entirely in the computations of Table 9.2. Either way of

By themselves, these findings do not necessarily mean that TARP payments acted as work disincentives. TARP members in payment groups may have been using the resulting freedom from pressing economic need to engage in a more leisurely search for better jobs at higher wage rates. However, there is more than a slight hint in Table 9.4 that such was not entirely the case. Among TARP members who were eligible for 26 weeks of payments, 35% in Georgia and 18% in Texas never held any jobs at all during the postrelease year. For those eligible for 13 weeks of payments, the corresponding proportions who never held jobs were 14% in Georgia and 10% in Texas. In contrast, among control-group TARP members who were not eligible for any payments, only 17% in Georgia and 9% in Texas never held any jobs in the postrelease year. In short, TARP payments appeared to operate as work disincentives at least for some participants. Furthermore, the disincentive effects persisted throughout the year, and for some persons, went beyond the point at which they had exhausted their benefit eligibilities.

Getting a job is only part of the battle, and most TARP participants won at least that preliminary skirmish. Keeping jobs and remaining employed in one or another job are other major parts of the battle. Table 9.5 presents the number of weeks worked by TARP members throughout the year following release.[3] On the average, Georgia TARP participants worked 18.4 weeks, or 35% of the time. As we will see consistently throughout this section, Texas TARP members did much better, working an average of 26.2 weeks, or about 50% of the time.

The postrelease employment records of TARP participants were hardly encouraging. Being employed half the time or less could hardly have produced much income, especially given the kinds of jobs TARP participants were likely to hold. Not only was it difficult for TARP participants to get hired; they also had difficulties working steadily.

Table 9.6 shows the average numbers of jobs held by TARP members in each of five time periods. These time periods were formed by breaking the postrelease year into the first 6 weeks after release, the next 7 weeks, the second quarter of the year, and the last 6 months. The final time

---

handling those who never went to work leads to somewhat unsatisfactory results: If omitted, the average is misleadingly low; if added as 52 weeks, the average is still lower than likely actuality since some of those who did not obtain jobs in the postrelease year may still not have obtained jobs. Either way leads to underestimations, although the averages shown in Table 9.4 are less of an underestimation than those shown in Table 9.2.

[3] It should be noted that Table 9.6 contains only persons from whom complete follow-up interview sets were available. Hence, only 752 persons were available under this restriction in Georgia and 935 in Texas.

TABLE 9.5
Weeks Worked in Postrelease Year

	Georgia	Texas
Did not work at all	24%	11%
Worked less than 13 weeks	19%	19%
Worked 14 to 26 weeks	27%	20%
Worked 27 to 39 weeks	16%	19%
Worked 40 to 52 weeks	14%	31%
100%	(752)[a]	(935)[a]
Average number of weeks worked in year	18.4	26.2
Median number of weeks worked in year	16.0	26.6

SOURCE: All follow-up interviews in both states.

[a] N consists of persons from whom information on employment was available for every week of the postrelease year.

period shown in Table 9.6 is the entire postrelease year. It can be anticipated from the rather large proportions who never worked at all during the year that in any one time period the number of jobs held was quite small. Compared to Georgia, Texas TARP members held more jobs in every time period, but mainly because more of them were employed. In each time period, except for the total year, most TARP members held one job, if they were employed at all.

Over the entire year, employed TARP members held about two and one-third jobs in Texas and one and one-third jobs in Georgia. It is difficult to calibrate these numbers against what might be expected for "normal" members of the labor forces of their respective states. On one hand, excessive labor mobility can be a sign of employment in casual labor or tem-

TABLE 9.6
Number of Jobs Held by TARP Members in Postrelease Year

	Texas			Georgia		
	Average number[a]	Percentage holding one job	N	Average number[a]	Percentage holding one job	N
First 6 weeks	.74	83	(971)	.50	73	(897)
Next 7 weeks	1.18	82	(975)	.61	72	(897)
14 to 26 weeks	1.00	70	(966)	.74	66	(801)
Last 6 months	1.14	60	(936)	1.05	52	(779)
Entire year	2.32	28	(833)	1.37	43	(692)

SOURCE: Follow-up interviews.

[a] Computed as a proportion of those who held at least one job during the period in question.

porary jobs and, hence, can be another indicator of hard times for TARP members. On the other hand, job changes are means of enhancing one's employment situation; thus, moderate amounts of job mobility may be indicators of upgrading. Indeed, the signs appear to suggest the latter rather than the former interpretation. Texas TARP members, who by and large did better than their Georgia counterparts, were more likely to change jobs and less likely to have held only one job throughout the postrelease year. It seems as if Georgia TARP members had a more difficult time finding jobs and also experienced a correspondingly more difficult time moving from one job to another in search of better opportunities.

A still different view of employment throughout the postrelease year can be obtained by examining average weeks worked and the proportion of participants who did not work at all in each of four periods following release. For each of the time periods, Table 9.7 presents three statistics—the average number of weeks worked during a period, the proportion of time worked during that period, and the proportion of persons who did not work at all. Panel A of Table 9.7 presents findings for the entire TARP contingents in each of the two states. Several trends stand out. First, as usual, Texas TARP participants worked more weeks in each period; they also worked a larger proportion of the time in each period, and the proportions who did not work at all were smaller. Second, there was a trend in each state for TARP members to work greater proportions of the time during each successive time period, the proportions rising from 38% to 53% in Texas and 25% to 36% in Georgia.[4] Some steps toward obtaining steady employment were clearly being made by TARP members as a whole.

In Panels B, C, and D of Table 9.7 the statistics are shown separately for experimental groups as compared to controls.[5] Evidence of the work-disincentive effects of TARP payments is fairly clear in these three panels. Experimental groups given 26 weeks of payment eligibility worked less in every period; they also worked a smaller proportion of the time and contained larger proportions of persons who never worked in that period. Those eligible for 13 weeks of payments worked a bit more than those eligible for 26 weeks but much less than controls, who were not eligible for any payments. Finally, control group members in both states worked more

---

[4] This trend actually underestimates the proportion of time worked by those who were eligible to work. Since as time went on some TARP members ended up back in prison and others became disabled or were in the hospital for significant periods of time, the base of work-eligible persons declined.

[5] The two 13-week-eligibility payment groups (2 and 3) have been combined for this purpose as well as groups 4 and 5, the two nonpayment groups. Thus, this table facilitates the comparison between the two lengths of eligibility (26 and 13 weeks) and payment groups versus nonpayment groups.

TABLE 9.7
Weeks Worked in Various Periods of Postrelease Year for All TARP Members and by Experimental Group

TARP group and period	Texas				Georgia			
	Average weeks worked	Percentage of time worked	Percentage who did not work	N	Average weeks worked	Percentage of time worked	Percentage who did not work	N
A. All TARP members								
First 6 weeks	2.3	38	38	(971)	1.5	25	59	(897)
Next 7 weeks	3.4	48	35	(971)	2.3	33	55	(897)
14 to 26 weeks	6.8	52	26	(966)	4.5	35	45	(824)
Last 6 months	13.8	53	25	(936)	9.4	36	42	(852)
Entire year	26.2	50	11	(935)	18.4	35	24	(752)
B. Group 1: Eligibility for 26 payments								
First 6 weeks	1.8	30	49	(174)	1.0	17	72	(167)
Next 7 weeks	2.2	31	52	(174)	1.4	20	72	(167)
14 to 26 weeks	4.5	35	43	(174)	2.5	19	68	(157)
Last 6 months	12.4	48	29	(169)	6.8	26	53	(152)
Entire year	20.8	40	19	(169)	12.3	24	40	(142)
C. Groups 2 and 3: Eligibility for 13 payments								
First 6 weeks	2.0	33	44	(398)	1.1	18	67	(374)
Next 7 weeks	3.1	44	50	(398)	1.9	27	63	(374)
14 to 26 weeks	7.1	55	22	(395)	4.3	33	45	(342)
Last 6 months	13.7	53	24	(380)	10.0	38	39	(350)
Entire year	25.9	50	10	(380)	17.6	34	23	(310)
D. Groups 4 and 5: Control groups: no payments								
First 6 weeks	2.9	48	27	(399)	2.2	37	44	(356)
Next 7 weeks	4.2	60	22	(399)	3.2	46	39	(356)
14 to 26 weeks	7.5	58	23	(397)	5.8	45	33	(325)
Last 6 months	14.5	56	24	(387)	10.0	38	39	(350)
Entire year	28.9	56	8	(386)	22.0	42	17	(300)

weeks, worked a greater proportion of the time, and contained fewer persons who did not work at all.

All TARP participants experienced extremely high rates of unemployment. In Texas, over the entire postrelease year, TARP members worked about 50% of the time, and 11% had no employment at all. In Georgia, TARP participants worked, on the average, only 35% of the time, and 24% never found work (or never looked). Experimental groups receiving payments experienced even greater levels of unemployment. Group 1 (26 weeks of TARP-payment eligibility) worked only 40% of the time in Texas and 24% of the time in Georgia. Groups 2 and 3 (13 weeks of eligibility) worked 50% of the time in Texas and 34% of the time in Georgia. Those not eligible for any payments (controls) were employed for 56% of the year in Texas and 42% of the year in Georgia.

Although in Table 9.7 a trend may be discerned that apparently indicates increasing proportions of time spent in work as the year progresses, this trend was to some degree underestimated. TARP members spent significant amounts of time too sick to work or in the hospital (as shown in Chapter 8); they also spent significant amounts of time in jail or prison in the postrelease year. Since a person who is either in jail or in the hospital is not able to work, a more appropriate calculation of proportions of time spent working would take these two factors into account. It is especially appropriate to do so since, as the year goes on, increasingly larger proportions of TARP members end up back in prison and hence should not be counted among those who are eligible for work.

The proportions of time spent working, corrected for time spent in the hospital or in jail, are shown in Table 9.8. Here the trends toward in-

TABLE 9.8
Proportion of Time Available Spent Working

| | Proportion of time worked | | | |
| | Georgia | | Texas | |
All TARP Members	Proportion	N	Proportion	N
First 6 weeks	.254	(897)	.390	(966)
Next 7 weeks	.336	(897)	.500	(966)
14 to 26 weeks	.379	(795)	.557	(936)
Last 6 months	.462	(770)	.596	(886)
Entire year	.328	(743)	.570	(883)

SOURCE: Follow-up interviews.

NOTE: Time available is defined as total time during the period specified less weeks spent in hospital and/or in jail or prison.

creasing proportions of time worked were more pronounced, as one would expect, as compared to the proportions in Table 9.7. In particular, note that in the last 6 months of the year, Georgia TARP members spent 46.2% of eligible time working, and Texas members spent 59.6% of the time working. In short, for those who managed to stay out of prison, employment increased with time. Alternatively, those who managed to get jobs also may have managed to stay out of trouble with the law. The intricacies of this mutual interaction between work and criminal activity are at the heart of the counterbalancing theory of TARP effects described in Chapters 5 and 11.

EARNINGS FROM EMPLOYMENT

It is quite critical to consider the returns from working obtained by TARP members. Since employment for this group competes with illegitimate activities, the competitive strength of employment needs to be measured. The TARP data bases provided two independent ways to estimate employment earnings received by TARP members in the postrelease year. The follow-up interviews probed weekly wages received from each of the jobs recorded, providing a record of earnings based essentially on respondent reports. Estimates of earnings are also provided by the employment service system's files, which contain amounts earned by each TARP member who provided a valid social security number and who worked in employment that was covered by unemployment insurance taxes.

Both estimates each leave much to be desired in the way of accuracy and coverage. Indeed, as will be shown later in this section, the two sets of reports do not fit very well with each other.

The wage data obtained from the follow-up interviews suffered from a number of defects, each of which contributed to some degree to the problems that arise in dealing with these data. First, there is some ambiguity over whether the "recalled earnings" (as these data will be called in this chapter) refer to gross or net earnings, essentially the difference between income before or after deductions. In each of the follow-up interviews, persons who had worked during the previous period were asked how much they had earned as weekly wages on each of the jobs held. In Texas, interviewers had been instructed to obtain gross earnings, but in Georgia apparently no specific instructions were given. As a consequence, the earnings differences between Georgia and Texas TARP members are confounded with these possible differences in measurement. Second, the information asked for in the interviews was some *estimate* of weekly wages, not wages actually earned, which could have varied from week to week depending on hours worked and amount of overtime. Given the types of jobs held by TARP members, which tend ordinarily to vary considerably in those two respects, the weekly wage measure is subject to some ambiguity. This is so whether it is some sort of informal average over the length of time the job in question was held or whether it is wages that would have been earned for a full week of work without overtime, or some other kind of "average." Finally, there are the usual problems of recalled data, subject to memory error, especially for events that took place months before the time of the interview. The consequences of these method defects is that the recalled earnings estimate of employment earnings is subject to some error that is likely to be large.

The second source of earnings information comes from the wage files of the unemployment benefit systems of each of the states. These files are generated from quarterly reports of employers whose contributions to taxes on employees' earnings help to support the unemployment benefit system. These files record the gross earnings of individuals during each calendar quarter. Wages of individuals are filed by social security number. These files are used routinely by the Employment Security Agency to determine the eligibility of persons applying for unemployment benefits.

The defects of the unemployment insurance (UI) wage files are also potentially large and difficult to estimate. First of all, matching these files with TARP members was successful only when a valid social security number was available for a TARP member. In some cases, such numbers were not available. In other cases, social security numbers may have been recorded incorrectly by prison clerks either by error or because the TARP member made recall errors. In still other cases, several social security numbers may be held by a TARP member under various aliases. In addition, some employers attempt to evade paying UI taxes by paying wages in cash, contracting with employees as if they were subcontractors (taxicab drivers, for example, are often paid that way), or simply by filing false returns. Given the types of employment of TARP members, it is likely that at least some would find employment with firms on the edge of legality. Finally, the wages recorded in the UI wage files are aggregated for calendar quarters, time periods that did not coincide with the postrelease year. This made it necessary to make arbitrary adjustments to obtain estimates of UI wages for the postrelease year and for subperiods within that year.

It was difficult to decide whether recalled or UI wages constituted the better source of information about the employment earnings of TARP members. The data from the two sources are not consistent, as Table 9.9 indicates. The total amounts of recalled wages were higher in both states, slightly more than 1.6 times greater. The correlations computed between the two sources also left much to be desired, R^2 being .24 in Georgia and

TABLE 9.9

Comparisons between Unemployment Insurance Wages
and Recalled Earnings over Total Postrelease Year

	Georgia	Texas
A. Estimated average annual earnings		
Average UI wages	$1339	$2618
Average recalled earnings	2230	4180
Regression of UI wages on recalled earnings		
b	.494	.526
SE	.0288	.025
Intercept	344.4	419.49
SE	92.7	139.09
$R^2 = .244$	.244	.336
$N = 747$	(747)	(907)
B. Estimated average weekly earning		
UI wages	$ 85	$101
Recalled earnings	141	157

SOURCES: Follow-up interviews and UI wage files.

NOTE: Computations were made for persons for whom both total recalled earnings and UI wages were available. Thus averages vary from those shown in other tables that are based on larger portions of Georgia and Texas TARP groups.

.34 in Texas. Because of the differences in the time periods involved, very high correlations between the two sources were not to be expected. However, these correlations were too low to be accounted for by that factor alone.

Particularly distressing was the fact that UI earnings were lower than recalled earnings. Since there is some reason to suspect that persons in payment groups might have withheld some information on earnings in order to cover up for some payments received while working and that persons might have reported net rather than gross earnings through misunderstanding, one would expect that recalled earnings would have tended to be smaller than UI earnings.

Inspection of the scatter plots of the two variables brought to light that much of the problem was caused by UI wage files that registered zero earnings when recalled wages indicated otherwise. Such would be the case if incorrect social security numbers were used in searching the UI wage files. The files would falsely register no wages when in fact the TARP member in question actually had had some earnings. While it would have been possible to remedy this defect by eliminating all persons with zero wages in the UI file, such a move would also have removed persons who actually had had no wages and whose correct social security number was at hand. Given these problems we have decided to use the recalled wages as the basis for the discussion in this chapter.[6]

Panel C of Table 9.9 contains estimates of the average weekly earnings of members for each of the states based on the two data sources. Georgia TARP members earned either $85 per week or $141 depending on whether you believe the UI wages or recalled earnings. The corresponding estimates for Texas were $101 and $157. *It should be noted that any and all of the estimates indicate that TARP members earned very little over the post-release year.* These low earnings were, to a very large extent, due to high rates of unemployment, as the previous section of this chapter indicated. However, low earnings also indicated that wage rates were low.

Given the patterns of unemployment described and the low occupational skills of TARP members, it can be anticipated that their annual recalled earnings would not be high. Indeed, as Table 9.10 shows, on the average TARP members earned considerably less over the year than the poverty-level amounts for either single or married persons. Georgia TARP members earned an average of $2230; Texas members earned $4120 (shown in Panel A of Table 9.10). Note that median earnings were considerably lower than the averages, reflecting in large part the fact that large proportions of persons in each state had zero or very low earnings (representing, of course, the levels of work effort described in the preceding section).

TARP members who were eligible for payments earned considerably less than control group members, especially in the early periods when they were apparently using up their benefit eligibility. The reader will note that this pattern is another manifestation of the disincentive effect of payments on work.

Of course, earnings were not the only source of income for TARP members. Those in the experimental groups that were eligible for benefits could and did receive payments in significant amounts. To obtain another measure of their total average incomes, we have added together average recalled earnings and average TARP payments (see Chapter 4) to form estimates of total annual income, as shown in Table 9.11.[7]

The findings of Table 9.11 are rather surprising. They indicate that TARP participants in groups that received payment eligibility had slightly larger incomes than control-group members. In Georgia the benefits pro-

---

[6] In Chapter 13 we use the UI wage files, but only for persons who have some wages registered for the postrelease year.

[7] It should be noted that there may well be other sources of income that should be added, including support in money or kind from spouses and relatives, other forms of transfer payments (e.g., welfare, veterans' benefits, etc.) as well as income derived from interest payments, illegal transactions, and the like. No attempt was made to measure these other sources of income.

TABLE 9.10
*Recalled Earnings for All TARP Participants
and Experimental Groups, by Period*

	Georgia			Texas		
	Average total earnings	Median total earnings	N	Average total earnings	Median total earnings	N
A. All TARP Members						
First 6 weeks	$ 176	$ 0	(897)	$ 309	$ 158	(971)
Next 7 weeks	276	0	(897)	483	339	(971)
14 to 26 weeks	554	72	(824)	1005	857	(966)
Last 6 months	1164	380	(852)	2330	1763	(936)
Entire year	2230	1550	(752)	4120	3233	(935)
B. Group 1: 26 weeks' eligibility						
First 6 weeks	$ 108	$ 0.05	(167)	$ 242	$ 17	(174)
Next 7 weeks	163	0.17	(167)	311	0	(174)
14 to 26 weeks	302	0.00	(157)	666	77	(174)
Last 6 months	838	1.31	(152)	2147	1255	(169)
Entire year	1472	602	(142)	3335	2404	(169)
C. Groups 2 and 3: 13 weeks' eligibility						
First 6 weeks	$ 128	$ 0.0	(374)	$ 254	$ 49	(398)
Next 7 weeks	226	0.1	(374)	434	219	(398)
14 to 26 weeks	529	45.7	(342)	1057	945	(395)
Last 6 months	1250	480	(350)	2343	1731	(380)
Entire year	2169	1500	(310)	4100	3471	(380)
D. Groups 4 and 5: No payment eligibility						
First 6 weeks	$ 259	$ 98	(356)	$ 394	$ 357	(399)
Next 7 weeks	380	193	(356)	607	603	(399)
14 to 26 weeks	703	503	(325)	1101	1004	(397)
Last six months	1221	500	(350)	2398	2114	(387)
Entire year	2652	2040	(300)	4483	4029	(386)

SOURCE: Follow-up interviews.

vided a difference of about $400 in total income in favor of the treatment groups (1 through 3). In Texas, Group 1 participants had total incomes that were almost $100 more than control-group members, and Group 2 and 3 members received about $300 more. In short, TARP payments more than made up for earnings lost because of lowered levels of work effort.

In addition, since the TARP payments were considerably below average weekly earnings in each state, there is some evidence in these findings that

TABLE 9.11
Totals of Earnings and Payments for Postrelease Year

| | Georgia | | Texas | |
	Average	N	Average	N
Group 1: 26 weeks of eligibility	$2908	(142)	$4571	(169)
Group 2 and 3: 13 weeks of eligibility	3006	(310)	4798	(380)
Groups 4 and 5: Controls— no payments	2653	(300)	4483	(386)
All TARP participants	2847	(752)	4627	(935)

SOURCE: Follow-up interviews and payment files.

TARP members in the experimental groups, when they worked, earned better wages than persons in the control groups. The freedom from absolute want that was provided by TARP payments apparently allowed those in the experimental groups to find better jobs. Indeed, as is shown in Chapter 13, such was the case.

EMPLOYMENT AND EARNINGS CONDITIONAL ON WORK

The findings shown thus far concerning work and wages were based on averages computed over all participants from whom we had apparently valid data. In many cases these averages were not necessarily typical, being unduly influenced by extreme values. In particular, average incomes, wages, and weeks worked were very much influenced by the fact that many TARP participants registered essentially zero on all the measures in question. Indeed, a very good case can be made that TARP participants divide themselves into two main groups: those who did not manage to make *any* job arrangements during the postrelease year, and those who found some sort of work. Mixing the two groups together in the same calculations produces measures of central tendencies that are representative of neither.

Table 9.12 presents some work measures computed only for persons who were employed at some time during the postrelease year, omitting from the calculations those who did not work at all during that period. Panel A shows average and median numbers of weeks employed during the postrelease year. It may be noted that the work-disincentive effect was not quite as strong among those who worked at all. Group 1 members in Georgia and Texas worked about 6 weeks less than controls. This finding hints that a major portion of the disincentive effect was manifested in in-

TABLE 9.12
Selected Work Measures for TARP Participants
Ever Employed in Postrelease Year

	Georgia			Texas		
	Average	Median	N	Average	Median	N
A. *Weeks employed*						
All TARP Members	24.0	23.0	(574)	29.4	30.4	(833)
Group 1 (26 weeks)	20.6	20.0	(85)	25.6	23.9	(137)
Groups 2 and 3 (13 weeks)	22.7	22.0	(240)	28.8	29.3	(342)
Groups 4 and 5 (No payments)	26.5	26.0	(249)	31.5	34.7	(354)
B. *Total wages*						
All TARP Members	$2922	$2439	(574)	$4624	$4034	(833)
Group 1 (26 weeks)	2459	1960	(85)	4114	3029	(137)
Groups 2 and 3 (13 weeks)	2801	2242	(240)	4556	4031	(342)
Groups 4 and 5 (No payments)	3196	2850	(249)	4889	4461	(354)
C. *Average weekly wages*						
All TARP Members	$115	$112	(574)	$146	$128	(833)
Group 1 (26 weeks)	111	114	(85)	150	136	(137)
Groups 2 and 3 (13 weeks)	116	111	(240)	146	130	(342)
Groups 4 and 5 (No payments)	116	113	(249)	145	126	(354)
D. *Weeks to first job*						
All TARP members	10.2	4.6	(574)	6.5	2.2	(833)
Group 1 (26 weeks)	12.1	5.9	(85)	9.0	2.9	(137)
Groups 2 and 3 (13 weeks)	13.9	9.1	(240)	7.5	3.1	(342)
Groups 4 and 5 (No payments)	6.0	2.4	(249)	4.6	1.8	(354)
E. *TARP payments*						
Group 1 (26 weeks)	$1430	$1820	(85)	$1245	$1226	(137)
Groups 2 and 3 (13 weeks)	836	910	(240)	703	704	(342)
F. *Number of TARP payments*						
Group 1 (26 weeks)	21.2	25.6	(85)	20.5	25.7	(137)
Groups 2 and 3 (13 weeks)	13.2	13.2	(240)	12.8	13.3	(342)

NOTE: Measures are based on TARP members who were employed at least once during the postrelease period.

creasing the numbers of persons who did not work at all. As usual, Texas members worked a larger proportion of the time than their counterparts in Georgia.

The remainder of Table 9.12 presents no surprises. The figures shown are different from those calculated over the entire TARP group and in the directions expected. The closest to a striking finding is the considerable difference between the two state contingents in time to first job. TARP members who worked in Texas got to their first job on the average much sooner than Georgia members—6.5 weeks as compared to 10.2. Typically, it took 2.5 months for Georgia members to find their first job and only 1.5 months for Texas members.[8]

Also, we may note that TARP members who worked received quite significant increases in total income (wages and payments) when they were eligible for payments—close to $500 additional income for Group 1 and about $350 for Groups 2 and 3. This increment added about 14% to the total income for Group 1 in Georgia and 10% to Groups 2 and 3 in that state; the comparable percentages for Texas members were 10% and 8%, respectively.

Finally, the readers' attention is directed to the average wages received by TARP members. These weekly wage rates reflect annual incomes of about $6000 a year in Georgia and close to $8000 per year in Texas, assuming steady work over a 52-week period. At that level, the jobs were clearly, on the average, below the poverty level for single persons in that region. But, they were not jobs in which an incumbent can expect steady employment for a full year; hence, earnings in fact fell considerably below full annual earnings.

CONTROL GROUPS: DETERMINANTS
OF EMPLOYMENT

For the TARP participants who were eligible for payments, the effect of the payments on work and wages appears to be strong. Any analysis of work in those groups (1, 2, and 3) will have to take into account the impact of payments on work effort. We will pursue those issues in detail in the next section, in which the counterbalancing theory will be tested.

For the present, however, it is appropriate to consider some findings concerning employment in the control groups, whose members did not receive any payment. Because they were unaffected by any payments, the experiences of Groups 4 and 5 can be regarded as representative of how prisoners released from the state prison systems of Georgia and Texas typically fare in the year beyond release.[9]

---

[8] The perceptive reader will note that the average weeks to first job presented in Table 9.12 varies from the figures presented in earlier tables, especially Table 9.2. These differences reflect the fact that different case bases are involved in the computations. In particular, Table 9.2 presents data on all TARP participants, showing weeks to first job ever recorded for a participant. In contrast, the computations in Table 9.12 are computed only for those for whom all interviews were completed. These discrepancies are a dramatic illustration of the sensitivity of findings to the amount of missing data, particularly in the Georgia data set.

[9] Although Group 4 did receive an experimental treatment, namely job placement, they did not receive any payments and hence can be regarded as controls in this context.

In Table 9.13 we present an analysis of what determined how quickly TARP members in Georgia and Texas found their first jobs.[10] In the multiple-regression analysis presented in that table, the dependent variable is "number of weeks to first job." The regression coefficients indicate how each of the independent variables affects number of weeks to first job. Thus, the coefficient .388 for age in Georgia is to be interpreted as follows: For each additional year of age, a TARP member in Georgia took .388 weeks longer to find a job, holding everything else in the table constant. Coefficients which are statistically significant are starred (*) in the table. Those that cannot be statistically distinguished from zero are not starred. The independent variables were selected on two grounds. First, there should be good reason—on theoretical or prior-knowledge grounds —why a variable should be related to employment. Second, variables that were present in more or less the same form in the data bases of the two states were also selected in order to enhance the comparability of analyses for the two states.

Several findings stand out. First, only modest success can be claimed for the ability of this set of variables to predict how long it took a TARP member to land a first job. The R^2 statistic at the bottom of the table is .236 for Texas and .145 for Georgia. While these values are statistically quite distinguishable from zero, their sizes indicate that there are a great many factors that determine length of time to first employment that are not included here.[11]

A second set of findings concerns the sign patterns of coefficients. For comparable independent variables the signs were almost always identical in the two states, indicating that characteristics of TARP members tended to act in a consistent manner in both TARP states.[12] A major exception, of

---

[10] The analyses in Tables 9.13 and 9.14 are presented mainly to fill out the presentation in this chapter. In fact they do not fit the theoretical model for the experiment. They differ slightly from results that we will present in chapter 12, which is based on the theoretical model outlined in Chapter 5 (and presented in greater detail in Chapter 11). Fortunately not too much distortion is presented in the analyses. In addition, the dependent variables "weeks to first employment" and "total weeks worked" are truncated by the fact that no case can be less than zero, a condition that lumps a large number of cases at that point. Attempts to take this truncation effect into account and to adjust for it are discussed in Chapters 11 and 12, in which the full structural forms of the TARP model are presented along with better versions of the reduced forms of which Tables 9.13 and 9.14 are examples.

[11] It should be pointed out that measurement error also plays a role in lowering R^2. Indeed, the major difference between Georgia and Texas may be largely due to the fact that the Georgia data set has many more missing values and, more generally, shows that measurements were taken in a less careful fashion in that state.

[12] In the two cases where signs differ, one of the coefficients could not be considered statistically significant.

TABLE 9.13
Regression of Weeks to First Job on Selected Prerelease
Characteristics: Groups 4 and 5 Only

Independent variables	Control groups			
	Texas		Georgia	
	b	SE	b	SE
Age (years)	.019	.082	.388**	.135
Male	−14.459***	2.72	−12.05**	5.11
Black	4.458**	1.53	−.867	2.45
Chicanos	4.336*	2.072		
Education (years)	−.160	.348	−.601	.489
Married	−.011	1.89	−.510	2.83
Number of previous convictions (Texas)/Number of years of prior confinement (Georgia)	.080	.091	.445	1.05
Gate money	.000	.001	.003	.006
Handicap prison classification	7.363**	2.257	−.119	3.78
Houston/Atlanta	−4.671**	1.444	−.485	2.54
Postrelease job arranged[a]	−.209**	.067	−7.46**	2.56
Expected number of weeks to first job	2.819***	.760	2.70*	1.31
Total PIP points/prison security code[b]	−.0367	.023	.055	1.17
Constant	16.689*	6.50	23.59*	9.65
R^2	.236***		.145**	
N	(397)		(231)	

NOTE: Dependent variable = number of weeks to employment on first job postrelease.

[a] Coded in Texas data as gradation of certainty about postrelease job arrangements. Georgia code is a dummy variable (1 = job arranged; 0 = not arranged).
[b] Texas prison system points given for good conduct, work within the system, etc. Code for Georgia is degree of security classification within prison, ranging from minimum security to maximum security.

* $p < .05$
** $p < .01$
*** $p < .001$

course, is the difference between Houston and Atlanta as home destinations of the released prisoners. TARP members going to Houston managed to get jobs almost a month sooner than other Texas TARP members. The reader may recall that the difference in unemployment rates between Houston and other parts of Texas are consistent with this finding. In contrast, Georgia prisoners returning to Atlanta did not fare any better (or worse) than those with other destinations in Georgia, a finding that is also consistent with the unemployment rates for places in Georgia, discussed earlier in this chapter.

Third, one may note a set of specific findings: In Texas, males went to

TABLE 9.14

Regression of Weeks Worked in Postrelease Year on Selected
Prerelease Characteristics: Groups 4 and 5 Only

	Control groups			
	Texas		Georgia	
Independent variables	b	SE	b	SE
Age (years)	.171	.100	.030	.131
Male	10.741**	3.35	8.52	4.95
Black	−4.493*	1.89	−0.64	2.37
Chicanos	−1.545	2.57		
Education (years)	1.080*	.429	.549	.474
Married	3.000	2.32	3.33	2.74
Number previous convictions	−.239*	.112	−.461	.914
Gate money	.000	.001	−.011	.006
Handicap prison classification	−5.67*	2.78	−3.9	3.15
Houston/Atlanta	2.74	1.78	3.21	2.46
Postrelease job[a] arranged	−4.37**	.934	5.40*	2.48
Expected number weeks to first job	−.192**	.082	−1.39	1.27
Total PIP points[b]	−.077**	.028	−.845	1.13
Constant	8.98	7.99	9.36	9.36
R^2	.219***		.107[a]	
N	(384)		(231)	

NOTE: Dependent variable = total weeks worked in postrelease year.

[a] Coded in Texas data as gradations of certainty about postrelease job arrangements. Georgia code is dummy (1 = job arranged; 0 = not arranged).

[b] Texas prison system points given for good conduct, work within the system, etc. Code for Georgia is degree of security classification, ranging from minimum security to maximum security.

* $p < .05$
** $p < .01$
*** $p < .001$

work sooner, and blacks and Chicanos tended to find work later. The findings about males also obtained in Georgia, and the coefficient for blacks was of the opposite sign but not large enough to reach statistical significance. Handicapped TARP members in Texas took longer to find jobs, but not so in Georgia. There were strong indications that having a job arranged prerelease meant obtaining a job earlier, not a surprising finding but one which indicated that at least some prerelease-arranged jobs were likely to have been real commitments on the part of an employer. Finally, persons who did not do well in prison did not do noticeably worse on the outside. Texas subjects who had low scores on a scale measuring conduct and performance in prison took slightly longer to get jobs. Prisoners in Georgia who were kept under stricter security also obtained jobs later, but these coefficients were not significant.

The factors that predict how long a person will take to obtain a job also predict the total amount of work effort made during the postrelease year, as Table 9.14 shows. In that table the dependent variable is the total number of weeks worked in the postrelease year associated with the same set of independent variables presented in Table 9.13. While the findings were similar, the total level of prediction afforded by the independent variables taken together (as indicated by the R^2 values at the bottom of the table) was somewhat lower, and fewer of the regression coefficients reached significance in either state. Males worked a greater number of weeks, along with those of greater educational attainment. Blacks, handicapped TARP members, and those with poor prison records and previous convictions worked less over the year.

SOME CONCLUSIONS

This chapter has presented abundant evidence documenting the serious employment and earnings problems faced by ex-prisoners after their release. Sizable minorities never worked at all, and the average proportions of time worked did not exceed half of the available time. As a consequence, earnings over the year were considerably below poverty levels.

The patterns of employment and earnings shown in this chapter are the results of many conditions and factors. Clearly, ex-prisoners are not attractive employees because they have little in the way of human capital. Even those prisoners who were well educated and who had acquired job skills in previous employment were not that much better off than the average released prisoner. If it were somehow possible to raise the level of educational attainment and provide job experiences to the ex-prisoners, levels of employment postrelease would rise, but certainly not enough to wipe out the large differential in employment that exists between this group and persons who have not been imprisoned. To some degree, the situation of ex-prisoners reflects the tendency of employers to weed out released prisoners from among job applicants. Unfortunately, the TARP data did not contain any information that would enable any estimates of the effects of employment discrimination.

Finally, there are the ex-prisoners themselves. Clearly, work per se did not mean much to them since they were so easily swayed from working by the small TARP payments. This negative appraisal of working may be the outcome of years of bad experiences, a function of the types of jobs available to them, or some combination of the two. Whatever the causes, it appeared that ex-prisoners do not find the employment opportunities available to them as attractive as reduced income and no work.

10

Arrests and Arrest Charges

INTRODUCTION

As shown in Chapter 7, many of the TARP participants in both states had extensive criminal records at the time they were released, had been arrested at least several times, and had served a large part of their adult lives in state prisons. Consequently, there was every expectation that participation in criminal activities would again continue in the postrelease year. Indeed, given the patterns of employment and earnings shown in earlier chapters of this report, there were additional reasons to expect that some TARP members again would choose property crimes as alternatives to the jobs available and that still others would supplement their meager legitimate earnings with some illegal enterprises. For the largest group, who returned to their parental families, there may have been the additional motivation of lessening the financial burdens their presence imposed on households with meager resources.

We can never know just how much criminal activity TARP members engaged in during their postrelease year. All we can observe is that tip of the iceberg that surfaced in the form of arrests. Since each arrest usually represented one suspected crime—at most, that and only a few others—the total number of actual crimes, both detected and undetected, is probably some multiple of the number of arrests.[1] Of course, a multiplier, or multipliers, would have to be varied according to the type of crime—crimes against persons would have lower multipliers than crimes against property. Multipliers would also differ according to the police jurisdiction

---

[1] Although we could estimate this multiplier, taking into account the ratios of arrests to crimes reported to the police or claimed through victimization surveys, a multiplier, or multipliers, would be based on all crimes committed, not on those committed by persons with extensive criminal records. For the latter group, an argument can be made both for larger and smaller multipliers, depending on whether one accepts the idea that those caught and arrested are those who commit extensive crime or the incompetents among professional criminals.

involved, because it is reasonable to assume that in some jurisdictions larger proportions of crimes would be cleared by arrests. In any event, the arrests experienced by TARP members that will be discussed in this chapter were only some fraction of the total amount of crime committed in the postrelease year by TARP members.

Of course, some arrests may have been unjustified, reflecting a more-than-usual suspicion of ex-felons by the police. The vulnerability of ex-felons in this respect would lead one to expect a certain amount of inflation in arrests. Most likely, however, the amount is slight, especially in larger jurisdictions where ex-felons were not well known to the police.

Finally, an arrest may involve several charges (and hence several criminal acts), or an investigation following an arrest may lead to the clearance of several reported crime incidents. This possibility further obscures the relationships between arrests and crime.

ARREST RATES

Table 10.1 presents arrest rates by period for charges that involve serious crimes, felonies, and major traffic violations.[2] (Omitted from the tabulations are such minor infractions as public drunkenness, disturbing the peace, loitering, minor traffic violations, and the like.) The bottom line of Table 10.1, containing arrest rates for all serious charges over the entire postrelease year, presents a disheartening story. More than one-third of the TARP members in each state were arrested on relatively serious charges at least once during the year: 35% in Georgia and 36% in Texas. Since the average number of arrests per TARP member was .559 in Georgia and .567 in Texas, it is also clear that many were arrested more than once during that period.

It should be noted that the rates shown in Table 10.1 are not mutually exclusive. In other words, a person may have been arrested once or several times during the year, but within each period if he was arrested on the same charge more than once, he is counted only once in the column headed "Percent of persons arrested." However, if he was arrested more than once but on different charges he is counted separately under each charge. Thus a person who was charged with two arrests for burglary is counted only once in Panel A, but if he was also arrested for assault he would be counted as well in Panel B during the same period.

---

[2] Major traffic violations include driving while intoxicated and driving without a license, charges included mainly in the Texas data.

TABLE 10.1

Arrests of TARP Members by Time Periods during Postrelease Year

	Georgia		Texas	
	Average number of arrests	Percentage of persons arrested	Average number of arrests	Percentage of persons arrested
A. *Arrest for crimes against property*				
First 6 weeks	.027	2.6	.016	1.4
Next 7 weeks	.044	4.0	.033	3.0
14 to 26 weeks	.109	9.9	.087	8.2
Last 6 months	.155	12.6	.181	14.0
Total year	.334	23.6	.317	22.8
B. *Arrests for other (nonproperty) crimes*				
First 6 weeks	.016	1.6	.022	2.0
Next 7 weeks	.042	3.6	.028	2.4
14 to 26 weeks	.057	5.4	.071	6.4
Last 6 months	.103	9.0	.130	10.8
Total year	.219	17.1	.250	18.1
C. *Total arrests for all significant charges*				
First 6 weeks	.043	4.3	.038	3.5
Next 7 weeks	.086	7.6	.061	5.3
14 to 26 weeks	.166	14.5	.158	13.5
Last 6 months	.264	20.1	.311	23.2
Total year	.559	35.3	.567	35.8
N	(976)		(975)	

SOURCE: Criminal justice information system computerized files, supplemented by manual searches of arrest records in local jurisdictions. (See Chapter 3 for description of records.)

NOTE: Data include significant charges only, which are arrests exclusive of those on petty charges; for example, minor traffic violations, loitering, and drunk and disorderly.

Theft crimes of all sorts were the more frequent charges lodged against TARP members, a pattern that resembled that of the crimes for which they served prison terms. The average number of theft arrests for Georgia TARP members was .334, involving about 24% of all persons; the corresponding numbers for Texas were .317 and 23%.

Arrests for non-theft-related charges were lower, the average number of such arrests being .219 in Georgia and .250 in Texas, involving 17% and 18% of TARP members, respectively.

There appeared to be no particular time pattern to the arrests, other than a somewhat lower arrest rate for the first 6 weeks after release than for

TABLE 10.2

Weeks to Arrest for First Significant Charge and Weeks to First
Jail or Prison Stay during Postrelease Year

	Texas	Georgia
Average number of weeks to first significant arrest charge (among those ever arrested)	25.2	22.4
Average number of weeks to first jail or prison time (among those ever serving time in jail or prison)	22.3	24.4
N	(975)	(976)

SOURCE: Criminal justice information system tapes.

NOTE: Jail or prison time is counted as time resulting from all arrests, including those for misdemeanors, traffic violations, and other minor infractions, whereas arrests include only "significant" charges—mainly felony charges and major traffic violations.

later periods. Indeed, for those arrested, the average number of weeks before a first arrest was 25 in Georgia and 22 in Texas, as Table 10.2 indicates. In short, the typical arrestee was booked a week or two before the middle of his postrelease year.

Time trends in property arrests are presented with greater precision in Table 10.3, in which time eligible for arrest in each period is taken into account. In this table we present *property-related arrests per week of eligible time*, a measure that takes into account the fact that while sick or in hospital or in jail or prison, TARP members were incapacitated and could not contribute to arrest rates. This correction becomes of some importance

TABLE 10.3

Property Arrests per Week of Eligible Time
(Total Time Less Time Spent in Hospital or Prison)

Time period	Georgia		Texas	
	Arrests per week	N	Arrests per week	N
1. First 6 weeks	.006	(897)	.005	(967)
2. Next 7 weeks	.009	(897)	.007	(967)
3. 14 to 26 weeks	.014	(818)	.020	(936)
4. Last 6 months	.014	(843)	.019	(886)
5. Entire year	.012	(743)	.017	(883)

SOURCE: Criminal justice information system files and follow-up interviews.

NOTE: "Eligible" time is defined as total time minus time spent in hospital and time spent in jail and/or prison.

TABLE 10.4
Total Arrests per Week of Eligible Time

Time period	Georgia		Texas	
	Arrests per week	N	Arrests per week	N
First 6 weeks	.010	(897)	.016	(967)
Next 7 weeks	.016	(897)	.016	(967)
14 to 26 weeks	.030	(818)	.021	(900)
Last 6 months	.021	(843)	.035	(886)
Entire year	.018	(743)	.025	(883)

SOURCE: Criminal justice information system and follow-up interviews.

NOTE: Total arrests include only significant arrests as defined in Table 10.1. Eligible time is defined as total time less time spent in hospital or prison.

particularly in the last six months, when a fair proportion of the TARP members were back in either jail or prison. It may also be remembered that TARP members spent significant amounts of time sick or in hospital.

Arrest rates did show a time trend when computed as in Table 10.3: They tended to increase in the second quarter of the year and in the last 6 months as compared to arrest rates in the first quarter. This trend seemed particularly pronounced in Texas, where the arrest rates for the later quarters were more than double those in the first quarter. The same trend was apparent in the Georgia arrest rates, though the increase in arrests from the first half of the year to the second was lesser in magnitude than in Texas.

Total arrests per week of eligible time accentuated the trend toward increasing arrest incidents over the year following release (see Table 10.4). The pattern of increasing arrests over time was particularly noticeable in Texas.

The reader will note a disparity between this table, which shows differences in yearly arrest rates across states, and Table 10.1, in which there is essentially no difference in average number of arrests across states. Two points bear mention in this regard. The arrest rate per week of eligible time in Texas for the last 6 months was much greater than the corresponding rate in Georgia, a difference that was not apparently as large from a casual scan of Table 10.1 (though even there the pattern of difference existed). The reason for the accentuation in Table 10.4 is that Texas releasees had less eligible time "on the street" than Georgia releasees. The Texas criminal justice system apparently had shorter elapsed times between arrests and imprisonment. Thus a similar number of arrests in the two states resulted in a greater Texas arrest rate per eligible time.

ARREST CHARGES

Since arrest records were available for all TARP participants, including
Group 6 (those who were not interviewed during the postrelease year),
detailed information on the types of arrest charges is recorded for all arrests
among all 2000 TARP participants in each state. Such a detailed breakdown is shown in Tables 10.5 and 10.6. If more than one charge appeared
on the arrest records, only the most serious charge is included in these
tables.

Note that the arrest charges resembled the distribution of crimes for
which the members were imprisoned. The most common charge was burglary, followed in frequency by larceny. The charges ran the gamut from
homicide to considerably less serious charges involving possession of "soft"
drugs and similar minor transgressions.

TABLE 10.5
Georgia TARP: Postrelease Arrest Charges

	First arrest	Second arrest	Third to sixth arrests	Total arrests
Homicide and manslaughter	6	3	0	9
Kidnapping	6	1	0	7
Rape	9	3	2	14
Sodomy	6	0	0	6
Robbery	41	20	14	75
Assault	111	30	21	162
Arson	3	2	2	7
Burglary	150	77	19	246
Larceny	119	32	29	180
Vehicle theft	24	11	6	41
Forgery and fraudulent activity	58	29	19	106
Stolen property	13	5	4	22
Damage to property	10	0	3	13
Drug offenses	51	22	11	84
Sex offenses	5	2	1	8
Family offenses	21	4	3	28
Gambling	4	2	2	8
Commercial sex	5	3	2	10
Obstructing justice, police	32	2	6	40
Flight, escape	6	2	4	12
Weapons charges	23	16	3	42
Other charges	7	9	5	21
Total arrests	(710)	(275)	(156)	(1141)

NOTE: Table includes all six experimental groups; thus, $N = 2007$. Data include most serious charges only.

TABLE 10.6
Texas TARP: Postrelease Arrest Charges

	First arrest	Second arrest	Third to sixth arrest	Total arrests
Homicide and manslaughter	12	4	1	17
Kidnapping	3	1	1	5
Sex assault	4	0	0	4
Robbery	65	21	5	91
Assault	30	10	5	45
Arson	1	0	1	2
Burglary	132	51	47	230
Larceny	113	46	44	203
Stolen vehicle	24	15	4	43
Forgery and fraudulent activity	30	10	4	44
Stolen property	11	4	3	18
Damaging property	3	3	4	10
Dangerous drugs	88	29	14	131
Obstructing police, justice	33	16	11	60
Weapons	24	6	3	33
Traffic offenses	69	18	6	93
Other miscellaneous offenses	18	10	5	33
Total offenses	(660)	(244)	(158)	(1062)
Charges not known	(40)	(17)	(26)	(83)

NOTE: Table includes all six experimental groups; thus $N = 1975$. Data include most serious charges only.

In order to facilitate discussion we have summarized the recorded charges in Table 10.7. Sixty percent of the arrests in both Georgia and Texas involved theft-related offenses, and in both states 22% of these offenses were burglary charges. Crimes against persons were involved in charges filed in 17% of the arrests in Georgia but only 7% in Texas, the major difference between the two states being that assault charges were much more frequent (14%) in Georgia as compared to Texas (4%). If such small proportions can be trusted, Texas TARP members were about twice as likely to be charged with homicide and/or manslaughter.

Of course, part of the difference between the two states arose out of the ways in which police jurisdictions customarily handled arrests. It may well be that the Georgia police preferred to enter "assault" as a charge when this was an alternative available to them. Certainly, Georgia arrest records recorded few major driving offenses, and the Texas records contain a fairly large proportion.

Since these arrests were recorded throughout the year following release, we do not have full information on the eventual disposition of the charges. A large proportion were still being adjudicated when the search of the state

TABLE 10.7

Summary of Significant Arrest Charges during Postrelease Year

	Percentage of arrests	
	Georgia	Texas
A. *Theft-related charges*		
Burglary	22	22
Robbery	7	7
Larceny	16	19
Forgery and fraudulent activity	9	4
Other theft-related charges	6	8
Total theft-related charges	60	60
B. *Crimes against persons*		
Homicide and manslaughter	.8	1.6
Assault	14	4
Other crimes against persons	2	1
Total crimes against persons	17	7
C. *Other offenses*		
Drug-related offenses	7	12
Weapons charges	4	3
Miscellaneous	11	18[a]
Total other offenses	22	33
Number of total arrests	(1139)	(1062)

[a] Includes large proportion of vehicle and traffic violations (see Table 10.6).

arrest records ended. Some had already ended with recommitment to prison. Indeed, the sentences meted out as of midsummer 1977 included one death sentence and close to 50 life sentenes. The TARP members were going back to prison in a small but steady stream.

During the year, TARP members were no strangers to jail or prison.[3] As Table 10.8 shows, on the average, Georgia TARP members spent 3.25 weeks in jail or prison during the year and Texas TARP members spent 5.8 weeks. It should be noted that these periods included postarrest detention for minor as well as serious charges and included time spent in jail awaiting trial or release on bail. More than a third of Georgia TARP members (38%) experienced some jail or prison time and half of Texas TARP members spent some time in jail or prison. Typically, the average TARP member experienced his first jail or prison residence shortly before the middle of the

[3] These data come from criminal justice official records. It can also be expected that these averages are underestimates, since self-reports from TARP members record more jail time in the aggregate than appears in the criminal justice records.

TABLE 10.8

Time Spent in Prison or Jail during Postrelease Year, by Periods

	Georgia			Texas		
	Average weeks	Percentage of persons	N	Average weeks	Percentage of persons	N
First 6 weeks	.051	5	(976)	.064	6	(967)
Next 7 weeks	.192	11	(976)	.225	14	(967)
14 to 26 weeks	.709	19	(976)	1.006	24	(957)
Last 6 months	2.303	27	(976)	4.537	41	(927)
Total year	3.255	38	(976)	5.834	50	(922)

postrelease year. At the end of the year following release, 15% in Texas and 12% in Georgia were back in prison serving time for convictions on felony charges or because their paroles were revoked.

SOME OBSERVATIONS ON REARREST

The overall pattern of postprison rearrests is clearly a recapitulation of patterns manifested throughout the adult years of the TARP members. While a bare majority have escaped arrest on one charge or another throughout the year, there are additional years to come. Of course, not all the arrests will lead to convictions and recommitment. Some are minor and involve fines and confinement in local jails for short periods of time. In addition, some of those arrested will have charges against them dismissed for lack of evidence or win acquittal in trials. Nevertheless, the signs point quite strongly to a large proportion of the ex-prisoners studied returning to prison within a few years of release.

Property crimes remained the major source of arrest charges. Property crime apparently competed successfully with alternative ways of earning income. Coupled with the information presented in Chapter 9, it is apparently the case that at least some large minority of TARP members had decided that it was easier to get along by stealing than by working.

III

MODELING AND ESTIMATING
THE EFFECTS OF
THE TRANSITIONAL AID
RESEARCH PROJECT

11

Model of the Effects of the Transitional Aid Research Project: Theoretical Foundations

INTRODUCTION

In Part III we discuss the reasoning that went into the construction of the counterbalancing model of TARP effects, which model was described in Chapter 5, and describe the way in which the model parameters were estimated. Chapter 11 describes the social science theory of, and knowledge about, criminal behavior that serves as the foundation for the model. Chapter 12 presents details on how the model was fitted, using data from the two experiments.

Although the discussion in this chapter does rely very heavily on previous writing on crime, borrowing particularly from economic theories of crime, we believe it is written in a nontechnical vein. Its content should therefore be understandable without detailed knowledge about relatively sophisticated statistical methods. More technical expertise is required for a full appreciation of Chapter 12, in which some of the computations that bolster the plausibility of the TARP model are shown.

The TARP counterbalancing model described in this chapter is partially a priori and partially ex post facto. It was certainly not postulated from the beginning of the experiment as the mechanism through which the TARP payments were to function. Indeed, if this had been the way in which payments were anticipated to work, then a much different program would have been designed and tested. The basic outlines of the model were first formulated after early tabulations of findings from both Georgia and Texas indicated a fairly heavy work-disincentive effect of payments and a slight tendency for arrest rates in the payment groups to be higher in both states. It was at this point (approximately February 1978) that the two senior authors of this book began to lay out a mechanism that would account for both positive and negative effects of TARP payments on arrests. At the outset the model was a simple framework of postulated effects, much as shown in Figure 5.1 (see Chapter 5). At the same time we began to construct the theoretical rationale laid out in this chapter. It was only somewhat later, when the full data set became available for analysis in the summer of 1978, that empirical tests could be made of the model. Empirical testing proceeded through the summers of 1978 and 1979, and the model was constantly modified in specification terms until we were satisfied that some of the difficult and obstinate characteristics of the data had been understood and taken into account in the specification shown in Chapter 12.

The approach in this chapter is eclectic. Borrowing heavily from both economics and criminology, we have put together a theoretical rationale for the model that we believe rests upon what is currently best known about criminal behavior and upon relevant social phenomena from the appropriate social sciences. Of course, we realize that we run the risk of satisfying no one by drawing on sources of ideas that may be too diverse. Nevertheless, what we have done seems to us to be closer to the particular circumstances faced by TARP participants than are more general theories of criminal behavior.[1]

Indeed, because the TARP participants were a rather special and highly selected group, it is worthwhile at this point to remind the reader of some of their salient characteristics, especially those that condition the applicability of current social science theories about criminal behavior.

First of all, it must be remembered that all of the TARP members had been convicted at least once of felonies or serious demeanors and that many had served several stretches of time in state prisons. This means that TARP members were persons who have opted for participation in criminal activities before and who in the past have been *undeterred* by the prospect of imprisonment and other punishment. It is difficult to say whether this means that as individuals they were more inclined to take the risks involved in participating in criminal behavior than other persons or whether they were in circumstances where illegitimate activities appeared more attractive. For present purposes, clearly TARP members on the basis of past behavior were especially prone to engage in criminal behavior.

Second, the crimes for which TARP members were incarcerated were largely crimes against property, that is, crimes from which one can derive income. Two or three of the TARP members were jailed for offenses that had provided a source of income that either supplemented their legitimate earnings and/or was their sole source of support.

---

[1] More generally, all three authors share a commitment to interdisciplinary research. It is obvious to us that the empirical world is not organized into neat cubbyholes of sociological phenomena, economic phenomena, psychological phenomena, and the like. Yet the balkanized social sciences each seem so invested in their own unique brand of truth that they in effect routinely misspecify their causal models in services of disciplinary purity. End of sermon.

Third, if there is anything to the notion of a criminal subculture composed of circles of persons who derive a livelihood from illegitimate activities, all TARP members by virtue of having spent some time in state prison had been in close and prolonged contact with members of that subculture. If they had wanted to learn how to live from illegitimate activities, prison provided a rich and diversified learning environment.

Fourth, as we have seen in the chapters in the last section, TARP members were recruited from the bottom levels of the local societies in which they lived. If crime is an alternative way of life for any strata of American society, it is most nearly so among the poor and disadvantaged. TARP members were fairly homogeneous in class origins, coming from poor families with little in the way of resources. On the average, the skills they had accumulated and the training they had received were meager. Their preprison employment records had been so skimpy, partially because they had spent so much of their adult lives in prison, that they had little to offer to prospective employers. Levels of educational attainment were considerably below the averages for their age groups, another characteristic that handicapped any attempts to find positions in the labor market that were average or better in wage rates and working conditions. These characteristics meant that sources of legitimate earnings available to TARP members through the labor market were likely to be relatively unattractive, especially when viewed in comparison to illegitimate activities. In short, for TARP members, legitimate activities were not as competitively attractive when compared to illegitimate activities as sources of earnings and income.

Finally, because they were out of step with the typical life-cycle progressions of their age peers, TARP members tended to have few responsibilities for family support, as is typical for men in their middle and later twenties. This meant that they had lower needs for income by reason of having few or no persons dependent upon them for support. By the same token they were also low in the need for a steady and uninterrupted flow of income. In short, the pressure to obtain jobs and to retain them was considerably less than for young married men with small children, a stage that is quite typical for most young men of the age group to which most TARP members belonged.

The implications of these characteristics are twofold. First, theories that have been constructed to explain *criminal behavior in general* have to be modified to take into account these characteristics. For example, sociological theories that rely on explanations along class lines or in terms of relative deprivation are not very useful in explaining differential participation in criminal behavior among persons all of whom came from the lower levels of the class system or all of whom were relatively deprived. Theories of differential association, which explain criminal behavior in part through exposure to persons pursuing criminal careers, also do not help much in explaining why some of the TARP members returned to crime, since all TARP members had been exposed through their prison experiences to career criminals.

Second, the circumstances facing released prisoners were ones in which participation in criminal activities was relatively attractive. The legitimate means of earning income that were available to released prisoners were not very attractive or very remunerative compared to average employment and earnings. In addition, given the family circumstances of ex-felons, there was little need for steady sources of earnings. TARP members were therefore particularly vulnerable to whatever was attractive about participation in illegitimate activities.

THE THEORETICAL FOUNDATIONS OF THE TARP MODEL

One of the roots of the theoretical rationale for the TARP counterbalancing model lies in utilitarian models constructed to explain criminal behavior. While a number of variations are proposed by different utilitarian writers, the basic idea is one of individuals faced continually with choices between legitimate and illegitimate activities.[2] Individuals participate more heavily in illegitimate activities as the anticipated returns from illegal actions exceed the anticipated returns from legal ones. The content of these returns can vary depending on the particular views of the utilitarian theorist, but money, possessions, and excitement are the sorts of things that may be treated as benefits, whereas arrest, imprisonment, and guilt may be treated as costs. In addition, it is usually assumed that the returns from legal activities can be fully anticipated, but the returns from illegal activities are uncertain. Since an individual cannot know in advance

---

[2] See, for example, G. S. Becker, *The Economic Approach to Human Behavior* (Chicago: University of Chicago Press, 1976); M. K. Block and J. M. Heineke, "A Labor Theoretic Analysis of the Criminal Choice," *American Economics Review* 65, no. 3(1975): 314–325; A. Blumstein, J. Cohen, and D. Nagin (eds.), *Deterrence and Incapacitation: Estimating the Effects of Criminal Sanctions on Crime Rates* (Washington, D.C.: National Academy of Sciences, 1978); W. A. Bonger, *Criminality and Economic Conditions* (New York: 1916; reprint ed., Agathon Press, 1967). I. Ehrlich, "Participation in Illegitimate Activities: An Economic Analysis," in G. S. Becker and W. M. Lantes (eds.) *Essays in the Economics of Crime and Punishment* (New York: Columbia University Press, 1974); P. Letkemann, *Crime as Work* (Englewood Cliffs, N.J.: Prentice-Hall, 1973); L. Radzinowicz, "Economic Pressures," in L. Radzinowicz and M. E. Wolfgang (eds.), *The Criminal in Society* (New York: Basic Books, 1971); and D. L. Sjoquist, "Property Crime and Behavior: Some Empirical Results," *American Economics Review* 63, no. 3(1973): 439–446.

whether a particular illegitimate action will lead to sanctions from the criminal justice system, some of the most important costs associated with crime are necessarily weighted by the probability of incurring sanctions. For example, if the chances of apprehension and conviction are very slight, the net anticipated returns from illegal activities may be significantly enhanced.

Since legitimate and illegitimate activities are not mutually exclusive, the problem faced by individuals is that of choosing an optimal mix of such activities so as to maximize net returns. Thus, one might envisage a full-time career criminal whose only income-producing activities are illegitimate, or a part-time criminal who uses illegitimate income to supplement earnings from legitimate sources, or, at the other extreme, a person who always chooses to use his time in legitimate employment or other legal income-producing activities.

Translated into the circumstances faced by ex-felons upon release, the utilitarian framework sees the income needs of the ex-prisoners as satisfiable by some mix of employment, illegitimate activities, transfer payments, and donations from family and friends. No one has successfully managed to estimate the expected returns from illegitimate activity, and TARP data are unfortunately silent on the issue.[3] However, TARP data did allow some appreciation of the prospects from legitimate activities. First, jobs were not easily obtained, so the job-search costs were high. TARP members reported experiencing considerable difficulty in finding employment, and such difficulties have been reported uniformly by other investigators.[4] Second, it is clear from the findings of Chapter 9 that the wage rates commanded by TARP members were toward the bottom of the wage scale. Average weekly wages in Georgia were $115 and in Texas $148, corresponding respectively to hourly wage rates of $2.88 and $3.70, rates that either as gross or net were close to minimum wage levels.[5] Third, given the economic circumstances of families and friends, their donations, however generously given, cannot have been large, considering the straitened circumstances of such persons. Finally, as noted earlier, transfer payments through most of the welfare and other income-maintenance programs were either unavailable or difficult to obtain. Indeed, this unavailability of transfer payments from ongoing social programs was one of the major justifications for extending unemployment benefits as in the TARP plan.

---

[3] A pioneering attempt to do so, at least for habitual or "career" criminals is J. Petersillian, P.W. Greenwood, and M. Lavin, *Criminal Careers of Habitual Felons* (R–2144–D01) (Santa Monica: Rand Corporation, August, 1977).

[4] Daniel Glaser *et al., Money against Crime* (Chicago: John Howard, 1961).

[5] Although interviewers were instructed to obtain gross rather than net weekly earnings, there is considerable internal evidence that net earnings were often recorded.

In short, the prospects from employment and other legitimate activities were grim at best. In terms of the economic-choice models of criminal behavior, TARP members faced choices in which the anticipated returns from legitimate activities were low.

In this context, the formal status of ex-felons per se produced some puzzling complications. First, about half of the TARP members had been released on parole, a condition that made it very easy for them to be returned to prison without going through the usual routes of arrest and trial. In addition, because of their criminal records, it was more likely that they were known to the police as probable suspects, and to their neighbors, local shopkeepers, and the like as untrustworthy persons. Hence, they were possibly more likely to be suspected of criminal activities and therefore more likely to be frisked, picked up on suspicion, interrogated by the police, and so on.

Yet, being an ex-felon had ambiguous implications for the balance of incentives. On one hand, being an ex-felon appears to raise the probability of being apprehended and punished, given a transgression. Hence, anticipated returns from illegal activities should be modified downward.[6] On the other hand, since ex-prisoners were also likely to be picked up and returned to prison whether or not they had actually committed any illegal acts, the anticipated returns from legitimate activities appear to be correspondingly lowered. While the net impact of these competing forces cannot be estimated in the TARP data, suffice it to say that being an ex-felon complicates the decisions faced by TARP participants.

Another source for the theoretical underpinnings of the TARP model is the sociology of occupations and work, a speciality that has been concerned with the interpretation of the roles that jobs, occupations, and work play in the social psychology of the individual. From this theoretical tradition is obtained a conception of work as more than the earnings derived. Perhaps the most well-established set of socially defined valuations is composed of the prestige ratings of jobs and occupations. Being invariant over time and across subgroups of the population, as well as being quite comparable across different national cultures, ratings based on sample surveys place every well-known job and occupation into a stable hierarchical order.[7] It is important to note that the invariances noted mean quite literally that the valuations of occupations and jobs do not vary significantly

---

[6] Perhaps this explains why only minorities of ex-felons are rearrested and/or returned to prison.

[7] Robert W. Hodge, Paul M. Siegel, and Peter H. Rossi, "Occupational Prestige in the United States: 1925–1963," in R. Bendix and S. M. Lipset (eds.), *Class Status and Power*, 2nd ed. (New York: The Free Press, 1966).

by sex, age, ethnicity, and social class (among other subgroupings). It is also clear from studies that have included the status of being unemployed or that of being a transfer-payment recipient that these two positions are regarded as considerably worse than the lowest of the occupations on the scale. In short, the position of the unemployed, even those for whom transfer payments have compensated for lack of income, is clearly and sharply at the bottom of the heap in the consensus of all groups in the population. To the extent that such valuations have some direct benefits to individuals over and beyond the earnings provided, employment provides some status in the society at large and in the local society in which the TARP members live.

In addition, most occupations provide a set of social contacts—a social environment. The social context of work also has an impact upon a worker. It is composed of a group of persons with attitudes and values to which a jobholder may be exposed more than to any other group in the society. It provides contacts that may be the basis of friendship, and so on. For example, there is some evidence that the voting choices of individuals are influenced by the predominant candidate preferences of co-workers.[8] In short, the world of work is an important connecting institution that provides links between the individual and a society that extends beyond kinship and neighborhood. For ex-prisoners, this connectivity function may be especially important.

From the sociology of occupations and work, we are alerted to the fact that employment is more than earnings—that it provides individuals with a valued position in society and a set of supporting social contacts.

Both the microeconomic and sociological views of work acknowledge that work occupies time. Indeed, the choice situation envisaged by some of the economist commentators on crime directly involves individuals constantly making decisions about the appropriate mix of discretionary time between legitimate and illegitimate activities. The sociologists of work, especially those who have studied unemployment, have also emphasized the deleterious effect of unemployment through increasing the leisure time of individuals without appropriate substitutes.[9] The effect of work time on illegitimate activity is both in the form of direct competition—time spent at work cannot be spent on crime—and in the form of avoiding superfluous leisure.[10]

---

[8] Bernard Berelson, Paul F. Lazarsfeld, and William M. McPhee, *Voting* (Chicago: University of Chicago Press, 1954).

[9] Herbert Hyman, "Studies of Unemployed," in R. K. Merton, J. S. Coleman, and P. H. Rossi, *Qualitative and Quantitative Social Research* (New York: The Free Press, 1979).

[10] This is not quite true, since crime-on-the-job in a variety of forms is possible, ranging from pilfering to outright embezzlement.

Now it is necessary to build the connections between these theoretical considerations and the ways in which TARP payments affected those eligible. First, TARP payments were designed to fulfill minimum income needs so that illegal activities would not be necessary as a source of income or would be rendered less attractive. This effect implicitly assumes that the first few dollars of income are worth more than the next, a direct application of the theory of declining marginal utility. In other words, given the $63 or $70 per week available through the payments, additional income that could be derived from illegal activities is diminished in utility; hence, the eligible ex-felons would be less likely to engage in such illegal activities. This anticipated effect postulates a rather rapid decline in marginal utility such that the first $60 to $70 per week is "worth" a great deal more than additional money that can be obtained from illegal activities.

Second, TARP payments may also be viewed as raising the costs of crime by imposing an additional "fine" if incarceration occurs. That is, TARP payments are lost (or forfeited) if the TARP member returns to jail or prison. Hence, the opportunity costs of crime are increased.

Third, TARP payments may only seemingly reduce crime by providing incentives for eligible ex-felons to be more careful in planning their crimes and thereby reduce the chances of apprehension. With basic income needs provided for through TARP payments, ex-felons may avoid high-risk criminal opportunities. They may also plan crimes with potentially higher returns (in order to counteract the declining utility of additional income).

The considerations listed above are addressed primarily to the effects of TARP payments on economic crime. But there are also effects that can be anticipated for noneconomically motivated illegal activities, such as crimes against persons, drunkenness, drug abuse, and the like. First, TARP payments raise the opportunity costs of such crimes. Ex-felons may be less likely to, say, become drunk in public, because they do not want to forego eligibility for the remainder of their TARP payments. Second, the income provided by the TARP payments may make relationships with family and friends easier and hence reduce the level of interpersonal friction that leads to crimes against the person. Thus, the ability of TARP members to contribute something to their households may reduce the amount of quarreling over money that leads to assaults.[11]

TARP payments also affect participation in illegal activities through affecting employment. Hence it is necessary to consider how employment affects crime. Some of the same mechanisms are at work with respect to the effect of employment on illegal activities, but there are additional ones as well.

---

[11] See Appendix B for evidence on this point.

To begin with, because work produces income, the returns from additional illegal activities are diminished in value through the declining marginal utility mechanisms. Persons earning $100 to $150 per week are less likely to engage in illegal activities than persons whose income is zero.

Second, work preempts time: Time spent at work reduces the amount of time available to engage in illegal activities. Note that since TARP payments do not require any time investment on the part of recipients, this mechanism is not at work with regard to the effect of TARP payments on participation in illegal activities.

Third, work raises the opportunity costs of illegal activities. Persons jailed or incarcerated cannot work, obviously, but also their being arrested might lead to dismissal from employment, especially in jobs where trustworthiness is a job qualification. It should also be noted that the opportunity costs of losing a job rise over time as the benefits of seniority accumulate.

Finally, there is more to employment than either earnings and time investments. Besides the psychic rewards and costs associated with work (which most economists would acknowledge), the way in which a person obtains his living affects his social status and self-esteem (as we noted in Chapter 8 for TARP members). In addition, the work environment provides a setting in which the actions of ex-offenders may be differentially reinforced by fellow workers and supervisors. Such effects may be regarded as simply another set of incentives that can be incorporated as part of the benefits recognized in economic theory. They also may be thought of as effects that last beyond the *immediate* outcomes in so far as the social aspects of the work setting lead to learning that can carry over into other aspects of life, and hence provide a social context that affects attitudes toward a broad spectrum of issues. TARP payments, of course, do not compensate for the employment effect of working. Hence to the extent that TARP payments and working are mutually exclusive, the income effects of working can be captured by TARP payments, but the employment effects cannot.

The final link between TARP payments and criminal activities is provided by the tax rates applied to TARP payments within each of the experimental groups that were offered eligibility for payments. Within the first two groups, the tax rate was 100%; that is, each dollar earned, beyond the small forgiveness amounts in each state, lowered TARP payments by a dollar.[12] Those in the third experimental group were faced with a 25% tax rate and no forgiveness feature. Thus in Texas, an ex-felon in Groups 1 and 2 earning $78.75 or more, or in Group 3 and earning $252 or more in a

---

[12] See Chapter 4 for a detailed description of experimental treatments.

given week, was not eligible to receive any benefit payment for that week. In Georgia the corresponding amounts were $78 and $280. It should be noted that since these amounts for Groups 1 and 2 were less than minimum wages for a full week of work in either of the two states, virtually the only way a person could have qualified for partial payments was by working less than full time. In effect, the rules of the TARP experiment defining eligibility made any significant amount of employment in Groups 1 and 2 mutually exclusive with TARP payments. In short, TARP payment provided a work-disincentive effect that was particularly strong in Groups 1 and 2.

The strength of the TARP work-disincentive effect for Groups 1 and 2 depends largely on the wages anticipated from employment. Given the average weekly wages earned by TARP members when working, in Texas the choices faced were working and receiving $145 per week or not working and receiving $63. In Georgia the choice was between $110 and working and $70 and not working. Another way of putting it is that during the period of eligibility for TARP payments, Texas members worked, on the average, for $82 per week (or a little more than $2 per hour), and Georgia members worked for $40 per week (or $1 per hour). These were the amounts over and above the payments they would have received by working and receiving average wages as compared to being unemployed and collecting benefits. Certainly for Groups 1 and 2 the incentive for working that derived from earnings was severely undercut by TARP payment eligibility.

The work disincentive faced by Group 3 members in both states was somewhat less. Persons earning the average amounts of $110 in Georgia were entitled to $42.50 in payments, in Texas those earning average amounts of $145 could receive $33.75 in TARP payments.[13] Thus in Texas, persons in Group 3, if they worked, received $82.50 more than the benefits receivable under unemployment, or they worked at a wage rate of a bit more than $2 per hour. Similar calculations for Group 3 members in Texas led to a wage of $115.75 on the average, or $2.89 per hour.

Of course, the calculations outlined above only make sense to the extent that the various experimental plans were administered faithfully and to the extent that participants were able to act on the provisions of the plans. In Chapter 4, it is shown that TARP members in the experimental groups knew how much their full benefits came to but were quite unlikely to know much about the tax rate and partial payment provisions of the eligibility

---

[13] Georgia payments were computed according to the formula

Payment = Full payment amount − (.25)(Average earnings or $110)

rules.[14] Especially discouraging was the fact that few members of Group 3 knew very much about the partial-payment provisions of their plan. It seems likely that Group 3 members, in effect, faced the same tax rate that was faced by Groups 1 and 2.

The point of the discussion in the last two paragraphs is to bolster the argument that a large work-disincentive effect was built into TARP experiments both by the nominal tax rates and by the way in which the payments were administerd.[15] In effect, being paid benefits and working were made mutually exclusive.

To summarize the discussion so far, five hypotheses can be written as follows:

1. TARP payments and employment reduce property arrests by lowering the marginal utility of income derived from illegal activities.
2. Employment will reduce all arrests by withdrawing time from illegal activities, by opening up new options, and by shaping the preferences and enhancing the self-regard of employed ex-offenders.
3. TARP payments and employment will directly reduce the number of arrests, property and nonproperty, by raising the opportunity costs of engaging in illegal activities.
4. TARP payments will compete with employment and will therefore reduce the time spent on employment.
5. TARP payments will *indirectly* increase participation in illegal activities by lowering work effort.

Note that both property and nonproperty crimes (and arrests on such charges) are included in the above summary, even though it would seem that property crimes were more directly affected through the income derived from either TARP payments or employment.[16] We will have more to say on this score later on in this chapter.

---

[14] It should be recalled that the measurement of plan knowledge was made at the end of the postrelease year, and some degree of knowledge may have been lost in the normal deterioration of memory over time. That some of the participants received part payments can also be shown in the records of the payment files. The tax rates were applied to some extent. Whether they were administered to the fullest possible extent seems unlikely (but that is a speculative statement).

[15] Indeed, our findings, reported in Chapter 12, indicate that there were few differences between Group 2 and Group 3 TARP members in their behavioral reactions to the TARP payments.

[16] Nonproperty crimes are defined residually as all charges that do not involve the theft or appropriation of property. As such, this is a considerably heterogeneous set, including crimes of passion such as murder and assault, as well as crimes involving the possession of drugs, manslaughter charges arising out of vehicular accidents, and so on. (See Chapter 10 for tabulations of specific charges involved.) In addition, the charges lodged against a person may

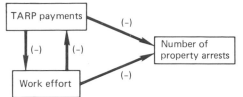

FIGURE 11.1 *Schematic representation of TARP counterbalancing model.*

The five hypotheses are summarized in the diagram of Figure 11.1. Note, however, that this diagram makes no reference to any other factors that affect payments, working, or arrests. It is abstracted from the concrete matrix of processes that determine the factors shown. To model the relationships we have hypothesized requires that a more elaborate set of factors be specified. In addition, the system shown in Figure 11.1 is one in which elements are allowed to influence each other reciprocally and thus defines a nonrecursive system.

The hypothesized relationships can be estimated statistically, provided that one can correctly specify a set of equations linking together the factors shown in Figure 11.1 with each other and with other variables in a system of equations that make sense theoretically. The system constructed is described in detail in the next section of this chapter. Chapter 12 shows the results of computations made.

THE SPECIFICATION OF THE NONRECURSIVE TARP MODEL

Since the primary concern of the TARP experiment was with lowering property arrests through TARP payments, the variables to be designated as the endogenous (or to-be-explained) variables are those that are intimately interrelated with payments and arrests. The preceding section of this chapter, plus our general knowledge of the experiment and of the workings of criminal justice, brought the model construction to focus on five endogenous variables: property arrests, TARP payments, time worked, nonproperty arrests, and time in prison. The theoretical discussion in the last section set the framework for considering that the first four are interrelated either by administrative definition or by theoretical considerations. The last listed endogenous variable—time in prison—has been added for fairly

represent primarily the charge that the prosecutor believes is most likely to result in either a guilty plea or a conviction. Hence some of the nonproperty arrests may actually involve property offenses along with other offenses.

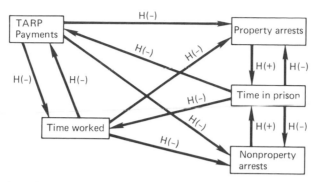

FIGURE 11.2 *Hypothesized relationships among endogenous variables in TARP counter-balancing model.*

obvious reasons: Persons in prison can neither work nor obtain payment checks. Time in prison in turn is affected mainly by arrests, and arrests are hypothesized to be affected by both TARP payments and time worked. The hypothesized relationships among the endogenous variables (marked "H") are shown in Figure 11.2 along with the expected signs of the relationships.

Since the five endogenous variables do not simply interact with each other but are related to outside processes, it is necessary to add a set of exogenous factors. Theoretical considerations as well as commonsense understanding dictated the exogenous variables to be added. These have been grouped into five broad categories: human-capital variables, or characteristics of TARP members that relate to employability; measures of income needs; indicators of criminal justice practices; measures of past criminal behavior; and indicators of the demand for labor on local labor markets.

A set of five equations defines the nonrecursive system whose parameters are to be estimated. Each of the equations defines one of the endogenous variables as a function of relevant other endogenous variables, as shown in Figure 11.2, and of a set of exogenous variables that relate primarily to the endogenous factor in question. Each of these five equations, along with the rationale for its construction, is described in detail in the following sections.

An Equation for the Number of Property Arrests

The number of property arrests is taken to be a function of a set of exogenous variables (to be discussed later) and three endogenous variables: the amount of money received from TARP, the number of weeks employed, and the number of weeks in jail or prison.[17] The justifications for designating each will be addressed in turn.

Whatever else we may consider, the impact of the TARP payments is, of course, the critical issue. A priori, we expect the payments to reduce the number of property arrests. But at least four mechanisms may be involved. First, TARP payments lower the utility of illegitimate activities by providing a kind of larger initial "endowment." Second, on the basis of the insights of Becker, Ehrlich, Sjoquist, Block, Heineke, and other economists, TARP payments may increase the opportunity costs of illegal behavior.[18] Ex-offenders in payment groups had more to lose (i.e., TARP payments) if they were caught committing crimes and would therefore be less likely to invest time in illegitimate activities. Third, if (as economic models assume) the commission of property crimes can be viewed as a "job" much like legitimate employment, TARP payments may in part by understood within a job-search framework.[19] TARP payments may have subsidized a "job" search, so that illegal opportunities with high risks and low payoffs were bypassed.[20] That is, TARP ex-offenders in payment groups could have afforded to avoid less desirable illegitimate opportunities and, therefore, these kinds of property crimes would decline. The result is that, overall, the number of property crimes would have decreased. Finally and somewhat cynically, the subsidized job search may not have reduced the number of property crimes committed, but since "better" crimes were undertaken, the number of property *arrests* may have been reduced. A higher proportion of low-risk property crimes were initiated, and fewer arrests were recorded. In summary, although at least four mechanisms may have been involved, one would nevertheless predict a negative relationship between money received and the number of property arrests.

The impact of employment on property arrests should be much the same. More specifically, we are assuming that ex-offenders selected some mix of legal and illegal activities to maximize their returns. Legal and illegal pursuits are not mutually exclusive. This assumption is reinforced by the com-

---

[17] An alternative specification would have been to consider whether or not a TARP member was ever arrested, reasoning that any arrest is a "failure" and that arrests beyond the first arrest are simply redundancy. However, the view taken here is that the TARP experiments were concerned to reduce the amount of property crime, postrelease, and that this desirable outcome is better indicated by the number of arrests. Moreover, we did estimate models with "success" and "failure" as outcomes, the results of which are described in Chapter 12.

[18] See footnote 2 for full citations.

[19] S. Lippman, and J. McCall, "The Economics of Job Search: A Survey," *Economic Inquiry* 14, no. 1 (1976).

[20] This interpretation was first suggested to us by Professor Thomas Cooley, University of California, Santa Barbara.

mon observation that for subjects such as ours the line between crime and work is often ambiguous.[21] Consequently, one may view employment as a source of income, somewhat like the TARP payments. However, employment involves more than income, and in this context, it may also be understood as reducing the time available for illegal activities. In short, given the time constraint of a 24-hour day, time devoted to legitimate jobs must necessarily reduce the time available for other pursuits.

If time invested in legitimate jobs reduces the time available for crime (among other things), time spent in jail or prison should have similar effects.[22] While we will consider time spent in jail or prison as a single variable, it is nevertheless important to understand that the kind of time involved may vary. An arrest will often lead to a few days in jail before the case is considered by a local magistrate. In addition, once an indictment is filed, an offender may spend a month or more in jail awaiting trial. Both of these processes should be distinguished from a return to prison after conviction. For our purposes, however, the critical issue is a reduction in time available for illegal activities, so separate variables are unnecessary.

Turning to exogenous variables affecting the number of property arrests, a first set of predictors may be viewed as indicators of economic need (i.e., demand): the amount of money an ex-offender had in hand upon release, the amount of money saved at home, the amount of money owed at time of release, and the number of dependents. We will also include a variable indicating whether the ex-offender is returning to live with a spouse, although it is not clear whether this measures financial need or a source of support.

If property crime can be viewed as an occupation, human-capital variables should be relevant. Therefore, we include the number of previous convictions for property offenses to measure "experience" with property crime. As with other sorts of "on-the-job-training," we expect that higher levels of human capital will encourage continued participation in the relevant economic activities. Of course, it is also possible to view such variables as measures of a "taste" for property crime, which is closer to the way sociologists approach criminal behavior. For whatever reason (culture, socialization, differential association), some individuals develop a preference for criminal behavior that gets played out in everyday activities. In any case, the predicted effects on the number of property arrests is much the same.

---

[21] Letkemann, *Crime as Work;* Petersillian *et al., Criminal Careers.*

[22] Actually, since jail or prison time precludes any other activity, such time reduces the opportunity to commit property thefts even more drastically than an equivalent amount of time spent working.

Another human-capital variable we shall use is whether or not an ex-offender was physically handicapped.[23] While many property crimes may not require unusual physical skill, many do demand strength, speed, agility, and an appearance of physical competence. Thus, handicapped ex-offenders may commit fewer property crimes.

Finally, there are several variables that should have some impact on property crimes but may be hard to fit within a human-capital framework. In particular, we will include sex and age as predictors, relying primarily on a legion of empirical studies showing that persons who are young and male commit more crimes than any other group. Unfortunately, the precise causal mechanisms have never been convincingly specified. Within an economic perspective, perhaps men are more likely to possess the kinds of skills that facilitate effective criminal activities, much as men are more likely to gain the kinds of skills that make them more desirable employees, at least for some legitimate jobs. Age may reflect the changing value of time. Younger offenders may anticipate a long life ahead and be more willing to risk time in prison.

Our last variable is the number of weeks spent sick and/or in the hospital.[24] The more days lost in sickness the more such episodes may reflect serious injuries or illnesses, perhaps lowering an ex-offender's abilities to effectively commit property crimes upon recovery. In addition, time spent ill or in hospital is much like time in jail or prison; the amount of time available for crime is reduced.

To summarize, our specification for the number of property arrests relies heavily on ideas from economics and past empirical work. For the vast majority of TARP subjects, we are assuming that the decision to invest in legal or illegal activities is a matter of likely returns, and that the balance of economic incentives is critical. To facilitate our discussion of findings in the next chapter, these ideas can be represented in an abbreviated equation form as follows:

(1)   Number of property arrests $= f$(TARP payments, employment, incarceration, exogenous variables)

An Equation for the Number of Nonproperty Crimes

Property crimes, as indicated, are assumed to be a source of earnings and hence motivated by the prospect of economic gain. Nonproperty crimes, being defined residually, are a miscellaneous category that cannot be

---

[23] Our definition derives from prison classifications. See Chapter 8 for a detailed discussion of this classification.

[24] See Chapter 8 for a detailed discussion of this variable.

assigned to a single motivational theme. Although murders and homicides are relatively rare, many of the nonproperty crimes were assaults, perhaps representing crimes of passion or the outcomes of heated arguments among friends, neighbors, relatives, and lovers. Another large component are vehicle-related offenses (at least in Texas) as well as drug possession, and so on.

While nonproperty crimes are not defined here as a source of monetary income, they are certainly a source of psychic rewards (and costs) and just the sorts of "noneconomic" factors we earlier linked to employment: self-esteem, status in the eyes of one's peers, information about alternative life styles, and the like. Presumably, therefore, participation in nonproperty crime responds to the balance of incentives, and in this context TARP payments may have an important impact.[25] If TARP payments increase the opportunity costs of property crime, why not also of nonproperty crime? The TARP experimental design was blind to the kind of offense that led to incarceration; incarceration from either type of crime would eliminate TARP payments. Therefore, TARP payments can be viewed as raising the opportunity costs of nonproperty crime (conditional on incarceration) and hence reducing the number of property arrests.

Whatever the common theme may be in nonproperty offenses, it is clear that time spent employed reduces the opportunities to commit nonproperty offenses. In addition, we anticipate that nonproperty offenses are considerably influenced by the types of law enforcement activities taking place in a jurisdiction. Some police departments may stress drug-related offenses; others may define interpersonal fracases differently than do typical jurisdictions. Indeed, a typical scenario that could lead to an arrest on assault charges or on disorderly conduct charges might be described as follows. It is a Friday night, and a number of local people are gathered in a neighborhood bar. Some individuals drink a bit too much, and a loud argument develops. At that point the police are called, for serious violence appears likely. The police arrive and arrests follow. Now, however, whether any person or which person is arrested are highly discretionary police choices. The police present must make a number of rapid decisions about whether (in the context of this particular neighborhood) the blows exchanged were assaults or simply arguments-as-usual and whether a significant breach of the public order has occurred. They must also weigh the risks of triggering a serious confrontation with neighborhood residents

---

[25] Indeed, within the framework of the "New Home Economics," nonproperty crime is "just" another household commodity that yields utility and that requires time inputs as a factor of production. For an overview of the New Home Economics, see Richard A. Berk, "The New Home Economics: An Agenda for Sociological Research," in Sarah F. Berk (ed.), *Women and Household Labor* (Beverly Hills, Calif.: Sage Publications, 1980).

by overreaction, and they must decide whether it is better to make arrests or simply warn the crowd to tone it down![26]

If nonproperty arrests depend heavily on the amount and kinds of leisure activities undertaken by TARP participants and an unusually high degree of police discretion, narrow economic variables should play less important roles in the specification. Rather, it would be more sensible to rely on indicators of the amount of leisure time, tastes in leisure time, and law-enforcement practices.

Turning first to endogenous variables, the number of nonproperty arrests is viewed as a function of TARP payments, the number of weeks employed, and the number of weeks in jail or prison. The assumption is that TARP payments raise the opportunity costs, and employment and time in jail or prison limit the amount of time available for leisure. The exogenous variable reflecting time sick or in hospital should also reduce the time available for nonproperty crimes.

We have no direct measures of law-enforcement practices. However, it was "common knowledge" in both Texas and Georgia that major cities differed substantially in the degree to which arrests for disorderly conduct or assaults were routinely made. In addition, minority group status made one more likely to be arrested. Consequently, dummy variables are included for minority group membership and for the major cities in each of the two cities.

The remaining exogenous variables can be roughly conceptualized as indicators of tastes for nonproperty crime, although calling something a "taste" is hardly an explanation. Nevertheless, we include sex, age, the age at first arrest, the number of previous arrests, the prison adjustment score (for Texas), and the number of residences reported by respondents. The last is included based on impressionistic observations that individuals with unstable living arrangements are likely to undertake leisure activities ouside their homes and consequently to be more likely to experience arrests for their leisure preferences.[27]

As in the case of property crimes, the equation for nonproperty crimes can be summarized as follows in the form of an abbreviated equation:

(2)   Number of nonproperty crimes $= f$(payments, employment, time in jail or prison, exogenous variables)

---

[26] For a detailed discussion of police discretion, see A. J. Reiss, Jr., *The Police and the Public* (New Haven: Yale University Press, 1971).

[27] That is, they "hang out" a great deal of the time.

An Equation for the Number of Weeks Employed

Given our discussion so far, the equation for the number of weeks employed holds few surprises. We will draw heavily from the labor force participation literature coupled with a few ideas from the field of criminal justice.

To begin, we assume that TARP payments act as a work disincentive although this does *not* mean that TARP participants are necessarily behaving irresponsibly. While some "freeloading" is no doubt going on, much of the support may well be directed toward productive ends. For example, some may use TARP payments to begin the process of buying a car, without which finding and keeping a job is often impossible. Or, the money may be used to move to a new neighborhood in order to start afresh. But perhaps most important, TARP payment recipients may use the money to enhance their job search so that more stable and higher-paying jobs are obtained.[28] (We will address this final possibility in detail in Chapter 13.)

We are *not* including the number of property or nonproperty arrests as predictors of employment. The reason is that arrests per se probably have little impact on the time available for employment. An arrest usually takes little more than a few hours, and many arrests occur at times of the day when most people would not be working. However, time in jail or prison following an arrest may be substantial and clearly may take a significant bite out of a working week. Hence, time in jail or prison will be included as an endogenous predictor.[29]

Turning to the exogenous variables, a relatively large number reflect the usual human-capital concern, although as critics of human-capital theory have emphasized, common indicators of productivity may have more to do with credentialing and the need to sort workers into convenient organizational categories.[30]

The following human-capital variables are included in the employment equation: experience in the military, IQ (for Texas only), an educational-achievement test score (for Texas only),[31] years of education, being of

---

[28] For a review of job-search models, see Lippman and McCall, "The Economics of Job Search."

[29] The same rationale holds for not including the number of property arrests as a predictor of nonproperty arrests and vice versa.

[30] S. Rosen, "Human Capital: A Survey of Empirical Research," in R. G. Ehrenberg (ed.), *Research in Labor Economics: An Annual Compilation of Research* (Greenwich: JAI Press, 1977). It is also probably worth mentioning that such complications are probably irrelevant to the specification of the property-crime equation since most individuals who invest time in illegal behavior are "self-employed."

[31] Although these variables were available in Georgia, up to a third of Georgia TARP members had missing entries for IQ and educational achievement.

prime working age (21–40), being employed at the time of the arrest for which the TARP member had been imprisoned, being handicapped, having a drivers license, and having vocational training in prison.

There are, of course, other factors that affect the ability to find work. We include the unemployment rate in the county of residence as an indicator of the demand side of the labor market, although overall unemployment figures no doubt seriously understate the problems faced by TARP subjects. Our hope is that, nevertheless, *variation* in these rates corresponded to variation in the actual rates *experienced* by TARP subjects. For Georgia we also include whether the individual is a member of a union, since union membership often provides entry into certain kinds of jobs. In addition, not belonging to a union may effectively exclude individuals from those same jobs. (We did not have this measure for Texas.) Unfortunately, for many of the jobs actually available for TARP participants, union membership is probably unimportant. Finally, we also include a variable indicating whether TARP participants claimed to have a job arranged for them upon release.

In the real world faced by our subjects, one must also consider the role of discrimination. Even economists who fervently believe in a competitive labor market acknowledge that discrimination often exists.[32] Consequently we introduce race and sex into our employment equation. For Texas, blacks and Chicanos will be distinguished from whites. In Georgia, blacks and whites only will be distinguished.

Much as in the case of the equation for the number of property arrests, employment should respond to financial need. Hence, the same measures of need are included here: money in hand at release, money saved at home, debts, the number of dependents, and whether or not the individual is planning to live with a spouse after release. We also include the number of weeks sick or in hospital as before, since illness or injury will no doubt take TARP participants off the labor market.

Finally, we include a dummy variable for whether or not the individual is released on parole. Parole officers require a large number of things from their charges, but perhaps the most common concern is that parolees are at least actively seeking work. Hence, release on parole should increase the number of weeks employed. Placing parole status solely in the employment equation also implies that if parole status reduces the number of arrests for property or nonproperty arrests, it operates *through* employment. While other more direct mechanisms may also be involved, we felt that the clearest case could be made for indirect effects.

---

[32] G. S. Becker, *The Economics of Discrimination* (Chicago: University of Chicago Press, 1971).

As before, one can represent the employment specification in an abbreviated equation form:

(3)   Number of weeks employed $= f$(TARP payments, incarceration, exogenous variables)

An Equation for the Number of Weeks in Jail or Prison

Compared to our previous three equations, the equation for the number of weeks in jail or prison is simple. For obvious reasons, incarceration time is taken to be a function of the number of property arrests and the number of nonproperty arrests. In addition, it is known that courts take a number of offender characteristics into account when setting bail and thereby determining pretrial detention; similar considerations influence sentencing. Clearly, a very large number of characteristics might be relevant, but equally important, since their impacts are felt *conditional* upon one or more arrests, they must be modeled as interaction effects. One important consequence is that one risks building serious multicollinearity into the equation. Acordingly, we include only two interaction effects: previous conviction record (first offense or multiple offender) by the number of property arrests, and previous conviction record by the number of nonproperty arrests. Whether or not the TARP member had been a first offender most simply reflected the role of an individual's previous record. Previous record is widely recognized to be a highly critical variable affecting bail setting and sentencing.[33]

In equation form, then:

(4)   Number of weeks in jail or prison $= f$(property arrests, nonproperty arrests, interaction effects)

An Equation for the Money Received from TARP

Since TARP benefits are experimental treatments, the equation for TARP payments represents the design of the TARP experiment, capitalizing on the random assignment to experimental and control groups. Eligibility for payments was contingent upon membership in one of the groups eligible for unemployment benefits. In addition, payment eligibility varied by treatment group. Hence, dummy variables are included for membership in Group 1, Group 2, or Group 3. In addition, payments were also contingent on earnings and availability for employment. However, since the impacts of each of these two contingencies was *conditional* on be-

---

[33] R. A. Berk, and P. H. Rossi, *Prison Reform and State Elites* (Boston: Ballinger, 1977).

ing in one or another of the treatment groups, an appropriate specification required interaction effects.[34] Six interaction terms follow: employment[35] or incarceration by each of the three treatment conditions. In equation form:

(5)   TARP payments received $= f$(Group 1, Group 2, Group 3, interaction effects)

SOME COMPLICATIONS AND CAVEATS

Although the specification for each question was based as much as possible on social science theory, it was necessary all too frequently to improvise. In some instances, the necessary theory did not exist or was articulated in far too general terms to be of much use. For example, discrimination along race, ethnic, or sex lines in the labor market is the subject of lively debate and considerable research, but the critical mechanisms remain poorly defined. Similarly, researchers agree that criminal behavior varies considerably by age, although no one is quite sure why.[36] The equations incorporate both labor-market discrimination measures and TARP-member ages even though the theoretical grounds for doing so are less than adequately developed. Specification errors undoubtedly exist, arising out of failing to include variables that conceivably play important roles in one or more of the equations. Certainly such errors are consistent with the modest size of the proportions of explained variance shown in the reduced-form equations displayed in Chapter 12.

In addition, we were also severely limited by the kinds of data available in TARP files. Some important variables are poorly measured (e.g., our measures of law-enforcement practices) and some important variables are missing altogether (e.g., friendship and kin networks by which jobs are often obtained). This is, of course, a common problem, but it introduces some uncertainty into our findings that must be acknowledged.

---

[34] This was pointed out to us by Professor Marilynn Brewer, University of California, Santa Barbara.

[35] Weeks employed and weeks in jail or prison represented the major contingencies of eligibility.

[36] As can be seen in the results of Chapter 12, the influence of age on either employment or arrest is scarcely large enough to sustain the attention given to this factor in the current literature on recidivism. Older ex-felons may be less likely to commit crimes that lead to re-arrest, but it apparently is not age per se that matters but factors that are associated with that condition.

We have consciously followed a strategy of developing "lean" specifications, keeping the models as simple as possible by using mainly variables whose roles seemed particularly salient on a priori grounds. In this manner, we avoided additional equations of dubious relevance and additional variables that might muddy the results. If there was any doubt an equation or variable was excluded. The reader will see later that the specter of multicollinearity hangs over the entire analysis and such restraint was essential.

Within the general confines of our model, we experimented with slightly different specifications. Building the model was accomplished on the data from Texas. Fine tuning of the model often led to the testing of alternative specifications—for example, trying out competing indicators of the same underlying concept. Had we data only from Texas, the model would be rather vulnerable to Type I and Type II errors. But after settling on the Texas model, *the very same specification was employed on the Georgia data* subject to a few minor alterations depending on differences in the variables available. *In other words, the Georgia analysis is a replication of the Texas analysis.* Since the results for both states are quite similar, it appears unlikely that the model has capitalized on chance (although nonchance specification errors remain).

Finally, we were able to take advantage of the longitudinal nature of the data. Substantively similar models were estimated for the year as a whole, for each of the four quarters, and for the first two quarters coupled with the last 6 months. In addition to permitting the examination of lagged effects, similar findings across all of the models further undercuts the problem of chance findings.

ESTIMATION PROCEDURES

The model specification and the nature of TARP data created a number of complications for estimation. A thorough discussion of the issues would take us well beyond the scope of this book, but some brief discussion is clearly warranted.

The use of endogenous variables as predictors means that our equations are nonrecursive; some variables are subject to reciprocal causation. For example, employment is viewed as affecting TARP payments and, in turn, as affected by TARP payments. Under these circumstances ordinary least squares estimates yield biased and inconsistent estimates of the regression coefficients, and alternative procedures are required. We initially resorted to two-stage least squares because that approach is relatively inexpensive to compute and (given that the structural forms are estimated one equation at a time) and because that approach is relatively robust to specification errors across equations.

We were also keenly aware that previous research had not been especially successful in explaining large amounts of variance in recidivism, and that two-stage least squares often produce high multicollinearity. Moreover, the findings of the Baltimore LIFE experiment suggested that only relatively small treatment effects might be found. In other words, we were searching for small effects in a statistical environment plagued by large standard errors. Consequently, it seemed necessary to improve our statistical efficiency, and we supplemented the two-stage least squares procedures with three-stage least squares. Besides the possibility of improved efficiency, substantively similar findings for both the two-stage and three-stage techniques promised to make our specifications more credible. In three-stage least squares, specification errors in one equation affect the estimates in other equations. But, if the substantive results from the two approaches were roughly the same, one might infer that specification errors were not serious. Of course, some disparities should surface (since the algebra is clearly different), but we hoped the story would be largely unchanged.[37]

Several additional technical problems at one time or another arose to plague the model-estimation efforts. For example, when one constructs interaction variables between an exogenous and an endogenous variable, the resulting interaction variable is subject to the same simultaneous equation bias as "pure" endogenous variables. We missed this point in some of our initial work, and a few rather misleading findings surfaced. For example, in an early version of the equation for property arrests, the TARP payments seemed especially effective for individuals between the ages of 20 and 30 as measured as an interaction term between group membership and being in that age group. The proper solution rests on techniques much like two-stage least squares, in which the interaction variable is "purged" of its correlation with the error term. Unfortunately, this serves to further exacerbate multicollinearity. In the end, however, it seemed more important to obtain consistent estimates, even at the cost of somewhat inflated standard errors.

---

[37] For example, both two-stage and three-stage least squares estimators of the regression coefficients are consistent. This means that asymptotically the sampling distribution of each will converge on the true value of the population parameter (or, alternatively, that the bias in both will disappear) and that, therefore, the two estimators are asymptotically equal. However, we live in a nonasymptotic world, even with samples as large as ours, and, therefore, since the estimators in fact rest on different algebra, they will yield slightly different results (hopefully) in practice.

Another set of problems emerged when we attempted to see how payments operated over time. We attempted to define sets of equations estimated over quarters of the postrelease year, introducing lagged endogenous causal variables. However, the presence of correlated residuals across equations led to inconsistent estimates. Again, a purging process was required, a solution that created additional multicollinearity. In addition, the multicollinearity somewhat limited the number of lagged endogenous effects that could be considered at one time and, given the large standard errors, it was difficult to find significant effects. It appeared that lagged equations tended to obscure the overall importance of processes that were clearly present when the data were analyzed over the entire postrelease year.

Most troubling, it became apparent that many variables are subject to both truncation and censoring.[38] For example, one cannot observe a negative number of property arrests, which means that if a large number of individuals have no arrests, the scatter plot is flattened. This truncation means that in the flattened part of the scatter plot, residuals cannot be symmetrically distributed around the population regression line, and the result is that correlations are often built in between one's regressors and the error terms. Inconsistency may follow.[39] Censoring is also a problem since one can only observe time in jail or prison, for instance, for individuals who have been arrested. While the substantive mechanisms are somewhat different, the result is the same; resulting estimates are often biased and inconsistent.

Unlike the previous difficulties discussed, we were unable to produce a fully satisfactory solution to the problems of truncation and censoring. The problem is that with a large number of equations and variables, currently available solutions are not feasible. Thus, we resorted to a combination of partial solutions. To begin, serious truncation often implies that one has made a specification error. Basically one has employed the wrong functional form. Therefore, we experimented with a number of functional forms that approximated to varying degrees the tobit model favored by some econometricians.[40] That is, we tried to capture the essence of Tobin's likelihood function model without estimating a combined probit and linear

[38] This problem was first pointed out to us by Professor Ann Witte, University of North Carolina.

[39] T. Amemiya, "Multivariate Regression and Simultaneous Equation Models When the Dependent Variables Are Truncated Normal," *Econometrica* 42, no. 6 (1974).

[40] J. Tobin, "Estimation of Relationships for Limited Dependent Variables," *Econometrica* 26, no. 1 (1958); R. C. Sickles and Peter Schmidt, "Simultaneous Equations Models with Truncated Dependent Variables: A Simultaneous Tobit Model," *Journal of Economics and Business* 31, no. 1 (1978).

model. By and large, the story did not change much, although the absolute size of some regression coefficients was significantly affected (as one would expect). In other words, the direction of the relevant coefficients remained the same, and a few switched from statistically insignificant to significant (or the reverse).

In a second step, we focused on the reduced forms. We hoped that in the simpler statistical environment of ordinary least squares where, in addition, multicolinearity was less problematic, we could get some sense of the possible biases. Basically, we "pretended" that each reduced-form equation could be treated in isolation such that we had only to adjust for the truncation/censoring reflected in the single endogenous variable being predicted. (This is, of course, false, since the error term in the reduced form included the errors from each of the structural forms.) We then employed two related adjustments, building on Heckman's sample selection perspective.[41] In not a single instance did the adjustment variable attain statistical significance, and in not a single instance did the story in the reduced form change. While we will review these results in a bit more detail later, suffice it to say we were encouraged.[42]

Finally, we redefined the number of property arrests and nonproperty arrests as dummy variables and reestimated the models. Again, the pattern of coefficients did not change, although t-values for a few important variables dropped below 2 (to about 1.5).

In short, we tried a number of different strategies and, by and large, few findings changed. We take this as evidence that whatever the biases introduced by truncation and censoring, they are probably not serious. On the other hand, we must fully acknowledge that in technical terms, proper adjustments were not fully made.

---

[41] J. J. Heckman, "Sample Selection Bias as a Specification Error," *Econometrica* 47, no. 1 (1979).

[42] Our efforts here were greatly aided by conversations with Thomas Cooley, Charles Mallar, Ann Witte, Peter Schmidt, and particularly James Heckman. We suspect that at least some of these individuals may still be unhappy with our partial solutions, and we are, of course, responsible for any errors in implementing their suggestions.

12

Estimating Transitional Aid Research Project Models for Texas and Georgia

INTRODUCTION

In many ways, this chapter represents the climax of the story of our attempts to unravel the findings of the TARP study. Using the equations and the rationale presented in Chapter 11, the parameters of each are estimated. Whether or not the postulated TARP model of counterbalancing effects is a reasonable interpretation of the data can be judged by assessing whether the results presented in this chapter adequately bolster such an interpretation.

Since the model was first fitted to the Texas TARP data, we will present the findings from that state first. Then we will look at the results obtained by transferring the model, with some modifications, to the Georgia TARP data.

In discussing the results, we will pursue the strategy of concentrating our attention on the structural equations and their parameters. Although the reduced-form equations will be presented, most of the interesting findings displayed in those equations have been discussed in other forms throughout the earlier chapters of this volume and, therefore, have been discussed previously in detail.

Although the model was also computed by quarters of the postrelease year, we will concentrate on presenting results for the year as a whole. That is, we will be concerned with summary measures of behavior over the entire postrelease year—the number of arrests over the postrelease year, number of weeks worked, etc. As we hinted in the last chapter, there were some problems with analyses for subperiods within the year, and we will discuss them at a point later in this chapter.

TARP RESULTS IN TEXAS

At the risk of incurring Type I and Type II errors, adjustments were made to the model when fitting it to the Texas TARP data. This risk was undertaken because such errors could be counteracted by applying the resulting adjusted model to the Georgia data. If the adjusted model did not fit in Georgia, then perhaps the adjustments had capitalized too much on chance and idiosyncracies, especially if there was good reason to believe that the two states were not different in the relevant respects.

The major adjustment made in fitting the model to Texas TARP data was in the selection of specific indicators. When faced with multiple indicators for the same underlying concept with likely multicollinearity among indicators, we selected subsets of indicators yielding the smallest set of standard errors, hopefully thereby producing the most stable results.[1] The success of these adjustments can be judged best when we apply the Texas-derived model to the Georgia data.

Reduced Form Results for Texas

In the first stage of computations, a set of *reduced form* equations are estimated. One important purpose of this set of computations is to provide a set of estimates for each of the endogenous variables that are in effect each free of the biasing influences of the other endogenous variables. These new "instrumental" variables are then used in the next stage. The method for accomplishing this purpose is to regress each of the endogenous variables on the *full* set of exogenous variables used in the system. The resulting equations are then used to compute an estimated value for each observation on each of the endogenous variables.

One usually estimates reduced form equations with ordinary least squares. However, since none of the observations on the dependent variables can be negative, in effect, "zero" provides a lower boundary that not only constrains the observations but also by implication their deterministic and stochastic components. Hence, errors cannot be normally distributed around the *true* regression line; indeed, they also cannot be symmetrically distributed around the true regression line.[2] Consequently, the assumptions of ordinary least squares are violated and biased, and inconsistent results occur.

---

[1] The alternative of confirmatory factor analysis (Karl G. Jöreskog and Dag Sörbom, *Advances in Factor Analysis and Structural Equation Models*, Boston: Abt Book, 1979) was simply not feasible for the complicated models required by our theory.

[2] An introductory discussion of these issues can be found in Richard A. Berk, "A Didactic Review of Some Recent Statistical Developments with Implications for Criminal Justice Evaluations," in M. Klein and K. Tielman (eds.), *Handbook of Criminal Justice Evaluations* (Beverly Hills: Sage Publications, 1980).

Perhaps the most important question raised by such truncation is how serious is the inconsistency in practice. Two important factors are whether the observations tend to "clump" at the boundary (i.e., whether there are a great many observations at zero) and whether after the boundary is exceeded, the observations "jump" to significantly higher values. (The latter is true for employment and not true for arrests.) A more subtle issue involves one's model of how the observations manage to exceed the boundary, although we shall not go into that here (see Heckman's work cited earlier in Chapter 11).

Given the possibility of significant truncation/censoring bias, there are, in principle, several ways in which one may alter the estimation procedures to adjust for the distortions. Perhaps the most practical adjustments rely on first estimating an equation predicting which cases exceed the boundary (e.g., an equation predicting which individuals have at least one arrest). Then a new variable is constructed from this equation, much as in the instance of two-stage least squares, which captures the likelihood of exceeding the boundary. Finally, this new variable is inserted in the equation one really cares about (e.g., an equation predicting the number of arrests). One includes only cases that have exceeded the boundary in this second equation, and the new variable in essence controls for bias. We employed this approach with three alternative forms of the "new variable," and in every case the new variable was not statistically significant.[3] Equally important, the story did not change in any important fashion. In short, for the reduced forms at least, the truncation/censoring biases may not be serious, and the ordinary least squares results are not misleading.[4]

The reduced form equations and estimated parameters are presented in Table 12.1, along with adjusted R^2s for the equations. Substantively, there is not very much new to be learned from these equations beyond findings already discussed in earlier chapters.

In the entries in rows at the bottom of Table 12.1 one can see that, by and large, membership in one of the groups eligible for TARP payments made

---

[3] Heckman suggests using a probit form for the selection (first) equation and then constructing a variable he calls a "hazard rate." We used a logit form in the selection equation from which we constructed both an "adjusted log odds" and the "predicted probability" of exceeding the boundary. All three of these new variables correlated with one another well over .90 (in absolute value), so it did not matter in practice which we used (Subhash Ray, Richard A. Berk, and William Bielby, *Logit Based Truncation Adjustments*, working paper, Group for Research on Social Policy, University of California, Santa Barbara, 1979).

[4] Recall however, that by focusing only on a single reduced form, as if the truncation/censoring was solely a function of the given endogenous variable being predicted, the adjustment is at least incomplete. A technically proper adjustment in this context would have required estimating sample selection equations (equations explaining which cases exceed the boundary) for each truncated/censored endogenous variable, constructing a set of adjustment variables, and then working with the structural forms.

TABLE 12.1
Five-Equation Texas Model, Reduced Form Results

	Regression coefficients				
	Property arrests	Nonproperty arrests	Weeks employed	Weeks incarcerated	Money received (hundreds)
Intercept	0.951	0.795*	−4.928	17.969*	−0.233
Number of residences during year	−0.013	0.020	−0.130	−0.011	0.0647
Male (dummy)	−0.060	0.130	10.267*	1.446	−0.931*
Age (years)	−0.010*	0.002	0.226	−0.150*	0.023
Money at release (hundreds)	−0.002	0.010	−0.122	−0.043	0.007
Money in savings (hundreds)	0.003	0.004	−0.026	0.052	−0.017
Debts (Hundreds)	−0.001	−0.004	0.002	−0.030	0.013
Intending to live with spouse (dummy)	0.022	−0.071	4.846*	−1.997	0.110
Physical handicap (dummy)	0.020	−0.090	−2.008	1.081	−0.130
Number of dependents	−0.016	0.005	0.268	−0.300	−0.015
Number of previous property convictions	0.042*	−0.025	−0.113	−0.420	0.022
Number of weeks sick or in hospital	−0.009	0.000	−0.541*	−0.202*	0.006
Age at first arrest	−0.003	−0.001	0.093	−0.019	−0.010
Times arrested	0.004*	0.000	−0.209*	0.128*	−0.006
Black (dummy)	0.099	−0.043	−3.119*	1.085	0.646
Chicano (dummy)	−0.091	0.161*	−2.645	0.996	0.557
Prison adjustment score[a]	−0.000	−0.000	0.046*	−0.042*	−0.002
Bexar (San Antonio) (dummy)	0.201	0.529*	−3.866	−2.422	0.741
Dallas (dummy)	−0.014	−0.099	0.245	−0.088	0.328
Harris (Houston) (dummy)	−0.093	−0.219*	2.801	−1.048	0.464
Tarrant (Fort Worth) (dummy)	−0.050	−0.159	−0.170	−0.538	0.52
Average unemployment[b] (percentage)	−0.018	−0.049	0.582	−0.263	0.08
Previous military service (dummy)	−0.037	0.073	−0.229	−0.949	0.42
Achievement test score[c]	0.001	−0.000	0.145	0.002	−0.00
IQ	−0.001	−0.002	0.076	−0.020	0.00
Years of education	0.005	0.002	0.254	−0.159	−0.0
Age 21–40 (dummy)	−0.159*	0.024	1.122	0.133	0.5
Employed at pre-TARP arrest (dummy)	−0.108*	−0.024	3.982*	−1.077	0.0

TABLE 12.1 (cont.)
Five-Equation Texas Model, Reduced Form Results

	Regression coefficients				
	Property arrests	Nonproperty arrests	Weeks employed	Weeks incarcerated	Money received (hundreds)
Job arranged at release (4-point scale)	−0.028	−0.006	1.946*	−0.379	0.052
Driver's license (dummy)	−0.070	0.020	1.320	0.094	0.020
Prison vocational training (dummy)	−0.045	−0.035	0.053	0.119	−0.003
Released on parole (dummy)	−0.147*	−0.073	7.277*	−2.025*	−0.337
Group 1 (26 wks./100%)	−0.032	0.068	−7.469*	−0.690	12.343*
Group 2 (13 wks./100%)	−0.031	−0.047	−1.777	−0.548	6.749*
Group 3 (13 wks./25%)	0.101	−0.042	−4.633*	0.389	7.258*
R^2	.088	.118	.291	.115	.750

[a] Scores given to Texas prisoners based on conduct, work effort, and other measures of behavior in prison.
[b] Average of monthly unemployment rates for county to which TARP member returned. Averages obtained from Texas employment security agency estimates.
[c] Achievement test scores derived from test are scored in terms of years of equivalent schooling.
* $p < .05$ (two-tailed test).

little difference in the number of property or nonproperty arrests.[5] Four signs are negative and two signs are positive, but none are significant at the .05 level (for a two-tailed test). Indeed, t-values hover around 1. At this level TARP payments did nothing to avert rearrest. Experimental group membership also had no effect on the number of weeks in jail or prison, as again the signs are mixed and t-values are around 1. In contrast, group membership had the predicted effects on payments and the number of weeks employed. For payments, group membership yields TARP participants between $675 (Group 2) and $1234 (Group 1) over the course of a year. Membership in Groups 1, 2, or 3 produced a work disincentive of between about 2 and 7 weeks.

There are also few surprises among the other exogenous variables. Persons with longer criminal histories tended to experience more property arrests. Older individuals tended to have fewer arrests. Nonproperty arrests seemed especially sensitive to locality and, therefore, perhaps, to local law-enforcement practices. TARP members who worked more were male, white, healthy, and living with a spouse. In addition, they had had fewer previous arrests, a better adjustment in prison, a better job history, a job

[5] These findings are also shown in the ANOVA results presented in Chapter 5. They are also not the final diagnosis of the role of TARP payments, as later tables will show.

arranged, and were on parole. Being on parole also appeared to reduce in-carceration time. And individuals who were older, who were likely to spend time in the hospital, who had had fewer previous arrests and a more satisfactory prison adjustment, and who were on parole were less likely to spend time in jail or prison. Finally, besides membership in one of the control groups, being male and of prime working age reduced the TARP money received. While one might be tempted to dwell on such findings, it is important to stress that reduced form equations reflect the impacts of exogenous variables with mediating links through endogenous variables ignored. That is, *causal mechanisms* are neglected so that substantive interpretations are obscured.

For policy purposes, however, reduced form findings often can provide important information in the form of an overall assessment of the net impact of exogenous variables and hence can yield important policy conclusions. In this instance, perhaps the most important message is that membership in any of the three groups eligible for payments had no net effect on property and nonproperty arrests, while employment was reduced.[6] In addition, parole status appeared to reduce the number of property arrests (by nearly 15%), to increase the number of weeks employed (by about 7 weeks), and to reduce the number of weeks in jail or prison (by about 2 weeks). Since group membership and parole status are presumably amenable to policy manipulation, these findings take on special relevance.

Finally, in the context of our structural form results that will be considered below, the R^2s warrant some attention. In essence, low R^2s mean that instruments constructed in the first stage of our three-stage procedures (i.e., the "purged" endogenous variables) will have relatively small variances and will therefore produce large standard errors. This means that statistically significant results for these variables will be difficult to obtain and, overall, the structural forms will be less "stable."

Estimating the Structural Equation for TARP Payments

The structural equation concerned with TARP benefit payments addresses the amount of money received over the course of a year from membership in Groups 1, 2, or 3. This equation represents the design of the experiment and on a priori grounds should yield sensible results. Indeed, if such results were not forthcoming, the entire analysis is in doubt.

Table 12.2 shows that the experiment was implemented largely as de-

---

[6] This is, of course, the identical message shown in the ANOVA findings presented in Chapter 5.

TABLE 12.2
Five-Equation Texas Model:
Amount of TARP Benefit Money Received

	Regression coefficient	t-value
Intercept	0.08	0.663
Group 1 (26 wks/100%)	1681.12	10.816
Group 2 (13 wks/100%)	990.90	4.367
Group 3 (13 wks/25%)	738.88	4.670
Group 1 × employment	−17.08	−2.858
Group 2 × employment	− 7.93	−1.083
Group 3 × employment	− 0.35	−0.070
Group 1 × jail	−15.23	−1.643
Group 2 × jail	−18.29	−1.812
Group 3 × jail	− 0.00	−0.001

signed. The intercept is indistinguishable from zero; control groups received virtually no money. In contrast, Group 1 members received, on the average, about $1700; Group 2 members about $1000; and Group 3 members about $700. Perhaps the only surprise is that Group 3 members, who were subject to the smaller 25% tax, actually obtained somewhat less money, although, given the complicated nonrecursive impact of the payments, far more then the tax rate alone is involved. Moreover, the interaction effects in Table 12.2 appear partly to right the balance. All are in the predicted direction, and if one uses a one-tail test, three of the six are statistically significant. Group members lose about $17 for each week employed and about $15 for each week in jail or prison. Group 2 members lose about $18 for each week in jail or prison. Note that Group 3 members are least affected by these deductions.[7]

In summary, there is good evidence that the experiment was implemented as designed, at least in terms of the provision of unemployment benefits. Perhaps the only problem with the result is that interactions with weeks employed, *rather than wages,* are included. This, of course, is in contradiction to the experiment's design, but our data on wages were so poor (see Chapter 9 and also Chapter 13) that employment was used as a reasonable surrogate. Fortunately, no really serious interpretative problems seem to have surfaced.

---

[7] Note that these estimates are for amounts of payments lost over *the entire year* for each week of employment or week in jail or prison. Eligibility rules call for much larger amounts of payment loss (see Chapters 4 and 10) but since there were limits to the number of benefits and the total amount of benefits that could be disbursed, some periods of unemployment and some periods of incarceration occurred after the benefit eligibility had been exhausted.

TABLE 12.3
Five-Equation Texas Model:
Number of Property Arrests

	Regression coefficient	*t*-value
Intercept	1.189	5.399
Weeks employed	−0.029	−5.152
Weeks incarcerated	−0.011	−0.860
Payments (hundreds)	−0.019	−3.188
Male (dummy)	0.278	2.331
Age (years)	−0.005	−1.983
Money at release (hundreds)	−0.008	−1.207
Money in savings (hundreds)	0.001	0.453
Debts (hundreds)	0.000	0.175
Live with spouse (dummy)	0.085	1.025
Physical handicap (dummy)	0.016	0.304
Dependents	−0.016	−1.009
Property convictions	0.021	1.484
Weeks sick or in hospital	−0.029	−3.958

Estimating the Structural Equation for Property Arrests

Table 12.3 presents an equation of more substantive interest—the regression coefficients and *t*-values for the structural equation predicting the number of property arrests during the year after release. Since, with one unimportant exception, directional hypotheses were posed, *t*-values in excess of 1.64 will be deemed statistically significant at the .05 level and will be so interpreted. There is nothing magical about the .05 level, and we (among others) have argued that in policy research other decision rules are often more relevant.[8] Nevertheless, the Baltimore LIFE Experiment used the .05 level (one-tail) and comparisons will be facilitated if we follow suit. In addition, without some cost function for the consequences of Type I and Type II errors, no other decision rule seems any more appropriate. Finally, using a more conservative alpha level (e.g., .01) does not substantially change the overall conclusions.

To begin with endogenous predictors, every additional week of employment appeared to reduce the number of property arrests by nearly .03 over the course of 12 months. Since Texas ex-offenders were employed on the average about half the time during their first year after release, this implies

[8] R. A. Berk and M. Brewer, "Feet of Clay in Hobnail Boots: An Assessment of Statistical Inference in Applied Research," in Thomas Cook (ed.), *Evaluation Studies Review Annual,* Vol. 3 (Beverly Hills: Sage Publications, 1978); and R. A. Berk, and P. H. Rossi, "Doing Good or Worse: Evaluation Research Politically Re-examined," *Social Problems* 23, no. 3 (1976).

that, other things being equal, employment may have reduced the *number* of property arrests by about .75 for the "typical" TARP member. After the intercept is adjusted for unreasonable extrapolations (e.g., an age of zero), this means that about 75% of a property arrest was averted. However, as the year progressed, ex-offenders tended to fall into two groups: those with regular jobs and those without. Hence, perhaps a more reasonable interpretation is that the difference between an ex-offender investing heavily in legitimate activities and those not investing in legitimate activities is about 1.5 property arrests. This is clearly a nontrivial impact, about which we will have more to say.

The impact of the number of weeks in jail or prison is in the correct direction, but is not large enough to be distinguished from chance. However, given the low "leverage" in the purged value of weeks in jail or prison, it may be worth noting that at least through incapacitation, every week incarcerated reduces the number of property arrests by about .01. Over the course of their first year, Texas ex-offenders spent about two weeks on the average behind bars, which translates into a .02 reduction in the number of property arrests. However, much as in the case of employment, by the end of the first year the distribution becomes somewhat bimodal, so that it is perhaps more reasonable to say that compared to individuals who stay out of jail, individuals who spend most of the year behind bars experience about .05 fewer property arrests (other things being equal). Of course, such individuals are almost certainly arrested at least once before being removed from circulation. In any case, the meaning of all this will become clearer when we later examine the equation for the number of weeks spent in jail or prison. And it must not be forgotten that the null hypothesis of no effect cannot be rejected.

The TARP payments appear to have an effect much like employment. Every $100 reduces the number of property arrests by about .02, and the large t-value makes chance an unlikely explanation (-3.188). On the average, Texas TARP participants received about $500 over the year, which means that the number of property arrests was typically reduced by about .10. For Group 1 members receiving the highest amount possible, the reduction in the number of property arrests appears to have been as large as .20. Again, this is clearly a nontrivial impact, consistent with a priori predictions.

Three exogenous variables are statistically significant and, in each case, in the predicted directions. Men experience about .28 more property arrests than women, and every additional year of age reduces the number of property arrests by about .005. These coefficients are, of course, consistent with a considerable array of previous studies. Finally, each additional week in the hospital reduces the number of property arrests by about .03.

Our other exogenous variables do not do as well. In particular, the measures of economic need fare poorly. Yet, this might have been expected. The measures of money at release, savings, and debts were not the subject of careful questioning. Living with a spouse was a priori thought to be an ambiguous sign, and the number of dependents is a somewhat indirect indicator of need. For example, a working spouse is treated as a dependent. In short, we would have been somewhat surprised had statistically significant results surfaced for the need variables.

By and large the kinds of physical handicaps experienced by our sample of ex-offenders had no effect on the number of property arrests, other things being equal (e.g., time sick or in the hospital).

Under some specifications, the number of previous property-crime convictions did produce statistically significant increases in the number of property arrests. Moreover, the number of previous property-crime convictions is statistically significant in the two-stage least squares results. Consequently we are inclined to conclude that despite the t-value of 1.48, the impact of previous property crime convictions is "real."[9]

To summarize, it seems clear that variables subject to policy manipulation had important effects on the number of property arrests.[10] Although the precise mechanisms are somewhat ambiguous, theoretical predictions from Bonger to Becker were supported. Equally important, these findings would not have surfaced had we neglected a *causal model* for the TARP experiment. By itself, the analysis of variance approach would have been very misleading. Finally, the structural equation results provide a quantitative estimate of the *size* of important causal effects, estimates that are absolutely critical for policy manipulation.

Estimating the Structural Equation for Nonproperty Arrests

Table 12.4 displays the regression coefficients and corresponding t-values for the structural equation predicting nonproperty arrests. As discussed in the previous chapter, the predictions about effects of employment and TARP payments on nonproperty arrests were at first not entirely obvious.

---

[9] Both the impact of employment and the impact of TARP payments had t-values well over 2.0 in the two-stage least squares results.

[10] We also tried several interaction effects with the TARP payments that seemed reasonable on a priori grounds (e.g., with the number of previous property-crime convictions, education, employment). However, in part because of increased multicollinearity, noting of interest surfaced and, indeed, other results became quite unstable. Subsetting the data to search for interaction effects (e.g., those over 30 years of age and those under 30) also led nowhere but, again, reduced statistical power was in part responsible. We suspect that "good risks" made better use of the TARP payments, but we cannot make a strong statistical case with these data.

TABLE 12.4
Five-Equation Texas Model:
Number of Nonproperty Arrests

	Regression coefficient	*t*-value
Intercept	1.407	3.291
Weeks employed	−0.029	−3.680
Weeks incarcerated	−0.062	−2.639
Payments (hundreds)	−0.016	−2.208
Male (dummy)	0.452	3.010
Age (years)	−0.001	−0.302
Residences (number over year)	0.017	1.438
Weeks sick or in hospital	−0.026	−2.589
Age at first arrest	0.011	−2.183
Times arrested	−0.000	−0.094
Black (dummy)	−0.067	−1.167
Chicano (dummy)	0.107	1.381
Prison adjustment score	−0.000	−0.306
Bexar (San Antonio) (dummy)	0.391	3.119
Dallas (dummy)	−0.054	−0.808
Harris (Houston) (dummy)	−0.152	−2.332
Tarrant (Fort Worth) (dummy)	−0.211	−2.225

On the one hand, since nonproperty arrests by definition were not motivated by income needs, whether a person was working or receiving TARP benefits appeared irrelevant. On the other hand, however, because arrests on a nonproperty charge could lead to loss of employment (and corresponding earnings) or loss of benefits, TARP payments and employment raised the opportunity costs of engaging in all sorts of crime. In addition, employment reduced the amount of leisure time. Thus it may have reduced the amount of opportunity to get into the sort of trouble that could lead to an arrest on a nonproperty related charge. Finally, interpersonal friction with spouse, friends, neighbors, and the like may be reduced when an individual holds down a job that provides him with some status and degree of independence. It may also be the case that the receipt of TARP benefits provided a financial independence that also reduced interpersonal friction, especially with family members.

In any event, both employment and TARP benefits tended to reduce nonproperty arrests. Employment has virtually the same effect (i.e., about a .03 reduction per week) as that found for the number of property arrests. This suggests that sheer economic need may be less relevant to the impact of employment on *all sorts of crime* but that employment raises the opportunity costs of apprehension (i.e., loss of income). In addition, given the obvious time constraints of a 24-hour day, employment may avert both property and nonproperty arrests by simply reducing the time available and, hence, the opportunities.

These interpretations become all the more important in the context of the statistically significant *reduction* in the number of nonproperty arrests for the TARP payments. Again, the impact is almost identical as found for property arrests (i.e., about .02 reduction per $100).

Now, given our findings that TARP payments reduce both property and nonproperty arrests, some of the above causal mechanisms apparently are more important then others. To begin, even if the TARP payments increase leisure time (which we will see shortly is likely), nonproperty arrests are *not* increased. This means that concerning nonproperty crimes, at least, the increase in opportunity costs brought about by TARP payments and the reduction of interpersonal friction apparently outweighs the effects of increased leisure. Second, since the effects of the TARP payments on property *and* nonproperty crimes are so similar, perhaps very similar processes are operating for both (although this is not necessarily the case). Possibly the most important implication is that the reduction of interpersonal friction and the increased opportunity costs may be the critical causal mechanisms reducing arrests; the impact of declining marginal utility of income coupled with the subsidized search for better opportunities in jobs or less risky crime may be less significant. This is especially important for our interpretation of TARP payment effects on property crime as being a *real* and not just an *apparent* effect. Third, if the effects of employment on property and nonproperty crimes are as similar as they appear, common mechanisms may be responsible here as well. Shifts in the time available, reduction of interpersonal friction, and opportunity costs are probably most relevant.

Returning now to Table 12.4, we find that our last endogenous predictor also has an important effect on the number of nonproperty arrests. Every additional week in jail or prison leads to about a .06 reduction in the number of nonproperty arrests. In contrast to the findings for property arrests, the coefficient is statistically significant at the .05 level. Given the average of about 2 weeks in jail or prison for Texas TARP participants over the first year after release, incapacitation appears to reduce the number of nonproperty arrests by about .12.

Finally, the statistically significant exogenous variables behave largely as expected. Males experience about .45 more nonproperty arrests. Each week in the hospital reduces the number of nonproperty arrests by about .025. Individuals who had been first arrested at a later age also experienced fewer nonproperty arrests. But perhaps more interesting were the effects of the county dummy variables. Consistent with impressionistic evidence, ex-offenders living in San Antonio (Bexar County) experienced nearly .40

more arrests, and ex-offenders in Houston (Harris County) and Fort Worth (Tarrant County) experienced about .15 fewer arrests and .21 fewer arrests, respectively. While the precise mechanisms were not clear, these dummy variables may well have reflected the impact of local law enforcement practices. In contrast, however, there is no evidence that blacks and Chicanos were higher risks, other things being equal. Also, age had no effect when other variables were held constant.[11]

Estimating the Structural Equation for Number of Weeks Employed

The equation for the number of weeks employed yields results that are rather consistent with expectations. Table 12.5 indicates that every week in jail or prison reduces employment by about one and one-half weeks. Ex-offenders lose more than a week of employment for every week in jail or prison. This makes sense, since for many, even a brief incarceration may well mean loss of a job. We will see shortly that this is in contrast to other constraints on available time for work.

TARP payments also have the predicted effects. Ex-offenders reduced their work effort by about two-thirds of a week for every $100 of support received.[12] Over the course of the year, typical TARP payment recipients may therefore have worked about three fewer weeks, but for those receiving the maximum amount of financial support, employment may have been reduced over seven weeks. However, the timing of work loss was as important as the total work disincentive: For example, withdrawal from the labor force late in the year after several months of steady work may have had very different implications than an initial reluctance to seek employment. The data indicate that by and large, Texas ex-offenders used up their eligibility early in the year (see Chapter 4). The TARP payments appear to have been used to cushion the initial transition back into the community. One might see this as an appropriate outcome, since it is in the first few months that financial need may be the greatest.

The statistically significant exogenous effects behaved as expected. Men

---

[11] The two-stage results were generally consistent with the three-stage results reported in Table 12.4. There are no sign changes for statistically significant effects, and by and large the regression coefficients are very similar in both estimation procedures (as one would expect). The main difference is that overall, t-values are reduced (again, as one would expect) so that in particular the t-values for the impacts of the TARP payments and weeks in jail or prison drop to about -1.30. These lower t-values should not be of any special concern given the lower efficiency of two-stage estimates.

[12] Note that this reduction is about what one would expect given the 100% tax rate on earnings.

TABLE 12.5
Five-Equation Texas Model:
Number of Weeks Employed

	Regression coefficients	*t*-value
Intercept	28.745	6.657
Weeks incarcerated	−1.691	−9.891
Payments (hundreds)	−0.639	−6.489
Male (dummy)	10.987	5.741
Money at release (hundreds)	−0.212	−1.678
Money in savings (hundreds)	0.038	0.590
Debts (hundreds)	−0.007	−0.120
Live with spouse (dummy)	2.371	1.437
Physical handicap (dummy)	0.002	0.002
Dependents	−0.321	−1.006
Weeks sick or in hospital	−0.866	−8.670
Black (dummy)	−0.764	−0.897
Chicano (dummy)	−1.072	−0.970
Unemployment rate (percentage)	−0.651	−2.053
Previous military service (dummy)	−1.481	−1.520
Achievement test score	0.005	0.214
IQ test scores	0.047	1.603
Years of education	−0.024	−0.142
Age 21–40 (dummy)	1.302	1.455
Employed at pre-TARP arrest (dummy)	1.883	2.576
Job arranged at release (4 levels)	0.957	2.341
Driver's license (dummy)	1.338	1.840
Prison vocational training (dummy)	0.258	0.310
Released on parole (dummy)	3.185	3.679

worked about 11 weeks more than women. Individuals who had been employed when arrested before their recent incarceration (i.e., pre-TARP arrest), worked nearly 2 weeks more. Compared to ex-offenders who claimed to have no job arranged prerelease, ex-offenders who were sure they had a job arranged before release worked about 4 weeks more. And, each week sick or in the hospital led to a reduction of a little less than a week's work. In contrast to the impact of weeks in jail or prison, there seems to be no additional penalty for being sick; loss of a job did not seem to be typically involved.

Probably more important are the statistically significant exogenous variables subject to policy manipulation. First, every $100 immediately available upon release (e.g., gate money) reduced employment by about one working day. Given the superficial manner in which the amount of money at release was measured, the statistically significant result was somewhat surprising (although consistent with a priori predictions). In short, there appears to be an additional source of work disincentive.[13] Second, every 1% increase in the overall unemployment rate in the county of residence led to about two-thirds of a week less employment. This may seem to be a very small effect, but county unemployment rates varied between about 3% and 12% across Texas counties. Hence, a disparity of as much as 6 weeks of employment could well have been involved. Looking back to the property-arrest equation, 6 weeks of unemployment translated into nearly .20 more property arrests, other things being equal. Clearly, this was nontrivial, and the effects on nonproperty arrests were similar. In addition, the unemployment rates used reflected the experiences of the labor force as a whole. It is likely that a 1% change in the unemployment rate for the labor force as a whole translated into a somewhat larger change for individuals with backgrounds like the TARP participants. In other words, we may well be understating the impact of unemployment rates. Third, being released on parole increased the number of weeks employed by about three. Again referring back to the two arrest equations, parole status reduced the number of arrests by nearly .10, other things being equal. Again, we have an important effect with policy implications.

Finally, several nonsignificant variables warrant brief mention. Perhaps most interesting, race or ethnic background had no impact on employment after the other variables in the equation were considered. For TARP participants, we found no evidence of discrimination. Yet, one must also keep in mind that most TARP participants were on the fringes of the legitimate labor market and were competing for jobs that a very large number of other individuals would not have considered. That is, we found no evidence for discrimination in such jobs as washing cars, janitorial work, day labor, unskilled factory work, and farm work. In this context, we also did not find much in the way of effects for our human-capital variables: education, IQ, achievement test scores, prison vocational training, prime working age, and the like. Witte and Schmidt[14] reached similar conclusions in their ex-offender study, which in turn raised the fundamental question of whether human-capital perspectives have much relevance for the kinds of jobs typically sought by ex-offenders. For the least dsirable jobs offered by society, employers may want little more than warm bodies.

---

[13] This effect, however, is not large when we consider the range of differences in money at hand at time of release among Texas ex-offenders. Almost every offender received $200 in gate money, and very few had more than that amount when they left. A handful of releasees had as much as $1000 upon release, but even this very large amount meant being unemployed about a week more than was typical for all ex-offenders. The work-disincentive effect of money at hand on release was considerably less than the effect of TARP payments as well.

[14] A. D. Witte and P. Schmidt, "An Analysis of Recidivism Using the Truncated Lognormal Distribution," *Journal of the Royal Statistical Society*, series C, vol. 26, no. 3, (1977).

To summarize, we have found clear evidence for the predicted work disincentive of TARP payments; time is shifted away from employment. We have also found important effects for parole status and the overall unemployment rate. In contrast, human-capital variables seemed largely irrelevant. These patterns have important policy implications that will be addressed in a later chapter.

Estimating the Structural Equation for Number of Weeks in Jail or Prison

Our final equation shown in Table 12.6 examines time spent in jail or prison. The risk of serious multicollinearity dictated a very simple model, and the results are easily communicated. Every additional property arrest leads to about 17 weeks in jail or prison, on the average. Basically, these are the study's failures. In contrast, there is no evidence that nonproperty arrests make any statistically significant difference in incarceration. If nothing else, this serves to further justify our distinction between relatively serious property arrests and the many nuisance arrests included under the nonproperty characterization.

Both interaction effects operate in the predicted direction; first offenders who are arrested tended to receive shorter jail or prison terms. The impact for property arrest is statistically significant (barely) and indicates that arrested first offenders have their incarcerations reduced by about 5.5 weeks.[15]

It is perhaps important to stress that important causal variables have probably been excluded. Our four-variable model is certainly not the whole story. However, besides the impact of arrests, the model for time in jail or prison is not central to our analysis and, in any case, our data on actions of the criminal justice system beyond arrest are virtually nonexistent.

Estimating Overtime Models

Besides a model for the year as a whole, we estimated larger models in which the five equations reported here were "moved" through each of four quarters. We also estimated a system of equations using three periods: the first quarter, the second quarter, and the last 6 months. In both cases, this allowed (among other things) for the consideration of lagged effects. For example, we explored the possibility that TARP payments not only pro-

---

[15] Note that "first offender" refers to the offense for which the TARP member served his prison term. Hence "first offenders" really means persons with relatively short previous records. Any "first offender" who gets arrested appears as a "second offender" when he or she appears before the courts.

TABLE 12.6
Five-Equation Texas Model:
Number of Weeks in Jail or Prison

	Regression coefficients	*t*-value
Intercept	0.671	0.916
Property arrests	17.093	7.888
Nonproperty arrests	0.909	0.534
First offender × Property	− 5.630	− 1.640
First offender × Nonproperty	− 2.054	0.491

duced a work disincentive immediately, but also a work disincentive lagged by one quarter. Similarly, we examined whether an arrest in an earlier quarter led to an increase or decrease in arrests in later quarters.

Unfortunately, the larger overtime models were subject to a number of statistical problems. First, many reduced form R^2s fell below .05, which meant that the variances of constructed instruments were severely constrained. Low statistical power (and hence instability) resulted. Second, for a few of the low R^2 reduced-form equations, virtually all of the explained variance was attributable to a very small number of variables. If these happened to then be included in a structural form with the relevant instrument, multicollinearity sometimes reached unacceptable levels. Third, the use of lagged endogenous variables required yet more instruments (for the lagged endogenous variables) since residuals were correlated across equations. As a consequence, multicollinearity was further heightened.

Coupled with the statistical problems were some serious interpretative difficulties with some variables. For example, time in jail or prison in the first and second quarter was primarily a function of short stays behind bars while awaiting bail or trial. Consequently, the variable of incarceration time was really little more than a surrogate for contact with the criminal justice system. It did not actually capture "time at risk."

These and other complications led to a sequential analytical strategy. First, we estimated overtime models (with three-stage least squares) that were as similar as possible to the model estimated for the year as a whole.[16] However, we also included some especially important lagged effects, justified on a priori grounds (e.g., the lagged effects of TARP payments). The results were heartening, but certainly not compelling. For example, TARP payments reduced the number of property arrests in the first quarter and second 6 months by a statistically significant amount but showed no ef-

---

[16] One model involved 20 equations over 4 quarters, and the other model involved 15 equations over the first 2 quarters and the second 6 months.

fect in the second quarter. The impact of employment on property arrests followed the same pattern. More distressing was the total failure of TARP payments or employment to influence the number of nonproperty arrests. Yet, work disincentives from the TARP payments surfaced in both a simultaneous and lagged form.

It was apparent from some very large standard errors and high correlations estimated among some of the regression coefficients that the overtime models were being undermined by several nearly redundant variables. In particular, the instrument for time in jail or prison (i.e., the purged endogenous variable) was suspect, especially in the equations for property and nonproperty arrests. Correlations for the estimated coefficients in excess of .85 were common, and rather counterintuitive results sometimes appeared. For example, in the case of nonproperty arrests in the first quarter, every week in jail *increased* the number of arrests by .06. This implied that individuals who were behind bars for most of the quarter (13 weeks) would experience about .80 *more* property arrests. Clearly we were not tapping the effects of incapacitation, but rather (at best) the tendency to get into trouble. Therefore, we reestimated the initial overtime models dropping time in jail or prison from all of the arrest equations.

With a few minor exceptions, the new overtime models fully reproduced the findings for the model based on the year as a whole, despite some remaining problems with multicollinearity. We found, for example, that the TARP payments had roughly the same effects in the property, nonproperty, and employment equations in each of the time periods and that these were quite similar to the effects estimated for the full year. Moreover, these surfaced in the face of markedly reduced variance in TARP payments during the second half of the year (since most of the money was given out by then). On the other hand, little of any importance was learned from the overtime models that was not apparent from the model for the year as a whole. By and large, lagged endogenous variables had small effects, and the large effects that appeared were not particularly interesting. The fact that incarceration time in an early quarter predicts incarceration time in a later quarter, for instance, is hardly stunning, given jail terms of over 13 weeks in length. Still, it is important to keep in mind that the lagged (purged) variables were highly correlated with other variables in the models and perhaps more was actually going on than our statistical procedures could effectively reveal.

In summary, the story of the TARP experiment can be accurately told from the full-year model alone. The overtime models essentially reproduced these results and added little new information. We suspect, however, that with better data properly tied to the passage of time, some new findings would emerge. There are almost certainly significant dynamic processes that we have missed.

Truncation and Censoring Effects

In the last chapter we discussed the likely existence of problems stemming from truncated and/or censored variables. In particular, all of our endogenous variables are characterized by a lower bound of zero and some degree of clumping at those lower boundaries. That is, a number of observations pile up at zero. As demonstrated by Tobin, this may imply a specification error, and one's regression estimates may be misleading (inconsistent).[17] In addition to such truncation problems, censoring is also a factor, since only people who have been arrested (presumably) can serve a jail term. And if one is interested in projecting our results beyond the 1-year follow-up, a second source of censoring is apparent.

We have no full solution to these difficulties, but we tried a variety of strategies that, as a group, may help to discount concerns that our findings are seriously in error. First, we make no claims that our conclusions are fully appropriate for time periods beyond 1 year after release. We are, for example, obviously underestimating the total number of property arrests for periods longer than 12 months postrelease. This in turn implies that the regression coefficients in the property-arrest equation may be somewhat misleading if formal extrapolations are attempted. In other words, while there is good reason to believe that the overall results would be much the same over a far longer follow-up (in part because recidivism is reputed to be most common soon after release), we will undertake no such projections. In one sense, the censoring problem generated by the 1-year follow-up is being defined away.[18]

Second, there *may* be little reason to be especially concerned about the effects of the censoring for time in jail or prison when that variable is the dependent variable. The censoring process is being tapped by the instruments for the number of property and nonproperty arrests. On the other hand, since these predictors are truncated, the implicit relationship between them (that in turn affects the estimates of their regression coefficients) is not being properly handled. This requires some consideration of more general truncation problems.

---

[17] J. Tobin, "Estimation of Relationships for Limited Dependent Variables," *Econometrica* 26, no. 1 (1958).

[18] In addition, the earlier Baltimore LIFE experiment employed a 2-year follow-up finding that first-year effects were not eroded by second-year events.

As an initial cut at the implications of truncation, we attempted to approximate the functional form of the tobit model with various powers of the relevant variables. For example, the combined probit–linear form can be roughly approximated by transforming all of the truncated endogenous variables into their square roots. That is, when each truncated endogenous variable *was being predicted*, its square root became the dependent variable. Other fractional exponents were also tried, but all implied that the impacts of exogenous variables were greater as the values of the exogenous variables increased. In other words, we were trying to model the impact of clumping and truncation near the zero boundary.[19]

The results from these transformations were encouraging. Although the size of the regression coefficients necessarily changed in response to the transformation, the signs were consistent with the untransformed results. Moreover, *t*-values were quite similar. In other words, the story did not fundamentally change when we tried to take the piling up at zero into account.

Next, we redefined the number of property and nonproperty arrests as dummy variables (i.e., arrested or not arrested).[20] In effect, we hoped to trade inefficiency and inconsistent standard errors for consistent regression coefficients. Again, the results were encouraging. For example, TARP participants who received the full amount of money possible experienced nearly a .07 reduction in the probability of arrest. Note that this is almost the same reduction found in the Baltimore LIFE experiment. Similarly, each week of employment reduced the probability of a property arrest by a little more than one-half percent. This implied that ex-offenders who worked most of the year had less chance, by more than 30%, of being arrested for a property crime. Slightly larger effects were found for the impact of employment on nonproperty arrests. On the other hand, the use of dummy variables for property and nonproperty arrests also introduced greater instability into the equations, so that some of the results were not fully comparable to earlier findings. We did not find, for example, a statistically significant effect for the TARP payments on nonproperty arrests (although the sign was negative and the regression coefficient nontrivial).

Finally, we attempted to use adjustments roughly consistent with the suggestions of Heckman.[21] In brief, we focused on the equation for property arrests and constructed a logit-derived instrument for whether or not an ex-offender was arrested. Then, we examined only the subset of of-

---

[19] In slightly different terms, we were trying to overcome the attenuation of effects caused by the truncation at zero.

[20] Piling up was most serious for these variables.

[21] J. J. Heckman, "Sample Selection Bias as a Specification Error," *Econometrica* 47, no. 1 (1979).

fenders with one or more arrests, using the instrument as a "control" variable. Basically, we transformed a truncation problem caused by a fixed boundary at zero to a censoring problem. Then, we tried to control for the processes by which that boundary was exceeded.

In spite of (or because of) our unorthodox procedures and the fact that only the variable for the number of property arrests was considered, we again found that TARP payments and employment significantly reduced the number of property arrests. Indeed, regression coefficients for payments approximately doubled (to about a .04 reduction for every $100). And we found this in the face of greatly reduced sample sizes as a function of the subsetting process ($N = 223$).

To summarize, because of the large number of equations and the large number of variables subject to truncation/censoring, we could not use the recommended procedures to make the proper adjustments. However, our basic findings appeared to hold under each of our alternative analytic strategies. Hence, we are inclined to treat our original results as real although we fully admit that the preferred adjustments were not made.

GEORGIA TARP RESULTS

There can be little doubt that in Texas the TARP experiment altered the behavior of ex-offenders during the first 12 months after release. Perhaps the major policy-relevant conclusion is that after controlling for the work disincentive produced, unemployment benefits appeared to reduce the number of property and nonproperty arrests. Perhaps the most parsimonious explanation is that in both instances, TARP payments increased the opportunity costs of arrest and provided income competing with property crime. In addition, we found striking direct effects on crime for employment and indirect effects through employment for parole status and the overall unemployment rate. In short, rearrest rates respond dramatically to the mix of incentives with which ex-offenders are presented.

A priori, there is some reason to be a bit skeptical that the findings for Georgia will be the same as those in Texas. First, the data are of lesser quality. For a variety of reasons, described in earlier chapters, Georgia had more missing data, and there is reason to believe that errors in data were frequent. Second, the economic climate in Georgia was very different from that of Texas. In particular, overall unemployment rates were approximately twice as large. This means that Georgia ex-offenders faced greater difficulty in finding jobs, and jobs available were less desirable. Among the many implications for our analysis, the work disincentives from TARP payments should have been heightened. Third, there is no reason to assume that the criminal justice systems in the two states functioned in identical fashion. More specifically, Texas was known to send offenders to prison readily and for long periods of time. This was less true in Georgia. One important implication is that our equation for weeks in jail or prison will be more difficult to estimate. Finally, we "fine tuned" our structural equation model with data from Texas, not Georgia. Hence, even if Georgia was an exact replication of Texas, the models will fit less well in Georgia by chance alone. And of course, Georgia was not an exact replication of Texas.

With these complications in mind we estimated equations in Georgia that were identical in form to those estimated in Texas, except where comparable variables were not available. For example, in Georgia there were no measures of prison adjustment, many IQ scores were missing, but union membership was ascertained. By and large, however, the equations were much the same.

Unfortunately, while the overall results were rather similar to those in Texas, several important differences appeared. Perhaps most troubling, TARP payments had only small (negative) effects on the number of property and nonproperty arrests, and in both equations the number of weeks in jail or prison dramatically *increased* the number of arrests. For example, each \$100 reduced the number of nonproperty arrests by about .005 ($t = -1.09$), and each week in jail or prison increased the number of nonproperty arrests by .04 ($t = 2.96$). The latter meant that Georgia ex-offenders who spent most of the year in jail would have been expected to experience about two more nonproperty arrests then ex-offenders with no jail time.

Perplexed by such findings, we carefully scrutinized a range of diagnostics. We noticed, for example, that compared to Texas, the R^2s for the reduced-form equations for nonproperty and incarceration were reduced by about 50%. Weak instruments necessarily resulted. In addition, the variance that was explained in these reduced forms could be attributed to a very few variables, most of which appeared in the same structural forms with the instruments. This led to serious multicollinearity. Finally, it was apparent that compared to Texas, the correlations among the residuals across equations were very large. In Table 12.7 we show the correlations for Texas (Panel A) and Georgia (Panel B). Note the high correlations in Table 12.7, Panel B, for the residuals of the property-arrest equation with the residuals of the nonproperty equation and the residuals of the equation for incarceration (.74 and $-.77$, respectively). Although such correlations can result from a number of problems, they typically stem from serious specification errors or instability caused by multicollinearity. Since there is no reason to believe that suddenly our model is grievously in error, and since there is ample evidence of multicollinearity, we are inclined to accept the second explanation.

TABLE 12.7
*Correlations between Residuals
across Equations*

		Equation				
		1	2	3	4	5
A. *Texas*						
Number of property arrests	1	1.00	.252	.528	−.349	.060
Number of nonproperty arrests	2		1.00	.471	.354	.043
Number of weeks employed	3			1.00	.316	.053
Number of weeks incarcerated	4				1.00	−0.025
TARP money received	5					1.00
B. *Georgia*						
Number of property arrests	1	1.00	.738	.130	−.770	.014
Number of nonproperty arrests	2		1.00	.145	−.424	.021
Number of weeks employed	3			1.00	.149	.078
Number of weeks incarcerated	4				1.00	−.059
TARP money received	5					1.00

The next problem was to reduce the multicollinearity. Estimated correlations between coefficients within equations and residuals across equations suggested that a substantial part of the instability could be attributed to the inclusion of weeks incarcerated in the property and nonproperty arrest equations. In particular, correlations between incarceration and other endogenous predictors often topped .70; this was, of course, somewhat expected. Consequently we dropped weeks incarcerated from the property and nonproperty equations and reestimated the entire model. The results that follow are taken from this second pass over the data.

Georgia Reduced Form Results

Table 12.8 shows the reduced form results from Georgia. As before, there is little to say beyond the material covered in earlier chapters. Perhaps the most useful figures can be found near the bottom of the tables where, once again, several coefficients for the employment equation are statistically significant. In particular, being released on parole leads to an extra 5.5 weeks of employment over the course of the year. However, membership in Group 1 reduces the work effort by 10 weeks, membership in Group 2 reduces work effort by 6 weeks, and membership in Group 3 reduces work effort by 4 weeks. Although these coefficients tell much the same story as found in Texas, the more difficult job market also affected

TABLE 12.8
Five-Equation Georgia Model:
Reduced Form Results

	Regression coefficients				
	Property arrests	Nonproperty arrests	Weeks employed	Weeks incarcerated	Money received (hundreds)
Intercept	0.719*	1.131*	8.531	5.597	−0.362
Male (dummy)	0.135	0.013	4.286	4.096*	0.237
Age (years)	−0.008	−0.011*	−0.024	−0.069	−0.003
Money at release (hundreds)	−0.004	−0.006	−0.334	0.004	−0.138*
Money in savings (hundreds)	0.004	0.008	−0.162	−0.039	0.022
Debts (hundreds)	−0.002	−0.006	0.099	−0.049	−0.002
Live with spouse (dummy)	0.103	0.156	2.096	−1.188	0.126
Physical handicap (dummy)	0.037	0.032	−2.008	0.737	−0.170
Number of dependents	−0.023	−0.006	−0.497	−0.259	−0.092
Number of property convictions	0.164*	0.202*	−0.210	0.476	−0.030
Number of weeks sick or in hospital	−0.004	−0.005	−0.409*	−0.081	0.007
Age at first arrest	−0.005	−0.009	0.188	0.022	−0.001
Times arrested	0.006	0.009*	−0.048	0.115*	−0.006
Black (dummy)	0.040	0.023	0.165	−0.479	−0.004
Savannah (dummy)	0.162	0.044	−1.570	3.844*	−0.101
Atlanta (dummy)	0.122*	0.164*	−1.396	1.366	0.471*
Bibb County (dummy)	0.030	0.153	−2.891	1.653	0.881
Banks County (dummy)	−0.025	−0.195	0.185	0.243	1.078*
Unemployment rate (percentage)	−0.001	−0.002	0.023	0.014	0.011
Previous military service (dummy)	−0.062	0.014	0.141	−1.200	−0.098
Union member (dummy)	−0.020	−0.001	0.640	−0.655	0.645*
Number of residences	−0.002	0.039	0.400	0.235	−0.052
Years of educations	−0.011	−0.006	0.107	−0.001	−0.066
Age 21–40 (dummy)	−0.042	−0.089	0.332	−0.324	0.266
Employed at pre-TARP arrest (dummy)	−0.012	−0.001	2.367*	−0.752	−0.023
Job arranged at release (4-point scale)	−0.094	−0.062	5.715*	−0.417	−0.368
Driver's license (dummy)	−0.072	−0.089	3.676*	−2.392*	−0.055*
Prison vocational training (dummy)	0.047	0.034	1.958	0.563	−0.111
Released on parole (dummy)	−0.053	−0.133*	5.461*	−1.034	0.078
Group 1 (26 wks/100%)	0.078	0.037	−10.103*	−0.079	13.826*
Group 2 (13 wks/100%)	0.079	0.122	−6.221*	0.245	7.518*
Group 3 (13 wks/25%)	0.086	0.094	−4.026*	−0.352	8.301*
R^2	.084	.088	.226	.073	.765

* $p < .05$ for two-tailed test (since our one-tailed hypothesis referred to structural forms).

findings. The effect of parole in Georgia was smaller than in Texas by about 2 weeks. Correspondingly, the work-disincentive effect in Georgia is generally several weeks larger than in Texas.

Table 12.8 also indicates that on the average, Group 1 members received about $1400, Group 2 members received about $750, and Group 3 members received about $800. These figures are roughly comparable to those in Texas, once we take into account that benefit levels were higher in Georgia ($70 per week as compared to $63 in Texas).

The impact of TARP experimental group membership on property and nonproperty arrests was once again virtually zero. Indeed, the signs are all positive; hence, if anything, membership in one of the experimental groups makes things worse (t-values average around 1.20). Perhaps once again we are seeing the impact of poorer job prospects in Georgia. The work disincentives and their consequences for crime may be nearly making the treatment appear harmful.

Finally, at the very bottom of the table, the R^2s are reported for the reduced-form equations. The R^2s for the property, nonproperty, and incarceration equations are quite low, and the latter two are considerably lower than for the Texas reduced-form equations. It is difficult to know why these reductions occur, although we anticipated more problems with the data in Georgia. However, the low R^2s mean that the instruments for the number of weeks in jail or prison will have little variance and will perhaps, therefore, mask important causal effects. This should be kept in mind as we proceed through the tables that follow.

Georgia Equation for the Amount of TARP Money Received

Once again there is no evidence that the experiment was significantly subverted. Table 12.9 indicates that, on the average, Group 1 members received nearly $1700, Group 2 members received over $1000, and Group 3 members received over $600. These figures are rather close to the figures for Texas, which means that once we take employment and incarceration into account, very similar amounts of money were received. Only one of the interaction terms is statistically significant.[22] Each additional week in jail or prison for Group 1 members costs them an average of nearly $27. Nevertheless, four of the six have signs in the predicted direction, and

---

[22] Note that even though random assignment was employed, group membership is necessarily correlated with the interaction terms. Moreover, with all of the interaction terms, multicollinearity mitigates against finding statistically significant results for anything but main effects.

TABLE 12.9
Five-Equation Georgia Model:
Amount of TARP Money Received

	Regression coefficient	*t*-value
Intercept	2.321	0.153
Group 1 (26 wks/100%)	1691.11	7.602
Group 2 (13 wks/100%)	1021.99	5.266
Group 3 (13 wks/25%)	621.80	3.799
Group 1 × Employment	−11.59	−1.027
Group 2 × Employment	−10.65	−1.207
Group 3 × Employment	3.90	0.575
Group 1 × Jail	−26.93	−2.018
Group 2 × Jail	−14.59	−1.072
Group 3 × Jail	28.21	1.600

hence there seems no grounds for special concern. In short, we can proceed with some confidence that we are examining the effects of an experiment implemented substantially as planned.

Georgia Equation for the Number of Property Arrests

Table 12.10 shows the results for the equation in which the number of property arrests for one year after release are predicted. Much as in the case of Texas, every week employed reduced the number of property arrests by .022 (.029 in Texas). Since ex-offenders in Georgia were employed about 40% of the time, an average of half a property arrest was averted. For ex-offenders employed for the full year, an average of about one property arrest was averted. Given a mean number of property arrests of well under one, these are clearly nontrivial effects.

The TARP payments also have substantial and statistically significant effects ($t = 2.207$). Every $100 reduces the number of property arrests by a little over .01. This is about half the effect found in Texas ($b = .019$) but given the amount of money paid out, still of practical importance. The average TARP participant received nearly $600, which means that typical reduction in the number of property arrests was about .06. Assuming a maximum of about $1700 in Group 1, for some the number of property arrests could have been cut by .17.

Among the exogenous predictors, less of interest is revealed. Tables 12.10 and 12.3 show that men experienced about .32 more property arrests in Georgia and .28 in Texas, and that each additional week in the hospital reduced the number of property arrests by about .014 in Georgia and .029 in Texas. There is also a suggestion that older people experience about .005 fewer arrests for each year of age in both states. Finally, the number of

TABLE 12.10
Five-Equation Georgia Model:
Number of Property Arrests

	Regression coefficient	t-value
Intercept	0.788	5.745
Weeks employed	− 0.022	− 6.173
Payments (hundreds)	− 0.011	− 2.207
Male (dummy)	0.320	3.220
Age (years)	− 0.005	− 1.857
Money at release (hundreds)	− 0.003	− 0.621
Money in savings (hundreds)	− 0.003	− 1.470
Debts (hundreds)	0.001	0.432
Live with spouse (dummy)	− 0.014	− 0.364
Physical handicap (dummy)	− 0.023	− 0.738
Dependents	− 0.023	− 2.188
Property convictions	0.036	1.544
Weeks sick or in hospital	− 0.014	− 3.512

dependents had a statistically significant effect in Georgia. Each additional dependent reduced the number of property arrests by about .023 (t = 2.19). In Texas the sign was the same but the t-value was about − 1. The theoretical expectation for this variable is somewhat ambiguous. We had taken the number of dependents to reflect need, but if that is true, we find that greater economic need leads to fewer arrests. Perhaps the need manifested is for certainty and steadiness of income. An alternative explanation within an economic framework would view dependents as a source of utility forgone with arrest and conviction. This interpretation would yield the sign actually found, and the effect might be enhanced to the degree that ex-offenders consider the welfare of their dependents when time allocation decisions are made.

In summary, whether by luck or skill, we have managed to effectively replicate with data from Georgia the findings from Texas. We find again that TARP payments and employment had important effects on the number of property arrests.

Georgia Equation for the Number of Nonproperty Arrests

In Table 12.11 we turn to the equation for the number of nonproperty arrests. It is immediately apparent that we have replicated the key findings from Texas (see also Table 12.4). Every week employed reduced the number of of nonproperty arrests by .026 (.029 in Texas). Every $100 of

TABLE 12.11
Five-Equation Georgia Model:
Number of Nonproperty Arrests

	Regression coefficient	t-value
Intercept	1.187	6.433
Weeks employed	− 0.026	− 5.351
Payments (hundreds)	− 0.014	− 2.143
Male (dummy)	0.248	1.903
Age (years)	− 0.006	− 1.877
Weeks sick or in hospital	− 0.016	− 3.130
Age at first arrest	− 0.005	− 1.320
Times arrested	0.002	0.903
Black (dummy)	− 0.021	− 0.545
Residences	0.046	2.673
Savannah (dummy)	− 0.161	− 1.826
Atlanta (dummy)	0.045	1.128
Bibb (dummy)	0.101	1.104
Banks (dummy)	− 0.154	− 1.643

TARP benefits reduced the number of nonproperty arrests by .014 (.016 in Texas). Both regression coefficients have t-values over 2, so that chance is not a likely explanation. In short, the story is virtually the same.

We also find once again that each week sick or in the hospital reduced the number of nonproperty arrests (in Georgia by .016), and that women and older individuals experienced fewer arrests. Perhaps the only surprise was that in Georgia, in contrast to Texas, the number of residences lived in over the postrelease year managed to reach statistical significance. Each additional move leads to a rather large .046 increase in the number of nonproperty arrests. In Texas, the regression coefficient was .017 and the t-value was 1.43. Finally, some null effects are probably worth noting. First, in Georgia there did not seem to be particularly large effects for the county or city dummy variables (with the possible exception of Savannah). Perhaps there was less place-to-place variation in law-enforcement practices in Georgia. Second, we once again find no statistically significant effects for race. If Georgia blacks committed more crimes and/or if police were more likely to arrest blacks, it was not apparent in our data.

In short, so far we are batting two for two. We have managed to replicate our most important effects for the number of property and nonproperty arrests. It would appear that something rather important occurred between employment and TARP payments, on the one hand, and the number of property and nonproperty arrests, on the other. Moreover, the fact that the effects were so similar in both states suggests that common causal mechanisms were involved.

Georgia Equation for the Number of Weeks Employed

Table 12.12 shows the results for the number of weeks employed, and it is clear that by and large the Texas findings were reproduced. Whereas the intercept in Georgia was somewhat lower than in Texas (as one would expect from the difference in employment rates), the marginal effects of the important variables were quite similar. To begin, each week in jail or prison reduced the number of weeks employed by about 1.3. The figure for Texas was 1.7 (see Table 12.5), but in both cases 1 week in jail or prison cost more than 1 week of work. Most likely, jobs were being lost.

Once again we find large work disincentives. Each $100 of payments reduced the number of weeks worked by .68 (in Texas the figure was .64). As we argued earlier, this is clearly nontrivial and, given the effect of unemployment on arrests, serves to undercut the reduced form effects for membership in any of the three groups eligible for payments. For example, ex-offenders receiving $600 (about the mean) would have been expected to work about 4 weeks less over the course of a year. This would have led to about .09 more property arrests and about .10 more nonproperty arrests.

We also find a large effect for release on parole. Ex-offenders on parole worked about 3.6 weeks more during the first year after release (in Texas the effect was 3.2 weeks). While it is entirely possible that we have not effectively controlled for selection biases in who obtained parole, the effects seem far too large to simply be dismissed. At the very least, the impact of parole status on employment needs to be studied further; parole is, after all, a variable that may be manipulated.

Other statistically significant variables include savings, money at release, sex, the number of dependents, weeks in the hospital, and having a job arranged upon release. Every $100 of savings reduced the work effort by about .2 weeks. We are not inclined to make too much of this since no such effects surfaced in Texas.[23] On the other hand, the sign is in the predicted direction, and money held at release had a similar effect (t-value of -1.89). In short, there is a hint of work disincentive here as well.

The impact of weeks sick or in the hospital and having a job arranged replicated the Texas findings and seems rather sensible. The former reduced work effort, while the latter increased it. However, we do not know quite what to make of the finding that each additional dependent *reduced* the work effort by nearly 1 week. The effect in Texas was also negative, but about one-third as large and not significant.

---

[23] It should be noted that since few ex-offenders had any savings at all, this effect is scarcely an important one.

TABLE 12.12
Five-Equation Georgia Model
Number of Weeks Employed:

	Regression coefficient	t-value
Intercept	18.792	4.860
Weeks incarcerated	−1.320	−4.241
Payments (hundreds)	−0.684	−7.786
Male (dummy)	8.557	3.387
Money at release (hundreds)	−0.346	−1.887
Money in savings (hundreds)	−0.199	−2.571
Debts (hundreds)	0.041	0.764
Live with spouse (dummy)	0.499	0.374
Physical handicap (dummy)	−1.436	−1.374
Dependents	−0.798	−2.342
Weeks sick or in hospital	−0.507	−6.053
Black (dummy)	−0.717	−0.776
Unemployment rate (percentage)	0.005	0.209
Previous military service (dummy)	−0.630	−0.594
Union member (dummy)	0.124	0.116
Years of education	0.196	1.001
Age 21–40 (dummy)	−0.045	−0.051
Employed at pre-TARP arrest (dummy)	1.281	1.338
Job arranged at release (4-point scale)	4.633	4.941
Driver's license (dummy)	1.156	0.977
Prison vocation training (dummy)	1.767	1.610
Released on parole (dummy)	3.556	3.596

It is also worth noting that as in the case of Texas, men worked more (10.99 weeks in Texas and 8.6 weeks in Georgia), but minority status had no impact. At least in the case of race, no evidence of discrimination surfaced. Again, however, one must keep in mind that the kinds of jobs open to ex-offenders were hardly the kinds of jobs most people would find desirable. Finally, in marked contrast to Texas, the overall unemployment rate in an ex-offender's county of residence had no effect. This violates common sense, and we have no ready explanation. Unemployment rates certainly varied widely across counties, and these should have affected the prospects of our subjects. On the other hand, it is equally true that the correspondence between overall unemployment rates and the rates faced by ex-offenders is unknown, and perhaps in Georgia the relationship was more problematic than in Texas.

In summary, probably the major findings from Table 12.12 are that large work disincentives surfaced once again and that parole appeared to increase work effort. We stress these since they were large and clearly relevant to policy. In contrast, the fact that males, for example, worked substantially more than females may be interesting, but gender is obviously not a manipulable variable.

Georgia Equation for Time in Jail or Prison

As in the case of Texas, the equation (shown in Table 12.13) for the number of weeks in jail or prison was neither particularly interesting nor important. Indeed, not a single statistically significant effect appeared. In Texas we at least found that property arrests affected incarceration, but for Georgia, the 10 days for each property arrest was not distinguishable from chance (the effect in Texas was 17 days per property arrest). Recall that in Georgia the measure of incarceration was a constant source of trouble, and apparently we were victimized once again. Perhaps the problem lay in quality of the data on incarceration and/or incarceration responded to factors we have missed. It is worth noting, for example, that overall, Georgia ex-offenders spent less time behind bars during their first year after release. Although any explanation we may offer is highly speculative, we may also look to the working of the criminal justice system for an explanation. It appears that the prosecutors and the courts operated with considerably greater dispatch in Texas, with less time intervening between arrest, trial (or other form of judgment), and imprisonment. Hence the imprisonment consequence of arrest is a closer connection in that state. In contrast, for many of the Georgia TARP members who were arrested, particularly in the last half of the postrelease year, the criminal justice system was still grinding away in processing. Because we measured arrests and imprisonment only in the postrelease year, we may have been severely underestimating the connection between the two in Georgia, where so many cases had yet to be brought to ultimate disposition.

Georgia Overtime Models

As in the case of Texas, we estimated several models in which longitudinal patterns could be more effectively addressed. Some models moved the five-equation formulation used for the year as a whole through each of four quarters, and some models moved the five-equation formulation through the first two quarters and then the second 6 months (three sets of five equations). The main asset of these large structural equation models is the ability to address dynamic and lagged effects.

However, much as for Texas, the longitudinal models were fraught with statistical problems. For example, the R^2 for the reduced form property-arrest equation over the second 6 months after release was .028. For non-property arrests it was .042. This is hardly the raw material upon which to

TABLE 12.13
Five-Equation Georgia Model:
Number of Weeks in Jail or Prison

	Regression coefficient	*t*-value
Intercept	0.244	0.324
Property arrests	10.299	1.362
Nonproperty arrests	0.480	0.089
First offender × Property	7.036	0.694
First offender × Nonproperty	−3.087	−0.446

construct powerful instruments. To make matters worse, the residuals from the structural form of the property arrest structural equation in the first quarter were correlated .85 with the residuals from the structural form of the nonproperty arrest equation in the first quarter. Clearly the equations leave something to be desired. While these are somewhat extreme examples, they provide some sense of the difficulties faced.

Despite these and other problems, the general story told by the five equations for the year as a whole was supported in the overtime models. For example, TARP payments reduced the number of property and nonproperty arrests in the first quarter and second 6 months (but not in the second quarter, as in Texas) with *t*-values averaging around −1.40. The employment effects were also replicated, and here *t*-values averaged around −3 (again, except in the second quarter). We also found rather consistent work disincentives as a result of the TARP payments. In short, the general form of the counterbalancing model surfaced once again.

There were also some lagged and dynamic effects, although given all the statistical problems, we are inclined not to make too much of them. There was, for example, a substantial tendency for arrests in an earlier period to predict arrests in a later period. There was also some evidence that TARP payments lagged by one period produced an additional work disincentive. Finally, there was a general pattern in which arrests and incarceration time in earlier periods predicted incarceration in later periods. While none of these findings is surprising, they give the overall results additional credence and suggest that future studies might well consider in some depth dynamic models of recidivism.

Truncation and Censoring Effects in Georgia

There is no need to review the problems with truncation and censoring and our efforts to make the proper adjustments. Basically, the issues in Georgia were the same as in Texas, and the same range of strategies were employed. We appeared to have the greatest success with use of nonlinear forms when endogenous variables were used as dependent variables and with dummy variables for property and nonproperty arrests. For example, each $100 of TARP payments reduced the probability of a property arrest by .006 ($t = -2.17$). This means that ex-offenders receiving the maximum amount of money possible were about 10% less likely to experience arrest. For nonproperty arrests the regression coefficient was .0057 ($t = -1.76$), clearly a very similar effect. Each week employed altered the probability of a property arrest by $-.012$ ($t = -5.45$). This implies that ex-offenders working full time for the entire year might have been expected to have a 60% lower probability of experiencing an arrest. The comparable regression coefficient for nonproperty crimes is $-.013$ ($t = -5.26$ When these effects were coupled with the work disincentive produced by the TARP payments, the counterbalancing model remained intact.

Unfortunately, in contrast to our models for Texas, our two-step truncation/censoring adjustments did not yield much evidence of treatment effects. Our greatest success came with the effect of employment on nonproperty arrests, and even here the t-value was only -1.49. We find this perplexing, since corrections for censoring in Texas actually increased the treatment effects. On the other hand, we argued earlier that this was inherently our weakest response to the problem (in part because so much of the data is discarded in the subsetting process), and we are inclined to downplay the lack of findings. Moreover, the weight of evidence from our other strategies strongly supports the counterbalancing model.

SOME CONCLUSIONS

Where does this leave us? While there were genuine problems with the data and the estimation procedures we have employed, the findings for Georgia by and large replicated the findings for Texas. TARP payments reduced the number of property and nonproperty arrests in a substantively and statistically significant manner. TARP payments also produced a work disincentive which in turn served to increase the number of property and nonproperty arrests. These findings explain why no reduction in arrests were found in the reduced forms (and the earlier analyses of variance). They also support a perspective on recidivism in which economic incentives play a critical role. Later we will return to these conclusions and consider a range of policy implications.

13

Transitional Aid Research Project Payments, Job Search, and Weekly Wages

INTRODUCTION

In our initial conceptualization of TARP payments, one of our major assumptions was such payments would help ex-prisoners adjust to civilian life by subsidizing their search for employment. A recipient could use the payments to conduct a longer and more thorough search for employment with higher wages and better working conditions. This search could also result in "better" crime as well as better legitimate employment, since better opportunities for property theft presumably require an investment in time to search for theft opportunities that have high payoffs and low risks of apprehension.

Unfortunately, the TARP data sets contain no direct information about job search or the earnings from criminal activities.[1] However, it is possible to examine the earnings of those who were eligible for TARP payments in comparison to control cases. If TARP payments were used to subsidize more thorough job searches, that fact should show up in higher wages for TARP experimental groups as compared to the controls. Indeed, there have been hints in the data presented earlier, particularly in Chapters 5 and 9, that such might well have been the case. In those chapters it was shown that the aggregate earnings of persons in the payment eligibility groups were not different from the earnings of ex-felons in the control groups, although it was abundantly clear that because of the work-disincentive effects of TARP payments, persons in such groups worked considerably less.

Initial efforts to address the issue of whether TARP payments had any positive effects on wages and earnings turned out to be more sophisticated

---

[1] It should be noted that there is very little evidence, if any, that TARP payments were used in ways that subsidized illegitimate activities. These are mentioned here and in previous chapters because they are logical possibilities given the theoretical foundations. Although direct data on illegitimate activities were not collected, the arrest-averting effect of TARP payments certainly casts some strong doubts on such undesirable side effects.

than the grain of the data could sustain. Employing a structural-equation approach similar to that used in Chapter 12, we attempted to estimate the impact of TARP payments on wage rates. This strategy failed in part because we could not develop good measures of wage rates (dollars per hour).

As discussed in greater detail in Chapter 9, two sources of information were available in TARP data files on earnings. The unemployment insurance (UI) computerized files contained earnings by calendar quarter for each TARP participant who had provided a usable social security number. These files consisted of earnings reported by employers for work covered under the relevant unemployment insurance regulations. No information was available in this file on the number of hours worked. Hence, in order to obtain wage rates it was necessary to go to the interview files, in which weeks worked had been calculated from retrospective accounts obtained from TARP members. The interview data were adequate for estimating weeks worked, as used in Chapter 12. However, because the data contained no information on the number of hours worked, either actually or typically per day or per week, we could only make assumptions that TARP workers worked full-time during the periods when they reported having worked. Employment at the bottom of the occupational structure abounds in part-time work. Moreover, is often punctuated by layoffs, and it is often controlled by employers who either are not covered by the unemployment insurance system or who attempt to evade paying the taxes that support the system. Given these factors, the efforts to translate weeks worked into hours worked were bound to produce considerable error. In addition, it was necessary to translate the calendar-quarter earnings recorded in the UI files into periods that coincided with those covered in interviews, a conversion that required making unrealistic assumptions about how earnings were distributed over time within a calendar quarter.

Attempts to use interview data on employment earnings also foundered. Often interviewers did not sufficiently distinguish between gross and net pay, nor did the questions asked focus on earnings actually received as distinguished from "typical" or "average" weekly earnings.[2] In addition, the interview data on employment earnings had many missing values.

It also turned out that the structural-equation approach ran up against serious specification and multicollinearity problems. A structural-equation approach for an analysis of wage rates required that we specify an equation for employment and an equation for wages, with both embedded in a model much like that estimated earlier. Unfortunately, this led to some serious identification problems, and it also yielded equations crippled by

---

[2] A typical question asked was "How much did you earn per week on that job?"

multicollinearity. The results we obtained were simply not believable; substantively impossible coefficients surfaced in a number of places.

Faced with poor wage measures, large amounts of missing data, and serious statistical problems, the structural-equation approach was abandoned. However, all was not lost. Instead of examining the effects of TARP payments on wages, we addressed the effect on wages of membership in one of the three experimental groups eligible for payments. That is, we returned to the analysis of variance approach supplemented with a number of other exogenous predictors (i.e., ordinary least squares—OLS). Moreover, within this approach, the censoring problems associated with estimates of the impact of group membership on wages could be partially addressed with analogies to Heckman's procedures.[3] The remainder of this chapter reports the resulting analysis.

As measures of wages received from employment, it was necessary to abandon the attempt to measure wage rates in terms of amounts per hour and to resort to weekly wages. We used adjusted data from the UI files and data on number of weeks worked from the interview data and restricted the analysis to those TARP members who had worked at least 1 week during the year and who also had some earnings recorded in their UI files.[4] The approach regressed the resulting weekly wages on a set of variables representing membership in one or another of three payment groups and a set of exogenous variables that represent human-capital factors and labor market and discrimination variables that were used in the model presented in Chapter 12.

It should also be noted that while the analyses presented in this chapter bear a superficial resemblance to analyses of randomized experiments (i.e., membership in a payment group appears to be a randomized variable), in fact they do not resemble such analyses. Although randomization has placed TARP members in experimental and control groups, nonrandom processes that took place after that assignment brought the members into the labor force at least for a minimum period of time and thus into consideration in these analyses. Hence, the ex-felons under analysis are individuals who were likely to have had configurations of characteristics that predicted success on the job market.

To elaborate on the argument about the nonrandom nature of member-

---

[3] The censoring occurs because one can only observe the wages of those ex-offenders who find work. This in turn creates the selection bias described by Heckman and others. (Heckman, "Sample Selection Bias.")

[4] The data were adjusted for the lack of fit between calendar quarters and the postrelease years of the ex-felons. Note that the restriction limits the sample size considerably and treats only persons from whom we have data recorded in the two files involved (UI files and periodic interviews).

ship in experimental groups: Group 1 members who faced a strong work-disincentive effect from the 26 weeks of eligibility for TARP payments offered them are included in these analyses only if they worked at least 1 week during the postrelease year. Because these persons managed to find work, under conditions of being offered strong work disincentives, they were quite likely to have been different in important motivational ways from their confreres who never entered the labor market. In addition their human-capital levels may have been more attractive to employers, and thus they may have found jobs more easily than other members of Group 1. In short, in the ordinary least squares analyses presented in this chapter, membership in one or another of the three payment groups is not orthogonal to other variables (as would be the case in most of the other analyses in this volume). This also means that there are some positive correlations (hopefully slight) in these analyses between membership in the payment groups and predictors of employment.

If all that we faced were a few small correlations between group membership and other predictors, there would certainly be no cause for alarm. OLS estimates would in principle be perfectly sound. However, the selection bias can under some circumstances cause OLS estimates to be biased and inconsistent. In this instance, if the random shocks that affect an ex-offender's employment chances (e.g., a local contractor getting a large project underway) are associated with the random shocks that affect an ex-offender's wages (e.g., a temporary scarcity of laborers or a new union wage settlement), an equation regressing wages on some set of exogenous variables will typically yield inconsistent estimates of the regression coefficients; correlations between the exogenous variables and the error term are built in. One solution is to construct an adjustment variable capturing the selection process (in this case the process by which jobs are obtained) and then include this variable in the wage equation. Basically, this "controls" for the selection bias. This procedure will be used in the analyses.[5]

The analyses will be presented in two steps. First, OLS results without the censoring adjustment will be presented, primarily because these

---

[5] Unfortunately, this procedure may not be fully satisfactory in this instance. In particular, there is good reason to treat any single equation that predicts wages as a function of treatment groups and other exogenous variables as a reduced-form representation derived from models much like those in Chapter 12. Then, the error term implicitly includes the errors from the full set of structural forms, and if their endogenous variables are subject to truncation/censoring, adjustment variables for each must be constructed and included. This was simply not feasible here. (The process of subsetting for those cases exceeding the threshold in each instance would have virtually eliminated all of the data.) In short, our logit-based adjustment variable, constructed to capture the selection process into jobs, does not control for analogous processes in other implicit equations (e.g., being "selected" into imprisonment).

statistical procedures are more familiar and because the adjustment does not change the story a great deal. Then we will briefly consider how the results are altered after the adjustment, and along the way we will explain how the adjustment variable was constructed.

TEXAS WAGE ANALYSIS

Table 13.1 contains the results of regressing weekly wages on membership in the three payment groups. It also presents a set of exogenous variables representing individual and community characteristics that are related to earnings. A glance at the variables included in Table 13.1 readily indicates the strategy used in the model specification. We included a full complement of human-capital variables along with race, sex, the unemployment rate, and four county dummy-variables. Race and sex are meant to capture discrimination, while unemployment rates and the dummy variables are meant to capture the local labor market.

TABLE 13.1
Wage Analysis for Texas (in Dollars per Week)

	Regression coefficient		*t*-value
Intercept	−102.128		−2.228
Male (dummy)	40.391		2.108
Physical handicap (dummy)	12.770		1.481
Black (dummy)	−4.742		−0.541
Chicano (dummy)	−4.696		−0.382
Bexar (San Antonio) (dummy)	−2.854		−0.162
Dallas (dummy)	15.330		1.384
Harris (Houston) (dummy)	37.035		3.402
Tarrant (Ft. Worth) (dummy)	7.806		0.058
Unemployment rate (percentage)	2.694		0.643
Previous military service (dummy)	−3.578		−0.402
Achievement test score	0.921		3.697
IQ test score	0.016		0.049
Years of education	2.459		1.397
Ages 21–40 (dummy)	16.308		1.662
Employed at pre-TARP arrest (dummy)	6.580		0.897
Driver's license (dummy)	2.913		0.387
Prison vocational training (dummy)	−15.333		−1.698
Group 1 (26 wks/100% tax)	31.694		2.991
Group 2 (13 wks/100% tax)	17.554		1.889
Group 3 (13 wks/25% tax)	32.065		3.326
R^2		.15	
N		459	

No doubt, the specification is subject to disagreement.[6] However, for present purposes the biases are probably not large regardless of what variables have been neglected. The main interest here is in the impact of the experimental groups. Despite the selection process, these dummy variables are in fact nearly independent of (uncorrelated with) both the variables included and virtually all others one might choose to include. While we no longer have a randomized experiment, we still approximate it rather well.

Several statistically significant regression coefficients surface. For example, men earned an average of $40 more a week, and ex-offenders living in Harris County (Houston) earned an extra $37. Somewhat surprisingly, each additional point on the educational-achievement tests yielded nearly an extra dollar a week in wages.

Probably the most important finding concerns the effects of membership in each of the three experimental groups eligible for TARP payments. Group 1 and Group 3 members obtained a little over $30 a week more, and Group 2 members earned about $18 more. All three effects are statistically significant at the .05 level for a one-tailed test, although the effect for Group 2 members would fail under a two-tailed test. Clearly, there is good evidence that membership in one of the three experimental groups increases wages and the job-search predictions are supported.

The regression equation of Table 13.1 explains only a modest amount of the total variance in weekly wages, R^2 being .15. Given the amount of measurement error that was involved in constructing the dependent variables, weekly wages, the R^2 is as impressively large as most shown in this volume for similar variables.

If the selection bias described earlier is really important, the results reported in Table 13.1 are biased and inconsistent. Consequently, we resorted to adjustments for the selection process. In a first step we specified a logit equation with a dummy dependent variable for whether wages were "observed" for each individual in the full sample. The specification rested heavily on the reduced forms used in the employment equations reported earlier. As one would expect, much the same substantive results appeared as for the previous reduced forms in which the number of weeks employed was the endogenous variable. We then constructed our adjustment variable as a function of the predicted probability of "observing" wages.

With the adjustment variable from the employment equation (i.e., the

---

[6] Since this specification is close to that used for the weeks-worked equation of Chapter 12, the same arguments apply for its inclusion here. Indeed, in our developmental work on the logit-based adjustment variable, we experimented with several variations of the specification reported in Table 13.1, and as one would expect, some minor differences surfaced. However, the overall story did not change materially, with the exception that the impact of membership in Group 2 became nonsignificant (though still positive).

predicted probabilities of employment) inserted in the wage equation estimated before, the overall picture was much the same. No new statistically significant predictors surfaced (and none was lost). However, the impact of group membership was enhanced. Group 1 members earned an average of $36 more a week; Group 2 members earned an average of $23 more a week; and Group 3 members earned an average of $36 more a week. In other words, the treatment effects were increased by about $5 a week, or about 15%.[7]

GEORGIA WAGE ANALYSIS

Table 13.2 shows the OLS results for Georgia without the selection adjustment. With a somewhat smaller sample size (296) and a slightly smaller R^2 (.12), it is not surprising that fewer effects were found.[8] For reasons that are not at all clear, previous military service reduced weekly earnings by about $22. More important, only one of the treatment groups showed a statistically significant improvement in weekly earnings. Group 2 members earned an additional $34 a week. Although Group 1 members earned about $9 more, and Group 3 members earned about $14 more, neither of these effects could be distinguished from chance. One may take some solace in the fact that the signs are in the predicted direction, that the magnitude of the effects is nontrivial, and that these patterns surface despite the small sample and considerable problems with the quality of Georgia data.

The selection adjustment improved matters somewhat. In the employment equation, we used the same strategy as we did with the Texas data. After the adjustment variable was inserted in the wage equation, the impact of military service was about the same, but the impact of group membership was heightened. Group 1 members earned about $13 more a week ($t = 1$), Group 2 members earned about $39 more a week ($t = 3.76$), and Group 3 members earned about $19 more a week ($t = 1.67$). Again, the improvement brought about by the adjustment was around $5 a week. Note also that using a one-tail test (which is appropriate since the hypothesis was

---

[7] Actually, a great deal more effort was involved than this brief summary suggests. To begin, there are actually two possible forms of the adjustment variable, and in practice one can work with either the logit or linear probability model in the first step. Moreover, we experimented with several different specifications to explore the sensitivity of our results and adjustments to somewhat different causal perspectives. (Ray, Berk, and Bielby, op. cit.). Suffice to say that membership in the treatment groups (especially Groups 1 and 3) always increased wages nontrivially, and the adjustments always enhanced these effects.

[8] The Georgia sample size is smaller because a larger proportion of TARP members in Georgia never worked during the postrelease year (see Chapter 9), and more gaps existed in the data files on weeks worked.

TABLE 13.2
Wage Analysis for Georgia
(in Dollars per Week)

	Regression coefficient	*t*-value
Intercept	1.791	−0.038
Male (dummy)	14.943	0.446
Age (years)	0.463	0.801
Physical handicap (dummy)	2.212	0.235
Black (dummy)	−13.280	−1.626
Savannah (dummy)	8.684	0.447
Atlanta (dummy)	6.859	0.722
Bibb (dummy)	−5.336	−0.280
Banks	−21.733	−1.360
Unemployment (percentage)	0.306	1.312
Previous military service (dummy)	−19.955	−2.067
Union member (dummy)	5.685	0.569
Years of education	2.781	
Age 21–40 (dummy)	12.649	1.508
Employed at pre-TARP arrest (dummy)	11.220	1.359
Driver's license (dummy)	12.503	0.708
Prison vocational training (dummy)	15.958	1.676
Group 1 (26 wks/100% tax)	8.725	0.708
Group 2 (13 wks/100% tax)	34.424	3.485
Group 3 (13 wks/25% tax)	14.029	1.284
R^2	.15	
N	296	

one-tailed), the Group 3 effect is now statistically significant. In addition, had we been able to capitalize on a sample size at least as large as we had in Texas, and had we been able to explain just a bit more variance, the results would have been stronger. Consequently, we are inclined to take the effects as real and conclude that in both Texas and Georgia TARP eligibility improves the wages of ex-offenders who find employment.

CONCLUSIONS

For those TARP members who found some work during the postrelease year, TARP payment eligibility apparently served to subsidize a more effective job search. Although the results of analyses presented in this chapter were not always consistent in finding this effect in all of the payment experimental groups, given the known data-quality defects, we are confident that the effects shown are real and substantial. Increments to weekly wages of $13 to $39 a week in Georgia amount to percentage increases of 12% to 35%, a substantial increase at the lower end and a quite remarkable increase on the upper end. The corresponding percentage increases for Texas were 16% and 25%, also substantial increases.

In a dramatic way these results illustrate the serious problem faced by released prisoners. The usual meager resources available to them upon release, in effect, force them to make suboptimal choices in employment. Finding any work they can means finding work that pays less well and likely involves poor working conditions. The impact of such suboptimal jobs on the choice for legitimate as opposed to illegitimate activity is easy to project: This process is another source of pressure to recidivism.

IV

CONCLUSIONS

14

The Policy Implications of the Transitional Aid Research Project

INTRODUCTION

The TARP experiments were not academic exercises: They were carried out for the purpose of testing a promising change in an established social program. As the preceding chapters have shown, the results of the test indicate that the version of the proposed changes tested left much to be desired. A simple extension of unemployment benefits, *as tested* in the Georgia and Texas TARP experiments, would not accomplish the desired end result of reducing crime.

Were this disheartening finding the only outcome of the experiments, it would be difficult to do more than lament the obstinacy of the crime-reduction problem, and one would turn elsewhere for guidance in formulating social policy about crime. But, TARP yielded a great deal more information than the simple documentation of the failure of the specific social-policy change being tested. The earlier chapters also contain information on the question of why the TARP version of the policy failed to produce results as well as findings that suggest policy strategies that appear very promising.

The positive policy implications of the TARP experiments rest on two important findings:

1. Limited amounts of financial aid appropriately given to ex-felons can help them to avoid reverting to crime.
2. Employment for ex-felons is clearly the strongest antidote to reengaging in criminal activities.

These two findings give rise to two promising strategies directed at reducing the rate of return to crime among ex-felons. These two strategies are discussed in detail in the sections that follow.

THE EMPLOYMENT STRATEGY

An employment strategy is one that provides some means for increasing both the proportion of ex-felons who are employed in the postrelease period and the steadiness of that employment, once achieved. The attractiveness of this strategy is based on the very firm findings of the TARP experiment that working clearly lowers the probability of arrest on all sorts of charges. In the preceding chapters we speculated on why this was so for TARP participants, but there is no speculative or tentative flavor to the assertion that, however it may work, being employed and the length of such employment has a very direct effect of lowering arrests.

The attractiveness of the employment strategy is somewhat offset by the fact that the TARP experiments did not directly either supply employment opportunities or pursue a set of policies designed to foster employment directly. To be sure, one of the experimental groups, Group 4, was offered intensive job placement and counseling services, but the evidence is that so few TARP members in that group took advantage of the services offered that such a program, delivered at the level of effort experienced in the two states, must certainly be regarded as an implementation failure.

Those TARP members who became employed during the postrelease year did so through their own efforts. Hence, the statement concerning the efficacy of employment in averting arrests should be qualified to take into account that in the TARP experiments the act of getting and keeping a job was a voluntary one. About the best one could say is that the TARP payments experimentally created unemployment among those eligible, and hence indicated that unemployment led to more arrests under somewhat experimental conditions.

There are several difficulties in pursuing an employment strategy. First, efforts to help ex-felons to obtain jobs have not been very successful. In the earlier Baltimore LIFE experiment, as indicated in Chapter 2, one of the treatments was intensive job placement and counseling, a treatment that did not consistently lead to higher levels of employment among those offered it. At a much lower level of effort, the TARP experiments also offered somewhat the same services, also without any impact on employment. Similar unsuccessful experiences have been encountered by others. The bulk of the evidence leads one to conclude either that the counseling and placement mode of proceeding is simply generally ineffective or that investigators have not employed placement and counseling methods that are most appropriate. Considering that so many different projects and demonstrations have been shown to be ineffective, the search for effective job counseling and placement techniques will be difficult.

Second, it is extremely difficult and expensive to provide employment opportunities directly. The essence of a job is that an employer pays someone for doing a set of activities from which the employer will benefit. One method of providing employment is to subsidize employers, thereby raising the benefit to employers of employing certain classes of workers, classes from which it is believed the employers would not get their ordinary level of benefits. Subsidized work is expensive, and it is especially attractive to employers who are running marginal business enterprises and hence who offer quite poor jobs. Another method is for a public or quasi-public agency to create jobs and to hire target persons for those positions. This last method was employed by the Manpower Demonstration Research Corporation's national experiment with supported work.[1] This program contracted with a fairly large number of public and quasi-public agencies to provide jobs for more than 2000 persons, about one-third of whom were ex-felons. Jobs provided for the mostly male ex-prisoners were mainly construction employment involving rehabilitation of dilapidated housing. The positions provided were temporary, restricted to a tenure of 12 to 18 months.

The supported work experiment has not been very successful in dealing with ex-felons, especially in reducing arrests among participants: At least such was the case in the first report of results. These preliminary findings from the supported work experiment do not contradict the conclusions drawn from TARP concerning the efficacy of employment. There are considerable differences between the employment obtained by the TARP participants on their own and the "supported work" provided under the supported work program. This is not the place to spell those differences out in detail.[2] The main point to be drawn is that it is difficult to provide work experiences through this program that will have the same effects as employment obtained by the ex-felons themselves.

An effective employment strategy would be one that provides jobs that capture all of the positive effects of working. As discussed in earlier chapters, these positive effects are partially obvious and partially specula-

---

[1] Mathematica Policy Research, Inc., *The National Supported Work Demonstration Effects during the First 18 Months after enrollment* (Princeton, 1979).

[2] Several differences stand out. First, persons referred to the supported work program were likely those who could not find, or would not find, work on their own. Hence, a strong self-selection factor may be at work. Second, the work environment provided under the supported work program consists of persons very much like the ex-felons themselves and hence unlikely to provide the kinds of interpersonal ties and modeling available in "regular" employment. Third, supported work is also "make work," however socially useful, and hence not as meaningful in some sense as "regular" employment. Finally, it is explicitly temporary. There may also be elements of the administration of supported work (e.g., ways of assigning persons to positions, supervisory patterns, and the like) that further exacerbate the differences between "regular" employment and the jobs provided under the supported work program.

tive. On the obvious side, employment provides income and hence lowers the utility of earnings from illegal activity. Clearly, the better paying the job, the more earnings offset the attractiveness of illegal activities. The second obvious effect is that the time spent on the job reduces the amount of time available for pursuing illegal activities. Any employment can provide this effect. The final obvious effect of employment is to raise the opportunity costs of illegal activities; the better the job's pay and working conditions, the higher these costs.

On the less obvious and more speculative side, employment reduces illegal activities through providing social supports for legality. Thus the status of being employed may mean achieving respectability among family, kin, friends, and neighbors. In addition, the social context of most work provides ties to others that may provide reinforcement for legality, new networks of friendship, possibilities for meeting potential mates, and so on.

It is difficult to envisage the specific employment strategy that could capture all of the positive effects of employment as discussed above. It is even more difficult to imagine such a strategy being relatively inexpensive. Arranging employment in existing organizations for ex-felons would require considerable amounts of time and would, in any event, be difficult to carry out. It is also abundantly clear that no promising specific strategy currently exists.

For these reasons, we believe that an employment strategy is not a very promising direction to pursue. Certainly, it should not be pursued on any but research and development lines. That is to say, it is worthwhile at this point to fund on an experimental basis a number of promising pilot studies that will test out alternative ways of pursuing an effective employment strategy.[3]

EFFECTIVE TRANSITIONAL FINANCIAL AID STRATEGIES

Our analyses provide ample evidence that limited amounts of financial aid do lower the number of arrests from all causes. Unfortunately, these positive effects were offset by the negative impact of the unemployment induced by the work-disincentive effects of the way in which payments were administratively linked to employment. In effect, the 100% tax rate administered made work and receiving payments mutually exclusive.

---

[3] Since the supported work experiment is currently under way, it is important that this experiment be thoroughly analyzed from the point of view of examining differences among sites. Such analysis would maximize the possibility of detecting specific features of the programs, at various sites, that lead to success in capturing the positive effects of employment through the supported work modality.

The positive effects of TARP can be fully recovered, we assert, if the work-disincentive effects of such payments could be removed or substantially reduced. That it is possible to do so is demonstrated by the experience of the earlier Baltimore LIFE experiment in which no work-disincentive effects were found. The effective strategy pursued in the Baltimore experiment was to insure that LIFE participants received all the partial payment benefits to which they were entitled. The Baltimore LIFE experiment, as a consequence, had a low nominal and a low actual tax rate on earnings.

Several strategies for removing the work disincentive effect of transitional aid payments are suggested in the four sections that follow.

Low Actual Tax Rates

This is a strategy that sets tax rates low enough to provide some positive incentive for working and ensures that the tax rates are known to participants and enforced by the agency administering payments and determining payment eligibility. This mode of proceeding takes the Baltimore LIFE experiment as its model.

The main problem with the LIFE strategy is whether it is compatible with the existing unemployment insurance system (or any other large-scale government agency) and whether severe equity problems would assert themselves if ex-felons were given more generous tax rates on their benefits compared to the other clients of the unemployment benefit system. Although a case can be made that lowering the tax rate for all clients of the unemployment benefit system would be socially useful, it is not a likely change at least for the near future.

Severance Pay

A more promising strategy—at least in our view—is to extend the concept of severance pay to persons released from prison. Severance payments are not work conditioned but are paid out regardless of the work status of the recipient. Thus, a severance pay strategy might be designed consisting of 10 to 15 weekly payments that are mailed to the released prisoner as long as he or she remains out of jail or prison and does not have a parole revocation. Payments should be set high enough to meet the income needs of the ex-felons but not so high that the payments provide too much work disincentive.[4]

---

[4] That severance pay might provide work-disincentive effects can be derived in the first instance from microeconomic labor-supply theory that predicts that any transfer payment would lower work effort. In the second place, we noted that gate money in the analyses of Chapter 12 had a small but consistent work-disincentive effect. Note, however, that gate money is a lump sum payment whereas the severance pay proposal is envisaged as a set of payments spread out through time.

It should be noted that there are several attractive features to the severance pay proposal. First, it is not costly. Even if 10 payments of $100 each were paid out, the payment costs per individual would be $1000. Second, the administration of the program could be simple, since eligibility rules need not be applied to each of the payments.

Severance Pay Conditioned by Work in Prison

It is possible that severe equity issues might be raised by a severance pay proposal that appears to reward felons perhaps more than other persons who have experienced a period of involuntary withdrawal from the labor force; for example, persons experiencing severe disabling uncompensated injuries. A method of countering such an equity issue is to make the amount of the severance pay conditioned by work within prison.[5] The more a prisoner worked at some prison job the greater the benefits that he would be eligible for when released.

There are several difficulties that would be encountered with this modification of the severance pay proposal. First, some prison systems do not offer sufficient employment to accommodate all prisoners. In such systems, some prisoners would be deprived of eligibility for postrelease severance pay simply because of the inadequacy of the prison employment system. Second, short-term prisoners might suffer from not being able to accumulate enough credits before release. Since such prisoners are likely to be persons who could benefit from severance pay, work conditioning such payments might be to slight these good prospects for self-rehabilitation.

Severance Pay with Work Bonuses

It can be argued that severance pay by itself would contain work disincentives. To counter whatever disincentives severance pay would have and also to provide positive incentives for working, a modification of the severance pay proposal would provide bonus payments for persons who found employment. For example, one possible plan would be to pay the equivalent of 2 weeks' wages upon employment, the payment to be forgiven if the individual remained employed for more than a certain period of time. In the event that he or she left employment before that time the bonus amount would be deducted from total eligibility.

It should be noted that this modification has both its positive and

---

[5] Thus, the TARP-like payment authorized in California for released prisoners is made conditional upon work within prison. Prisoners receive a day of unemployment benefit eligibility for each day of prison employment. This program is currently being evaluated by Richard A. Berk.

negative aspect. On the positive side, besides providing positive incentives, the bonus payments provide the necessary funds to tide one over until the first paycheck appears, often a very necessary sum for persons who are so close to the margins of adequate income. On the negative side, the bonus payments would require an administrative mechanism, and some surveillance of compliance, features that would raise the costs of the proposal and be difficult to arrange.

The several proposals suggested above are clearly not definitively stated. They are presented primarily to outline a family of proposals that would appear, on the basis of the TARP findings, to be *likely* to capture the positive effects of transitional aid payments. Of course, details of amounts, mode of administration, and the like are not considered here, and would be critical in the workings of any specific program. It is for these reasons that we believe that additional developmental research should be undertaken.

A CALL FOR ADDITIONAL RESEARCH

If the TARP experiments were able to show a clear, unequivocal, and uncontaminated positive effect, there would be no need for this section. As it now stands, we do know that transitional financial aid can help to reduce recidivism, *under some circumstances*. What remains unclear is whether the facilitating circumstances can be translated into a workable program that can be faithfully administered in actual practice. Hence the need for further research.

There are two directions in which it seems fruitful for additional developmental research to turn. In the first place, since the employment strategy is so attractive on its face, any move in this direction ought to be preceded by a program of developmental research devoted to exploring different ways of delivering employment to released prisoners. As noted earlier, the authors of this report have little to suggest as promising programs along the lines of providing effective employment to ex-felons.

In the second place, it is much clearer what should be the research on stripping the work-disincentive effects from transitional financial aid. Experiments should be undertaken varying the amount of payments, the length of time over which payments should be made, tax rates and their administration, as well as the several members of the severance pay proposal family. While this may appear to be an ambitious developmental research program, it is justified in two ways. First, the crime problem in the United States is serious and obstinate; any program that shows promise ought to be given the best chance to succeed. Second, the costs of developmental research are several magnitudes less than the costs of a large-scale ineffective program, and the benefits of an effective program are likely to be several magnitudes greater than such costs.

V

APPENDICES

A

Data and Instruments

The many sources of the data used in the TARP research have been described in some detail in Chapter 4. All of the data collected for the TARP project (with personal identifiers stripped off) have been deposited with the Inter-University Consortium on Political and Social Research at the Institute for Social Research of the University of Michigan. The Consortium will make the data set available to any member institution at nominal cost.[1] Documentation that accompanies the data sets includes all the questionnaires used in the personal follow-up interviews as well as sufficient definition of the other data sets to allow anyone both access to the data and to the instruments that generated them.

The data generated specially for the TARP research included four personal interviews with members of the first five groups in the experiments. A total of eight different forms were used, amounting to more than 150 pages of material. To reproduce every instrument here, however, would raise the price of this book, and the instruments themselves are readily available through the Consortium for those readers who would like to inspect them in detail.

To provide the reader of this volume with a "sample" of the research instruments, we have reproduced in the pages that follow the instrument used in the 3-month follow-up interview in Texas. The main topics pursued in all of the follow-up interviews are taken up in this sample, which differs in only marginal ways from the Georgia schedule.

---

[1] Almost every university in the United States belongs to the Consortium, along with major not-for-profit research institutes.

TRANSITIONAL AID RESEARCH PROJECT

THREE-MONTH POST-RELEASE INTERVIEW

NAME OF MEMBER _____
                        (Last)   (First)   (MI)

TARP NUMBER _____   SEX _____

GROUP NUMBER _____   RACE _____

SOCIAL SECURITY NUMBER _____   DATE OF RELEASE _____

DATE OF BIRTH _____   METHOD OF RELEASE _____


```
┌─────────────────────────────────┐        ┌─────────────────────────────────┐
│    THIS INTERVIEW SCHEDULED      │        │    NEXT INTERVIEW SCHEDULED      │
│  Date _____   │        │  Date _____   │
│  City _____   │        │  City _____   │
└─────────────────────────────────┘        └─────────────────────────────────┘
```

```
┌─────────────────────────────────────────────────────┐
│              INTERVIEW COMPLETED                      │
│                                                       │
│   Interviewer _____   │
│                                                       │
│   Date _____   │
│                                                       │
│   Time:  From _____   To _____   │
│                                                       │
│   Location _____   │
└─────────────────────────────────────────────────────┘
```

```
┌─────────────────────────────────────────────────────────────────────────────
│   Comments on interview, including inconsistencies in responses:
│
│
│
│
│
└─────────────────────────────────────────────────────────────────────────────
```

Editing Completed _____   Coding Completed _____

Editor's Initials _____   Coder's Initials _____

CUE SHEET FOR THREE-MONTH INTERVIEW

1. Who member intended to live with:

   _____

2. Address from Pre-Release Interview:

   _____

   _____

3. Address at $5 contact:

   _____

   _____ Date

4. Most recent address:

   _____

   _____

5. Job Arrangements:

   Employer   _____

   Occupation _____

THREE-MONTH POSTRELEASE INTERVIEW

FIRST I'D LIKE TO ASK YOU SOME QUESTIONS ABOUT WHERE YOU HAVE LIVED

1. What is your current address and telephone number?

    ——————————   ——————————   ——————————
    Street #   City   Telephone

2. Is that a house or an apartment?

    ___ 1. House
    ___ 2. Apartment
    ___ 3. Halfway House
    ___ 4. Other (Specify) _____

3. Have you moved since the last time we saw you in _____?

    ___ 1. Yes   ___ 2. No

    IF YES: How many different places have you lived?

    _____ Month/$5 Contact

4. Have you lived outside of _____ City of Residence/$5 Contact ?

    ___ 1. Yes   ___ 2. No

    IF YES: How long and where? _____

5. (A) What is the house payment/rent per month where you live?

    ___ 1. Rent $_____
    ___ 2. House payment $_____
    ___ 3. Not applicable
    ___ 4. Other (Specify) _____

    (B) Is this with or without utilities? (water, gas, electricity)

    ___ 1. With   ___ 2. Without

    IF WITHOUT: What is the approximate utility bill per
               month? $_____

6. Is the place where you are living public housing?

    ___ 1. Yes
    ___ 2. No
    ___ 3. Do not know

7. Who are you living with now? (Check all that apply)

    ___ 1. Mother   ___ 10. Stepfather
    ___ 2. Father   ___ 11. Stepmother
    ___ 3. Wife/husband   ___ 12. In-laws
    ___ 4. Girl-/boyfriend   ___ 13. Second degree relation
    ___ 5. Son/daughter (adult) ___ 14. Male/female friend
    ___ 6. Son/daughter (minor) ___ 15. Halfway house
    ___ 7. Brother/sister   ___ 16. Other children
    ___ 8. Grandparent   ___ 17. Alone
    ___ 9. Aunt/uncle   ___ 18. Other (Specify)

    AFTER EACH ANSWER, ASK: Anyone else?

8. Altogether, how many adults are living there, including yourself?

    _____ How many children live there?

9. Who is the head of the household (breadwinner)?

    IF RESPONDENT CLAIMS SELF, ASK: Who was the head of the house-
                                   hold before you returned?

10. How does/did that person support the household?

    ___ 1. Works full-time: How much per week? $_____
    ___ 2. Works part-time: How much per week? $_____
    ___ 3. Welfare: How much per month? $_____
    ___ 4. Other (Specify) _____ How much? $_____

11. Do you have any dependents?   ___ 1. Yes   ___ 2. No

    IF YES: How many? _____

12. What is your current marital status?

    ___ 1. Single   ___ 5. Separated
    ___ 2. Married   ___ 6. Widowed
    ___ 3. Common Law   ___ 7. Other (Specify) _____
    ___ 4. Divorced

NOW I WOULD LIKE TO ASK YOU SOME QUESTIONS ABOUT YOUR MONEY SITUATION

13. Since you have been released, have you received any money from welfare (public assistance)?

___ 1. Yes ___ 2. No

IF YES: How much? $ ___
For how long? ___
When did it start? ___

IF NO LONGER ON WELFARE: Why aren't you receiving it any more? ___

14. Have you at any other time received any money from welfare?

___ 1. Yes ___ 2. No

IF YES: How many times? ___
For how long altogether? ___

15. Have you received any money from Unemployment Insurance since you have been released?

___ 1. Yes ___ 2. No

IF YES: How much? $ ___
For how long? ___

16. Have you received any money from friends or relatives--either as loans or gifts?

___ 1. Yes ___ 2. No

IF YES: How much and from whom?

RELATIONSHIP OF PERSON   AMOUNT
_____   _____
_____   _____
_____   _____
_____   _____

17. Have you received any money by pawning or selling anything?

___ 1. Yes ___ 2. No

IF YES: What have you pawned or sold, and how much did you get?

ITEM   AMOUNT
_____   _____
_____   _____
_____   _____

AFTER EACH ITEM, ASK: Anything else?

18. Of the gate money you had when you left TDC, how much did you still have when you got home? $ ___ .

IF LESS THAN $200: What did you spend it on?

ITEM   AMOUNT
___ 1. Clothes   _____
___ 2. Transportation   _____
___ 3. Food   _____
___ 4. Beer or liquor   _____
___ 5. Other (specify) _____

19. Did you find that you had any debts that you had to pay off after you got out of TDC? ___ 1. Yes ___ 2. No

IF YES: What were they for, and how much did you owe?

WHAT FOR   AMOUNT OF DEBT
_____   _____
_____   _____
_____   _____
_____   _____

291

NOW I WOULD LIKE TO ASK YOU ABOUT THE JOBS YOU HAVE HAD AND WHAT YOU HAVE BEEN DOING SINCE YOU GOT OUT.

(NOTE: If below statement is filled in, continue with Question 24. If it is blank, go to Question 25.)

You told us at the Pre-release Interview you had a job arranged with _____.

24. (A) When you got out, did you go to work there?

_____ 1. Yes   _____ 2. No

IF YES: IF NO:

(B) Are you still working   Why not? _____
    there?

_____ 1. Yes (Go to 26,   GO TO 25.
              PRESENT JOB)

_____ 2. No

IF NO:

(C) Have you had
    any other jobs?

_____ 1. Yes: How many? _____

_____ 2. No

GO TO 26, FIRST JOB.

25. Have you worked on a job since you got out of prison?

_____ 1. Yes: How many? _____ (CONTINUE ON NEXT PAGE, QUESTION 26)

_____ 2. No (SKIP TO QUESTION 27)

---

20. Besides these, do you have any other debts that you NOW owe?

_____ 1. Yes   _____ 2. No

IF YES: What are they for, and how much do you owe?

WHAT FOR   AMOUNT OF DEBT

_____   _____

_____   _____

_____   _____

21. Since you have been released, how much CASH have you spent altogether on:

ITEM   CASH SPENT

1. Clothing   _____
2. Furniture   _____
3. Television/stereo _____
4. Automobile   _____
5. Medical care   _____
6. Entertainment   _____
7. Child support   _____
8. Other (Specify)   _____

22. How much do you usually spend per week on eating out? $ _____

23. Do you contribute any money toward running the household either
as rent or room and board?

_____ 1. Yes   _____ 2. No

IF YES: How much for rent? $ _____
           How many weeks have you been paying rent? _____
           How much for board? $ _____
           How many weeks have you been paying board? _____

           IF LUMP CONTRIBUTION:

           How much? $ _____
           How long? _____

292

26.

	FIRST JOB	SECOND JOB	THIRD JOB	PRESENT JOB
1. When did you start on the job?				
2. How long did you work there?				
3. How much were you earning per week?				
4. How many hours per week did you work?				
5. What kind of work did you do?				
6. Did your employer provide any on-the-job training?				
7. Was the work connected with any training or work assignment you had in prison?				
No				
Vocational training				
On-the-job-training				
Regular job w/o training				
8. Was it a union job?				
9. What did you like most about the job?				
10. What did you dislike most about the job?				
11. How did you find this job? (Probe for information.)				

293

27. Have you looked for a job since you have been released?

    ___ 1. Yes
    ___ 2. No: Any particular reason why you have not looked? _____

IF YES:

	1st Job Effort	2nd Job Effort	3rd Job Effort
1. Where did you look for a job?			
2. How did you happen to go there?			
3. What kind of a job were you looking for?			
4. What happened?			

294

33. Who do you think was the one TDC person who helped you the most?

_____ 1. Warden
_____ 2. Chaplain
_____ 3. Vocational Instructor
_____ 4. Correctional Officer
_____ 5. Psychologist
_____ 6. Work Supervisor
_____ 7. Medical Officer
_____ 8. Physician
_____ 9. Other (Specify)
_____ 10. No one

34. Who was the one TDC person who you disliked the most?

_____ 1. Warden
_____ 2. Chaplain
_____ 3. Vocational Instructor
_____ 4. Correctional Officer
_____ 5. Psychologist
_____ 6. Work Supervisor
_____ 7. Medical Officer
_____ 8. Physician
_____ 9. Other (Specify)
_____ 10. No one

35. (A) How much money do you think you will need in the coming month to do the things you have to do and to live decently?
$ _____

(B) How much money do you actually think will be coming in next month?
$ _____

36. What would you say your chances are of staying out of prison this time--good, 50/50, or poor?

_____ 1. "Absolutely sure" (VOLUNTEERED RESPONSE)
_____ 2. Good
_____ 3. 50/50
_____ 4. Poor

37. Are you on parole, or have you discharged your sentence?

_____ 1. Parole   _____ 2. Discharge

IF ON PAROLE: When will you get off parole?

_____ Month   _____ Year

---

28. Do you have any occupational licenses or training certificates?

_____ 1. Yes   _____ 2. No

IF YES: Explain _____

29. Do you NOW have a valid Texas Driver's license?

_____ 1. Yes   _____ 2. No

30. Since you got out of prison, have you been attending school or a job-training program?

_____ 1. Attending school: What are you studying? _____
_____ 2. Attending job-training program: What kind of training is it? _____
_____ 3. No

31. (A) Since you got out of prison, have you been in a hospital or laid-up so you could not work?

_____ 1. Yes   _____ 2. No

IF YES: (B) What was the matter? _____

(C) When and how long were you in the hospital or laid up? _____

32. Have you been arrested since your release from prison?

_____ 1. Yes   _____ 2. No

IF YES: When were you arrested, for what, and how long were you detained in jail?

OFFENSE	DATE	LENGTH TIME IN JAIL
1.		
2.		
3.		
4.		

WE ARE ALMOST FINISHED

38. Now, I am going to mention some problems which persons sometimes have when they come out of prison, and I want you to tell me whether these were a serious problem for you, a minor problem, or no problem at all. Since you have been out, has:

	SERIOUS PROBLEM	MINOR PROBLEM	NO PROBLEM	DOES NOT APPLY
1. Finding a job	( )	( )	( )	( )
2. Finances and getting along on the money you have	( )	( )	( )	( )
3. Having enough clothes	( )	( )	( )	( )
4. Finding a good place to live	( )	( )	( )	( )
5. Staying out of trouble	( )	( )	( )	( )
6. Finding a good woman/man	( )	( )	( )	( )
7. Transportation and being able to get around town	( )	( )	( )	( )

IF DOES NOT APPLY IS CHECKED, EXPLAIN HERE:

39. (A) Roughly, how often do you see your mother?

____ 1. Daily
____ 2. Once a week
____ 3. Once a month or more
____ 4. Less than once a month
____ 5. Never (Go to Question 40)
____ 6. Does not apply (Explain) (Go to Question 40)

(B) Since you got out of prison, how often do you have diffi-culties with your mother--things like arguments, complaints, or nagging? Would you say that happens very often, sometimes, rarely, or never?

____ 1. Very often
____ 2. Sometimes
____ 3. Rarely
____ 4. Never

NOTE ANY COMMENTS:

40. (A) Roughly, how often do you see your wife/girlfriend?

	WIFE	GIRL-FRIEND
1. Daily	( )	( )
2. Once a week	( )	( )
3. Once a month or more	( )	( )
4. Less than once a month	( )	( )
5. Never	( )	( )
6. Does not apply (Explain)	( )	( )

(B) How often do you have difficulties with your wife/girl-friend--things like arguments, complaints, and nagging? Would you say that happens very often, sometimes, rarely, or never?

	WIFE	GIRL-FRIEND
1. Very often	( )	( )
2. Sometimes	( )	( )
3. Rarely	( )	( )
4. Never	( )	( )

NOTE ANY COMMENTS:

41. Since you were released, how often would you say you have felt (depressed)--very often, sometimes, rarely, or never?

	VERY OFTEN	SOMETIMES	RARELY	NEVER
1. Depressed	( )	( )	( )	( )

REPEAT THE QUESTION FOR THE FOLLOWING:

	VERY OFTEN	SOMETIMES	RARELY	NEVER
2. Lonely	( )	( )	( )	( )
3. People treated you as an Ex-convict	( )	( )	( )	( )
4. Strange and awkward in a group where you know few of the people	( )	( )	( )	( )
5. Uncomfortable about how to act in stores or restaurants	( )	( )	( )	( )

42. Since you have been released, what has been the worst thing that has happened to you?

43. And what has been the best thing that has happened?

44. Is there another address besides the one you gave me at the beginning where you might be reached?

_____

_____

WEEKLY SUMMARY OF FIRST THREE MONTHS AFTER RELEASE

WEEKS	SUNDAY	MONDAY	TUESDAY	WEDNESDAY	THURSDAY	FRIDAY	SATURDAY
1st							
2nd							
3rd							
4th							
5th							
6th							
7th							
8th							
9th							
10th							
11th							
12th							
13th							
14th							
15th							
16th							

Use the following codes to enter summary data:

E - Employed   U - Unemployed   S - School   T - Training

H - Hospital or laid up   J - Jail   P - Prison

B

"Nobody Knows the Troubles I've Seen": Postrelease Burdens on the Families of Transitional Aid Research Project

JEFFREY K. LIKER

Commentators on the experiences of men while in prison and after release have long recognized that family ties play important roles as communication links to civilian life during incarceration and as important sources of material and social support after release.[1] The great majority of letters to and visits with imprisoned men are from family members, predominantly mothers and wives.[2] In addition, as reported in Chapter 5, almost three-quarters of the TARP released prisoners went to stay with their parent(s), or if they managed to maintain a marriage during imprisonment, with their spouses.

It is also apparent from past research and TARP data that female relatives play considerably more important roles than male relatives.[3] Visits, letters, and postprison assistance generally come from mothers rather than fathers, from sisters rather than brothers, and from spouses rather than other persons. (Since the bulk of released prisoners are men, "spouse" generally means wife, legal or common law.)

A number of criminologists have suggested that family ties may play an important "rehabilitative" role for the ex-prisoner who is reentering the free

---

[1] For example, in *The Felon* (Englewood Cliffs, N. J.: Prentice Hall, 1970) John Irwin describes the family as "the most frequently used buffering agency" for released prisoners (p. 128).

[2] See Stanley L. Brodsky, *Families and Friends of Men in Prison* (Cambridge: Mass.: Lexington Books, 1939); and Norman Holt and Donald Miller, *Explorations in Inmate-Family Relationships*, mimeographed, California Department of Corrections, Research Division, Report 46, 1972.

[3] Data on prison visitors and letter writers in the studies by Brodsky and by Holt and Miller (*ibid.*) are consistent with this view. Data from TARP also suggest this is the case. For example, it was very common for the TARP ex-prisoners to return to live with their mothers, with fathers absent, but quite rare for them to move in with fathers where no mothers were present. There were also a nontrivial number of cases of participants returning to live with a mother and stepfather, but practically no cases of return to father and stepmother. (See also Chapters 7 and 8 of this book.)

world. For example, one study provides evidence of a correlation between the frequency of social contacts (i.e., visits) while in prison and subsequent success on parole after release.[4] Despite the obvious importance of the possible role of family support in reducing recidivism, this focus seems not to have led to research on the other side of the relationship—on the families providing the material and social support and on the impact of prisoners upon such families.[5]

While relatives, primarily women, clearly play important helping roles for convicted felons before and after release from prison, it is reasonable to assume that there are costs, possibly high, in so doing. Offering assistance typically means shouldering the burden of housing, feeding, and supporting an adult male who has little or no money and poor employment prospects. Prisoners' families who are living in poverty or hovering on the borders, are hardly in a position to afford to act as "buffering agencies."[6]

This appendix reports on a reanalysis of data from the Significant Woman study, a substudy of the TARP project (described briefly in Chapter 3). These data provide an opportunity to investigate the effects of the TARP payments from another vantage point, namely, from the viewpoint of women running the households to which a subgroup of TARP participants returned. In addition, these data provide information of some interest on the families who provided the backgrounds of the ex-felons. Some of these women respondents constitute another set of "innocent victims of crime." Others may be the not-so-innocent cause of crime, as persons responsible for the early experiences of the ex-felons. In either event, of course, their characteristics are of interest.

THE SIGNIFICANT WOMAN SUBSTUDY

Since this study is described in detail in the report prepared by the coprincipal investigators, Russell L. Curtis, Jr. and Sam Schulman, Jr., only a brief accounting of the methodology is presented here.[7]

The study, and therefore the interview schedule, was designed primarily

---

[4] Holt and Miller, *Explorations.*

[5] There are a small number of studies that look at the impact of *husband* imprisonment on wives and children left behind. A review of these studies is presented in Donald P. Schneller, *The Prisoner's Family: A Study of the Effects of Imprisonment on the Families of Prisoners,* mimeographed (California: R and E Research Associates, 1976).

[6] It is not surprising that this is the case. There is ample evidence from TARP and prior research that prison inmates come from impoverished backgrounds. In addition, studies of the wives of incarcerated felons show that the women involved are generally living at a subsistence income level. See for example, Pauline Morris, *Prisoners and Their Families* (London: George Allen and Associates, 1965).

[7] Russell L. Curtis, Jr. and Sam Schulman, Jr., *The Impact of Financial Aid on the Home Conditions and Family Relationships of Ex-Offenders,* mimeographed, Center for Human Resources, University of Houston, 1978.

to ascertain the way in which TARP payments affected relationships between TARP participants and their "significant" women. A subset of 200 male inmates from the larger pool of TARP participants was systematically sampled prior to release. Every inmate returning to either Atlanta or Houston to live in a household with at least one female present was included in the study if he agreed to participate.[8] Agreement in this case meant that the ex-felon had to name the woman who was the most "significant" or "important" in the household of return and provide her name, address, and phone number. By design, half of the men sampled were in payment groups and half in control groups; half intended to return to live in Atlanta and half planned to reside in Houston. The all female interviewers were successful in reaching 198 of the 200 significant women approximately 4 months (on the average) after the prisoners' release dates.

The coprincipal investigators, Curtis and Schulman, wrote their final report based exclusively on data from the significant women's interviews. Comparing the significant women of payment group members with those of controls revealed no discernible impact on family relationships attributable to *eligibility* for postrelease financial assistance.[9]

In the analysis presented here, data collected on and from the men were merged with the significant women's interviews. Records of the actual amounts of TARP money *received* by payment group members were included, enabling an assessment of the effects of amounts of benefits received. Also utilized in this analysis were official arrest records and the prerelease and 3-month interviews with the men.

CHARACTERIZING THE SIGNIFICANT WOMEN

Table B.1 describes ex-prisoners' relationships to the women designated as the most significant in the household. The more detailed relationship breakdown is collapsed into three more general categories: mothers–surrogate mothers (61%), wives (28%), and others (11%).[10]

---

[8] Almost everyone asked agreed. However, there was some deviation from this sampling procedure. After the interviewers were already in the field, it became apparent that there would be too few wives in the sample for meaningful analysis and that it would be difficult to get to payment-group members before they exhausted their eligibility. Thus, wives were oversampled and participants assigned to the 26-week-eligibility payment group were oversampled. These infield shifts in sampling procedures produced correlations between assignment to a treatment group and relationship to the significant woman, state of return, and time from release to the women's interviews. These correlations are small enough ($r \approx .30$) to be controlled for in regression equations See Jeffrey K. Liker, *The Return of the Felon: Money, Work, and Love* (M.A. thesis, University of Massachusetts, 1978).

[9] The finding of no difference between treatment group and control group members also held up in regression equations, with controls for possible sampling biases, in the analyses of Liker, *ibid.*

[10] The term "common law wives" is used in Table B.1 merely as a convenient way of describing the lovers TARP participants moved in with.

TABLE B.1
Relationships of Significant Women to TARP Participants

Relationship	Significant women	
	Number	Percent
Mothers–surrogate mothers		
Mothers	102	
Grandmothers	3	
Aunts	8	
Older sisters	8	
Total mothers–surrogate mothers	121	61
Wives		
Wives (legally married)	46	
Common law wives	9	
Total wives	55	28
Other relationships[a]	22	11
N	198	

[a] The "other" category consists of daughters, cousins, younger sisters, and women who claimed they were just friends of the released prisoners and never invited them to move in. These cases do not fit into either of the other two categories and are excluded from subsequent analyses.

The group of women designated as "others" consisted of daughters, cousins, younger sisters, and some women who claimed they were "just friends" of the released inmate. It seemed apparent that these others were women who were not in positions to assess the progress of TARP participants either because of youth or lack of commitment to the relationship. As expected, the interview schedules for these women tended to be filled largely with "don't know" and "not applicable" responses. Consequently, these women are not in the analysis.

The groups of women remaining for analysis were composed largely of mothers–surrogates (121 women, about two-thirds of the remaining sample), with a smaller group of wives (55 women, the remaining one-third). It is clear that the natural mothers dominated as helpers for the released prisoners.[11] As one commentator put it, "Mothers represent the island of relationship certainty in the ocean of insecure and changeable relationships."[12] Despite the fact that the recent incarceration of their sons was

---

[11] Since "natural mothers" (102) are so much greater in number than the women designated "surrogate mothers," the term "mother" will be used generically to include these latter women unless otherwise specified.

[12] Stanley L. Brodsky, *Families and Friends of Men in Prison.*

probably only the latest in a series of earlier arrests or jailings, mothers remained committed to helping.

Additional information on the mothers and wives of the TARP participants is presented in Table B.2. An examination of these statistics confirms what might have been expected: We are dealing with a group of women who were heavily burdened and economically deprived. Women in the lives of TARP released prisoners had seldom completed their high school education, had little household income, were generally working full time or part time, had children to care for, often without the assistance of a man around the house, and they had the additional burden of a dependent man released from prison. Note that a large majority of these were black women (67%). This figure exceeds somewhat the proportion of blacks for the entire TARP sample (Chapter 7) because of the decision to sample only men returning to the major metropolitan areas of Atlanta and Houston.

TABLE B.2

Characteristics of Significant Women by Relationship to Released Prisoner

Characteristics	Mothers/ surrogates (N = 121)	Wives/women friends (N = 55)
Average age (years)	50 (119)	31 (55)
Median education (last grade completed)	10.2 (119)	10.7 (54)
Completed high school (percent)	30% (119)	37% (54)
Women working, full or part-time (percent)	47% (121)	51% (55)
Median earnings (weekly)[a]	$103 (52)	/105 (24)
Median household income (weekly)[b]	$106 (69)	$130 (34)
Receiving public assistance (percent)	39%[c] (114)	28%[d](54)
Average weekly amount of public assistance	$57 (44)	$51 (15)
Female-headed households[e] (percent)	54% (95)	22% (55)
Black (percent)	67% (121)	67% (55)
Chicano (percent)	5% (121)	6% (55)
Had at least one child under 18 at home (percent)	56% (119)	60% (54)
Living in Houston (percent)	58% (121)	31% (55)
"Never visited" TARP member (percent)	11.5% (113)	17.0% (47)
Average visiting frequency visits per (month)[f]	1.64 (113)	2.20 (47)

NOTE: *N*s for each measure are given in parentheses.

[a] Based only on those women working.

[b] All "significant women" who responded to the question reported some household income. The small *N* is due to the large number of women who refused to answer the question about income.

[c] Principal form is social security. Other forms equally split among Aid to Families with Dependent Children (AFDC), Supplementary Security Assistance (SSA), unemployment compensation, and disability compensation.

[d] For the wives, social security assistance was relatively rare. Otherwise, the distribution of public assistance forms was comparable to the mothers.

[e] Released prisoners who were absent from their wives' homes at the time of the women's interviews.

[f] Women who never visited were coded as zero for the computation of average visiting frequency.

The most obvious difference between the mothers (and surrogate mothers) and the wives of TARP participants is that mothers were generally older (50 years old, compared to 31). However, the mothers of these TARP participants (whose average age was 26) were by no means very old women. Mothers were slightly less likely to be high school graduates and more likely to be heading their own home without a husband present (among mothers, 54% headed households). Nonetheless, the proportion of wives who headed households was also quite high (22%): A number of TARP ex-prisoners moved out only 4 months after returning home.

Another interesting difference between the mothers and wives is the lower household income figure for mothers of $106 a week compared to $130 a week for the wives. This income difference is partially attributable to the impact of the TARP participants who were more likely to provide for wives and be provided for by mothers (see Table B.3). However, even the wives were barely getting by. For a family of at least two adults and probably children, $130 a week certainly could not have stretched very far.

Finally, we see that these women demonstrated a continuing commitment to the TARP participants that extended back further than the day of a prisoner's release. Only a small minority of women reported "never visiting" the TARP members while they were still behind bars (11.5% of the mothers and 17% of the wives). Although the mothers were less likely than wives to report "never visiting," they visited less often than wives who reported going to see their husbands, on the average, about once every 2 weeks. These figures are remarkable considering the difficulties involved in visiting for these women, who were heaped with other responsibilities, particularly in Texas where the prisons are all centrally located in Huntsville—several hours of travel from Houston.

In short, the "typical" significant woman was the mother of a TARP released prisoner: a middle-aged black women heavily burdened financially and saddled with the responsibility of heading a household with children present and with the additional burden of a dependent adult male who had recently come home from prison.[13] She had demonstrated continuing com-

---

[13] It is difficult to convey through statistics the truly miserable conditions that many of these women face on a day-to-day basis. The following interviewer's notes help flesh out the skeleton provided by Table B.2. One worker who had just interviewed the 52-year-old mother of a TARP member at her home wrote: "Interview conducted under the constant, hostile gaze of the TARP participant's sisters while his many nieces and nephews swarmed over the porch, covered with sores and smeared with mustard. Have you seen children eat mustard and bread sandwiches for breakfast?" Another woman who interviewed an older sister whose husband was a "disabled vet" wrote: "The house was very small, in a low rent area. There were 7 rooms, but they were all very small. It was dirty and very cluttered, but considering 13 people live there it looked very lived in, not too cluttered for that many people. She was very cooperative and seemed very concerned about her brother and being able to help him."

TABLE B.3

Financial Impact of TARP Members on Significant Women's Households

	Mothers and surrogates	Wives
Proportion of men taking money[a]	46% (100)	18% (38)
Average amount of money taken ($)[a]	$44.14 (46)	$20.43 (7)
Proportion of men contributing money[b]	43% (113)	62% (45)
Average amount of weekly contributions ($)[b]	$25.58 (48)	$89.11 (28)
Net weekly financial impact (contributions less money taken)[c]	$1.64 (94)	$41.95 (33)

SOURCE: Significant Women's interviews.

NOTE: Ns for each measure are given in parentheses.

[a] Women were asked how much money they "gave or lent" the TARP member during the 3 to 4 weeks prior to the interview.

[b] Women were asked how much money the TARP member contributed weekly "for things like rent and running the house."

[c] Computed as the difference between weekly contributions and money taken divided by 3 (to convert the latter to a weekly basis).

mitment to helping the TARP ex-prisoner despite the repeated trials he undoubtedly put her through.

"OBJECTIVE" FINANCIAL DRAIN ON HOUSEHOLD RESOURCES

For the wives of TARP participants, the return of their husbands often meant additional income for the household. The mothers, however, were not nearly as fortunate, and the return of their just-released sons simply meant they had an additional mouth to feed.

The contrast between the financial impact figures for mothers and wives shown in Table B.3 is striking.[14] Less than one-fifth of the returned husbands took loans or gifts, in average amounts of $20, from their wives. By contrast, close to half of the returned sons took money, in average sums of $44, from their mothers.

This difference in financial impact is accentuated further when we consider the incidence and amounts of money TARP members contributed toward household expenses. Whereas 62% of the husbands were contributing

[14] We caution the reader that these "objective" financial drain figures are based on the women's self-reports. It is quite possible that there was some tendency for wives more than mothers to present their men in a favorable light to the interviewers, thus exaggerating the differences between mothers and wives. Note, however, that even the more favorable picture presented by wives is dismal.

average amounts of $89 a week, only 43% of the sons were contributing average sums of $26 a week.

Another way to look at financial impact is to subtract the weekly amounts borrowed from the weekly contributions, thereby arriving at the net weekly financial impact. On this basis, the husbands had a net positive impact of $41.95 a week, but sons returning to their mothers added a net amount of only $1.64 a week to the household income—hardly enough to cover the additional costs incurred by an adult male.

The statistics discussed in this section show quite clearly that TARP members who returned to live with their mothers placed a much greater financial burden on the households than did the released prisoners who returned to live with their wives. Essentially, the released prisoner sons were getting room and board for free. Nonetheless, we should bear in mind that the wives were not getting off lightly either. Recall that almost 40% of the wives reported that their husbands were making *no* contributions toward household expenses. These women continued to pay the bills and support the children despite the fact that the father had come home from prison.

FROM THE SUBJECTIVE SIDE

When asked in the interview whether initially they had "looked forward to [the TARP member's] coming home" from prison, 90% of the women responded, "Yes, very much!" However, for many—particularly the mothers—this positive feeling was short-lived. When asked how they felt at the time of the interview about the actual impact these men had had on the household, a much larger proportion expressed dissatisfaction (see Table B.4). Apparently, the reality of the day-to-day burden their released-prisoner sons or husbands placed on them was not what they had been looking forward to.

Presented in Table B.4 are the responses to interview items asking the women to assess the impact of the TARP member on the household in a variety of respects. The response categories were "very satisfied, okay, and not satisfied," and Table B.4 shows the proportions of mothers and wives who responded "very satisfied." There is considerable variation in the proportion of women expressing satisfaction across items and across relationship types. In general, the wives were more satisfied than the mothers regardless of the specific content of the item. However, the rank ordering of how problematic these various problems seemed is fairly consistent across mothers and wives. The greatest difference between wives and mothers is shown in the item asking about "help around the house": Of the wives,

TABLE B.4

Significant Women's Satisfaction With the TARP Participant Four Months After Release

Items with which women were asked to indicate relative satisfaction[a]	Percent "very satisfied"		Included in Satisfaction Index?
	Mothers	Wives	
"The friend he sees regularly"	41 (114)	63 (51)	yes
The general "influence on the other people living here"[b]	42 (118)	57 (51)	yes
"The amount of help he gives around the house"	43 (110)	73 (51)	yes
"The amount of money he contributes to the house"	46 (100)	66 (47)	no
"The number of times he asks you for money"	52 (118)	67 (52)	no
"How he spends his time"	53 (119)	69 (54)	yes
"His effort in trying to find a job"	74 (117)	82 (50)	no
"How he treats the children or his brothers and sisters" (if applicable)	75 (88)	81 (36)	yes
Mean score on Satisfaction Index (range from 0–100)[c]	65.5 (119)	77.5 (55)	

NOTE: Ns for each measure are given in parentheses.

[a] Response categories were "very satisfied, okay, not satisfied."

[b] Response categories were "extremely good influence" to "very bad influence," with three additional categories in between. For computation of the Satisfaction Index, the categories "no influence, bad influence, and very bad influence" were combined, leaving three categories as in the satisfaction items.

[c] Constructed from all answered items above which are demarcated with a "yes" in the far right column. The index is simply the sum of the answered items standardized to range from 0–100, where 100 represents the response of "very satisfied" to all answered items.

73% responded that they felt "very satisfied," but only 43% of the mothers claimed great satisfaction. This may indicate that wives more than mothers felt that it was their own role to take care of the house.

Among the items to which mothers and wives responded with the least satisfaction were the items asking about financial matters. Nonetheless, approximately half the mothers and a majority of the wives said that they were "very satisified" with the TARP member's tendencies to borrow money and the financial contributions he made. These figures seem remarkably high considering the objective realities of these women's lives which, as we saw in the last two sections, were fraught with financial difficulties.

There were fairly strong correlations among the satisfaction items. That is, women who expressed dissatisfaction in one area tended to report dissatisfaction in the other areas asked about. The average intercorrelation among items was close to .50, suggesting that these items were actually tapping into some more generalized attitude toward the ex-prisoner.

Accordingly, a number of items were summed to form a satisfaction index to capture this underlying assessment. The means of the resulting index are shown at the bottom of Table B.4. Since the satisfaction index was to be treated as a dependent variable, predicted by a set of independent variables that included measures of the ex-prisoner's "objective" work experiences and financial impact on the household, items asking about satisfaction with his work efforts or financial impact were excluded from the satisfaction index (as noted in Table B.4). The five remaining items were summed, with the resulting score transformed so that the index had a possible range of zero to 100. As computed, 100 was the best score and would result from a woman answering all applicable items with the response "very satisfied."[15]

From the means of the satisfaction index across mothers and wives, we see that both groups tended to report more satisfaction than not (means equal 65.5 and 77.5 respectively). Nonetheless there was considerable variation around the mean responses (standard deviations of 28 and 21 for mothers and wives), and it is that variation that we attempt to explain via regression results presented in a later section. Before proceeding with those results, we will briefly discuss correlates of the satisfaction index.

WHAT DOES THE SATISFACTION INDEX MEAN?

The satisfaction index was created under the assumption that the component items were all indicative of some underlying sense of generalized satisfaction with the returned TARP member. It may help clarify what this generalized satisfaction means if we examine the way the index correlates with other interview items. Correlates of the satisfaction index are presented in Table B.5.

First, we see that there is a negative correlation ($r = -.39$) between expressed satisfaction and the recent incidence of quarreling between the significant woman and the TARP member. Thus, a low score on the index is indicative of overt tension that existed in the relationship and thus in the home.

Second, the index is most strongly correlated ($r = .61$) with the woman's assessment of her son's or husband's chances of staying out of prison, and there is a somewhat lower correlation ($r = .45$) with her feeling that she could help him "make it" this time. Thus, we sense feelings of despair,

---

[15] "Applicable" in this case simply means the woman was able and willing to answer the item. Obviously if there were no children around, the item asking about the influence on the children could not be answered. Thus, the satisfaction index was based on the items that each woman did answer.

TABLE B.5
Correlates of the Satisfaction Index

Significant women's statements[a]	Correlation
Whether quarreled with TARP member recently[b]	− .39 (174)
Estimate of chances TARP member will stay out of prison[c]	+ .61 (172)
Judgment of own ability to help TARP member "Make it now that he's out of prison"[d]	+ .45 (174)
Assessment of personal well-being of TARP member (0–100)[e]	+ .43 (174)
Whether gave money to TARP member recently[f]	− .31 (137)
Amount of TARP member's weekly household contributions ($)	+ .31 (156)

NOTE: Ns for each measure are given in parentheses.

[a] All measures were derived from the women's interviews, which took place approximately 4 months after the TARP member's release.

[b] Women were asked if they "quarreled" with the TARP member in the 3–4 weeks prior to the interview. (Scored as 1=yes, 0=no.)

[c] Response categories went from "poor, 50/50, good" to the top response category, which was some expression of certainty (e.g., "absolutely sure").

[d] Response categories were "not at all, not sure, somewhat, a great deal."

[e] The women were asked to agree or disagree with 10 items asking how the ex-prisoner was getting along in the 3–4 weeks prior to the interview (e.g., he feels kind of angry, lonely, happy, scared, etc.). The responses were combined into an index computed such that 0 represents a woman's perception of a TARP member as doing very poorly and 100 her perception of a man who seems to be doing very well.

[f] Scored as 1=yes, 0=no

worry, and helplessness coming through in the index. These women had been through enough, and the last thing they needed was to suffer through the imprisonment of their sons or husbands once again.

There is also a sizable correlation ($r = .43$) between the satisfaction index and the women's assessments' of their sons' or husbands' own personal well-being (e.g., whether he felt angry, lonely, disorganized, etc.). This can be interpreted in part as a sense of concern, but also as a realistic appraisal of the depressing influence created by the addition to the household of an adult man who was feeling down and bringing others in the household down with him.

Finally, we see that the satisfaction index is sensitive to the "objective" financial burden these men were placing on scarce household resources. Women expressed dissatisfaction with men who took financial gifts or loans ($r = - .31$), and they felt more satisfied ($r = .31$) the more money he was contributing toward household expenses. The correlations of the index with these measures of objective financial drain are especially impressive when we consider that items specifically asking about work or financial considerations were excluded from the satisfaction index.

It appears from the pattern of correlations in Table B.5 that the satisfaction index is a good measure of the general burden the returned TARP participants placed on these women and their households. A low score was indicative of incidents of open quarreling between the woman and man and of a feeling of despair that the TARP member was going to get himself into trouble again and that she could do nothing to prevent it. The expressed dissatisfaction was also a response to the negative influence on the "harmony" of already troubled homes created by the addition of adult men who felt down and were possibly bringing others in the household down with them. Furthermore, there is advanced indication that the women's dissatisfaction stemmed in part from the objective reality of the financial strains these men were placing on an already financially depressed household. This latter "hint" at a bivariate level is given further support by the results of regression analyses presented in the next section, which looks at the effects of this objective financial burden, holding other factors constant.

DETERMINANTS OF SATISFACTION

This section examines the "objective" factors underlying the women's expressed feelings of satisfaction or dissatisfaction with their returned son or husband as measured by the satisfaction index.

The results of regression analyses are presented in two slightly different models, as shown in Table B.6. The two models are identical, with one exception: In Model 1, a binary variable, which equals one if the TARP member had taken money, is entered into the equation, whereas Model II treats weekly household contributions as the measure of financial impact.[16] Each measure reflects different aspects of the ex-prisoner's financial impact on the woman's household, and each has a direct effect on her satisfaction with the TARP member. There is a net drop of 11 satisfaction points if the TARP member took money during the weeks prior to the woman's interview, and a net increase of 1.6 points for each additional $10 contribution to household funds. These are rather large effects, especially considering that the satisfaction items comprising the index never specifically asked about financial burdens.

Of all the additional factors thought to affect the women's satisfaction level, only a few crossed thresholds of statistical significance. These are

---

[16] Due to the correlation between these two measures of financial impact ($r = -.37$) and their multiple correlations with other independent variables, entry of both simultaneously into the equation resulted in neither showing a significant effect (i.e., because of multicollinearity). Another way of putting this is that given the relatively small sample size, there was not enough information to disaggregate the effects of these two measures of financial impact. Thus, two models are presented in Table B.6 in which each variable is entered separately into regression equations.

TABLE B.6

Regression of Satisfaction Index on Selected Characteristics

Independent Variables[a]	Model I		Model II	
	b	SE	b	SE
TARP member took money (1=yes)[w]	−10.84*	5.08	Excluded	
TARP member's weekly contributions ($)[w]	Excluded		.16**	.06
Number of weeks member worked first 3 months[m]	.58	.60	.88	.53
Total TARP cash received first 3 months ($)[m]	.003	.008	.001	.007
Member's friends are "ex-offenders"? (0–3)[b]	−8.11**	3.14	−9.76**	2.91
Frequency visited member in prison (0–4)[c]	4.29*	1.84	3.54*	1.66
Black dummy (0=white)[w]	7.47	5.25	8.16	4.89
Chicano (0=white)	25.34*	11.39	24.77*	10.57
Dollars per Week Public Assistance[w]	.11	.07	.10	.06
Relationship dummy (1=wife)	3.77	5.43	−1.42	5.78
Time to interview (days)[w]	.09	.06	.10	.06
Home in Houston[w]	−3.56	5.45	−7.98	5.07
TARP member moved out? (1=Yes)[w]	−7.26	5.28	−3.10	5.17
TARP member's age (years)[m]	.02	.28	−.04	.26
Number of arrests first 3 months[m]	−5.40	7.01	−4.73	6.49
Number of prior arrests[m]	−.17	.12	−.08	.11
Constant	52.87**	17.32	48.78**	15.76
R^2	.330**		.336**	
Adjusted R^2	.239		.257	
N	(126)		(143)	

SOURCES: Variables marked with "w" are derived from the the significant women's interviews. Those marked with "m" are derived from either the TARP member's 3-month interview or official records.

Note: Pair-wise deletion used for regression analysis.

[a] Dependent variable is Satisfaction Index, which ranges from 0–100, where 100 is the case of indicates a response of "very satisfied" to all applicable items.

[b] Response categories are 0=none, 1=one to two, 2=most, 3=all.

[c] Response categories are 0=never, 1=once in 6 months, 2=once a month, 3=every 2 weeks, 4=once a week.

* $p < .05$

** $p < .01$

marked with asterisks in Table B.6. First, there was a marked drop in the woman's assessment if she knew that her son or husband was associating with other ex-offenders.[17] For the women involved, this was certainly a cause for real concern, since the influence of these friends with a record of getting into trouble could have led the TARP member back into trouble

[17] This item had four response categories, as follows: "none, 1–2, most, all." Thus, the variable ranged from 0–3. Most of the women reported that the TARP members were associating with no ex-offenders (71%), with a minority reporting 1–2 (20%), and even fewer (10%) claiming "most" or "all" of their husband's friends were ex-offenders. Thus, most of the variation that exists is between the 0 and 1 categories.

with the law. This added psychological burden on the women may have in fact been even more stressful than the financial burdens created by the TARP member's return.

Second, women who visited their husbands or sons often while they were in prison felt more satisfied with them after they returned home. If we take visiting as a measure of the women's a priori commitment to the relationship, this finding suggests that committed women were more willing to shoulder the burdens created by the return of the TARP participant.[18]

The only other factor that significantly affected the women's satisfaction level was race. Chicanos were considerably more likely than whites to feel satisfied with their released prisoner sons or husbands (a difference of 25 points between Chicanos and whites), other things equal. This finding bolsters evidence from previous research on family relationships of imprisoned men that family ties among Chicanos are particularly strong.[19]

Two factors that clearly did not directly affect the women's satisfaction were the TARP member's work stability (i.e., weeks worked) and the amount of TARP cash received. Nonetheless, this is not particularly surprising since these equations control statistically for the objective financial drain the released prisoner placed on household resources. One would expect that if the TARP financial assistance and wages from work did affect the women's satisfaction, they would operate through a reduction in the financial burdens the TARP member placed on the household. The next section investigates this issue.

DETERMINANTS OF FINANCIAL IMPACT

This section investigates the question of whether TARP members with greater financial resources of their own had a more favorable financial impact on the households they returned to live in. In other words, did the money received from working and/or from TARP help reduce the financial burdens the ex-prisoners placed on the families they returned to live with? If the answer is yes, it logically follows that wages from stable employment

---

[18] An alternative interpretation is that prison visiting helped maintain the relationship during the prison term. Women who, for whatever reason, were able to see imprisoned men face-to-face may have found their reentry into the home less abrupt and easier to deal with.

[19] Holt and Miller, *Explorations in Inmate–Family Relationships*. Holt and Miller found that Chicano mothers and sisters were much more apt to visit their imprisoned sons or brothers than women in other ethnic groups.

and TARP payments indirectly increased the significant women's satisfaction with the returned men.

The measures of TARP members' financial resources used for the analysis were the number of weeks worked and the total amount of TARP cash received during the first 3 months of freedom.[20] These and a number of other relevant characteristics are the independent variables in the regression equations shown in Table B.7.[21] The dependent variables are three different measures of the financial impact of TARP participants: weekly household contributions in dollars; a binary variable equal to one if the member took money from the significant woman in the 3–4 weeks prior to her interview; and the total amount of money he took.

There clearly was no effect either of working or of the TARP payments on the weekly financial contributions of TARP members. However, both factors strongly affected the ex-prisoner's propensity to take money from significant women. Since this latter dependent variable is binary in form, the coefficients are interpretable as the incremental probability of taking money for each unit change in the independent variable of interest. Thus, based on average amounts of work (about 5 weeks) and TARP cash received (about $500) during the first 3 months out, these results show that wages from work reduced the ex-prisoners' tendencies to place cash demands on the women by 23%, whereas TARP payments reduced the propensity to take cash handouts by 15%.[22]

When we move from the binary form of presence or absence of borrowing to the amount of money borrowed, the effects of both working and TARP cash are attenuated. The work effect just barely crosses conventional levels of statistical significance (significant at .052 level), and the TARP cash effect moves out of the realm of statistical significance

---

[20] Since the TARP member's wages were all relatively low and did not vary greatly, weeks of work is a good proxy for the amounts of wages earned during the first quarter of the year. The time period chosen—the first 3 months after release—was selected because it was just prior to the women's interviews (about 4 months after the men's release).

[21] Measures of weeks worked, TARP cash received, and other characteristics of the men came from interviews and official records independent of the dependent variables based on the women's reports. Thus, effects cannot be attributed to response biases of the women or men interviewed.

[22] There are at least two possible explanations for the stronger effect of work on the tendency to take money from the significant women. First, since weekly wages from work exceeded the TARP weekly payments, the additional income may have enabled the working ex-prisoners to refrain more often from taking money from the women. Second, there may be something about working itself over and above the wage effect (e.g., a steady job requires responsibility, which transfers to the members being more responsible in the home, or perhaps unemployed men simply have more time to spend money and thus a greater "need" for supplementary cash from family members).

TABLE B.7

Regression of Financial Impact of Returned TARP Members on Selected Characteristics

Independent variables	Dependent Variables					
	Weekly household contributions ($)[w]		Member took money? (1=Yes)[w]		Dollar amount of money taken[a]	
	b	SE	b	SE	b	SE
Number of weeks member worked first 3 months[m]	.81	.71	−.046**	.010	−2.15*	1.08
Total TARP cash received first 3 months ($)[m]	.00	.01	−.0003**	.0001	−.017	.014
Frequency visited member in prison (0–4)[w]	−.57	2.29	.070*	.003	.66	3.48
Relationship dummy (1=mother-surrogate)[w]	−45.64**	6.67	.250**	.098	20.45*	10.15
Chicano dummy (0=white)	25.58	14.32	−.379	.21	−50.90*	21.79
Black dummy (0=white)	−7.39	6.57	.045	.096	−26.84**	10.00
Dollars per week earnings for working women[w]	.00	.04	.001	.001	.08	.06
Time to interview (days)[w]	.03	.08	−.002	.001	.03	.12
Home in Houston[w]	13.21	7.05	.207*	.103	15.48	10.72
TARP member moved out? (=yes)[w]	−23.18**	6.64	.008	.100	−3.70	10.11
TARP member's age (years)[m]	.89*	.43	−.009	.006	1.80	.65
Number of arrests first 3 months[m]	2.81	8.80	−.082	.129	−7.17	13.39
Number of prior arrests[m]	−.54**	.15	.001	.002	.36	.22
Longest job ever held (months)[m]	−.16	.12	.003	.002	−.30	.18
Constant	34.77	21.10	.695	.309	−18.40	32.11
$R^2=$	.434**		.286**		.256**	
Adjusted R^2	.372		.196		.162	
N	(143)		(126)		(126)	

Source: Variables marked with "w" are derived from the significant women's interviews. Those marked with a "m" are derived from either the TARP members' interviews of official records.

[a] Based on women's reports, this is the total amount of money the TARP member borrowed in the 3 to 4 weeks prior to interview.

* $p < .05$
** $P < .01$

altogether (both were significant at the .01 level, using the binary specification of money taken). This finding suggests that wages and financial assistance reduced the tendency of the ex-prisoners to place cash demands on family members, but did not affect the amounts taken by those who took money.[23]

Of the remaining factors entered into the equations in Table B.7, only a few have a direct bearing on the financial impact of the TARP participants. First, we see confirmation that, *ceteris paribus*, ex-prisoners placed a much greater financial burden on their mothers (or surrogate mothers) than on their wives. They contributed on the average $46 a week more to wives than to mothers' households; they borrowed money from mothers 25% more often; and the average cash demands placed on mothers exceeded that on wives by $20.

Second, there is evidence that Chicanos had a considerably more favorable impact on their families compared to white ex-prisoners: they contributed on the average $26 a week more; they borrowed money in 38% fewer cases; and the average cash demands placed on women were $51 less.[24] As we saw earlier (Table B.6), even when Chicano men were compared to blacks and whites equivalent in their financial impact (i.e., holding financial impact measures constant), they were regarded more favorably than whites and blacks by the women.

Third, blacks were comparable to whites in their contributions to the household and their tendency to take financial loans or gifts; however, the amounts of money taken were less than for whites (by $27 on the average). This probably reflects the harsher economic conditions faced by the black women involved who were unable to provide as much money as the white women.

Fourth, participants who returned to Houston, where the economic conditions were more favorable than in Atlanta, received money from the women interviewed 21% more often. The weekly contributions of Houston men also appear to be greater ($13 a week), although this latter effect can be regarded as real only if we relax the significance criterion to the .06 level.

Fifth, men who moved out of a woman's home (prior to her interview)

---

[23] When the amount of money borrowed was entered into the women's satisfaction equation (not shown in Table B.6) as a measure of financial impact, the estimated effect was not even close to significance. Thus, what seems to matter is whether or not the men refrained from making cash demands altogether, not differences in the amounts taken.

[24] The coefficients for "Household contributions" and "member took money" for Chicanos can be considered significant only if we relax the conventional criterion to the .075 level. Given the substantive magnitudes of the effects and their consistency with other findings concerning Chicanos, I have discussed these as real effects.

essentially stopped contributing money toward household expenses (reduction of $23 a week, which is almost equal to the average household contribution).[25] It is interesting to note, however, that while moving out meant that the flow of financial contributions into the women's home stopped, the flow of money leaving the household continued. Men who moved out borrowed money from the women left behind as often as men who remained in the home.

Finally, two characteristics of the men were significant predictors of their financial impact on the women's home. Older men contributed more money on a weekly basis but also borrowed greater sums of money from the women. Men who had a history of repeated arrests contributed substantially less money to the household than men with less extensive criminal histories.

Results from this section showed that TARP financial assistance did reduce the tendency of the released prisoners involved to place cash demands on family members. However, as in the main analysis of recidivism, treatment effects could be detected only when we shifted our measure of the treatment from eligibility for TARP payments to the amounts of benefits received, and when we included a measure of employment stability in the regression analysis, thereby controlling for the work-disincentive effects of the TARP program.

CONCLUSIONS

In this appendix our focus has shifted away from the TARP ex-prisoners and their lives to take a brief look at a group of women who were very much involved in the TARP members' lives. As far as we know, these women, mothers and wives of the TARP members, have done nothing "wrong" yet each time their sons or husbands are taken away to be punished the women too are punished. We have seen that for this group of women who have expressed continuing commitment to the TARP members, the "punishment" often continues after their husbands or sons are released from prison as they attempt to absorb these financially dependent adult males back into their already overburdened households.

Current social policy involves releasing men from state prisons with few or no resources with which to find their way back into civilian life. This

---

[25] A total of 24% of the men (42 out of 176) left women's homes before their interviews. The percent absent was about the same for mothers and wives (26% and 22% respectively). Of the 42 cases who were not living with the women when they were interviewed, 8 (19%) had never gone to live there after release from prison (5 of the 8 had claimed they were going to live with their wives after release).

social policy in effect forces released prisoners to rely on their kinship or marital ties. Since so few are married at the time of release (less than 25% in our two samples), the real burden of financing the transition back into civilian life is typically shifted onto the shoulders of mothers heading their own households. What this means to poor families—to absorb another adult who must be fed, clothed, housed, and provided with some cash—we can only surmise. It must mean tightening of belts, overcrowding, and doing without necessary expenditures on other household members. It should be noted that many of these households have additional dependent children at home. One can only admire the willingness of most of these women to shoulder this burden and claim more satisfaction than dissatisfaction with the TARP members.

It is also clear that TARP, a quite modest program providing minimum unemployment insurance payments to released prisoners for a short period of time, helps relieve some of the burden placed upon the prisoners' families. Men who used the money to cover their own incidental expenses and thereby refrained from placing cash demands on the significant women were regarded with more positive affect by these women. It should be noted that the sums involved are not very large. At the margins of poverty, small benefits are easily detected as having effects.

Another way of putting the message in this appendix is that we have uncovered another cost of crime in which extra burdens are placed on the families of ex-criminals on whom, by default, the responsibility of providing transitional postrelease aid is placed. We have shown that small amounts of postrelease financial aid can help relieve those burdens.

C

Women Ex-Offenders in the TARP Experiment

NANCY JURIK

INTRODUCTION

The analysis reported in the text has focused largely on the TARP subjects as males. This appendix deals with the less than 5% of the ex-offenders who were female and, it is to be hoped, provides a balance to the relative neglect of women in the text.

The number of women in the TARP experiments mirrors faithfully the proportion of females among the prisoners released during the period in question. A total of 256 women ex-felons took part in the experiment, but only those (126) in the five interviewed experimental groups—68 in Texas and 58 in Georgia—will be included in the analysis presented here. Since this group is too small to sustain an analysis as complex as that presented in Chapter 12, the best that can be done in this appendix is to show that the *trends* among this small group of female offenders were similar or dissimilar to those shown by the total group analyzed in the preceding chapters.[1]

There are many reasons for treating women separately. To begin with, the women ex-offenders were imprisoned, by and large, for different offenses: Among the most common were crimes against the person, drug offenses and prostitution. Second, the employment prospects for female offenders may be quite different, especially in the light of the heavier family obligations of women. Finally, some criminologists have argued that women offenders are motivated in their illegitimate behavior by quite different aims. We do not share the latter perspective. At the same time, it clearly cannot be taken for granted that the behavior of women ex-offenders simply mirrors that of their male counterparts.

---

[1] It should be borne in mind that the analyses in the main body of this volume were based on all ex-felons in the TARP experiment, including both males and females. Of course, since females constituted only 5% of the subjects, the processes described are dominated by the experiences of men.

Early criminologists who sought the roots of criminal behavior in biological factors believed that the nature of female criminals *ipso facto* must be different from that of males. In particular, they held that female criminality was not economically motivated.

The more recent literature on female criminality has abandoned the biological perspective but is still attempting to explain why women commit fewer crimes and why the crimes they commit are different from those of men.[2] Of particular interest are the very recent attempts to integrate womens' criminal behavior into the same framework used to explain that of males. Bartel has argued that Ehrlich's economic model can be applied with a few modifications that take into account the special position of women.[3] According to Bartel, in the study of female criminality some special considerations must be included: "An analysis of female participation in criminal activities requires a model that considers not only the optimal allocation of time between legal and illegal activities, but also the optimal allocation of time between household and work activities (legal and illegal)." Bartel's analysis attempts to take into account the special effects that marital status and having children make on the choices made by women between legal and illegal activities.

Much of the recent criminological literature attempts to analyze the impact of increasing degrees of equality between the sexes. Thus both Simon and Adler argue that the criminal behaviors of men and women are converging as the greater employment of women increases illegal opportunities.[4] Other criminologists dispute this expectation, suggesting that recent egalitarian feminist ideologies have a long way to go to reach the very disadvantaged women who are typical felons.

From this disparate, somewhat contradictory literature several expectations can be formulated concerning how TARP payments might have affected women ex-offenders.[5]

First of all, since TARP females (like male TARP subjects) are overwhelmingly drawn from the bottommost socioeconomic levels of American

---

[2] For an extensive review of this literature see Nancy Jurik, "Women Ex-Offenders: Their Work and Re-arrest Patterns" (Ph.D. diss. University of California, Santa Barbara, 1979).

[3] Bartell, A. P. "Women and Crime: An Economic Analysis," *Economic Inquiry* 17 (1979); Ehrlich, I. "Participation in Illegal Activities: An Economic Analysis," in *Essays in the Economics of Crime and Punishment*, C. S. Baker and W. M. Lantes (eds.) (New York: Columbia University Press, 1974.)

[4] Adler, F. *Sisters in Crime: The Rise of the New Female Criminal* (New York: McGraw-Hill, 1975), and R. Simon *The Contemporary Women and Crime* (Washington, D.C.: National Institute of Mental Health, 1975).

[5] A more complete exposition of the derivation of these expectations can be found in Jurik, "Women Ex-Offenders."

society, TARP payments may be expected to have reduced rearrests for economic crimes, because payments can compete successfully with illegal economic activities.

Second, to the extent that female crimes are beginning to more closely approximate the nature of male crimes, a comparison of the distribution of charges for TARP female rearrests with those of TARP male rearrest charges should show some degree of convergence between the two distributions. Comparisons between female TARP participants and the total population are appropriate tests of this expectation. In addition, it is to be expected that the male and female recidivism rates would be about the same.

Because some women make choices among work, crime, and household activities, a special expectation can be formulated: Relative both to the other TARP females and to married males, married women and women with dependent children would be expected, *ceteris paribus*, to incur greater opportunity costs for criminal involvement. Because husbands are expected traditionally to be the breadwinners, marriage might also relieve the women of financial pressures and thereby decrease criminal activities.

As with male ex-felons, it is to be expected that legal employment would decrease female criminal involvement. The more weeks employed, the greater the costs of criminal acts. In addition, legal employment may lead to a change in social ties, which in turn may lead to increased exposure to anticriminal behavior patterns. At minimum, employment may help the ex-offender to avoid returning to exactly the same situation that, in the first place, produced her criminality.

With regard to noneconomic crimes, Simon has hypothesized that working women will encounter less frustration and will therefore, be less likely to commit drug or assault-related crimes. Conversely, she predicts that women who remain in the home will experience more frustration and commit more crimes. Both of these hypotheses can be examined.

Since studies have shown that for women as for men, the number of previous incarcerations is positively associated with recidivism, we can expect that multiple offenders will be more likely to be rearrested.

Concerning female employment patterns, several expectations can be formulated. Drawing on Bartel's analysis, it is expected that, holding constant human-capital investments, married women will allocate time away from the labor market. They may do so in order to allocate more time to household production and child care. Recall that married men were expected to allocate increasing amounts of time to the labor market.

It is also expected that married women with children would allocate time away from legal employment. Single women with children might be expected to allocate increasing amounts of time to the labor market;

however, given that TARP females are likely to earn low wages it is possible that the high prices of purchased child care would make it more reasonable to stay at home and rely on welfare and family support than to work. Consequently, it is expected that the greater the number of dependents, the more women would withdraw from the labor market.[6]

Additional hypotheses regarding the prediction of TARP female employment are consistent with those defined for the analysis of the total sample. Other factors included are indicators of human-capital investment, financial need, the demand for labor, and whether or not the individual was on parole.

CHARACTERISTICS OF TARP WOMEN:
PRERELEASE AND POSTRELEASE

As we have noted, like other felons across the country, TARP women are overwhelmingly drawn from the bottommost socioeconomic levels of society. By and large, the characteristics of the female TARP participants are not unlike those revealed by recent surveys of female prison populations across the country.[7]

The "typical" TARP woman can be described as impoverished, poorly educated, and about thirty years of age.[8] Less than one-third had obtained their high school diplomas. Like the men, they were of average intelligence but had educational achievement scores that fell below their reported years of schooling. Approximately 60% of the women in both states were members of a minority group. Their family backgrounds closely resembled that of the men: broken homes, often raised by relatives, etc. Between 50% and 55% of TARP females were single upon release.

If their educational backgrounds imply that TARP women might be less than successful in finding "good" jobs, their preprison employment histories fail to brighten the picture. Their longest held preprison jobs lasted between 20 and 25 months on the average as compared with a 32-month average for the entire sample of TARP participants. Like the men, approximately 60% of the women in each state were categorized as unskilled workers.

Compared with TARP males, the women had still other job liabilities.

---

[6] Ideally an interaction term should be included for marital status times the number of children. The sample size prohibits this addition, however.

[7] M. L. Velemesis, "The Female Offender," *Crime and Delinquency* 13, (1975).

[8] Note that this average age is about 5 years more than the average age of the total TARP sample. This considerable difference may be caused by the alleged greater leniency shown to women in their earlier offenses.

None of the women in Texas and only 9% in Georgia belonged to any sort of trade union. Since an important aspect of job search and employment involves transportation, the fact that only 22% of Texas women and 33% of Georgia women had valid driver's licenses could also be a tremendous liability to finding employment.

Given this description of the human-capital stock of the TARP women, their labor market prospects looked dim indeed. Moreover, relative to males, a larger proportion of females were married and a larger proportion of women indicated that they planned to support children after release (approximately 60%). Thus, combined with few job possibilities, is a set of special financial needs.

Somewhat more optimistically, TARP women had much less extensive criminal histories compared to TARP men. Thus, on the average, relative to men, women were arrested and convicted fewer times, had fewer recorded prison incarcerations, and had served shorter sentences in prison. A larger proportion were first offenders: 65% of Texas women as opposed to 33% of the men and 53% of the Georgia women as compared with 39% of the men. Security classifications revealed that no women in either state were categorized as high security risks.

Prior to imprisonment, the largest percentage of TARP female convictions was in the drug-related category. The next largest proportion occurred in the larceny–theft category, followed by forgery–fraud types of offenses.

From the preceding paragraphs, it is clear that TARP women came from social strata that are likely to be untouched by either changing female consciousness or expanding economic opportunities for women. The socioeconomic levels in which TARP females are located, however, will make them vulnerable to the stresses caused by inflation, recession, and correspondingly high unemployment rates. Minority status, limited job skills, poor employment records, and the stigma of a criminal record will limit their future employment plans. These considerations, together with the plans of many TARP women to care for children, will create serious economic pressures, particularly in the early days after release. Given such circumstances, TARP payments were no doubt likely a welcome relief to many women ex-felons.[9]

With females as with males there was a tendency to ease postrelease economic pressures by moving in with parents or other relatives immediately after prison. As the year progressed, there was also a general trend for women to leave the homes of parents and make their own homes

---

[9] Payments to female ex-offenders were almost identical, on the average, with those given to men.

with friends or spouses. However, at the end of the postrelease year, a larger proportion of females than males continued to remain with family and/or relatives. In addition, although females exhibited a net shift in marital status toward marriage, proportionately more women than men remained unmarried for the duration of the study. It appears that, particularly for TARP woman ex-offenders, aid from extended families is a crucial means of survival.

Employment figures for the year after release reveal that a large proportion of women in both states remained unemployed. Thirty-four percent of Georgia women and 28% of Texas women never worked; another 32% and 28%, respectively, worked 13 or fewer weeks. Compared to all TARP members (29% and 11% in Georgia and Texas, respectively, never worked), it is clear that women had considerably higher unemployment rates. Although it might be argued that many women did not work because they were supported by a spouse, it is also important to note that only about 8% of TARP females returned to live with a spouse after release. Wage information indicates that on the average, women earned anywhere from $200 to $500 less than men per quarter.[10]

Given the inferior economic situation of many TARP women, it would not be surprising to discover a high arrest rate for property-related crimes. Although fewer females then males were rearrested during the postrelease year, the percentage of women who were rearrested for property crimes is about the same as that for the total sample. The major sex differences were in noneconomic arrest categories. Twenty five percent of Texas females and 22% of Georgia females were rearrested one or more times during the study year, whereas the figures for the total sample were 38% in Texas and 36% in Georgia. Between 20% and 23% of females of the total TARP group were rearrested for property-related charges.

Although the female arrest rate for property-related crimes closely approximates that for males, the types of offenses for which TARP women are rearrested differ quite markedly from those of males, as shown in Table C. 1. It should be noted that these charges resemble closely those for which the women had been imprisoned. The largest proportion of offenses fell in the prostitution, larceny, and assault categories, while male charges fell predominantly into the burglary, larceny, and assault categories (see Chapter 10).

However, note that these findings do not support the predictions made by Adler and Simon, since the *types* of crimes that these women committed

---

[10] It is difficult to be too sure of these figures, however, because a large proportion of the female wage data were missing. These missing data problems precluded a more extensive analysis of female wages.

TABLE C.1
Charges on Postrelease Arrests of Texas and Georgia Women

Charge	Percent
Burglary	3
Robbery	8
Larceny (includes shoplifting and picking pockets)	27
Forgery (includes 3 hot checks, credit cards)	8
Joyriding	3
Miscellaneous property offenses	5
Drug offenses	7
Assault	12
Weapons	1
Drunk/disorderly	3
Obstructing justice	1
Escape/failure to appear	4
Parole violation	4
Prostitution/morals	14
N	(97)

were what have been termed in the literature "traditional" female crimes (i.e., larceny, prostitution, assault, and drug offenses). Although Adler and Simon may be correct about future trends, their predictions do not hold for this group of female offenders at this time.

REPLICATION OF THE COUNTERBALANCING MODEL

By applying the five-equation model developed in Chapters 11 and 12 to the subsample of TARP women, much additional information can be derived about female postrelease experiences. The specifications used in this effort are almost identical to those elaborated in Chapters 11 and 12, with modifications as described below.

First, instead of the property–nonproperty arrest categorization used in Chapters 11 and 12, female arrests have been redefined into economic and noneconomic offenses. Many crimes which are for women major sources of illegal revenue have traditionally been conceptualized as nonproperty as, for example, prostitution and drug-trafficking. In the classification used here, any offense that may serve as a means to achieve financial or monetary gain is defined as an economic-related charge. Thus such charges include property theft, fraud, prostitution, gambling, sale of drugs, extortion, robbery, burglary, and larceny. All other arrests were coded as "noneconomic arrests," including offenses such as assaults, drunkeness, petty gambling, disorderly conduct, obstruction of justice, and drug use. Among Texes females there was only one noneconomic arrest. On the other hand, 11% of Georgia women were rearrested for noneconomic offenses.

A second modification made for the female analysis involved the necessary exclusion of some variables included in the specification in Chapters 11 and 12. Several of the variables had either large percentages of missing data or had little or no variance among TARP females, as for example, "job prearranged at release," "union membership," and "money in savings." In addition, several variables were eliminated because they represented redundant information. The small sample size made these specifications particularly vulnerable to problems from multicollinearity. For related reasons it was also necessary to eliminate the number of weeks incarcerated from the model specifications for both types of arrest. From early model estimations it appeared that the incarceration variable was highly collinear with some of the other variables in the arrest equation. Similar problems in the analysis of the total Georgia data were encountered in Chapter 12.

Finally, given that some theoretically important variables had to be dropped because of insufficient variance, some alternative indicators of the same theoretical concept were added. For instance, in the equation predicting the number of weeks employed, an alternative human-capital indicator was included: the longest periods the women ex-felons had worked for a single employer prior to prison. In addition, the number of times a woman had been in prison was included in the arrest equations.

As in the Chapter 12 analysis, five structural equations were used to predict each of the following: the number of economic-related arrests, the number of noneconomic arrests, the number of weeks allocated to legal employment, the number of weeks spent in jail or prison, and TARP dollars received. The exogenous factors considered can be summarized under the following categories: previous criminal history, human-capital factors, measures of the demand side of the labor market, indicators of the criminal justice practices in a given area, family status, indicators of financial need, and release status.

In an effort to increase statistical power, the state data were combined to run a pooled three-stage least squares analysis of TARP females. Since the regression coefficients of the individual state analyses were quite similar, and since there were no theoretical reasons to predict different parameter estimates, this seemed a reasonable procedure. A dummy variable for Texas was included to capture state differences of an additive nature.

In spite of pooling efforts, the TARP female subsample of 126 still lacked the necessary statistical power to obtain significant treatment effects. In light of the fact that the female analysis is a replication of that for the entire sample, if the *b*-values for the women approximate in magnitude and sign those for the entire sample, the effects will be assumed to be significant. For other female-specific predictions, when direction is predicted, *t*-values in excess of 1.64 will be deemed statistically significant at the .05 level. When direction is not predicted, *t*-values in excess of 1.97 will be defined as statistically significant.

REDUCED FORM RESULTS

The reduced form equations shown in Table C.2 are quite similar to those shown in Chapter 12. One noteworthy difference is that the treatment effects for TARP females are in the predicted direction. The *t*-values are still not significant, however; the *t*-value for group 2 membership is −1.44, and those for the other group memberships are very small. In addition, work disincentives for treatment group membership also emerged. Individuals in Group 1, for instance, worked almost 8 fewer weeks, on the average.

Several other significant reduced form effects merit discussion. Texans have .17 fewer economic arrests on the average. Of course, more important will be the relationship observed in the structural form when other relevant endogenous influencers were held constant.

The reduced form results for employment show four other significant effects. Persons with debts worked more, persons with greater employment experience prior to prison worked more, and persons on parole worked more. Finally, the expected negative impact on employment surfaces for women living with a spouse.

One other significant reduced form effect was not hypothesized but is in line with other expectations for married women. Living with a spouse was negatively associated with the amount of payments collected. Such a finding supports the notion that married women are not actively seeking work and perhaps encounter less financial need than do nonmarried women.

STRUCTURAL EQUATION RESULTS FOR
TARP MONEY RECEIVED

The payment equation results, presented in Table C.3, offer no new findings for women. TARP treatments were correctly administered as per design to the female subjects.

TABLE C.2
Five-Equation Pooled Model: Reduced Form Results

	Economic arrests	Non-economic arrests	Weeks employed	Weeks incarcerated	TARP payment received (hundreds)
Intercept	0.060	0.122	18.924	1.500	−1.362
Number of residences	0.072	0.025	0.250	0.168	−0.193
Age (years)	−0.002	0.002	−0.294	−0.034	−0.004
Money at release (hundreds)	−0.003	−0.001	−0.058	−0.011	0.002
Texas (dummy)	−0.046	−0.174*	0.883	3.254	0.767
Debts (hundreds)	0.008	−0.004	1.297*	−0.104	−0.089
Living with spouse (dummy)	−0.007	0.118	−8.952*	0.401	−1.378*
Number of dependents	−0.028	−0.022	0.100	−0.134	0.101
Number of property convictions	0.126	−0.012	−0.885	−0.048	13.680
Number of weeks in hospital	−0.007	−0.003	−0.411	−0.007	0.014
White (dummy for race)	−0.058	−0.071	1.650	0.006	0.394
Number of previous in-carcerations	0.189	−0.009	−1.428	2.084	0.589
Years of education	0.019	0.017	0.189	−0.147	0.034
Employment experience (most months worked for one employer before prison)	−0.002	−0.000	0.142*	−0.019	−0.002
Prison vocational train-ing (dummy)	0.045	0.006	−3.236	1.237	−0.382
Released on parole (dummy)	−0.187	−0.084	11.083*	−2.697	0.074
Group 1 (26 weeks/ 100%)	−0.097	−0.007	−7.849*	0.217	13.680*
Group 2 (13 weeks/ 100%)	−0.256	−0.009	−1.931	−0.708	7.256*
Group 3 (13 weeks/ 25%)	−0.014	−0.111	−3.226	0.354	8.462*
R^2	0.228	0.165	0.347	0.123	0.852

* $p < .05$ (two-tailed test)

STRUCTURAL FORM EQUATION FOR THE NUMBER OF ECONOMIC ARRESTS

Drawing on our theoretical understanding of economic crime, it was argued earlier that employed women ex-offenders would incur increased opportunity costs for criminal involvements. Thus, it was hypothesized that employed women would allocate less time to economic crimes and thereby have fewer economic arrests.

TABLE C.3
Five-Equation Pooled Model: TARP Money Received
(Dollars)

	Regression coefficient	t-value
Intercept	0.01	0.042
Group 1 (26 weeks/100%)	1376.54	22.799
Group 2 (13 weeks/100%)	739.61	12.802
Group 3 (13 weeks/25%)	849.37	15.420

This expectation is upheld in the findings of Table C.4. The number of weeks employed reduced the number of economic arrests for each TARP female by about .01, on the average. The coefficient was slightly smaller than that estimated for the larger analysis (.03 and .01 for Texas and Georgia total sample analyses, respectively). The corresponding t-value of −1.29 was not significant at the .05 level. However, since the effect closely replicates that found in Chapter 12, the relationship is likely a real one. For women who work 40 or more weeks, the estimated coefficient implied that half an economic arrest may have been averted. These effects are non-trivial. These findings also indicate that the Adler–Simon expectations for higher economic arrests for employed women are not borne out.

In agreement with earlier total sample findings, each $100 of TARP payments decreased the number of economic arrests per woman by .02, on the average. Since the average amount of cash received by TARP women was $585, the effect implies that the number of economic arrests were decreased by .12 for the "typical" TARP female. The t-value of 1.39 was statistically significant, but again, since the sign and magnitude were close to those shown in Chapter 12, we assume it is genuine.

TABLE C.4
Five-Equation Pooled Model: Number of Economic Arrests

	Regression coefficient	t-value
Intercept	0.486	1.259
Number of weeks employed	−0.013	−1.285
Payments (hundreds $)	−0.163	−1.391
Age (years)	−0.010	−1.261
Money at release (hundreds)	−0.002	−0.535
Debts (hundreds)	0.021	1.010
Living with spouse (dummy)	−0.082	−0.392
Number of dependents	−0.012	−0.332
Number of property convictions	0.197	3.927
Number of weeks in hospital	−0.012	−1.419
Number of previous incarcerations	0.253	1.913

An additional female-specific hypothesis was that married women and women with dependent children would incur greater opportunity costs for criminal activities. This hypothesis met with mixed success. As is apparent from Table C.4, neither effect was statistically significant although negative in both cases. The number of dependents had a negative effect on arrests, but was never significant. Living with a spouse had a negative and statistically significant impact on the economic arrests of Texas but not for Georgia women. Texas women who were living with a spouse experienced about .48 fewer arrests on the average. Thus, there is some evidence that opportunity costs are higher for married women and women with dependent children, but the evidence is inconclusive.

One major difference that surfaced for females involves the role of criminal history variables in their rearrests for economic-related crimes. Although criminal background indicators failed to surface as important predictors in the total sample analyses, such factors were quite important in predicting female economic arrests. On the average, each prior property conviction leads to .20 additional economic arrests; each previous incarceration results in another .25 in arrests. Since about 60% of TARP females are first offenders, it appears that women may be divided into two groups: one that consists of one-time offenders and another that is made up of more habitual criminals. Habitual offenders contribute more than their proportionate share to rearrest rates.

Remaining effects for the number of economic arrests were much the same as those for the total sample analyses. Financial aid indicators were in the predicted direction but insignificant. "Age" and "time spent in the hospital" were negatively although nonsignificantly associated with economic arrests.

By and large, with the exception of the relationship found between criminal background and economic arrests, the findings of the Chapter 12 analysis have been replicated. TARP payments and the number of weeks employed were both negatively associated with economic arrests.

Living with a mate made some difference for Texas women only; living with children, on the other hand, had no significant impact on rearrests.[11]

The results for the equation predicting the number of noneconomic arrests are shown in Table C.5. Looking at the effects for employment, one can observe that each additional week worked resulted in .004 fewer noneconomic arrests. This effect was considerably smaller than that reported in Chapter 12. However, it is difficult to interpret this failure to replicate since the definitions of "noneconomic" offenses are different.

---

[11] Arrest and employment variables for females were also subject to truncation and censoring problems. Adjustments similar to those discussed in Chapter 12 were used for this analysis. Substantive implications of these reanalyses were basically the same as those reported here.

TABLE C.5
Five-Equation Pooled Model: Number of Noneconomic Arrests

	Regression coefficient	t-value
Intercept	0.303	2.081
Number of weeks employed	−0.004	−1.441
Payments (hundreds $)	−0.000	−0.008
Number of residences	0.005	0.479
Age (years)	−0.003	−0.993
Texas (dummy)	−0.103	−1.822
Living with spouse (dummy)	0.071	0.970
Number of weeks in hospital	0.002	−0.516
Number of previous incarcerations	−0.027	−0.486

Similarly, in contrast to a significant negative impact on total sample nonproperty arrests, TARP payments did not appear to have had much effect on female noneconomic arrests, being quite small and with a correspondingly small t-value.

STRUCTURAL FORM RESULTS FOR THE NUMBER OF WEEKS EMPLOYED

The findings for the equation predicting the number of weeks employed are shown in Table C.6. The major difference hypothesized for TARP females was a significant work disincentive for women who were living with a spouse and for TARP women with children. Other expectations conformed to those for the total sample analysis.

It is apparent that "living with spouse" has a significant work-disincentive effect, on the average, about 8 fewer weeks worked. From the reduced form tables, one may recall that married women also collected significantly fewer TARP dollars. Apparently, one way of coping with financial dilemmas was to rely on the income of a spouse.

A work-disincentive effect also emerged for TARP payments received, about the same magnitude as in the total sample analysis. For each hundred dollars received, TARP women ex-offenders worked about .5 weeks less. Thus, women who received the full amounts of payments could be expected to work an average of 5 fewer weeks.

The number of dependents also appeared to have a negative effect on employment. The t-value is so small, however, that chance is a likely alternative explanation. For Georgia women, the number of dependents did serve to significantly decrease the number of weeks worked. The sign in Texas was negative, but the t-value was not significant. Thus, for all TARP women, the relationship between children and employment is inconclusive.

TABLE C.6
Five-Equation Pooled Model: Number of Weeks Employed

	Regression coefficient	*t*-value
Intercept	9.718	1.206
Payments	−0.530	−2.079
Number of weeks incarcerated	0.124	0.107
Texas (dummy)	1.970	0.502
Money available at release (hundreds)	−0.059	−1.083
Debts (hundreds)	1.127	2.861
Living with spouse (dummy)	−8.478	−2.013
Number of dependents	−0.208	−0.234
Number of weeks in hospital	−0.499	−3.362
White (dummy for race)	0.454	0.155
Years of education	0.212	0.346
Employment experience (most months worked for one employer before prison)	0.103	1.711
Prison vocational training (dummy)	−2.829	−0.699
Released on parole (dummy)	10.640	2.287

By glancing at the coefficients for human-capital indicators, one can see that while education and vocational training failed to surface as significant predictors of TARP female employment, work experience before prison did appear to have a positive and statistically significant effect on the number of weeks employed. For each 10 months of previous experience at one job, the female ex-offender worked an average of 1 additional week. Thus, stable preprison work records appear to be one human-capital factor that is relevant to female ex-offender employment. As one may recall, no human-capital indicators were statistically significant in the total sample analyses.

Similar to the findings for the larger analysis, parole turned out to be an important predictor of the number of weeks worked by TARP women. Female parolees worked about 11 additional weeks, on the average.

Indicators of the structural demand for employment revealed no significant relationships. The dummy variable "Texas" did not appear to have a significant effect on the number of weeks worked, despite the relatively lower unemployment rate in Texas.

Of the financial aid indicators, "debts" appeared to increase the number of weeks worked. For each $100 owed by TARP females at release, about 1 additional week was worked. Although negative, the *t*-values for gate money and other funds at hand at release failed to attain significance.

Contrary to expectations, weeks incarcerated had no significant impact on the employment of TARP women. This variable was observed to have a negative and significant effect on employment in the separate-state female analyses. The anomalous finding in the pooled analysis appears to result from the multicollinearity of this variable with other predictor variables in the equation.

In summary, the major difference between the female-only analysis and that for the males is the observed work disincentive for married women. Two other unique female findings include the positive effects for employment experience and debts. Other findings that included the work-disincentive effect for TARP payments and a positive effect for parole were similar to those of the larger male–female estimations.

STRUCTURAL EQUATION RESULTS FOR THE NUMBER OF WEEKS IN JAIL OR PRISON

The findings for the equation predicting incarceration time are shown in Table C.7. Basically these findings reveal no surprises and have been discussed in detail in Chapter 12.

TABLE C.7
Five-Equation Pooled Model: Number Weeks Jail or Prison

	Regression coefficient	*t*-value
Intercept	0.891	1.183
Number arrests (economic and noneconomic)	3.478	2.396
First offender × Arrests	−0.323	−0.134

CONCLUSION

The findings of the female ex-felon analysis suggest, in contrast with traditional arguments made by some criminologists, that women will respond to economic incentives. Findings reported here indicate that TARP payments and legal employment reduced the number of economic-related arrests. Legal employment also appeared to reduce the number of noneconomic arrests, while TARP payments appeared to have no appreciable effect. The work-disincentive effect found in the male–female analyses also surfaced for TARP females. Thus, recommendations made from the analyses of the total sample also hold for TARP females: if the compensation were not tied to unemployment, TARP dollars would probably be more effective in reducing recidivism.

This analysis of women ex-felons did not support the hypotheses—deduced from the work of criminologists Adler and Simon—that suggested that legal employment will increase criminal opportunities and thereby increase female economic arrests. However, two additional hypotheses deduced from Simon regarding female noneconomic arrests did receive some support. Simon suggested that working women would experience less frustration and, therefore, fewer noneconomic crimes of violence and addiction. In addition, she suggested that married women who remain in the home will experience greater frustrations and commit more domestic and/or leisure-related crimes. In the TARP female analysis, each of these effects fell in the predicted direction. However, for the latter relationship, it was not possible to reject the null hypothesis of no effect.

On the whole, married women appeared to experience fewer economic problems. They worked significantly fewer weeks and collected significantly fewer TARP dollars. One source of relief for their financial stress was the support of a male breadwinner. There is a slight indication that TARP females who were living with a spouse also committed fewer economic crimes, but this finding was not consistent across states.

Contrary to Bartel's emphasis on the negative relationship between the number of children and female criminal involvements, such effects failed to surface for TARP females. Although the direction of influence was negative, as she suggested, it never attained statistical significance in either state.

Criminal background characteristics do serve as important predictors for female economic arrests. As noted before, this relationship may indicate that women who are imprisoned may be the more "hardened" cases.

Therefore, with noted exceptions the findings of the larger total sample study have been replicated. Although the small sample size for TARP females limits the strength of conclusions, the sensible character of the results inspires greater confidence in the analysis.

Basically, the findings for TARP women demonstrate that the same motivational factors are relevant to understanding male and female crime. Unlike some popular misconceptions, female criminal behavior is not primarily emotional, sexual, and/or irrational. We also find that differential male–female societal learning is not irrelevant, illustrating the importance of female role socialization in the criminal acts of women. The distribution of offenses for TARP women are quite representative of criminal acts which are referred to as "traditionally feminine."

QUANTITATIVE STUDIES IN SOCIAL RELATIONS

Consulting Editor: Peter H. Rossi

UNIVERSITY OF MASSACHUSETTS
AMHERST, MASSACHUSETTS

Peter H. Rossi and Walter Williams (Eds.), EVALUATING SOCIAL PROGRAMS: *Theory, Practice, and Politics*

Roger N. Shepard, A. Kimball Romney, and Sara Beth Nerlove (Eds.), MULTIDIMENSIONAL SCALING: *Theory and Applications in the Behavioral Sciences,* Volume I — Theory; Volume II — Applications

Robert L. Crain and Carol S. Weisman, DISCRIMINATION, PERSONALITY, AND ACHIEVEMENT: *A Survey of Northern Blacks*

Douglas T. Hall and Benjamin Schneider, ORGANIZATIONAL CLIMATES AND CAREERS: *The Work Lives of Priests*

Kent S. Miller and Ralph Mason Dreger (Eds.), COMPARATIVE STUDIES OF BLACKS AND WHITES IN THE UNITED STATES

Robert B. Tapp, RELIGION AMONG THE UNITARIAN UNIVERSALISTS: *Converts in the Stepfathers' House*

Arthur S. Goldberger and Otis Dudley Duncan (Eds.), STRUCTURAL EQUATION MODELS IN THE SOCIAL SCIENCES

Henry W. Riecken and Robert F. Boruch (Eds.), SOCIAL EXPERIMENTATION: *A Method for Planning and Evaluating Social Intervention*

N. J. Demerath, III, Otto Larsen, and Karl F. Schuessler (Eds.), SOCIAL POLICY AND SOCIOLOGY

H. M. Blalock, A. Aganbegian, F. M. Borodkin, Raymond Boudon, and Vittorio Capecchi (Eds.), QUANTITATIVE SOCIOLOGY: *International Perspectives on Mathematical and Statistical Modeling*

Carl A. Bennett and Arthur A. Lumsdaine (Eds.), EVALUATION AND EXPERIMENT: *Some Critical Issues in Assessing Social Programs*

Michael D. Ornstein, ENTRY INTO THE AMERICAN LABOR FORCE